DRIVE 18
pp180–189

Aran Islands
(Oileán Árann)

DRIVE 4
pp60–69

DRIVE 3
pp50–59

DRIVE 2
pp38–49

DRIVE 1
pp30–37

DRIVE 5
pp70–77

DRIVE 7
pp86–93

DRIVE 8
pp94–101

DRIVE 6
pp78–85

DRIVE 9
pp102–109

DRIVE 12
pp128–137

DRIVE 13
pp138–145

DRIVE 16
pp162–169

DRIVE 10
pp110–119

DRIVE 11
pp120–127

GALWAY

WESTMEATH

OFFALY

LAOIS

KILDARE

WICKLOW

DUBLIN

KERRY

CLARE

LIMERICK

TIPPERARY

KILKENNY

CARLOW

WEXFORD

WATERFORD

CORK

Galway Bay

Lough
Corrib

Lough
Derg

Wicklow
Mountains

Slieve Felim
Mountains

Knockmealdown
Mountains

Boggeragh
Mountains

Comeragh
Mountains

Macgillycuddy's
Reeks

Swords
DUBLIN
Dun Laoghaire
Bray
Greystones
Wicklow

Naas
Kildare
Gorey
Enniscorthy
Wexford
New Ross

Tullamore
Portlaoise
Carlow
Kilkenny
Waterford
Dungarvan

Athlone
Birr
Roscrea
Thurles
Cashel
Clonmel
Tipperary

Ballinasloe
Loughrea
Portumna
Nenagh
Mitchelstown
Fermoy
Mallow
Midleton
Cork

Gort
Ennis
Shannon
Limerick
Rathkeale
Castleisland
Clonakilty
Bantry

Kilrush
Tralee
Killarney
Dingle

EYEWITNESS TRAVEL

BACK ROADS
IRELAND

EYEWITNESS TRAVEL

BACK ROADS
IRELAND

CONTRIBUTORS

Donna Dailey, Brian Daughton,
John S Doyle, and Yvonne Gordon

LONDON, NEW YORK,
MELBOURNE, MUNICH AND DELHI
www.dk.com

PUBLISHER Douglas Amrine
LIST MANAGER Vivien Antwi
MANAGING ART EDITOR Jane Ewart
EDITORIAL Michelle Crane, Alastair
Laing, Georgina Palffy, Fay Franklin,
Dorothy Stannard, Vicki Allen,
Justine Montgomery, Nichole Morford
ART EDITORS Shahid Mahmood,
Kate Leonard, Maite Lantaron
PRODUCTION CONTROLLER
Linda Dare
PICTURE RESEARCH Ellen Root,
Rhiannon Furbear
DTP Jason Little, Jamie McNeill
CARTOGRAPHY MANAGER
Uma Bhattacharya
SENIOR CARTOGRAPHIC EDITOR
Casper Morris
CARTOGRAPHY
Stuart James, Schchida Nand Pradhan
JACKET DESIGN
Tessa Bindloss, Meredith Smith
ILLUSTRATIONS
Arun Pottirayil, Pallavi Thakur,
Dev Datta

Color reproduction by Media
Development Printing Ltd, UK

Printed and bound in China by
South China Printing Co Ltd

First American Edition 2010

12 13 14 15 16 10 9 8 7 6 5 4 3 2 1

First published in the United States by
DK Publishing, Inc., 375 Hudson Street,
New York 10014

Reprinted with revisions 2013

Copyright 2010, 2013 © Dorling
Kindersley Limited, London

Published in Great Britain by Dorling Kindersley
Limited.

A catalog record for this book is available from
the Library of Congress.

ISBN 978 0 7566 9590 3

Jacket Dingle peninsula, County Kerry, Ireland

CONTENTS

Above The Belfry Tower, known as the Yellow Steeple,
of St. Mary's Abbey on the River Boyne

Below left Iron Age Staigue Fort, near the
village of Castlecove on the Iveragh Peninsula

Below center View from the narrow road
over the Coomakesta Pass, Co Kerry

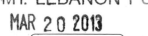

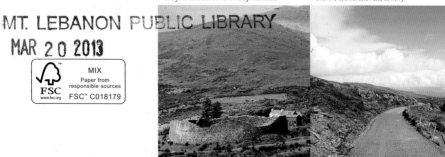

Above Howth Marina, near Dublin, full of clinking yachts and pleasure boats

Above Thatched cottage in the fishing village of Skerries, on Dublin's north coast

Above The picturesque road curving down to Coumeenoole Bay, Co Kerry

Below Hay bales in the countryside around Skerries, near Dublin

Below The entrance to 400-year-old Trinity College, Dublin, Ireland's oldest and most prestigious university

Title page: Horse-drawn caravan on the shores of Doolough, Co Mayo **Half-title page:** Quiet country road from Carran to Caherconnel in the Burren, Co Clare

About this Book

The 25 driving tours in this guide reflect the fantastic diversity of Ireland. Although it is a relatively small island – 303 miles (488 km) long and 189 miles (304 km) at its widest point – it has an amazing variety of terrain. The landscape ranges from rolling green pastures and fertile fields to mountain peaks, dramatic coastline, sandy beaches, tranquil lakes (loughs), great stretches of blanket bog, and rocky peninsulas jutting out to sea. Ireland has one of Europe's oldest cultures, glimpses of which can be found in its mysterious prehistoric sites, its quaint stone villages, and its ancient native tongue. These driving routes take visitors beyond the must-see tourist sights to lesser-known places that provide a more intimate experience of the people, customs, architecture, and cuisine of the island. Expect delightful surprises around every bend, packed with the sights, sounds, and flavors of the real Ireland.

Getting Started

The front section of the guide will give you all the practical information you need to plan and enjoy a driving trip in Ireland. It includes an overview of when to go and how to get there, advice on renting a vehicle, and details of any documentation required. In-depth motoring advice ranges from driving rules to road conditions, from buying gas to breakdown or accident procedures – the kind of background knowledge that helps to make a driving trip stress-free. There is information on money, opening hours, communications, health and safety, and other practical matters, as well as advice on accommodation and dining options, to ensure that you experience the very best of Ireland's legendary hospitality.

The Drives

The main touring section of the guide is divided into leisurely drives, ranging in duration from two to five days. All the tours can be driven in a standard vehicle, and no special driving skills are required.

The drives encompass every region of the country, from the gentle plains of Kildare to the rocky peninsulas of Cork and Kerry, from the remote and dramatic landscapes of Connemara and Donegal to Northern Ireland's stunning Causeway Coast.

Each drive begins with a list of highlights and a clearly mapped itinerary. There is advice on the best time of year to do the drive, road conditions, market days and major festival dates. The tour pages contain descriptions of each stop on the route, linked by clear driving instructions. Side panels have information on the most authentic places to stay and eat. Tinted boxes feature background information and anecdotes.

Each drive features at least one mapped town or countryside walking tour, designed to take a maximum of two hours at a gentle pace, with stops along the way.

The tours are flexible: some can be linked to create a longer driving holiday; or they can be dipped into as day trips while based in a region.

Using the Sheet Map

A pull-out road map of the entire country is supplied. This map contains all the information you need to drive around the country and to navigate between the tours. All highways, major roads, airports – both domestic and international – plus all the ferry ports are also easily identified. This makes the pull-out map an excellent addition to the drive itinerary maps within the book. The pull-out map also has a comprehensive index to help you find the places, and is further supplemented by a clear distance chart, so you can gauge the distances between the major cities in Ireland.

Top far left Devil's Pass near Lough Nafooey, Connemara **Top left** Rainbow over West Cork **Center far left** Fishing boats in Cobh Harbour, Co Cork **Center left** Old-fashioned truck, Sheep's Head Peninsula, Co Cork **Far left** Dublin's Temple Bar area **Left** Baldoyle Beach, near Dublin **Right** Road to Rossapena on the Fanad Peninsula

Introducing Ireland

With its quaint rural lanes, rolling green hills and stunning mountain vistas and seascapes, there can be few countries as rewarding for back-roads driving as Ireland. The winding lanes of Ireland run through lush pastures to the wildflower-studded pavements of the Burren and to the basalt columns of the Giant's Causeway. They weave their way into the glens of the Antrim Coast, along the wild peninsulas of Cork and Connemara, and around the calm loughs of Galway and Donegal. Along their leisurely way they pass by ancient stone circles and megalithic tombs, Celtic crosses and round towers, medieval castles, and stately homes. They afford ample opportunities to pause for a stroll in a pretty town or village and, for refreshment, a cozy pub is seldom far away. And, should a visitor ever stray too far off the unbeaten path, there are always friendly folk around who are more than happy to help with directions.

When to Go

The Gulf Stream ensures that Ireland enjoys a moderate climate all year round. However, summer not only has the warmest temperatures, but also has the longest days. With sunset as late as 11pm in midsummer, it's easy to pack in a lot more sightseeing and activities, from walking and cycling to boating and golf. If the goal of the trip is to take in the most popular attractions and beauty spots, however, there will be fewer crowds and yet still pleasant weather in both spring and autumn. Bargain-hunters will find the best deals on hotel and car rental rates in winter.

However, there's more than the weather to consider in deciding when to visit. Incorporating a music festival, a sporting event, or a local celebration can turn out to be the highlight of a trip to Ireland.

Times to Avoid

The busiest time to visit is during the summer school holidays (late Jun–early Sep). Prices will be highest, traffic heaviest, and lines longest. Dublin hotels quickly fill up during conventions and events, so check, and book, well ahead. Night falls as early as 4pm in winter, and many attractions have restricted opening times or may close entirely. Rural and smaller seaside resort hotels and restaurants often close completely from November until Easter.

Climate

Summer temperatures usually range from 60–68°F (15–20°C), with spring and autumn temperatures around 50°F (10°C). Winters generally average 41–46°F (5–8°C), although rain and wind can make it feel colder. It rarely snows, but expect rain at any time throughout the year. Ireland's "soft" rain is often interspersed with sunshine, so dress in layers and be prepared for sudden changes.

Festivals

St. Patrick's Day (Mar 17) is celebrated most enthusiastically in Dublin, but many fairs and festivals, from local food and livestock events to ancient festivities, to music, theater and arts events, are held throughout the country all year round. Full details of main festivals, where they are held and when, are supplied in each drive.

Public Holidays

New Year's Day (Jan 1)
St. Patrick's Day (Mar 17)
Good Friday
Easter Monday
May Bank Holiday (1st Mon May)
Spring Bank Holiday (last Mon May, Northern Ireland; 1st Mon Jun, Republic of Ireland)
July Bank Holiday (July 14, Northern Ireland only)
August Bank Holiday (1st Mon Aug, Republic of Ireland; last Mon Aug, Northern Ireland)
October Bank Holiday (last Mon Oct, Republic of Ireland only)
Christmas Day (Dec 25)
St Stephen's Day (Dec 26, Republic of Ireland)
Boxing Day (Dec 26, Northern Ireland)

Left A country road in County Cork, flanked by dry-stone walls **Right** Market stall in Macroom's Square, with its Norman gateway, County Cork

Getting to Ireland

Ireland is a popular destination for travelers worldwide, and its three major airports – Dublin, Shannon, and Belfast – are served by frequent, direct flights from Great Britain, Europe, and North America, as well as flights from major cities around the world. From these key gateways there are easy connections by air to regional airports, as well as good road and rail links throughout the country. Numerous ferry companies sail to Ireland from Britain and France, offering vehicle and foot-passenger services. Some connect with rail services to and from the ports. There are also low-cost combined bus and ferry routes to Ireland.

Above Republic of Ireland road sign indicating the route for Belfast Airport along a main road

DIRECTORY

AIRLINES

Aer Lingus
08 18 365 000 (Ireland); 0871 718 5000
(Northern Ireland and UK);
www.aerlingus.com

Ryanair
0818 30 30 30 (Ireland); 0871 246 0000
(Northern Ireland and UK);
www.ryanair.com

Delta Airlines
800 241 4141 (US); www.delta.com

United Airlines
1800 864 8331 (US); www.united.com

Air Canada
1800 709 900 (Ireland); 0871 220 1111
(Northern Ireland and UK);
www.aircanada.com

AIRPORTS

Dublin Airport
01 814 1111; www.dublinairport.com

Shannon Airport
061 712 000; www.shannonairport.com

Belfast International Airport
028 9448 4848; www.belfastairport.com

Tourism Ireland
www.discoverireland.com

Arriving by Air

Ireland is served by nearly all international airlines. The Irish national carrier, **Aer Lingus**, has non-stop flights from many British, European, and North American cities, including London, Manchester, Glasgow, Paris, New York, Boston, Chicago, and San Francisco. The Irish regional carrier **Aer Arann** flies to and from cities in Britain and Ireland. The Irish budget airline **Ryanair** offers direct flights to Ireland from many British and European cities. Ireland's major and regional airports are also served by other budget carriers from Britain and Europe. All three Irish carriers have flights to domestic destinations throughout the country. **Delta** and **United** also have direct flights from major US cities, and most other major airlines fly to Dublin with a stop in London. **Air Canada** has frequent flights to Ireland from Canada's main cities, but these may entail a stop in London. Ireland's three international airports handle most

long-haul flights. **Dublin Airport** is 6 miles (10 km) north of the city. Both regular city buses and the direct Dublin Bus Airlink run between the airport and the city center, with the latter stopping at Connolly and Heuston rail stations as well as the central bus station, Busaras. Many flights from North America land at **Shannon Airport**, 16 miles (26 km) west of Limerick on the west coast. There are bus connections into the city, as well as to Ennis and Galway. **Belfast International Airport**, located 15 miles (24 km) outside the center, is the main airport in Northern Ireland. Bus 300 runs a round-the-clock service between the airport and city center. Taxis are available at all airports.

The Republic of Ireland has seven regional airports at Cork, Kerry, Waterford, Galway, Knock, Sligo, and Donegal. Northern Ireland also has George Best Belfast City Airport and City of Derry Airport. The **Tourism Ireland** website has information on travel options from each of these.

Arriving by Sea

Ireland has six main ferry ports: Dublin, Dun Laoghaire (pronounced "Dun Larry"), Rosslare, and Cork in the Republic of Ireland, and Belfast and Larne in Northern Ireland. Four ferry companies operate car and foot-passenger services between Ireland and Britain. There are also ferry services to and from ports in France. The easiest way to compare routes and prices is online at the **Direct Ferries** website.

The Liverpool to Dublin routes (8 hours) are operated by **P&O Irish Sea** and **DFDS Seaways**. P&O also has crossings from Cairnryan (1 hour) and Troon (2 hours), in southwest Scotland, to Larne. In addition, DFDS Seaways runs crossings from Liverpool to Belfast (8 hours). There are also crossings to Belfast from Stranraer in southwest Scotland (2 hours) and to Larne from Fleetwood in northwest England (8 hours) with **Stena Line**. Stena also sails to Dublin and Dun Laoghaire from Holyhead in North Wales. **Irish Ferries** also operates crossings to Dublin from Holyhead (2 hours) as well as crossings from Pembroke in south Wales (4 hours) to Rosslare. Stena Line operates a daily 2-hour crossing to Rosslare from Fishguard in southwest Wales.

From France, **LD Lines** operates an overnight route (20–23 hours) from Le Havre to Rosslare, while Irish Ferries and **Celtic Link Ferries** operate similar overnight ferries between Cherbourg (18 hours) and Roscoff (20 hours) and Rosslare, and **Brittany Ferries** runs an overnight route between Roscoff and Cork (14 hours).

Arriving by Train and Bus

Trains run direct to most ferry ports, including Dublin, Dun Laoghaire, Fishguard Harbour in Wales, and Stranraer Harbour in Scotland.

If traveling by train, combination train-and-ferry tickets are usually available; these are convenient, and also often offer substantial savings. Several UK rail operators, Irish Rail, and ferry companies have teamed up with **SailRail**, which offers this deal from any UK train station to any station in the Republic of Ireland or Northern Ireland, using most ferry routes. Tickets can be bought at most train stations in the UK and Ireland and from the ferry operators, as well as from SailRail itself.

Stena Line has Rail-and-Sail fares from several British stations for the crossings between Fishguard to Rosslare, from Holyhead to Dublin and Dun Laoghaire, and from Stranraer to Belfast. Similar fares are available on routes operated by Irish Ferries. Check for deals with **British Rail**, **ScotRail**, **Irish Rail**, and **Northern Ireland Railways**. In Ireland, **CIE** has information on train and bus connections to the ferry ports.

The long-distance bus operator **Eurolines** offers a similar bus-and-ferry service, with routes to Dublin, Belfast, and beyond from most of the main British cities. Journey times may be long, but the fares are relatively inexpensive. In Ireland, Eurolines operates jointly with **Bus Éireann**.

Below far left The check-in area at Dublin Airport **Below left** The modern exterior of Dublin Airport **Below center** Sign for the Port of Belfast, Northern Ireland's biggest seaport **Below right** Irish Ferries ship loading up at Rosslare Harbour

Practical Information

Ireland may have an idyllic rural image but its infrastructure is thoroughly up-to-date. Public services operate smoothly and efficiently, and its health system is good. Communication networks, from Internet to mobile phone services, are widespread, and most banks have an ATM outside. What hasn't changed is Ireland's respect for religion and tradition, or the affable, laid-back nature of its people. Some shops and services are closed on Sundays, and the pace of life may feel slow, especially in the countryside.

Above Illuminated green cros indicating a pharmac

Passports and Visas

All visitors that are not EU citizens must have a passport with at least six months' validity remaining in order to enter the country. UK citizens do not need a passport or visa to enter the Republic of Ireland. However, it is advisable to have a valid form of photo identification, and most airlines and ferry companies will require a passport or driving license. Those hoping to travel without a passport should check with the carrier if another form of ID is acceptable. Nationals of EU countries should carry their passport, as some national ID cards are not accepted.

Travelers from the United States, Canada, Australia, New Zealand, and South Africa do not need a visa if they are staying for less than 90 days. For longer stays, or for student or working visas, apply well in advance of departure. Other nationalities may require a visa, and visitors should check with the **Irish Embassy** or Consulate in their own country prior to traveling. A list is available online.

The same rules apply for entry into Northern Ireland. For visa information and applications, anyone planning a trip should get in touch with the **British Embassy**, Consulate, or High Commission in their home country.

Travel Insurance

All travelers are strongly advised to take out travel insurance that offers cover for a broad range of possible emergencies. In addition to medical insurance, a comprehensive policy will normally cover the holder: for loss or theft of luggage and other belongings such as passports and money; damage or injury to a third party; personal accident; delayed or canceled flights; and in some cases even the cancellation of your trip due to personal illness or that of a family member. Most policies also cover legal costs up to a certain limit, as do comprehensive motor policies (see p16) in the event of any legal advice or action being needed, for example, after an accident. A standard policy will not cover hazardous or extreme sports, so if the plan is to go surfing, canoeing, or rock-climbing, check that it is covered; if not, many activities can be added for a small extra premium.

Read the terms and conditions carefully, because coverage, excess amounts, exclusions, and deductibles vary widely. Also check to see what kind of cover, if any, is offered under your home insurance policy. Some credit card companies also offer limited travel insurance benefits

if you use your card to book your trip or rental car. Check with the company.

Health

No vaccinations or immunization documents are required to enter Ireland, unless traveling from a country where infectious disease is widespread Tap water is fine to drink, and bottled water is widley available. Anyone planning to hike in boggy areas is advised to bring insect repellent to ward off the tiny biting insects, called midges, that are active in dull and damp weather.

Standard remedies can be bought ir pharmacies, but bring any prescription medications from home to last throughout the trip, otherwise it will be be necessary to visit a doctor for a prescription. Pack medications in carry on luggage with their original pharmacy labels in order to avoid any problems at airport security. If any condition requires carrying a syringe when traveling by air, get a formal letter of notification of the condition from the prescribing physician.

In the event of illness while traveling the **Irish Medical Council** can provide a referral to a doctor or dentist. Some hospitals have walk-in clinics for non-emergency cases. Most pharmacies are

Beware of the bull

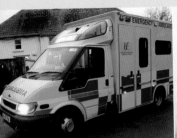

Above left Emergency ambulance **Above center** A tourist information sign **Above right** Main shopping street, Carlow Town

open Mon–Sat during business hours, and some are open 24 hours in larger towns and cities. Pharmacists can advise on minor medical matters.

Visitors from the US, Canada, and other countries are strongly advised to have private medical insurance, as Ireland does not provide publicly funded health care for foreigners from outside the EU. US medical insurance is generally not accepted outside the US, so it is best to consult with your insurance company and, if you are not covered, purchase a short-term health policy that will cover you while you are traveling. Visitors from Britain and other EU countries are covered for medical treatment in Ireland under EU social security regulations, but must see a physician who has an agreement with the Department of Health.

In Ireland, general practitioners charge fees for consultations and non-emergency treatment, and this must be paid at the time. Emergency hospital treatment will not be withheld or delayed, but will be billed later. The patient is expected to settle the bill and then seek reimbursement from their insurance company.

Police and Security

Ireland is a relatively safe country, but take the normal precautions against petty crime, especially in large towns and tourist areas. Leave all passports and valuables in the hotel safe. Keep an eye on your handbag or wallet in crowds and on public transport, and do not carry large amounts of cash. Never leave anything unattended or visible in a car, even if it is locked.

Victims of crime should contact the **Irish Tourist Assistance Service** in the Republic or the local police station in Northern Ireland. In the Republic, the police force is the **Garda Síochána**, known as the Gardaí. The **Police Service of Northern Ireland** is their counterpart in the North.

The Troubles are largely a thing of the past and any residual violence between Catholics and Protestants is infrequent and seldom affects tourist areas. If in doubt, check locally. Orange marches still take place in the fortnight around July 12, commemorating the Battle of the Boyne in 1690 (see p156). Avoid these gatherings, as they generate protests and sometimes violence.

Below far left Uniformed Gardaí in the Republic of Ireland **Below left center** Sign warning against entering field with dangerous bull **Below left** European Union passport **Below** Cycling on the narrow roads around Mount Leinster, Carlow

DIRECTORY

EMBASSIES AND CONSULATES

Irish Embassies Abroad
www.dfa.ie

US Department of State
www.travel.state.gov

American Embassy
42 Elgin Road, Ballsbridge, Dublin 4;
01 668 8777; http://dublin.
usembassy.gov

American Consulate
Danesfort House, 223 Stranmillis Road,
Belfast BT9 5GR; 028 9038 6100;
www.usembassy.org.uk/nireland

Australian Embassy
7th floor, Fitzwilton House, Wilton
Terrace, Dublin 2; 01 664 5300;
www.ireland.embassy.gov.au

British Embassy
29 Merrion Road, Ballsbridge,
Dublin 4; 01 205 3700; http://
britishembassyinireland.fco.gov.uk

Canadian Embassy
7–8 Wilton Terrace, Dublin 2;
01 234 4000;
www.canadainternational.gc.ca/
ireland-irlande/

HEALTH

Irish Medical Council
Kingram House, Kingram Place,
Dublin 2; 01 498 3100;
www.medicalcouncil.ie

EHIC
www.nhs.uk/EHIC/Pages/About.aspx

POLICE AND SECURITY

Emergency Services
In the Republic: 112 or 999;
In Northern Ireland: 999

Irish Tourist Assistance Service
1a Lower Grand Canal St, Dublin 2;
01 661 0562 (Mon–Fri); 01 666 8109
(weekends); www.itas.ie

An Garda Síochána
www.garda.ie

Police Service of Northern Ireland
www.psni.police.uk

Communications

Telephone service is provided by Telecom Éireann in the Republic, and by British Telecom in Northern Ireland. Irish phone numbers have a two- or three-digit area code beginning with 0 and followed by a local number of five to eight digits, depending on the region. When dialing within the country, use the full area code. It is only necessary to dial the local number when calling within the same area code.

When calling Ireland from abroad, dial the **international access code**, followed by the Ireland **country code**, and then the local area code (minus the initial 0) and number. The country code is 353 for the Republic and 44 for Northern Ireland. To make an overseas call from Ireland, first dial the international access code 00, then the country code, area code, and local number you wish to reach.

When dialing Northern Ireland from the Republic, dial the prefix 048, and then the local number. Calls to the Republic from Northern Ireland, however, are dialed in the same way as those from the rest of the United Kingdom: 00+353+area code (minus the initial 0) and then the number.

There are public pay phone booths throughout Ireland, which take coins or cards. The easiest and cheapest way to make calls is to purchase a pre-paid Callcard in the Republic or Phonecard in Northern Ireland. They are sold at newsagents, post offices, tourist offices, and other outlets, in several denominations. International phone cards are also available, and can be the cheapest way to call abroad. Some are rechargeable with a credit card, but note that the cards may not be interchangeable between the Republic and Northern Ireland.

Making calls from a hotel room is generally expensive, as most hotels add a high surcharge, particularly for overseas calls. Check before dialing whether there are any additional charges for local or toll-free calls.

Cell (mobile) phones are more convenient but can be very costly, depending on the roaming charges levied by your service provider. Only digital phones with GSM and a roaming agreement will work on the island. US phones need to be tri- or quad-band. Money can be saved by replacing the phone's usual SIM card with an Irish one, but the phone must be "unlocked" to do this.

There are Internet cafes in all the large towns and cities. Free access is often available at public libraries, though time may be limited and it may be necessary to reserve a computer in advance. Many hotels and guesthouses provide Internet access for their guests, through either a dedicated computer or via wireless access for laptop users. There may be a charge for this, but it is increasingly offered as a free service to guests. Wi-fi "hotspots" are becoming more common at coffee shops and other places around the country, including Dublin airport and Dun Laoghaire ferry port.

The Republic and Northern Ireland have separate postal systems. You must use Irish stamps to send mail from the Republic but British stamps to send mail from Northern Ireland. Mail boxes are painted green and red respectively. You can buy stamps at newsagents and in many shops, as well as at post offices.

Above Bord Fáilte (Irish Tourist Board) shamrock sign for approved accommodation

Currency and Cards

The currency in the Republic of Ireland is the Euro (€). One Euro is made up of 100 cents. Euro notes come in denominations of €5, €10, €20, €50, €100, €200 and €500. There are 1c, 2c, 5c, 10c, 20c, 50c, €1, and €2 coins. Sterling is the currency in Northern Ireland. One pound (£) is divided into 100 pence. There are £5, £10, £20, £50 and £100 notes, and 1p, 2p, 5p, 10p, 20p, 50p, £1, and £2 coins.

Traveler's checks are the safest way to carry money, with American Express checks widely accepted. However, it is more convenient to use a debit or credit card to withdraw local currency from ATMs, which are widespread. The card provider usually charges for withdrawing cash abroad.

Credit cards such as Visa, Mastercard, and American Express are widely accepted at hotels, restaurants, shops, and gas stations, but you will need cash at pubs, small businesses, and guesthouses or B&Bs. Credit card companies are increasingly vigilant against fraud, so it is wise to let them know you will be traveling and using the card abroad, so that they do not put a block on further use. It is also a

Above left Post office and *bureau de change* in Ventry, Co Kerry **Above right** Old-style red Northern Ireland phone box by the road, Fermanagh Lakelands

good idea to carry a different credit card as a back-up. Ireland uses the "chip-and-PIN" system, which requires you to enter the card's PIN number into the card reader rather than sign a slip. If your card only has a magnetic band, it is possible that it will not be accepted.

Tourist Information

Bord Fáilte (the Irish Tourist Board) and the **Northern Ireland Tourist Board** have regional offices that provide information about sights, activities, and accommodation in their area. There are also local tourist offices in most towns and tourist areas. **Tourism Ireland** covers the whole island. Along with general advice, its website has links to Irish Tourist Board offices worldwide.

Opening Hours

Most Irish shops are open Mon–Sat, 9am–6pm. Sunday trading hours are from noon to 5 or 6pm in the Republic, 1–5pm in Northern Ireland.

Banking hours are Mon–Fri, 10am–4:30pm. Post offices are generally open Mon–Fri, 9am–5:30pm, but main post offices in larger towns are also open on Saturdays, from 9am to 5pm in the Republic and from 9am to 12.30pm in Northern Ireland.

Museums and galleries are usually closed on Mondays and on public holidays.

Disabled Facilities

Many visitor attractions are now accessible to wheelchair users, and a growing number of hotels and restaurants also provide facilities for guests with disabilities. For more information, contact the **National Disability Authority** in the Republic, and **Adapt NI** and **Disability Action** in Northern Ireland.

Time

Ireland is on Greenwich Mean Time (GMT), with one hour's Summer (Daylight Saving) Time in effect from late March to late October.

Electricity

Ireland's electrical current is 230/240 volts. Plugs have 3 pins. Overseas visitors will need an adaptor to use their own appliances, but most hotels have built-in adaptors for shavers only, and also provide a hairdryer.

Below far left Republic of Ireland telephone box **Below left** Green postbox in the Republic **Below center left** Keep our beach tidy sign, Waterford beach **Below center right** Late bar sign, Kilkenny City **Below** Signs for Waterford Treasures Museum

DIRECTORY

COMMUNICATIONS

International Access Codes
Australia: 0011; New Zealand: 0170; UK: 00; US and Canada: 011

Country Codes
Australia: 61; New Zealand: 64; UK: 44; US and Canada: 1

Directory Assistance
In the Republic: 11811; in Northern Ireland: 118 118 (charges apply)

TOURIST INFORMATION

Fáilte Ireland South East Region
051 875 823;
www.discoverireland.ie/southeast

Fáilte Ireland East & Midlands Region
044 934 8761;
www.discoverireland.ie/eastcoast

Fáilte Ireland South West Region
021 425 5100;
www.discoverireland.ie/southwest

Fáilte Ireland West Region
091 537 700;
www.discoverireland.ie/west

Fáilte Ireland North West Region
071 91 61201;
www.discoverireland.ie/northwest

Northern Ireland Tourist Board
59 North Street, Belfast BT1 1NB;
028 9023 1221;
www.discovernorthernireland.com

Tourism Ireland
www.discoverireland.com

Dublin Tourism Centre
www.visitdublin.com

Shannon Development
061 361 555;
www.discoverireland.ie/shannon

DISABLED FACILITIES

National Disability Authority
01 608 0400; www.nda.ie

Adapt NI
028 9023 1211; www.adaptni.org

Disability Action
028 9029 7880;
www.disabilityaction.org

LATE BAR

WATERFORD TREASURES MUSEUM
Ireland's Museum of the Year
audioguide disponible en français

Driving in Ireland

Ireland has an extensive road network and in recent years there has been extensive upgrading and expansion of all main routes. However, it is only by driving the back roads that you'll discover the real Ireland. The relaxed pace is one of the greatest joys of driving here, and the further you get from the cities, the more likely you are to have the road to yourself. To travel safely and get the most from your trip, it is vital to familiarize yourself with the rules and requirements for driving in Ireland before you set out.

Above Premium, unleaded and diesel gas pump by a rural roadside in Co Tipperar

Insurance and Breakdown Cover

Third-party motor insurance is compulsory in Ireland. If you bring your own car, you must have an insurance certificate that is valid in the country. You do not necessarily need a "Green Card and Bail Bond," but you should check with your insurer prior to traveling that you are covered for the trip. Most companies give you automatic coverage in EU countries for up to 90 days. If your policy has breakdown cover, check whether it applies abroad. If not, it is worth considering purchasing additional breakdown and accident cover. Motoring organizations such as the AA *(see p19)* also offer single-trip policies of this type.

What to Take

In order to drive in Ireland, you must have a valid national driving license, issued in your country of permanent residence. By law you must have your license with you at all times while driving in the Republic. If your license does not have a photograph, be sure also to carry your passport or another form of official photo ID. If you are bringing your own vehicle, including trailers and motorcycles,

you should carry the registration document with you. If it is not registered in your name (for example, if it is a company car), bring a letter of authorization from the owner.

Visibility vests are compulsory in many EU countries and this may soon be extended throughout the EU. There should be one for every occupant of the vehicle. A warning triangle is compulsory and, while it is not compulsory to carry a first aid kit, it is a good idea. A flashlight (torch) and spare gasoline container are also highly recommended.

Road Systems

In the Republic, motorway or highway numbers are prefixed by an M. National Primary Routes have the prefix N, followed by numbers 1–50, while National Secondary Routes (also N) are 51 and above. Regional roads have an R prefix and a three-digit number; these range from stretches of multi-lane roads to narrow rural roads. Local road numbers are designated with an L, but often are not shown on road signs or maps.

Northern Ireland uses the British system of road classification: M for motorways, A for major roads, B for secondary roads and C for minor ones.

A barrier-free motorway toll system, called **eFlow**, was introduced in the Republic in the autumn of 2008. It currently operates on the M50 around Dublin. If your car is not registered, your vehicle license plate is recorded each time you pass the toll point and you must pay according to the distance traveled. Payment car be made online, through the call center or at Payzone outlets nation-wide, but the journey must be paid for by 8pm the following day. More information is available on the eFlow website. Some other motorways in Ireland also charge a fee, which is paid at toll plazas en route or as you leave

Speed Limits and Fines

In the Republic of Ireland, speed limits are given in kilometers per hour (km/h). In Northern Ireland the are posted in miles per hour (mph). Be sure to remember the change when near the border: it is unmarked and easy to cross without realizing.

Unless otherwise stated, speed limits are as follows:
• In the Republic: 120 km/h (74 mph) on highways; 100 km/h (62 mph) on national roads; 80 km/h (50 mph) on non-national roads; 50 km/h (31 mph) in towns and built-up areas.

ɔove left Slow sign on Lough Navar Forest Drive **Above center** Signs warning of changes in the road ahead **Above right** Double-decker buses, Dublin

n Northern Ireland: 70 mph (112 m/h) on highways; 60 mph (96 m/h) on the open road; and 30 mph 8 km/h) in towns and built-up areas. Police can levy on-the-spot fines r speeding violations in the epublic, and failure to pay incurs an ncreased penalty. Speed cameras e also widely in use; fines are utomatic, and tickets are sent to the ddress of the vehicle's registration. ɔu won't escape the penalty by riving a rental car. The car hire ɔmpany will bill you for the ticket, ong with an administration fee. ɔeed camera detectors are illegal nd will be confiscated.

The laws on drunk-driving are very rict and penalties are high. The gal limit is 80 mg per 100 ml of ɔood (about equal to a pint of beer). ɔlice are authorized to perform a reathalyzer test at any time, and the ɔenalty for refusal may be prosecution. ny accident that occurs while the river is under the influence of cohol or drugs is automatically ɔnsidered his or her fault.

ɹules of the Road

riving is on the left throughout eland. Most visitors get used to this uickly, but pay extra attention at ɔossroads and roundabouts, where it is easy (and dangerous) to forget or get confused. Always turn left into a roundabout, and yield to traffic already in the roundabout and approaching from the right.

Overtake on the right, but do not do so if there is a solid white line in the center of the road. At a junction where neither road has priority, yield to traffic coming from your right.

Seat belts must be worn at all times, by the driver and all passengers. It is illegal to use a hand-held cell phone while driving; this will incur a fine. The horn must not be sounded between 11:30pm and 7am.

At traffic lights, drivers must yield to pedestrians when the amber light is flashing, but if the crossing is clear they may proceed with caution.

Buying Gas

There are plenty of gas (petrol) stations throughout Ireland, and all grades of unleaded gas, as well as diesel and LP Gas, are available. Most stations are self-service, and nearly all take major credit cards.

Below far left Old-fashioned signpost near Leenane, Connemara **Below left** Sightseeing tour bus, Belfast **Below center** Sports car on the Coomakesta Pass, Iveragh Peninsula **Below** Signs for the Slea Head Drive near Dingle

DIRECTORY

HIGHWAY TOLLS

eFlow
www.eFlow.ie

IRISH PHRASES FOR DRIVERS

Géill slí
Yield

Mall
Slow

Bóthar dúnta
Road closed

Oscailt cheilte
Concealed entrance

Coisithe amháin
Pedestrian zone

Aire
Caution

Leanaí ag trasnú
Children crossing

Rampa romhat
Ramp ahead

Trácht aon líne
Single file traffic

Dromchla sealadach
Temporary road surface

Cloichíní scaoilte
Loose chippings

An lar
City center

Road Conditions

Most roads in Ireland are both well-surfaced and well-maintained. Distances are shown in kilometers on signs in the Republic, and in miles in Northern Ireland. In the Republic (and occasionally in Northern Ireland), road signs and place names are posted in both English and Irish. In the Gaeltacht (Irish-speaking areas), however, there are stretches where signs are in Irish only. Also be aware that road signs may be inadequate or confusing in rural areas and, on occasion, can be broken off or pointing in the wrong direction. It is essential to have a good road map.

Given the small size of the island, and the relatively short distances between towns, it can be easy to underestimate the time it takes to drive between two points. Back roads by their nature are often slow and winding, with reduced speeds through villages and hamlets, while traffic can become surprisingly congested in busy tourist towns such as Killarney. Unexpected things can slow movement down – a flock of sheep in the road, a farm vehicle, a beautiful view or even two locals stopping their cars for a chat in the middle of the road as they pass. Be extra careful on blind curves and look out for pedestrians walking on the roadway. An average of 30–40 miles (50–65 km) per hour is a sensible figure when planning your route.

Many country roads are so narrow that one vehicle will have to pull over to the side to let an oncoming car pass. Courtesy dictates that the one closest to a wide spot waits. Buses always have right of way, however.

It is wise to allow local drivers, who know the roads well and will drive much faster, to overtake. And be sure to give drivers who make way for you a friendly wave of thanks.

Taking a Break

If you are feeling tired or think you may be lost, it's a good idea to pull over and take a break. Many roads have marked areas where you can pull off and stretch your legs, have a snack, and consult your map. The glorious scenery can be a huge distraction so, if you find it hard to keep your eyes on the road, it's best to stop and admire the view. Parks and areas with nature trails also make good picnic stops. Ireland does not have US- or Continental-style rest areas, as distances are not great between towns with pubs, gas stations and other public facilities.

Breakdown and Accident Procedures

If you have a breakdown or accident, move the car safely off the road and turn on hazard lights or use a warning triangle (it is compulsory to carry one). Emergency telephones are sometimes located along the hard shoulders of the motorways, but along rural back roads it is best to have a cell phone.

Rental car companies will normally provide a number to call in case of breakdown or problems with the vehicle. They will advise or arrange for assistance, and can usually provide a replacement vehicle quickly. No repairs should be undertaken on a rental car without the company's authorization. If you are a member of the AA, RAC, or AAA, check whether reciprocal services are available in Ireland.

Above Dangerous bend warning sig[n]

If you are involved in an accident, you must stop and exchange name, address, and car registration details with the other parties involved. The police must be notified within 24 hours if anyone is injured and a report will be filed. Call the emergenc[y] services (see p13) if there are casualtie[s]. Be sure to get the insurance details of the other driver and give them yours. If your vehicle is rented, the company must be notified.

Circumstances can be confusing at the time of an accident, so do not admit fault, accept liability, or give money to any party. If possible, take down details from any independent witnesses. It is also a wise idea to tak[e] photographs of any vehicle damage.

Parking

Parking is allowed wherever you see a round sign marked with a red P. A diagonal line crossing the sign means that parking is prohibited. A red circle marked with an X means the road is a Clearway, and you may not stop on it during the hours indicated. Double yellow lines on the pavement mean no parking at any time. Parking lots and other parking areas are designated by a blue P sign. It is permissible to park on the street unless signs indicate otherwise.

Above left Cows on the road near Kells **Above center** Scenic drive sign, Gortin Glen Forest Park **Above right** Sign for Glenariff, Northern Ireland

However, check in case there is a parking scheme in operation, such as Pay and Display, in which you obtain a ticket from a nearby machine and display in on your windshield. Disc parking is another system used in many towns, whereby you must buy a scratch card from a nearby shop and scratch off the date and time before displaying it in your car. In many rural towns and villages, there is little room for parking in the center, but there are parking lots, usually free, situated at the edge of town. In the countryside, be sure not to block farm or other gates or private roads if you are leaving your vehicle for a walk or to explore archeological sites. On single-lane roads, never park in designated passing places, as this is a traffic hazard.

In the cities, where space is at a premium, parking regulations are strictly enforced, often by towing or wheel-clamping. These are strong deterrents to parking illegally or overstaying the time limit on a parking meter, as it is can prove very expensive to get a car released. In the Republic, traffic wardens and police can issue on-the-spot fines for parking offenses. Should you receive one, be sure to get an official receipt from the person collecting the fine. It is best to use a designated parking lot, and some now

accept credit cards. Drivers with disabilities can use their UK blue badge to park in designated spaces in Ireland. For further assistance and information, and for disabled drivers from other countries, contact the Disabled Drivers' Association of Ireland.

Maps

Free tourist maps are widely available, but they are seldom of much use for back-roads driving. It is useful to have a map that gives place names in both English and Irish, especially if traveling in Gaeltacht areas such as Connemara and Donegal. The *Ordnance Survey Complete Road Atlas of Ireland* is highly recommended. This can be purchased at gas stations, bookshops, newsagents, and tourist information centers. Even with the best map in the world, you are likely to have to stop and ask directions somewhere along the way. Locals usually refer to roads by their direction rather than their number, as in "take the Limerick road," so it's helpful to know which towns are near your destination.

Below far left Sheep on village street, Achill Island **Below left** Array of signs in the Glen of Aherlow **Below center** Yield sign in Irish **Below** Road through Galbally, Glen of Aherlow

DIRECTORY

MOTORING ASSOCIATIONS

Automobile Association (AA)
01 617 9999 (Republic of Ireland);
0870 600 0371 (Northern Ireland);
www.aaireland.ie

Aviva Ireland Breakdown Cover
1800 448 888;
www.aviva.ie

Trailers and Motorhomes/RVs

Trailers and motorhomes are subject to the same rules of the road as any other vehicle. However, camper vans or cars towing trailers are restricted to speeds of 50 mph (80 km/h) unless signs indicate otherwise. Trailer and motorhome drivers should also leave a greater space between them and the vehicle in front, to allow for the greater stopping distance required. Many of Ireland's country roads are very narrow and winding, and they may not be suitable for trailers and motorhomes. Signs are often posted, but they are easy to miss. It is worth inquiring locally about conditions before setting out on these roads. Narrow bridges, sharp curves, and bends and steep gradients can be potentially dangerous for large vehicles, so pay attention to road signs warning of such hazards.

If you are bringing your own trailer to Ireland, you must ensure that your LP Gas supply, used for cooking, has been turned off correctly for the ferry crossing.

You can also rent motorhomes and trailers that sleep several people, some fully equipped with sleeping bags, linens, and cooking utensils. For information on rental, repairs, and campsites, and trailer parks throughout Ireland, contact the **Irish Caravan and Camping Council**.

Motorbikes

By law, all motorcyclists and their passengers must wear helmets, and low-beam headlights must be used during the day at all times. To ride a motorcycle in Ireland you must have a valid driving license to cover a motorcycle, and an insurance policy. You may not carry a passenger if you hold only a provisional license; you must have a full license as well as an insurance policy that allows you to do so. Motorcycles must have a white or yellow headlamp, a red rear lamp, a red rear reflector, and rear number plate lighting. Ensure that your tires have adequate tread; the legal minimum is 1 mm. A current road tax disc must be displayed.

The rules of the road are the same for motorcyclists as for other drivers, though you should take additional safety precautions. Do not ride between traffic lanes, moving or stationary. Give other vehicles a wide berth when overtaking, and be alert to the fact that they may not see you.

Driving with Children

Child seats are legally mandatory for children aged between a year and 4 years 6 months. Children under the age of 12 are not allowed to ride in the front seat. Babies and small children must be placed in a restraint system suitable for their height and weight, such as a child seat or baby carrier. Infants must never be placed in a rear-facing child seat in the front passenger seat if there is an active airbag fitted. Children over the age of three who are under 5 ft (150 cm) tall and weigh less than 80 lb (36 kg) must use the appropriate child or booster seat or booster cushion. Remember to request any necessary child seats in advance when making a car rental reservation. It is the driver's responsibility to ensure that any passengers under the age of 17 comply with these laws.

Above Devil's Pass, near Lough Nafooe

Disabled Drivers

Drivers with disabilities who have a Disabled Parking card or UK Blue Badge can use designated disabled parking spaces around Ireland, either in their own vehicle or a rented one. The card or badge should be clearly visible on the dashboard. Contact the **Disabled Drivers' Association of Ireland (DDAI)** or the **Irish Wheelchair Association** for more details. If you are bringing your own vehicle to Ireland, you may be entitled to a discount from the ferry company on some sailings. Contact the company concerned, your motoring association, or the DDIA for more information.

Car and Motorhome/RV Rental

Most of the big international vehicle rental companies have branches at airports and ferry ports and in all the larger cities, and offer a wide range of vehicles. A good local firm with offices around the country is **Dan Dooley Car Rentals**. To rent a car in Ireland you will need a valid driving license and a credit card. Normally drivers must be between the ages of 21 and 70, but check with the company concerned before you make your reservation, regarding their age restrictions. It is highly recommended to book in advance,

Above Farmer driving cattle along an Irish country lane **Above right** Bikers stopping for a break at a café in Kinvarra, Co Galway

especially during peak season, and you will often get a better rate. Most rental cars in Ireland are manual (standard) shift. Automatic cars are available but they cost more and must always be booked in advance. Consider renting a smaller car than you may be used to at home, as they are much easier to handle on narrow country roads. If you require a child seat, this should be booked well in advance as well.

Always let the rental company know, for insurance purposes, if you plan to drive between the Republic and Northern Ireland. Third party insurance is compulsory and is included in the rate. Some rental agreements also include Collision Damage Waiver (CDW), which limits your liability for damages to the rented car, theft/loss cover, and personal injury insurance; others charge additional fees for these items. Read the agreement carefully if you are at all unsure about what your coverage and liabilities are. Some drivers may be able to use insurance from a personal credit card to claim CDW, but check carefully with your card company to make sure that they cover your trip to Ireland (many don't) and be prepared to show proof of cover. Further information

about car rental is available from the **Car Rental Council** in the Republic and the **British Vehicle and Leasing Association** in Northern Ireland. For information on motorhome rental, contact the **Irish Caravan and Camping Council**.

Driving in Rain and Fog

When rain, mist, fog, or cloudy conditions reduce light levels, low-beam headlights should be used. Turn on fog lights whenever visibility is less than 328 ft (100 m). If you bring a left-hand-drive vehicle over for your trip around Ireland, you will need to deflect the beam of your headlights. Beam-adjusters are simple to use; you can buy them at ferry terminals, or check with your motoring organization. Snow and ice are rare in Ireland, but you still may encounter them in mountain areas in winter. Reduce your speed in adverse conditions, as you will need a far greater braking distance, and poor visibility gives you less time to react to sudden hazards.

Below far left Mountain road near Portsalon, Fanad Peninsula **Below left** Main Street, Cushendall **Below center** Traditional horse-drawn trailer from Tralee **Below** Sheep crossing the road at the foot of Slievemore, Co Mayo

DIRECTORY

CAR AND MOTORHOME/RV RENTAL

Irish Caravan and Camping Council
www.camping-ireland.ie

Dan Dooley Car Rentals
062 53103; www.dan-dooley.ie

Car Rental Council
www.carrentalcouncil.ie

British Vehicle Renting and Leasing Association
www.bvrla.co.uk

CAMPING AND TRAILERS

Irish Caravan and Camping Council
www.camping-ireland.ie

Irish Horse Drawn Caravans
www.irishhorsedrawncaravans.com

DISABLED DRIVERS

Disabled Drivers' Association of Ireland
094 936 4054; www.ddai.ie

Irish Wheelchair Association
01 818 6400; www.iwa.ie

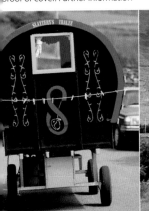

Where to Stay

Ireland offers some of the most romantic and special places imaginable in which to stay, from historic castles to traditional horse-drawn caravans, charming rural cottages to chic boutique hotels. The warm welcome that visitors receive in Ireland is like no other, and getting to know the hosts at a farmhouse bed-and-breakfast or family-run guesthouse is part of a memorable visit. The accommodation in this guide has been specially selected to reflect the unique Irish character of its back roads.

Above Youth hostel entrance, High Street, Kilkenny City

Hotels

Ireland has a fine range of traditional hotels across the country, with properties to suit all budgets. Some might be picturesque village inns; others may have been converted from former stately homes or other landmark buildings. Whether their decor is elegant and luxurious or modest and comfortable, these hotels have great character and charm, often with lovely features such as stone fireplaces or decorative plasterwork ceilings. Many also have a lively pub or acclaimed restaurant attached, making them a gathering place for the local community too. The websites of **Ireland's Blue Book** and the **Good Food Ireland** list many such traditional hotels.

Country-house hotels are set in beautiful grounds and are usually elegant and spacious. Food is often a highlight, with creative menus prepared by a top chef and served in a formal dining room. They may also offer a range of activities, from angling and horseback riding to cooking courses. Some do not accept young children. The **Hidden Ireland Guide** and **Manor House Hotels and Irish Country Hotels** list many of these special properties.

Ireland also has numerous resort hotels with impressive golf and other sporting activities available, as well as luxurious spa facilities.

Increasingly it is possible to find a choice of boutique hotels in towns and resort areas as well as in larger cities, with rooms and public areas featuring the best in modern design. They usually have hip and lively bars and restaurants, too.

As well as all these, Ireland also has a range of national and international chain hotels with accommodation in all price ranges, which can be found in the larger towns and cities or along the more major roads.

Depending on their rating (see opposite), most hotel rooms have private bathroom facilities, and some also offer family rooms and suites. Most include breakfast in the room rate, and larger hotels will normally have a restaurant and bar.

The **Irish Hotels Federation** publishes *Be Our Guest*, an annual guide to hotels and guesthouses in the Republic. The **Northern Ireland Hotels Federation** provides a similar service in the north. These properties have been inspected and approved by the tourist boards, and are identified by a green shamrock symbol.

Guesthouses

Guesthouses are smaller and usually less expensive than hotels. They are often family-run, with an emphasis on personal service. Many are set in large Georgian or Victorian houses, with all or several rooms converted for guests, often with simple but charming decor. Those with higher ratings will have private bathrooms; those in lower categories may have shared facilities for some rooms. Breakfast is usually included in the rate, but most guesthouses do not have a restaurant or bar, although they may have snacks and drinks available for guests.

In smaller towns and villages, pubs may have guestrooms available, and this can be an enjoyable way to experience the local nightlife without having to drive afterwards.

Bed-and-Breakfast

Bed-and-breakfast (B&B) is offered in private homes around the country, from busy town centers to remote villages. Traditional Irish farmhouse B&Bs are among the most popular. They have from one to three guestrooms, often with private but sometimes with shared bathrooms. Facilities and decor vary, but are

Above Picturesque café in Gowran, Kilkenny **Above right** Resort hotel with its own golf course near Lough Erne, Fermanagh Lakelands

usually clean and neat. Some hosts will offer an evening meal for an additional charge, but this must be arranged in advance, and is usually taken at a large communal table with the family and other guests. B&Bs are generally cheaper than hotels and guesthouses, and are a great way to meet local people. For a range of bed-and-breakfast options, contact the **Friendly Homes of Ireland**, **B&B Ireland**, and **Northern Ireland Bed&Breakfast Partnership**.

Castles and Historic Homes

The most stunning accommodation in Ireland can be found in castles and historic homes that have opened some of their rooms to overnight visitors. Although such an experience does not come cheap, a night or two in one of these landmark buildings can be the most memorable of any trip. For listings, see Ireland's Blue Book, Hidden Ireland, **Elegant Ireland**, and the **Irish Landmark Trust**.

Reservations

It is essential to book ahead for stays in July and August, as well as at other peak times. Reservations can usually be made by phone or online with a credit card. Alternatively, use the reservation service offered by the regional tourist boards (see p15) or the **Gulliver** reservation system, which lists all officially approved accommodation in Ireland.

Be sure to check if the rate quoted is per person or per room – B&Bs and guesthouses almost always charge per person, as do many hotels. Also check if the hotel rate includes tax.

Facilities and Prices

Irish hotel rooms generally have a double or twin beds; if a crib or child's bed is required, request it at the time of booking. Coffee- and tea-making facilities are standard. Most places serve a full Irish breakfast, with a lighter "continental" option available.

Hotels are rated from one to five stars. Few one-star properties have private facilities, while a five-star rating signifies luxury. Guesthouses are classified separately, from one to four stars. Generally, the higher the star rating, the more expensive the room, but prices also vary seasonally.

Below far left Pretty thatched cottage in Skerries, Co Dublin **Below left** Historic Ardgillan Castle, Co Dublin **Below** Clonmel, set on the banks of the River Suir, Co Tipperary

DIRECTORY

HOTELS AND HISTORIC HOMES
Ireland's Blue Book
01 676 9914; www.irelands-blue-book.ie

Good Food Ireland
053 915 8693; www.goodfoodireland.ie

The Hidden Ireland Guide
01 662 7166; www.hiddenireland.com

Manor House Hotels and Irish Country Hotels
01 295 8900; www.cmvhotels.com

Irish Hotels Federation
01 808 4419; www.irelandhotels.com

Northern Ireland Hotels Federation
028 9077 6635; www.nihf.co.uk

Elegant Ireland
01 473 2505; www.elegant.ie

Irish Landmark Trust
01 670 4733; www.irishlandmark.com

GUESTHOUSES AND B&BS
Friendly Homes of Ireland
01 288 9355; www.adamsandbutler.com

B&B Ireland
071 982 2222; www.bandbireland.com

Northern Ireland Bed & Breakfast Partnership
028 2177 1308

RESERVATIONS
Gulliver
1850 668 668 (in the Republic);
+353 (0)669 791 804 (in Northern Ireland and Great Britain and from abroad);
www.gulliver.ie or www.goireland.com

PRICES
The following price bands are for a standard double room in high season:

Republic of Ireland
Inexpensive – under €100
Moderate – €100–€200
Expensive – over €200

Northern Ireland
Inexpensive – under £100
Moderate – £100–£200
Expensive – over £200

Where to Eat

With its green pastures, fertile farmland, and clear coastal waters, Ireland enjoys an abundance of high-quality produce. In recent years, Ireland's restaurants have come into their own and now talented chefs are turning all that premium beef, succulent lamb, and fresh seafood into New Irish cuisine in acclaimed restaurants throughout the country. For those on a budget, there are hearty pub meals as well as that Irish favorite, fish and chips, not to mention endless delicious items for a memorable picnic.

Above One of the many pubs in the Temple Bar district of Dublin

Practical Information

A cooked breakfast – commonly known as a "Full Irish" or "Ulster Fry" – at your accommodation could easily keep you going throughout the day. If not, lunch is normally served from noon or 12:30pm until 2:30 or 3pm. Restaurants and cafés in larger towns and cities have longer hours than those in smaller towns and villages. Although it was once customary in Ireland to eat a large meal at midday, dinner is now the main meal for most people. Restaurants' evening hours vary. Most open between 5:30 and 7pm. In larger towns and tourist areas they may serve until 10 or 11pm, but in smaller towns and villages they often close at 9pm, with last orders 30 minutes earlier. Many pubs serve bar food from lunchtime until around 9pm. Restaurants often close for a day or two each week (usually Mondays), but many smaller establishments in busy areas stay open seven days. Off the beaten track, they may close out of season.

Credit cards are widely accepted, but pubs, cafés and take-out places may take cash only. Tax is always included in the bill. A service charge is often added as well; if not, expect to leave a tip of 10–15 percent.

Casual dress is acceptable in most restaurants, though you may want to dress smartly for more expensive establishments. Most places are wheelchair-accessible, but check in advance. Children are allowed into pubs with their parents until 9pm in winter and 10pm in summer. Smoking is banned in any indoor area, including restaurants and bars.

Menus are generally displayed outside, so it is possible to make an informed decision before entering. Fine dining establishments usually offer a set-price menu as well as à la carte. These can be excellent value, especially at lunchtime, and allow you to enjoy a top restaurant at an affordable price.

Restaurants

Restaurants in Ireland range from cozy, casual dining to trendy bistro-style hotspots to traditional dining rooms set with crystal and fine china. Many country house hotels offer outstanding dining in an elegant setting, and they are often open to non-guests who book in advance. Wild salmon, fresh seafood, oysters, and mussels feature on menus in season. The current trend is for New Irish cuisine, which uses accents from Europe, America, and the Pacific Rim to put a fresh spin on familiar dishes. However, it is also well worth seeking out small, local restaurants that serve traditional Irish dishes, such as boxty (potato pancakes) or the classic Irish stew. There are plenty of ethnic dining options too, from Indian and Chinese restaurants to Japanese noodle bars to Italian restaurants and pizzerias.

Nearly all restaurants feature at least one vegetarian option, often more. Fine dining establishments usually have impressive wine lists, as well as a good selection of Irish whiskeys and other spirits. It may be necessary to book well in advance for a table in a top restaurant. In Northern Ireland, look for restaurants with the Taste of Ulster designation, a symbol of quality.

Visitors returning to Ireland will be shocked to find that restaurant prices have risen significantly in recent years, and Ireland is no longer the bargain that it once was when it comes to quality dining. It may be possible to cut costs by opting for the "early-bird" specials at some restaurants, though this will, of course, entail dining rather early (between 5:30 and 7pm).

Above left A grocer's shop in the Boyne Valley **Above center** Pavement seating at a café in Carlow City **Above right** Shops along Malahide's main street

Pubs and Bars

The most reliable option for an inexpensive but delicious meal is the traditional Irish pub. An assortment of classic dishes usually features on the menu, along with burgers, lasagne, fish and chips, and other standards. Pubs serve hot meals at lunch and dinner. Some have table service, but it's more usual to order at the bar, in which case a substantial tip is not expected.

Hotel bars and wine bars may also serve snacks and light meals. Eighteen is the minimum legal drinking age in Ireland.

Cafés and Take-out

For snacks and light meals, there is an array of cafés, cafeterias, and bakeries. Cafés are generally open for breakfast and lunch, but many close by 6pm. Most museums and visitor attractions have cafeterias serving light refreshments. Ireland has not escaped the coffee craze. There are bustling branches of international chains, as well as individual coffeeshops, in larger towns and cities. Most sell sandwiches and pastries as well. Look out for traditional tea shops, where you can have a pot of tea or coffee along with homemade cakes, breads, and local specialities.

Ireland has all the usual fast-food chains, but far more enjoyable is take-out from the local "chippy," or fish and chip shop. On the coast, this is an experience not to be missed. Bakeries often sell pasties (a thick, enclosed pastry case filled with meat and vegetables) and other baked goods that make quick, filling, and inexpensive snacks on the go.

Picnics

Most towns will have a sandwich shop, where you can grab ready-made picnic supplies. More fun are the independent food shops and delicatessens that usually offer a great range of cured meats, patés, cheeses and other local delicacies.

Best of all are the colorful farmers' markets. These are a showcase for regional producers and you should be able to stock your picnic basket with home-baked breads, local cheeses, honey and preserves, and fresh seasonal fruit. Each driving tour notes the location and days of the week for markets around the region.

Below far left Old School House Café, Inistioge, Co Kilkenny **Below left** Pavement café in Dublin's Temple Bar **Below center** A pub in Temple Bar **Below** Fish specials at Howth Harbour

The Flavors of Ireland

For a small island, Ireland offers an amazing range of foods, and a high standard of both cooking and presentation. Some of Ireland's specialty dishes, such as boxty and colcannon, are based on its humble staple, the potato. Artisan breads and Irish cheeses are made to traditional recipes in time-honored fashion. Fresh salmon, oysters, and other seafood take pride of place on menus in season. And you can enjoy Ireland's best ales and stout, and its exquisite aged whiskeys, at any time of year.

Above Flower-decked storefronts along Main Street, Cashel, Co Tipperary

Irish Specialties
Ireland has a marvelous array of traditional dishes to try. Most are based on simple ingredients – potatoes, cabbage, bacon, and the like – that were important staples in the centuries when Ireland was primarily a rural country. A culinary resurgence has seen these basics being used in new ways by artisan food producers, and there is often great pride invested in their cooking.

Perhaps because they're mostly cooked at home, many traditional Irish dishes can be surprisingly hard to find on restaurant menus. They are most likely to appear as daily specials in family-run pubs or small cafés, or in independently owned restaurants that specialize in Irish home cooking.

Irish stew is the national dish, a slow-cooked casserole made with neck of mutton (mature lamb), potatoes, carrots, and onions, and served with fresh bread and butter. Dublin coddle is made with pork sausages, bacon, and vegetables cooked in a ham or apple cider stock. The magical combination of beef and Guinness makes for a rich, dark stew, sometimes with the addition of oysters for extra luxury.

Of Ireland's many potato dishes, a favorite is boxty, a griddled pancake made of grated raw and mashed cooked potato with buttermilk. Others to look out for include champ (or poundies), a mashed potato and spring onion dish served shaped like a volcano with warmed milk and a knob of butter in the "crater," and colcannon, made with mashed potatoes, onions, and cabbage.

Fish and Seafood
The abundance of fresh fish and seafood from the Atlantic, the Irish Sea and the country's many rivers is one of the delights of eating out in Ireland. Locally caught fish such as wild salmon and trout are highlights on many restaurant menus, and oak- or peat-smoked salmon is a popular starter. Herring, mackerel, and eels are also served smoked or fresh. Fish chowder is sold in most pubs and restaurants in coastal villages. Seafood and shellfish are plentiful along the coast: mussels from Bantry Bay, langoustines from Dublin Bay, and oysters from Galway Bay are the most renowned. Oysters are often served with Guinness at annual oyster festivals in the region.

Breads and Baked Goods
Bread is baked and served as proudly as any other food in Ireland, and there is a delicious assortment to try. A slice of warm, freshly baked bread, generously spread with butter, and a cup of tea is a traditional sign of hospitality. Homemade brown or soda bread is an accompaniment to most meals. Soda bread, which has a light texture, uses baking soda instead of yeast as a leavening agent, and also contains buttermilk. In Northern Ireland, soda bread is baked in the "farl" shape, with a cross slashed into the top of the dough, giving it a flatter form that is easily split into four sections. Soda farls are a key constituent in an Ulster fry. When made with wholemeal (rather than white) flour, soda bread is called brown bread in the Republic and wheaten bread in Northern Ireland. In Waterford, the traditional soft white doughy roll (bun) known as blaa was brought to the city by the Huguenots in the 17th century.

There is also a wide variety of sweet breads and cakes to try: scones; barm brack, a rich, fruity cake-bread traditionally eaten at Hallowe'en; and porter cake, which is made with dried fruit and stout.

Above Market in Moore Street, Dublin **Above center left** A perfect pint of Guinness **Above center right** Platter of oysters **Above right** Irish stew

Irish Cheeses

Cheese-making is a centuries-old art in Ireland, dating back to the time of the monasteries. Today, several dozen farmhouse-made cheeses are produced as local specialties, and are well worth sampling. There are just two blue cheeses produced in Ireland. Cashel Blue is a semi-soft, medium-strength unpasteurized cow's milk cheese with a creamy texture. Its sister cheese, Crozier Blue, is made from pasteurized sheep's milk and is as delicious young and crumbly as it is when mature and creamy. Both are from Tipperary. Durrus is a round, semi-soft raw milk cheese with a coral-colored washed rind, produced on the Sheep's Head Peninsula. Milleens is a similar style of cheese from the Beara Peninsula, as is Gubbeen, from Schull on Mizen Head. Another washed-rind cheese, with a rich, earthy flavor, Ardrahan comes from inland County Cork. Corleggy is a hard goat's milk cheese made in County Cavan. The same producers make Quivvy, a soft goat's milk cheese preserved in olive oil.

Stouts and Ales

Guinness is Ireland's most famous drink, and many believe that it tastes best on home soil, close to where it is brewed in Dublin, because the taste and texture of this dark, heavy beer, also known as "stout" is affected by how it is stored. A perfect pint is poured slowly and topped with a thick, creamy head. Other good Irish stouts are Beamish and the slightly milder Murphy's. Ales, made with malted barley, are also very popular. The best-selling brand is Smithwick's, produced at Ireland's oldest brewery, in Kilkenny. In pubs, be sure to try the excellent "real ales" that are produced by local micro-breweries.

Irish Whiskey

Whiskey has been made in Ireland since at least the 12th century. The first commercial distillery, Kilbeggan, was founded in 1757. Major brands include Bushmills, Jameson, and Powers, but Cooley Distillery is the only independent Irish-owned distillery left. Several working and former distilleries offer tours that explain the Irish triple-distillation process. Irish whiskey is matured in wooden casks for at least seven years, giving it a distinctive flavor.

Below far left Traditional Irish bar **Below left** Temple Bar, Dublin **Below center** Dublin coddle **Below center right** Irish coffee pudding **Below far right** High-quality Galway salmon

The Irish Pub

The archetypal Irish pub is noted for its friendly locals, genial staff and the *craic* (pronounced "crack," an Irish term for good times). Irish pubs date back to medieval taverns, coaching inns, and the *shebeens*, illegal drinking dens, that flourished under colonial rule. In the Victorian era, brewing and distilling were major industries. The sumptuous interiors of some city pubs are testament to these times, furnished with mahogany and marble bar counters. Snugs, or partitioned-off booths, are another typical feature of Irish pubs. Some rural pubs double as the village grocer's shop. The best pubs are not evenly distributed throughout Ireland. In the southeast, Kilkenny is awash with great pubs, while Cork and Kerry possess some of the most picturesque. The Lower Shannon region is noted for its boisterous pubs, especially in County Clare where spontaneous music sessions are common. The West has an abundance of typical pubs, and the many tourists and students guarantee a profusion of good ones in Galway.

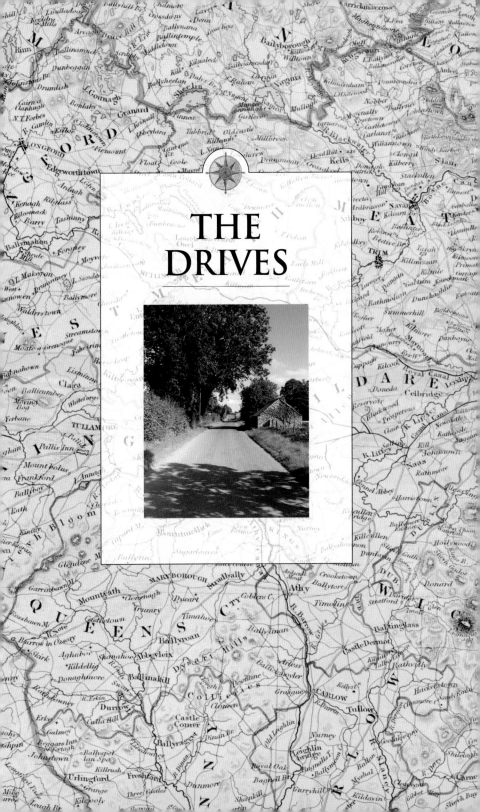

THE DRIVES

A Taste of East Cork

Cork City to Youghal

Highlights

- **Wonderful wildlife**
  See exotic and endangered species roaming free at Fota Wildlife Park

- **Maritime history**
  Learn about Irish emigration, the last days of the *Titanic*, and Sir Walter Raleigh in the old ports of Cobh and Youghal

- **Rare birds and heavenly coves**
  Spot rare sea and marsh birds on a walk along the cliffs to Paradise Cove from Ballycotton fishing harbor

- **Golden sands**
  Wander along the beautiful golden sandy beach at Youghal

- **Local flavours**
  Sample Jameson Irish whiskey and buy fabulous picnic fare from Cork's historic English Market

Cobh Harbor - one of the world's deepest natural harbors

A Taste of East Cork

East Cork is a relaxed and peaceful region to visit, with many beautiful places to enjoy, from the stately home and wildlife park of Fota to the golden beaches and clifftop walks of Youghal and Ballycotton. The expanse of coastline and harbors including historic Cobh has endowed the area with a rich maritime legacy. This short drive begins in lively Cork City itself, and follows the shores of lovely Cork Harbour to reach the spectacular bays of Ballycotton and Youghal. It also ventures inland from the fishing villages of the shore through the lush pastures that provide the fresh produce – from fine cheeses to pig's feet and oysters to corned mutton – for which the region is justly celebrated.

0 kilometers 5

0 miles

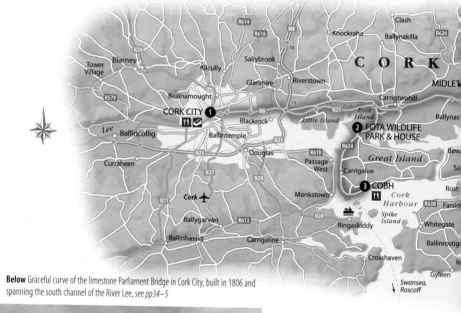

Below Graceful curve of the limestone Parliament Bridge in Cork City, built in 1806 and spanning the south channel of the River Lee, see pp34–5

KEY

Drive route

ACTIVITIES

Follow the Titanic Trail and undergo the Titanic Experience in historic Cobh

Watch a cooking demonstration at world-famous Ballymaloe House

Set sail for a sea-angling trip in lovely Ballycotton Bay

Enjoy a swim from the 5-mile (8-km) Blue Flag beach of Youghal

ew across Ballycotton Bay to the fishing village of Ballycotton and its sheltering island, *see p37*

PLAN YOUR DRIVE

Start/finish: Cork City to Youghal.

Number of days: 2, allowing half a day to explore Cork City.

Distance: 53 miles (86 km).

Road conditions: Roads are good, with most of the drive taking place on regional roads. There are some smaller, unclassified roads toward the end of the drive. On such roads there may not be a central line marked, and drivers should take care on bends in case of oncoming vehicles.

When to go: East Cork is lovely in every season, but be prepared for mixed weather – warm sunshine, rain, or cold winds – at any time of year, and pack appropriate clothing.

Opening times: Most shops and attractions open 9 or 10am–5 or 6pm. Shops open Mon–Sat; in large towns also 12–6pm on Sun. Convenience stores in villages open 8am until late.

Main market days: Cork City: Mon–Sat; Cobh: Fri; Midleton: Farmers' Market, Sat.

Shopping: In Cork City, explore the small shops of the pedestrianized Huguenot Quarter, and don't miss the English Market. Midleton is home to Jameson Irish whiskey, where visitors can purchase as well as sample.

Major festivals: Cork City: Jazz Festival, Oct; Film Festival, Nov; Cobh: Maritime Song Festival, May–Jun; Midleton: East Cork Early Music Festival, Sep; Food Festival, Sep; Youghal: Visual Arts Festival, Jul.

DAY TRIP OPTIONS

For **lovers of history**, a day divided between Cork City and Cobh would be time well spent. **Epicureans** will enjoy Midleton and Shanagarry, which offer both fine whiskey and fine food, while, for **families**, the wonderful beaches, clifftop walks and historic harbors of Ballycotton and Youghal would be hard to beat. For full details, *see p37*.

elow The peaceful promenade and bandstand in Cobh, on Great Island, *see p36*

Above The elegant English Market in Cork

❶ Cork City

Co Cork

Cork is a compact city with a lively atmosphere and plenty of historic sights. There are museums and churches to explore, and a church steeple to climb with bells to ring. Whether it's the impressive architecture of Cork Opera House, the bustling atmosphere and great local produce of the indoor English Market, or the little shops and cafés of the Huguenot Quarter, there's something for everyone to love in this friendly city.

A half-day walking tour

From the parking lot on Grand Parade by the **Tourist Office** ①, turn right. The **Cork City Library** ② *(closed Sun)* is across **Grand Parade** and further along on the same side is **Bishop Lucey Park** ③, which has remains of a 13th-century city wall. Cross Grand Parade again for the bustling indoor **English Market** ④. At the end of Grand Parade, turn right into St. Patrick Street. The pedestrianized streets of the **Huguenot Quarter** ⑤, running between St. Patrick Street and Paul Street, are worth exploring, with lots of small shops, cafés, and galleries. Turn left on Paul Street, then right into **Cornmarket Street** ⑥ where there is an outdoor market, especially good on a Saturday. Turn left into Kyle Street, then right into North Main Street and across the road to reach the **Cork Vision Centre** ⑦ *(open*

Giraffes at Fota Wildlife Park

Tue–Sat), with audiovisual displays about Cork City. Leaving here, turn left and, at the River Lee, turn right along the quays to **Cork Opera House** ⑧ and the **Crawford Art Gallery** ⑨ *(open Mon–Sat),* with work by Jack B. Yeats, Louis le Brocquy, and Paul Henry.

Cross the river here, turn left, then immediately right along Upper John Street, taking the first left onto Dominick Street for the historic Shandon area. Over to the right is the landmark **St. Ann's Church** ⑩. The bells in its 120-ft (36-m) steeple which is open to climb, are famous and, for anyone who ascends to the top, it is possible to try their hand at ringing them, and admire the views. Around the corner on O'Connell Square is the **Cork Butter Museum** ⑪ *(open daily),* in what was the world's largest butter market, telling the story of Ireland's most important food export

Below Tall, pastel-shaded buildings add character to the sweep of Popes Quay, Cork City

Where to Stay: inexpensive, under €100; moderate, €100–€200; expensive, over €200

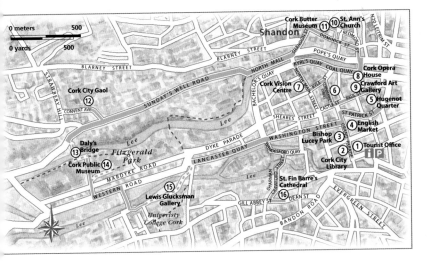

The English Market

Although there has been a market here since 1610, the current elegant covered market hall was built in 1786, and extensively restored after fires in 1980 and 1986. Despite its name (dating from the days of English rule) the best of regional and national produce is to be found here, from fine cheeses to pigs' feet, but there are also delicacies from around the world. The galleried upper level makes for great people-watching, and you can sample local fare at its cafés and restaurants (www.corkenglishmarket.ie).

Turn left and walk down Shandon Street to the river, turn right along North Mall and Sunday's Well Road and turn right into Convent Avenue for a tour of the 19th-century Gothic-style **Cork City Gaol** ⑫ *(open daily)*.

Return to Sunday's Well Road and cross the river via **Daly's Bridge** ⑬, a fine 1926 suspension footbridge (known as "the shaky bridge" because it moves as people cross it) into **Fitzgerald Park** for the **Cork Public Museum** ⑭ *(open daily)*, which tells the history of Cork and its most famous citizens.

From here, walk south, crossing Western Road, and over the South Channel of the River Lee to the campus of University College Cork. Don't miss the contemporary art at the **Lewis Glucksman Gallery** ⑮ *(open Tue–Sat, Sun afternoons)*; its cantilevered concrete design is an artwork in itself.

Turn right along the River Lee and Lancaster Quay, right again at the end onto Wandesford Quay, then right into Sharman Crawford Street. **St. Fin Barre's Cathedral** ⑯ was consecrated in 1870 on the site of a monastery founded by the saint in the 7th century. Its elegant spires are a city landmark. Walk back to the river, cross it, and turn right into Washington Street to return to Grand Parade.

🚗 *From Cork City, take the N8, then N25 signed to Waterford. Turn right on R624 to Cobh and continue on this for 2.5 miles (4 km) to Fota Wildlife Park.*

❷ Fota Wildlife Park & House
Carrigtwohill, Co Cork

Founded in 1983 as an adjunct to Dublin Zoo, and situated on lovely Fota Island, the **Fota Wildlife Park** *(open daily)* is a 70-acre (28-ha) conservation center where wildlife can roam free. It is home to rare species such as red pandas, as well as penguins, monkeys, cheetahs, marsupials, and many others. A train takes visitors through the varied habitats. **Fota House** *(open daily)* is the 19th-century Regency-style house at the heart of the estate, with a superb art collection and fine Neo-Classical interiors. Its arboretum includes rare trees and shrubs from around the world, and the lovely gardens also feature a fernery and an orangery.

🚗 *On leaving the Fota Wildlife Park, turn right and follow the R624 over the bridge to Great Island and Cobh.*

Above Cork City's lowering Gothic-style 19th-century Gaol

EAT AND DRINK IN CORK CITY

Farmgate Café *inexpensive*
Fresh ingredients are transformed into classic regional dishes – from oysters and chowder or corned mutton – in this lively market setting.
English Market; 021 427 8134; www.farmgate.ie; closed Sun

Jacobs on the Mall *moderate*
Foodies flock to this award-winning restaurant for delicious, modern European cuisine served in converted Turkish baths.
30a South Mall; 021 425 1530; www.jacobsonthemall.com; eves only, closed Sun

Jacques Restaurant *expensive*
The multiple award-winning Jacques attracts an elegant crowd with its quality Irish ingredients prepared in an imaginative way.
Phoenix Street; 021 427 7387; www.jacquesrestaurant.ie

Eat and Drink: inexpensive, under €25; moderate, €25–€50; expensive, over €50

Above The Old Distillery at Midleton
Right Huge copper pot still at the Jameson Experience, Midleton

VISITING COBH

Parking
Parking along the waterfront is free for the first hour, but then requires a disc available from local shops. There are two free parking lots: one on the waterfront; one above the cathedral.

Tourist Information
Old Yacht Club; 021 481 3301; www.eastcorktourism.com

WHERE TO STAY

AROUND MIDLETON

Barnabrow Country House *moderate*
This is a relaxed manor house set in its own grounds and on a clear day there are views all the way to Ballycotton Island in the distance. The walled garden supplies the kitchens.
Cloyne, Midleton (take R629 from Midleton, then left on R631); 021 465 2534; www.barnabrowhouse.ie

AROUND SHANAGARRY

Garryvoe Hotel *moderate*
This comfortable hotel has views over the stunning beach at Garryvoe, as well as Ballycotton Bay.
Ballycotton Bay, Castlemartyr (on drive route taking R632 from Midleton to Shanagarry); 021 464 6718; www.garryvoehotel.com

BALLYCOTTON

Bayview Hotel *moderate*
This is a comfortable and relaxing hotel in the quiet fishing village of Ballycotton, with views over the Bay.
021 464 6746; www.thebayviewhotel. com; closed Oct–Easter

③ Cobh
Co Cork
Cobh, once known as Queenstown, on Great Island is a pretty town with bright Victorian terraces overlooking Cork Harbour, one of the world's deepest natural harbors.

Cobh was the last port for the ill-fated *Titanic*, and the Queenstown Story at the **Cobh Heritage Centre** *(www.cobhheritage.com; open daily)* tells the history of the liner as well as that of Irish emigration to America – two and a half million people left from Cobh alone after the Famine. The **Titanic Trail** *(www.titanic-trail.com; departs Commodore Hotel daily at 11am)*, a guided walking tour, takes in sights such as the Titanic Memorial, the White Star Line office, and **Cobh Museum** *(Mar–Oct: open daily)*.
🚗 *Retrace route on R624 north to N25 junction. Here, take second exit for N25 to Rosslare. Continue on N25, then turn left onto R627 at the sign for Midleton.*

④ Midleton
Co Cork
Midleton is a busy commercial town, and the center of production for the majority of Irish whiskey. Find out how "the water of life" is distilled at the Jameson Experience in **The Old Distillery** *(www.jamesonwhiskey.com; open daily)*. There are guided tours, ending with a sample glass or tutored tasting *(book in advance)*. En route to Shanagarry are the magnificent golden sands of Garryvoe beach.
🚗 *From Midleton, return to the N25 and follow the road to Castlemartyr. Turn right at the bridge onto the R632 for Ladysbridge. Go through Garryvoe and follow the road to Shanagarry.*

Ballymaloe Cookery School
Ballymaloe attracts would-be chefs and keen cooks from far and wide. It was founded by Myrtle Allen in 1983 and today her daughter-in-law Darina, a renowned chef, is at the helm. Courses range from short demonstrations to half a day or a full 12-week Certificate Course for budding professionals. The school (and restaurant) kitchen is supplied with herbs, fruits, and vegetables from the 200-year-old gardens *(021 464 6785; www.cookingisfun.ie)*.

Below Gateway to Ballymaloe House

⑤ Shanagarry
Co Cork
Shanagarry was the birthplace of William Penn, the founding father of Pennsylvania. There are currently plans underway to create a Penn Story visitors' center at his ancestral home, Shanagarry Castle.

Shanagarry is probably most famous of all, however, as home to **Ballymaloe House** and its celebrated ulinary school (from the village ollow signs to the culinary school or ake the R629 toward Cloyne to the ront entrance). Non-guests may visit he **gardens** *(May–Sep: open daily)* and hop, which sells local produce, easonal plants, and fancy kitchenware. ⬛ *From Shanagarry, take a left turn t the gas station onto the R629 and ollow to Ballycotton.*

⑥ Ballycotton
o Cork

allycotton is a quiet fishing village verlooking a pretty island with a ghthouse that shelters its harbor rom Atlantic gales. Rare seabirds ake shelter at the marshland bird anctuary during stormy weather, ut around 300 species of bird in all isit Ballycotton during the year. A ishing fleet and sea-angling vessels re based in the harbor. There are arious coves and shore walks, and he cliff walk has great views, as well

as steep steps down to a rocky swimming cove, known aptly as Paradise. Take heed of warning signs and fenced-off areas on the walk. ⬛ *Take R629 back to Shanagarry, then turn right onto R632. On reaching Ladysbridge, turn right onto R633 to Ballymacoda. There, turn left onto R634 to Youghal, passing along its picturesque strand.*

⑦ Youghal
Co Cork

The 5 miles (8 km) of golden sandy beach at Youghal naturally play an important part in its popularity as a seaside resort. However, the town is also steeped in history and it is said that Sir Walter Raleigh planted the first Irish potato here in 1585. The ancient port retains original walls and towers from the 13th century. The Clock Gate over the main street dates from 1777; the Collegiate Church of Saint Mary the Virgin from 1220.

Above Ballycotton Island with its lighthouse, buffeted by Atlantic breakers

EAT AND DRINK

COBH

Jacob's Ladder *moderate*
Modern Irish cuisine in a lovely setting with views over Cork Harbour.
Waters Edge Hotel; 021 481 5566; www.watersedgehotel.ie/restaurant

MIDLETON

Farm Gate *moderate*
The store fronting this popular eatery gives a flavor of the delicious organic and home-baked produce it offers.
The Coolbawn; 021 463 2771; www.farmgate.ie; dinner served Thu–Sat only; closed Sun & hols

SHANAGARRY

Ballymaloe House *expensive*
Home of celebrity chef Darina Allen (*see Ballymaloe Cookery School box*), Ballymaloe is acclaimed for gourmet cuisine using local garden produce. Also offers luxury accommodation.
Shanagarry; 021 465 2531; www.ballymaloe.ie

YOUGHAL

Aherne's of Youghal *expensive*
Locally sourced seafood is a specialty in this cozy restaurant in historic Youghal.
163 North Main Street, Youghal; 024 92424; www.ahernes.net

bove The beautiful golden sands at the historic port town and seaside resort of Youghal, hich stretch for miles along the sheltered coast of Youghal Bay

---

DAY TRIP OPTIONS

Cork, Midleton, and Ballycotton are ideal bases to explore the local history, scenery and gourmet delights.

East Cork history trail
Spend the morning exploring historic Cork City ❶, then make the short drive out to Cobh ❸ to walk the Titanic Trail.

Follow the drive instructions but, instead of turning off to Fota Island, continue on the R624 direct to Cobh.

Fine Irish food and drink
Nominate a designated driver, or hire a taxi, to travel the short distance from the Jameson Experience at the Old Distillery in Midleton ❹ to the food-lover's paradise of Ballymaloe House at Shanagarry ❺.

Follow the drive instructions from Midleton to Shanagarry.

A day at the seaside
Go beach-hopping from Ballycotton ❻, ending the day with a seafood supper at Aherne's in Youghal ❼.

Follow the drive instructions or take the coastal road out to the rugged Knockadoon Head.

Eat and Drink: inexpensive, under €25; moderate, €25–€50; expensive, over €50

Islands and Lighthouses

Kinsale to Macroom

Highlights

- **Unspoiled beaches**
  Escape to a tranquil island and stroll on deserted, sandy beaches

- **Spectacular Sheep's Head**
  Walk around the tip of this peninsula for stunning vistas and perhaps a glimpse of whales or dolphins

- **Breathtaking peninsulas**
  Explore rugged scenery, coves, and mountains, stopping off at pretty fishing villages and historic sights

- **Lighthouse panoramas**
  Visit one of the region's many lighthouses and take in some panoramic coastal views

Rainbow over the lush green landscape of the Beara Peninsula

Islands and Lighthouses

West Cork offers some of Ireland's most scenic driving routes, with no fewer than three long, spectacular peninsulas to explore, each stretching southwest into the Atlantic. This drive encompasses a mix of wild forest and lush, cultivated farmland; unspoiled, golden beaches, rocky coves and inlets; and historic ruins and castles. There are opportunities to visit islands including Cape Clear, Sherkin, Hare, Bere, Dursey, and the lonely Fastnet Rock, the most southerly point in Ireland. And all along the route are the tall, imposing lighthouses and beacons that guide ships safely to secluded harbors and bays, from the moody Fastnet lighthouse to the stunning white beacon at Baltimore or the Mizen Head Signal Station perched high on the sea-battered cliffs. As if that weren't enough, every little village on the way has its share of lively pubs and great regional cooking.

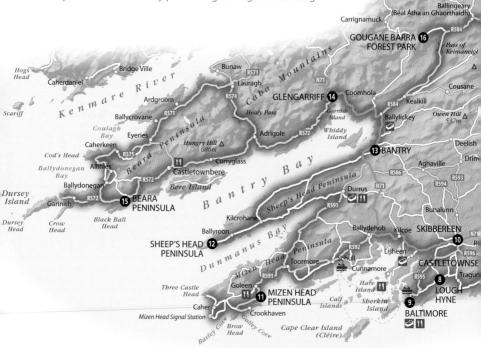

0 kilometers 10

0 miles

ACTIVITIES

Have a surfing lesson at Inchydoney Island

Look out for whales and dolphins from headlands such as Galley Head

Take a boat trip to an island such as Cape Clear, Sherkin, or the iconic Fastnet Rock

Walk part of the Sheep's Head Way, a marked track across rolling countryside and along rugged cliffs

Pedal a stretch of the Beara Way, a cycle route running along picturesque country roads

KEY

 Drive route

Above Pretty shops and houses lining the winding cobbled streets of Kinsale, *see p42*

PLAN YOUR DRIVE

Start/finish: Kinsale to Macroom.

Number of days: 4–5.

Distance: 210 miles (340 km).

Road conditions: Roads are generally good. However, some minor roads may not have central markings so take things slowly and watch out for oncoming vehicles.

When to go: West Cork can be busy at any time of year. It is most peaceful in the winter months, although some restaurants and sights may be closed. The climate is mild all year, but the weather can change quickly, so be prepared for sun or rain.

Opening times: Most shops and attractions open 9 or 10am–5 or 6pm. Shops open Mon–Sat; in large towns also 12–6pm on Sun. Convenience stores in villages open 8am until late.

Main market days: Kinsale: Tue; Clonakilty: Thu; Skibbereen: Fri, Sat; Schull: Sun; Bantry: Fri. These are among the country's best Farmers' Markets and an ideal way to sample the area's fine produce.

Shopping: With its temperate climate, lush famlands, and traditional farming methods, West Cork has become well-known for its excellent artisan food producers. World-class cheeses from Gubbeen and Durrus, cured meats from Gubbeen, and slow-smoked wild fish from the Woodcock Smokery are just some of the treats on sale in shops and on farms.

Major festivals: Kinsale: Arts Week, Jul; Gourmet Festival, Oct; **Baltimore:** Fiddle Fair, May; **Skibbereen:** Taste of West Cork, Sep; **Cape Clear:** International Storytelling Festival, Sep; **Bantry:** West Cork Chamber Music Festival, Jun–Jul.

DAY TRIP OPTIONS

Based in Baltimore, spend a day on one of the **islands**. Visiting one of the three **peninsulas** would also make a perfect day trip. For full details, *see p49*.

Left Empty, silken sands of lovely Barley Cove Beach on the Mizen Head peninsula, *see p45*

Above Traditional shop sign in Clonakilty

VISITING KINSALE

Parking
Pay-and-display in the parking lot next to the Tourist Office and along Pier Road. Free parking lots on Church Street and New Road.

Tourist Information
Pier Road; 021 477 2234; www.kinsale.ie

WHERE TO STAY

KINSALE

Acton's Hotel *moderate*
This is an old favorite in an excellent location near the harbor. Enjoy the lively bar and restaurant, or relax and admire sea views from the gardens.
Pier Road; 021 477 9900; www.actonshotelkinsale.com; closed Christmas–New Year

The Old Presbytery *moderate*
This is an atmospheric former presbytery, dating back to the early 1800s. Rooms are traditional but comfortable and some have brass and iron beds and claw-foot baths.
Cork Street; 021 477 2027; www.oldpres.com

INCHYDONEY ISLAND

Inchydoney Island Lodge & Spa *expensive*
This resort spa has rooms and apartments with sea views. Short break packages, with accommodation and treatments included, are popular.
023 883 3143; www.inchydoneyisland. com; closed 24–26 Dec

① Kinsale
Co Cork
Kinsale is a pretty town set around a harbor, with narrow streets full of small, eye-catching shops. Kinsale also has a reputation for fine food and gourmet dining, with plenty of atmospheric restaurants and pubs and gourmet-themed events. The tourist office is a good place to start exploring the town, with some great craft shops nearby. **Desmond Castle** in Cork Street, built in around 1500, has been used as a Spanish arsenal and a prison, and is now a **wine museum** *(open Easter–Oct: daily)*. On leaving town the road passes the 17th-century, star-shaped Charles Fort, its two huge bastions overlooking the estuary. This lovely stretch of waterway is the venue for international sailing events.

🚗 *Take the coast road past Kinsale Yacht Club and cross the river at the bridge, following the R600. At the junction with the R604, turn left. Then turn left again at the Speckled Door pub onto the L3233 for Old Head.*

② Old Head of Kinsale
Co Cork
This is the nearest point to the spot where the *Lusitania* was sunk by a German U-boat in 1915. It is possible to drive out to see the Old Head lighthouse from a distance, but the surrounding land is privately owned by a golf club and therefore not open to visitors. There is an ongoing campaign to restore public access but, for now, it is a lovely drive and worth the trip to admire the setting.

🚗 *Turn back along the L3233 and turn left onto the R604, passing two Blue Flag beaches at Garrylucas and Garretstown. Turn left, passing by Ballinspittle. At crossroads continue on R600, then turn left onto N71 (Convent Rd), entering Clonakilty. Go straight across roundabout at the edge of town, down to the harbor.*

③ Clonakilty
Co Cork
Clonakilty is a delightful heritage town that is a pleasure to explore, with colorful and traditional storefronts whose hand-painted, old-style signs reveal their contents, such as Knitwell Wools, Quirky Kitchen, and Harrington's Original Recipe Black Pudding. Spiller's Lane is a pretty, enclosed lane lined with little shops and galleries. The town is also a major center for live music.

The Michael Collins Centre *(open Mon–Sat)* tells the story of the famous Irish patriot, who was born here. The town center features a memorial in his honor and there is also a garden commemorating John F. Kennedy, whose ancestors came from the town. The **West Cork Model Railway Village** *(open daily)* is great for children, featuring four miniature West Cork villages linked by a 1940s-era model version of the now-closed local railway line.

🚗 *From the harbor, leave town with the bay on the left. On reaching a Y-junction, take the right-hand fork, then continue straight on at the next junction, following the road down to Inchydoney Beach and Island.*

Below Tranquil estuary of the River Bandon, just outside Kinsale

Above Inchydoney Beach, one of the loveliest on this stretch of coastline

Michael Collins

Michael Collins (1890–1922), the nationalist military and political leader, was born in Clonakilty at a time when West Cork was the nationalist heartland. He rose to prominence during and after the Easter Rising of 1916, but was assassinated aged 31. His monument in Clonalkilty was unveiled in 2002 by Liam Neeson, who played him in the film based on his life.

④ Inchydoney Island
Co Cork

This little island is linked to the mainland by a causeway, so you can drive on to it. The focal point is Inchydoney Island Lodge & Spa, a luxury resort spa with a thalassotherapy pool. Inchydoney is also home to the West Cork Surf School, which offers a range of surfing lessons provided the waves are good.

🚗 *Return to Clonakilty and take the N71 for Skibbereen. After Lisavaird, turn left at the sign for Long Strand. Take the right-hand fork at the Y-junction onto the R598. After Rathbarry, take the second exit at the roundabout by Castlefreke Post Office. Take the next right turn for Galley Head and go straight through the next crossroads, then turn right. Stop when the cliffs come into view.*

⑤ Galley Head
Co Cork

Galley Head is an attractive headland jutting out into the Atlantic Ocean. The **lighthouse** here dates back to 1873. It is on private property run by the Irish Landmark Trust; however visitors can book in advance for an entertaining tour by Gerald Butler,

a former keeper who grew up in the lighthouse. The rocks at the end are a good place from which to spot whales and dolphins. The drive to Dromberg passes some lovely beaches as well as the ruins, in private grounds, of Castlefreke Castle.

🚗 *Return along the road and take the first left onto the L4006, then go straight through the next crossroads. The Warren Blue Flag beach and Castlefreke Dunes are on your left. Turn left onto the R598 to Rathbarry for Castlefreke Castle and Wood. Continue on the R598, from which there is a lovely viewpoint on the left, overlooking headlands and islands. You'll also pass Owenahincha beach. Turn left onto the N71 to Rosscarbery, then left again onto the R597 toward Glandore. At Dromberg, take a left at the sign for the Stone Circle. There is a parking lot, from which the circle is just a short walk away.*

Above Lighthouse at Galley Head

Above left Ancient stone circle, Drombeg
Above center Boat in the Sound at Union
Hall **Above right** Baltimore's Beacon

VISITING BALTIMORE

Boat Trips and Other Activities
Sherkin Island Ferries make the
crossing from Baltimore daily between
June and October, hourly from 9:30am
to 8:30pm. The crossing takes 15
minutes *(028 20125).* **Cape Clear**
Island Ferry Service departs
Baltimore daily year-round *(028*
39153). **Heir Island MV *Tresher*** makes
the crossing to Heir Island year-round
(086 809 2447); more information can
be found at www.baltimore.ie.

WHERE TO STAY

BALTIMORE

Rolf's Country House *inexpensive*
This charming bed-and-breakfast is in
an old farmhouse with stone cottages
and converted outbuildings. The
whole complex, from the thriving café
and wine bar to the quiet garden with
sea views, has great character.
Baltimore Hill; 028 20289;
www.rolfsholidays.eu; closed Dec 21–27

Casey's of Baltimore *moderate*
This popular hotel, traditional pub, and
seafood restaurant *(see opposite)* is at
the entrance to Baltimore and makes a
great base for exploring the area. Many
of the rooms overlook the quiet bay.
028 20197; www.caseysofbaltimore.
com; closed Dec 21–26

SKIBBEREEN

West Cork Hotel *moderate*
This family-run riverside hotel is a
good base from which to explore the
surrounding coastline. Many of the
ensuite rooms enjoy views over the
river, as do the bar and breakfast room.
Ilen Street; 028 21277;
www.westcorkhotel.com

6 Drombeg Stone Circle
Co Cork

Known locally as the Druid's Altar,
and in a magnificent setting with sea
views, this circle of 13 (originally 17)
pillar stones dates back to around
900 BC. During excavation in the
1950s, a pot containing the cremated
remains of a young woman was found
in the center, dating from 150 BC.

🚗 *Continue on the R597 to arrive*
at the attractive village of Glandore,
on a picturesque bay. Drive through
the village and around the coast.
Turn left signed for Union Hall
and cross the bridge over the
Sound, turning at the sign for
Castletownsend. Take the next
right, toward Skibbereen, drive
through Rineen, and, at the
T-junction, turn left. Take a sharp
left at the next crossroads onto
the R596 for Castletownsend.

7 Castletownsend
Co Cork

This is a pretty village set on a steep
hill. Drive down the village to the
pier at the end. There is a secluded
cove with boats moored, and to the
left, the **Castle** *(open Apr–Sep),* which
dates back to the 1600s and is still
owned by the Townsend family. The
village was home for many years to
Somerville and Ross, authors of
Experiences of an Irish R M.

🚗 *Drive back through the village and*
turn left onto the L4218. There will be
lovely cliff views to the left. Toe Head,
off the road to the left, has great
views, and the village of Tragumna
has a fabulous bay and a Blue Flag
beach, but beware of the strong rip
and rocks. After Tragumna, turn left

at the first T-junction and take the
next right, then next left, then right
again, and then a slight left at the
next fork. Keep left at the next junction
and then left again for Lough Hyne.

8 Lough Hyne
Co Cork

Lough Hyne (also known as Lough
Ine) is a salt-water lake and Ireland's
only marine nature reserve. The lake
is fed by the sea through a narrow
channel that causes irregular tidal
movements. There are many species
of plants and animals, including sea
urchins and oysters, and the lake is
studied intensively by marine
biologists and scientists. A visitor
center in Skibbereen *(see right)* gives
more information on what is found
in the lake, which is also the subject
of poetry and local folklore.

🚗 *Follow the road left, marked for*
Baltimore, and turn left at the R595.

9 Baltimore
Co Cork

This tiny coastal village, set in lovely
scenery and with ideal conditions for
water sports, is the reason why there
are so many holiday homes in the
area. Nestled around a harbor, and
warmed by the Gulf Stream, it offers
sailing, angling, diving, kayaking,
whale- and dolphin-watching, and
boat trips to the islands (Sherkin,
Cape Clear, and Heir), Lough Hyne,
and the Fastnet lighthouse. The
harbor bustles with boats, especially
in summer. The small central "square"
offers plenty of dining options.
   Drive or walk to The Beacon (turn
left at the harbor) for fantastic views
out to sea and over to Sherkin Island.

Where to Stay: inexpensive, under €100; moderate, €100–€200; expensive, over €200

t's a steep climb, and it is dangerous to visit the Beacon in high winds.

🚗 Follow the R595 all the way from Baltimore to Skibbereen.

⑩ Skibbereen
Co Cork

The busy town of Skibbereen has strong ties to the Great Famine of the 1840s, which devastated the local community. There is a large famine graveyard at Abbystrowry, nearby. The **Heritage Centre** (open May–Oct: daily) has an excellent exhibition on the subject. The building also houses the Lough Hyne Visitor Centre, with information on the marine nature reserve, including an aquarium.

🚗 At the roundabout in Skibbereen take the N71 west, toward Bantry. Bear left onto the R592, entering Ballydehob, to begin the 23-mile (37-km) drive around Mizen Head Peninsula.

⑪ Mizen Head Peninsula

The first stop on the drive to Mizen Head is the village of **Schull**, with its busy harbor. Its Sunday market features crafts as well as a great selection of fresh local produce.

Stay on the R592 toward **Goleen**, then turn left onto the L4406 for the "coast road" (it actually runs a little inland). After the crossroads, keep left at the Y-junction. There are great views of Clear Island and the Fastnet Rock and lighthouse. After Toormore, stay on the R591 for Mizen Head. Just after Goleen is **Spanish Point**, where there is a lighthouse. Further on, the pretty village of **Crookhaven** can be

Skibbereen's famine memorial, in the form of a Celtic Cross

Fastnet Rock

Fastnet Lighthouse, 4.5 miles (7 km) out in the Atlantic from Cape Clear Island, is visible from much of West Cork's coastline, and is the tallest and widest lighthouse in Ireland and Great Britain. The Rock is Ireland's most southerly point, and is the rounding marker for the grueling Fastnet yacht race.

seen across a lovely sound. Ships stocked up on provisions here before setting sail for America. In 1837, there were 424 residents – now there are just 29. On the left you'll pass the secluded **Galley Cove**. Keep left onto the L4402 for Mizen Head. Further along on the left is the parking lot for **Barley Cove Beach**, a short walk away along a boardwalk through the dunes. This is a conservation area, full of birds, flora, and fauna. Turn left at the next junction, marked for **Mizen Head**, Ireland's most south-westerly point. There are great views down to Barley Cove and across to Brow Head. The 1909 **Mizen Head Signal Station** (open mid-Mar–Oct: daily; Nov–mid-Mar: weekends) is linked to the mainland by a 172-ft (52-m) suspension bridge and has a fascinating exhibition on its history as well as the building of the **Fastnet Rock** lighthouse. The surrounding cliffs are spectacular. Leaving Mizen, take the first left turn for Dunlough and **Three Castle Head**, which has some great Atlantic views.

🚗 Take main road back to Toormore and turn left onto the R591 to Durrus. Turn left here for Sheep's Head.

Above Clear tidal stream and pristine sands of Barley Cove Beach

EAT AND DRINK

BALTIMORE

Casey's of Baltimore inexpensive
Choose from an extensive menu of fresh seafood or West Cork meat and vegetables in the bright restaurant or cozy bar. The hotel has its own mussel farm in Roaringwater Bay and mussel and lobster dishes are a specialty. 028 20197; www.caseysofbaltimore. com; closed Dec 21–26

Chez Youen moderate–expensive
This smart French restaurant specializes in seafood including fresh lobster. It overlooks the harbor on a tiny square. The Square; 028 20600; www.waterfronthotel.ie

AROUND SKIBBEREEN

Island Cottage moderate–expensive
A short ferry journey from Cunnamore (take N71 west from Skibbereen and turn left at Church Cross) is Hare Island (also known as Heir Island), and The Island Cottage restaurant, run by chef John Desmond. The ferry runs year-round and must be booked in advance. Hare Island, Skibbereen; 028 38102; www.islandcottage.com; open Jun–Sep Wed–Sat

AROUND MIZEN HEAD PENINSULA

Heron's Cove B&B inexpensive
Enjoy fresh fish, game, and other local produce in a secluded tidal cove with lovely views, and choose your own wine from the collection on the rack. The Harbour, Goleen (on R591 between Toormore and Crookhaven); 028 35225; www.heronscove.com; closed Dec 25–26

Left Rocky cliffs at Mizen Head

Eat and Drink: inexpensive, under €25; moderate, €25–€50; expensive, over €50

Above Traditional shopfront in Kilcrahane on Sheep's Head

VISITING BANTRY

Tourist Information
The old courthouse, The Square, Bantry; 027 50229; www. discoverireland.ie/cork

Parking
Parking in the town center is free, but limited to 2 hours. Unlimited parking is toward the sea end of the square.

WHERE TO STAY

SHEEP'S HEAD PENINSULA

Blairs Cove House *inexpensive–moderate*
Dating from 1760, this relaxed country house is surrounded by lush gardens. It offers B&B, self-catering cottages and apartments, and has an atmospheric restaurant in a converted stable.
Durrus (located 3 km/1.5 miles south of Durrus on R591 to Goleen); 027 61127; www.blairscove.ie

BANTRY

Bantry House *inexpensive–moderate*
Staying in this historic stately home (*see p47*) is a treasured experience. The rooms, in the east and west wings, look out over the splendid gardens.
Bantry Bay; 027 50047; www.bantry house.com; open mid-Mar–mid-Oct

AROUND BANTRY

Ballylickey Manor House *moderate*
This lovely house (3 miles/5 km from Bantry on N71 to Glengarriff), is set in its own grounds with beautiful gardens and views over Bantry Bay.
027 50071; www.ballylickeymanor house.com; open Apr–Sep

GLENGARRIFF

Glengarriff Park Hotel *inexpensive–moderate*
Comfortable, modern hotel at the start of the Beara Peninsula.
The Village, Glengarriff; 027 63000; www.glengarriffpark.com

⑫ Sheep's Head Peninsula

At the start of the drive out to the end of Sheep's Head from Durrus, the road runs through Ahakista, which has a peaceful waterside memorial to those who died in the Air India disaster of 1985. From Kilcrohane onward, the road narrows and becomes more scenic, with stone walls, heather, craggy hills, and breathtaking views left to Three Castle Head and the Mizen Peninsula, and right over to the Beara Peninsula. On the way, there are lots of little side turnings and stopping-off points to explore the lakes, churches, beaches, holy wells, burial grounds, and secluded coves. Follow any of the brown signs. The road ends at the Toreen Turning Table, where there is a parking lot and a Visitor Centre with a small café. From here, there is a marked, circular walking trail out to the Sheep's Head lighthouse on the point and back. If the keeper is there, it may be possible to see inside the lighthouse.

A two-hour walking tour

This walk is a small part of the Sheep's Head Way, a stunning long-distance walk which runs around the entire peninsula. The walk goes around the very tip of the peninsula to the lighthouse, with spectacular panoramas of the neighboring peninsulas along the way.

A map is available from the **Visitor Information Centre ①**, but the path is marked all the way along with blue arrows, and the signposts are made from local stone or Irish oak, in keeping with the beauty of the surroundings.

The trail passes rocky outcrops until it reaches **Lough Akeen ②**. The easiest and safest way to cross the lough is via the wooden boardwalk to the right, but it can be skirted along the cliff edge as well. The path then goes up a rocky incline and across a helicopter pad. The views from here over the sea and over to Mizen Head are breathtaking, and whales and dolphins can often be spotted, especially between July and September.

At this point, follow the steps down to reach the **lighthouse ③** at the tip of the headland. On the return from the lighthouse, halfway up the steps, go around to the left-hand side of the green container and follow the path, which leads to the northern side of the Sheep's Head peninsula. The path passes along a scenic route, but the first part can be boggy, with a slightly uneven surface. Upon reaching the top, the path runs close to the cliff edge and could be dangerous, so extreme care is needed along this stretch of the route. There are spectacular views over to the Beara Peninsula, as well

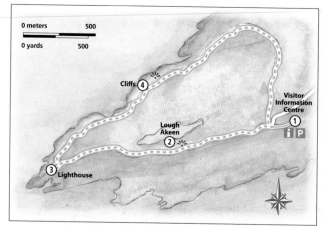

Lighthouse

Visitor Information Centre ①

Cliffs ④

Lough Akeen ②

Lighthouse ③

Where to Stay: inexpensive, under €100; moderate, €100–€200; expensive, over €200

as the chance of seeing whales or dolphins. The cliffs, which rise to some 400 ft (120 m), are home to nesting seabirds, and visitors might be lucky enough to spot the rare chough, which frequents Sheep's Head in significant numbers.

After the **cliffs ④**, turn right at the arrow, taking the marked path back across the headland to return to the parking lot and the café, which serves delicious home-baked treats.

🚗 *Drive back to Kilcrohane and then turn left onto Goat's Path Road, which winds up through the mountains. From the top of the hill pass, there are spectacular views over Roaringwater, Dunmanus, and Bantry bays and over to Castletownbere, Bere Island, and Dursey Island. The road then drops down to Bantry where there is free parking at the sea end of the square.*

⑬ Bantry
Co Cork

This large market town and fishing port is set at the head of picturesque Bantry Bay. There is an elegant open square in the center with seating, trees, and a fountain. One of Bantry's loveliest attractions is **Bantry House and Gardens** (open mid-Mar–Oct: daily), a Georgian stately home with impressive gardens and oustanding bay views. There are two woodland walks, a walled garden, and a tearoom, while the stable block houses a fascinating exhibition on the failed attempt by a French Armada to invade Ireland via Bantry Bay in 1796.

Take a ferry from Bantry pier to **Whiddy Island** for walking or cycling. There are some interesting historical remains on the island, as well as a pub-restaurant.

🚗 *Follow the N71 all the way to Glengarriff via Ballylickey.*

⑭ Glengarriff
Co Cork

Glengarriff is set in a lush, green area with lovely gardens and islands. The **Glengarriff Bamboo Park** (open daily) is an exotic coastal garden featuring bamboo and palms, with splendid views. From Glengariff harbor, boat trips operate to **Garnish Island** (open Mar–Oct: daily), where there are delightful subtropical Italian gardens with rare plants and a miniature temple. There is a seal colony on the island's rocky shore.

🚗 *Turn left onto R572, toward Castletownbere. At Adrigole, continue on R572 onto the Beara Peninsula.*

West Cork Garden Trail

Each June, a wide range of gardens feature on this well-established trail. Some are always open to the public but others open especially for the event. They range from country gardens, lakes and seaside gardens to mature and historical gardens. A leaflet, detailing which gardens are open, is available from any of the area's tourist offices, or see www.westcorkgardentrail.com.

Above left Rainbow over Bantry Bay
Above Reen Point, near Ahakista on the Sheep's Head Peninsula

VISITING WHIDDY ISLAND AND GARNISH ISLAND

Whiddy Island Ferries cross from Bantry Pier to Whiddy Island several times daily. The crossing takes 10–15 minutes (*www.whiddyferry.com; 086 862 6734*).

Harbour Queen Ferries cross from Glengarriff Pier to Garnish Island roughly every 20 minutes daily Mar–Oct (*www.harbourqueenferry.com; 027 63116*).

EAT AND DRINK AROUND THE SHEEP'S HEAD PENINSULA

The Good Things Café *moderate* Restaurant serving simple but elegant cuisine using top-quality seasonal and locally sourced ingredients, organic where possible. There is also an Irish cooking school on site. *Ahakista Road, Durrus, Co Cork; 027 61426; www.thegoodthingscafe.com; open Easter & mid-Jun–mid-Sep*

Below Majestic Bantry House with its marvelous view over Bantry Bay

Eat and Drink: inexpensive, under €25; moderate, €25–€50; expensive, over €50

Above Dramatic Dunboy Castle, set on the bay in Castletownbere

VISITING BEARA PENINSULA

Tourist Information
St. Peter's Grounds, Castletownbere, Beara; 027 70054; www.bearatourism.com

WHERE TO STAY

BEARA PENINSULA

Rodeen Country House *inexpensive*
Set within subtropical gardens in a secluded location, this guesthouse offers panoramic views of Bere Island and Bantry Bay.
Castletownbere; 027 70158; www.rodeencountryhouse.com

GOUGANE BARRA FOREST PARK

Gougane Barra Hotel *moderate*
The setting of this family-run hotel has to be one of the most picturesque in West Cork, with views out over the tranquil lake to St. Finbarr's Oratory on the island, and surrounded by forests and national parklands. Rooms are very comfortable and the home-cooked food is delicious.
Gougane Barra, Macroom; 026 47069; www.gouganebarrahotel.com; closed mid-Oct–early Apr

⑮ Beara Peninsula
Co Cork

The Ring of Beara is a scenic driving route that runs around the Beara Peninsula from Glengarriff to Dursey Sound and then back to Kenmare in County Kerry. Along the way are stunning coves, picturesque villages, islands, forests, and mountains. Whether the weather is sunny and warm or moody and misty, this peninsula leaves a lasting impression on visitors. For archeology enthusiasts, there are stone circles, cairns, and burial grounds, some dating back to 2500 BC, while walkers and cyclists will find plenty of routes, trails, and mountain paths on the Beara Way. Sea angling is also very popular. Visitors should take their time driving around the peninsula, stopping off at beaches, harbors, or historical sights along the way.

On the route from Glengarriff to Castletownbere the route passes through **Adrigole** ①, whose harbor affords plenty of opportunities for water sports such as sailing, kayaking, and powerboating.

Castletownbere ② is the main town on the Beara peninsula, with a busy port full of fishing trawlers. Its large natural harbor, Berehaven, is overlooked by the ruins of Dunboy Castle. Across the harbor lies **Bere Island** ③, accessible by ferry. It has an interesting military history, with parts of the island still used by the Irish army for training. There is a choice of places to eat, drink, and stay on the island, and panoramic views from its Ardnakinna lighthouse.

Further along, at the very tip of the Beara Peninsula, lies **Dursey Island** ④, a rugged, almost treeless place accessible only by cable car – strong tides make it unsafe for boats. Only about ten people live on the island and there are no cafés or shops, but it is a peaceful spot for walks and birdwatching, and there are great Atlantic views.

The area around **Allihies** ⑤, the last village on the peninsula, used to be dotted with copper mines and there is a fascinating Copper Mine Museum *(open Apr–Oct: daily)* telling of the history of copper-mining in the area. Allihies is on lovely Ballydonegan Bay, which has a quartz strand. Many artists are drawn to the area by its scenic beauty.

The village of **Eyeries** ⑥, with its brightly painted houses, overlooks the Atlantic. The surrounding area is rich in historic sights, including an Ogham Stone (a granite pillar carved with ancient writing) at **Ballycrovane** ⑦ standing over 17 ft (5 m) high.

At Lauragh, take the **Healy Pass** ⑧ though the Caha Mountains, back to Adrigole and on to Glengarriff, or continue on the R571 to Kenmare in County Kerry *(see p54)*.

🚗 *Return to Glengarriff on the R572, then take the N71 to Ballylickey. Turn left onto the R584 and head upward and through the spectacular Pass of Keimaneigh. At the end of the pass, turn left onto the L4643 following the signs for Gougane Barra.*

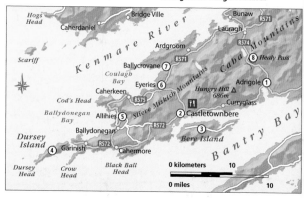

Coastal landscapes

A driving tour around this part of the world is lovely not only for the pretty towns and villages along the way, but for its stunning coastal scenery. Cliffs and peninsulas are almost sculpted, dotted by grazing sheep or cows. The lush green pastures and hedgerows here are in contrast to the more desolate scenery of the coastline further west. Mild Gulf Stream temperatures cause everything to flourish. It is no wonder that there are so many local artisan foods produced in this area, many of which can be sampled in atmospheric pubs and restaurants along the route.

16 Gougane Barra Forest Park
Co Cork

This is a stunning, peaceful national park set in a lake-filled valley and surrounded by mountains and forests. It is also home to the source of Cork's River Lee. In the center of the lake you'll see **St. Finbarr's Oratory**, set on the island where St. Finbarr, the founder of Cork city, built his monastery in the 6th century. The current chapel was built around 1900. The island is accessible by causeway and there are also circular cells and a well to be seen.

For those who do not have time to explore on foot, there is also a circular drive through the forest (3 miles/5 km). Follow the road with St. Finbarr's to the right. But to fully

appreciate the 350 acres (140 ha) of forest park, leave the car and try one of the many marked nature trails. In summer, the hotel *(see left)* stages a popular Theatre by the Lake series.

◖ *Return to the R584 and turn left following signs for Macroom.*

17 Macroom
Co Cork

Macroom is a busy market town on the River Sullane. It has several historical features, such as the remains of a gateway and Norman tower, both of which were part of Macroom Castle. The gate gives access to the castle grounds, with fine riverside walks. Nearby, **Bealick Mill Heritage Centre** *(open Apr–Sep: daily)* is a working corn mill with a water-powered wheel.

Above Colorful facades and market cross in Macroom's main square

Above St. Finbarr's Oratory, on the lake in Gougane Barra Forest Park

EAT AND DRINK AROUND THE BEARA PENINSULA

The Copper Kettle *inexpensive*
An atmospheric café offering sandwiches, salads, and hot dishes, plus mouthwatering desserts and home-baking.
The Square, Castletownbere; 027 71792; open daytime only; closed Sun

MacCarthy's Bar *inexpensive*
This is a lively pub with regular music sessions. Simple bar food is available during the day.
The Square, Castletownbere; 027 70014

DAY TRIP OPTIONS

Baltimore is a great base to visit one of West Cork's lovely islands. Take a trip to Sherkin, Cape Clear, Garinish, Whiddy, Dursey, or Bere Island to sample the relaxed pace of life, or take one of the peninsula drives.

Sherkin Island

Sherkin Island, just 3 miles (5 km) long and 1 mile (2 km) wide, is a peaceful and relaxed haven, with stunning beaches such as Silver Strand and Trabawn, which are safe for swimming, as well as the ruins of O'Driscoll Castle and a Franciscan Abbey dating back to 1460 to explore. There are places to stay on the island, and the two pubs, the

Jolly Roger and Murphy's Bar, often have live music sessions. The island is also well-known for its artists.

Take the ferry from Baltimore ❾ *(see p44).*

Cape Clear Island

This is a wild, rugged, and unspoilt island, and, with plenty of wild flowers, birds, and beaches, it is a haven of solitude. There are breathtaking views in all directions, from the Atlantic and Fastnet Rock, to Roaringwater Bay and Baltimore. Historic sights include St. Kieran's Church and O'Driscoll Castle. Walk to the 19th-century lighthouse and watchtower at the southern end of

the island – you may see whales and dolphins from here. Ireland's southernmost inhabited island is also home to a Gaeltacht (Irish-speaking area), with two Irish summer colleges. There are also craft shops, a café, two pubs, and a club that often hosts music sessions.

Take the ferry from Baltimore ❾ *or Schull; the journey time is 45 minutes.*

Peninsula drives

Explore one of the peninsulas – Mizen Head ⓫, Sheep's Head ⓬, or Beara ⓯ – from Baltimore ❾ or Bantry ⓭.

Follow the drive instructions.

Eat and Drink: inexpensive, under €25; moderate, €25–€50; expensive, over €50

The Majestic Ring of Kerry

Kenmare to Killarney

Highlights

- **Charming Kenmare**
  Soak up the atmosphere of this heritage town, gateway to the Ring of Kerry, and shop for fine local crafts

- **Remote monastic settlements**
  Go on a boat trip out to the island of Skellig Michael to view the early Christian monastery there, a UNESCO World Heritage Site

- **Island adventures**
  Admire awesome vistas from the Fogher Cliffs and the Martello tower at Bray Head on Valentia Island

- **Dramatic mountain drives**
  Take the high road through gaps in the Macgillycuddy Reeks range

Panoramic views from the dramatic Fogher Cliffs on Valentia Island

The Majestic Ring of Kerry

The Ring of Kerry is on the Iveragh Peninsula, the largest of five peninsulas jutting out into the Atlantic from the southwest of Ireland. The scenic promontory is famed for its vistas of sea and mountains – visitors have been coming here for centuries, drawn by the sheer abundance of natural beauty. It is a popular tourist route, so don't expect splendid isolation, but this drive offers plenty of opportunities to veer off the beaten track into a dramatic landscape of coves, cliffs, broad bays, and rugged countryside, all set against the Macgillycuddy Reeks, Ireland's highest mountain range. This ancient landscape is richly endowed with remnants of early Christian settlements and megalithic sites.

ACTIVITIES

Visit Iron Age Staigue Fort, the best-preserved in Ireland, set in a beautiful valley

Take a boat trip out to the island of Skellig Michael, a UNESCO World Heritage Site, to see the superb monastic ruins

Walk around Muckross Lake, through ancient forests, and have tea in an 18th-century hunting lodge

Go for an invigorating swim in the blue waters of Castlecove Bay, and canoe in nearby Derrynane Harbour

KEY

🛇 Drive route

0 kilometers   5

0 miles   5

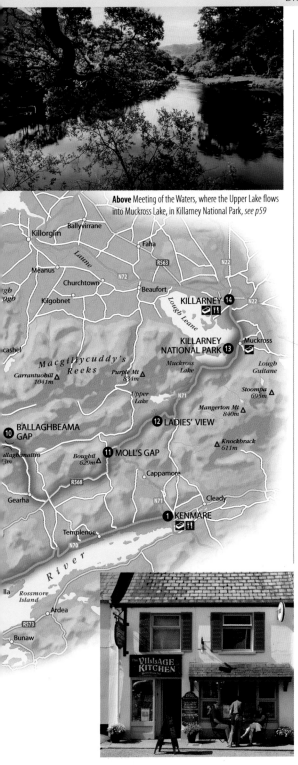

Above Meeting of the Waters, where the Upper Lake flows into Muckross Lake, in Killarney National Park, *see p59*

Left One of many attractive cafés in the village of Sneem, *see p54*

PLAN YOUR DRIVE

Start/finish: Kenmare to Killarney.

Number of days: 3, allowing half a day for Valentia Island and a trip to Skellig Michael island, and half a day for Killarney National Park.

Distance: 130 miles (210 km).

Road conditions: Roads are paved and well-marked, but there are some steep inclines on the passes. Turns off the main Ring of Kerry are not always as well marked.

When to go: July and August can be crowded, with tour buses dominating the main routes. The best months in which to visit are June and September. In the winter, many places beyond Kenmare and Killarney will be closed.

Opening times: Shops are generally open 9 or 10am to 5 or 6pm, but most close on Sundays except corner shops. Catholic churches stay open all day.

Main market days: Kenmare: Wed; Milltown: Tue–Thu & Sat; Killarney: Fri.

Shopping: Kenmare is renowned for its wide range of individual shops and galleries selling top-quality local art and crafts. Look out in particular for fine linen and lace.

Major festivals: Killorglin: Puck Fair (coronation of goat king), Aug 10–12; Cahersiveen: Cahersiveen Festival of Music, Jun/Jul–Aug; Killarney: Summer Festival, Jul.

DAY TRIP OPTIONS

For **nature and history lovers**, a day spent exploring Killarney and the National Park, with beautiful lakes and historic buildings, is a perfect choice. **Outdoor enthusiasts** will enjoy the rugged cliffs of Valentia Island and then a boat trip to the ancient monastery of Skellig Michael. If time allows, finish with a walk up to the Geokaun Mountain or Fogher Cliffs. For full details, *see p59*.

Above Handsome Derrynane House, set in subtropical gardens where flax grows

VISITING KENMARE

Parking
Park on either side of Main Street or in the Square opposite the Tourist Office.

Tourist Information
The Square; 064 664 1233; open Apr–Oct: daily; www.discoverireland.com/kerry

WHERE TO STAY

KENMARE

Lissyclearig Thatched Cottage
inexpensive
Charming traditional house in a quiet location with lovely countryside views.
Moll's Gap Road; 064 664 2562; www.lissyclearigthatchedcottage.com

Lansdowne Arms *moderate*
A welcoming family-run hotel.
Main Street; 064 664 1368

The Park Hotel *expensive*
This chateau-style hotel offers modern comforts in a traditional setting, and has exceptional estuary views.
High Street; 064 664 1200; www.parkkenmare.com

SNEEM

Parknasilla Hotel *expensive*
Set in swathes of subtropical parkland overlooking Kenmare Bay, this hotel may have the best location in Ireland.
Parknasilla Resort; 064 667 5600; www.parknasillahotel.ie; closed Jan–Mar

WATERVILLE

Butler Arms Hotel
inexpensive–moderate
One of Ireland's best-known hotels – Charlie Chaplin was once a regular. The restaurant offers fish and lobster.
Waterville; 066 947 4144; www.butlerarms.com

① Kenmare
Co Kerry
The picturesque heritage town of Kenmare on the mouth of the River Sneem regularly comes top of many Irish people's list when asked to nominate their favorite town. It isn't completely in thrall to tourism and goes about its business in a dignified and discreet manner. Its Irish name, Neidin, translates as "little nest," and is an apt description. It lies at the head of the River Kenmare, flanked by the Ring of Beara (see p48) and the Ring of Kerry, making it an ideal base from which to explore either peninsula.

The town center is compact, and its X-shaped street pattern converges in a triangular square at the junction of Henry Street and Main Street. Its narrow streets are lined with great shops and galleries, live music pubs, and some excellent restaurants and cafés. The library now houses the **Carnegie Arts Centre** (*www.carnegieartskenmare.ie*), whose state-of-the-art theater stages a wide range of top-quality drama and concerts. It is worth dawdling a while to make the most of this delightful town. An advantage to starting the drive around the Ring from here is that there is less chance of getting stuck behind a convoy of tour buses, as the majority of tours set off from Killarney, following a counterclockwise route around the peninsula.

Kenmare is also renowned for its traditional lace. During the famine years, nuns from the local convent, St. Clare's, introduced lace making to create work for the women and girls.

🚗 *Take the main N71 from the Square and over the Cromwell Bridge, marked for Moll's Gap and Killarney. Very shortly after the bridge, turn left onto the N70, toward Sneem. The drive from Kenmare to Sneem along the banks of the River Kenmare affords lovely views of the Caha and Slieve Miskish mountains on the opposite shore.*

② Sneem
Co Kerry
This quaintly pretty village, located at the head of an estuary flowing into Kenmare river, is built around a picturesque green on which stands a statue to the local hero Steve "Crusher" Casey, a world champion wrestler. This is a good place to stop for a quick bite or coffee. There are some nice shops, galleries, and cafés off the main square.

🚗 *Continue west on the N70 in the direction of Castlecove. At a junction just before the village, there is a tearoom and visitor center for Staigue Fort. Turn right here, taking the narrow road as indicated, which leads to the fort itself, and park by the fort.*

③ Staigue Fort
Castlecove, Co Kerry
This is an impressive ring fort, thought to date from 300–400 AD, set in a beautiful, remote valley. One of the best preserved Iron Age forts in Ireland, Staigue Fort has 16-ft (5-m) high drystone walls surrounded by a bank and a ditch. Access the two vaulted chambers within and climb up the ramparts. It's also well worth

Below The River Sneem before it flows into the estuary at Kenmare

walking a little way up the slopes of the valley to get a proper sense of the scale of the fort set against the surrounding landscape.

🔲 *Return to the N70 and turn right for Castlecove, then left for the beach.*

④ Castlecove
Co Kerry
The main attraction of this little resort is the beautiful white sandy beach that looks out across the River Kenmare toward the Slieve Miskish Mountains. This sheltered cove is ideal for safe swimming and is understandably popular with families. Children will also love to explore the deep rock pools for sea life when the tide is out.

🔲 *Return to N70 and continue to Caherdaniel. Turn left here, at the sign for Derrynane House.*

Blind Piper pub sign, Caherdaniel

⑤ Derrynane Bay
Co Kerry
The village of Caherdaniel sprawls along Derrynane Bay's eastern flank. At the heart of the village are two excellent pubs, the Blind Piper and Freddie's bar.

A little way beyond the village is **Derrynane House** (open May–Sep: daily; Apr & Oct–end Nov: Wed–Sun & public hols), set in a 300-acre (120-ha) wooded National Park. The former home of Daniel O'Connell (see p58), it is now a museum dedicated to "The Liberator" as he is sometimes called. A hugely popular and nonviolent campaigner, he championed the rights of the poor and helped bring

about Catholic emancipation in 1829. The house contains much important memorabilia, and there is a video presentation on his life and times. The lush subtropical gardens run down to the bay where there is a wide, sandy beach backed by dunes.

🔲 *Return to the N70 and turn left. Beyond Caherdaniel, the Ring of Kerry climbs steeply to the Coomakista Pass, with stunning views of Scariff Island and the mouth of the River Kenmare. Carry on to Waterville.*

⑥ Waterville
Co Kerry
Near Waterville, on the descent from the Coomakista Pass, the jagged silhouette of Skellig Rock (see p56) can be seen far out to sea. The town itself is located on a long strip of land between Lough Currane and Ballinskelligs Bay. Many visitors are attracted by its extensive beach, **Waterville Strand**; a championship golf course and superb angling are other notable attractions. The beach is on the left of the town, backed by a grassy promenade. Keep an eye out for the bronze statue of Charlie Chaplin, who was a regular visitor, staying at the Butler's Arms with his trademark bowler hat and cane. Waterville boasts many good places to eat and is an ideal stop off.

🔲 *Continue in the same direction on the N70, toward Cahersiveen. After New Chapel Cross turn left onto the R567, marked for Ballinskelligs. Shortly after the road crosses the River Inny there is a sign for the Skellig Ring Drive.*

Above left White sands and rocky outcrops of Castlecove **Above** Sturdy remains of the impressive Iron Age Staigue Fort

EAT AND DRINK

KENMARE

Packies *inexpensive*
The mainstays here include Irish stew and fish chowder, and they are very proud of their "real prawn cocktail."
Henry St; 064 664 1508; closed Mon

No. 35 Restaurant *moderate*
The menu at this informal restaurant features pizza and pasta dishes with an emphasis on local produce.
35 Main Street; 064 664 1559; www.no35kenmare.com

Lime Tree Restaurant *expensive*
One of Kenmare's best restaurants, with a loyal following. The food is classic Irish with a contemporary approach.
Shelbourne Street; 064 664 1225; www.limetreerestaurant.com

SNEEM

Sacre Coeur Restaurant *moderate*
Fresh fish features on the menu but local lamb is also a specialty.
North Square; 064 664 5186; open dinner only; www.sacrecoeur.com

WATERVILLE

Old Cable House *inexpensive*
The Old Cable House is blessed with clear views across the Atlantic, where the first transatlantic telegraph cable was laid from here to the USA in 1866. A guesthouse, it also welcomes non-residents for unfussy seafood with an emphasis on freshness and flavor. Local lamb and beef also on the menu.
Old Cable Station; 066 947 4233; www.oldcablehouse.com

Smuggler's Inn *inexpensive*
Adjacent to the golf course, this restaurant offers informal lunch at the bar or – on warm days – meals outside on the terrace. Seafood a specialty.
Cliff Road; 066 947 4330; www.the-smugglers-inn.com

Eat and Drink: inexpensive, under €25; moderate, €25–€50; expensive, over €50

Above Puffin Island, seen from Coonanaspig Pass on the Skellig Ring Drive

VISITING SKELLIG MICHAEL

The **Skellig Experience Centre** organizes a Sea Cruise to Skellig St. Michael (Great Skellig) and Small Skellig when the sea is not too rough. For details visit the center or its website, *www.skelligexperience.com*. Several independent boat owners can take you to the Skelligs too. On Valentia Island, try **Owen Walsh Skellig Boat Trips**, *066 947 6327*, or **Ocean Quests**, *066 947 6214* (Apr–Sep). Alternatively, try **Casey's Skellig Boat Trips**, *Portmagee*, *066 947 2437*, or **Waterville Boats**, *Waterville, 066 947 4800* (May–Sep only).

WHERE TO STAY IN BALLAGHBEAMA GAP

Blackstones House *inexpensive*
Situated at the foot of Carruntuohill, Ireland's highest mountain, and overlooking the Caragh River, this friendly family-run B&B enjoys a splendid location. All rooms are ensuite with views of the river and the soothing sound of its soft gurgling. *Blackstone Bridge, Glencar; 066 976 0164; www.glencar-blackstones.com*

Carrig Country House and Restaurant *moderate–expensive*
A former hunting lodge, owned by Lord Brockett, this manor house is the perfect hideaway – relaxed, and with a charming atmosphere. There are wonderful views over Caragh Lake, and a restaurant, which offers exceptional cooking (nonresidents are welcome). *Killorglin, Caragh Lake; 066 976 9100; www.carrighouse.com; closed end Nov–Mar*

⑦ Skellig Ring Drive
Co Kerry

Since there are no bus tours allowed on this stretch of the road – known as the Skellig Ring Drive – it is easy to enjoy the scenery in relative isolation. Where the R567 joins the R566, turn left and follow the road as it curves around the bay, leading to Ballinskelligs village, where there is a magnificent stretch of sandy beach. After the village, the road inclines sharply toward Bolus Head, before turning northward, skirting Bolus Mountain. Soon the landscape opens up into thrilling vistas of a patchwork of fields sweeping down to the headland and the jagged diamond of the Skellig Rocks, rising up from a vast expanse of sea. The road continues around, skirting the edge of Saint Finan's Bay before climbing again to Coonanaspig Pass. There follows an exhilarating descent into the harbor village of Portmagee. At the foot of the hill, on the left, is a family-run café, the Skellig Mist. From here, it is a 20-minute walk to the nearby cliffs, which offer a spectacular view across to Valentia Island.

🚗 *From the café turn left onto the minor road and follow it onto the R565 to the left to drive over the bridge that crosses the channel to Valentia Island. Coming off the bridge, the Skellig Experience Centre is on the left.*

⑧ Valentia Island
Co Kerry

Valentia Island has an enthralling mix of towering cliffs, rolling hills, and wild seascapes. Valentia is noted for the variety of subtropical plants that have taken root here: in the summer, many of the narrow lanes on the island are ablaze with the deep crimson of fuchsia hedges. History was made here in 1866 when the first transatlantic telegraph to the United States was laid here.

① Skellig Experience Centre
Housed in a striking, prize-winning stone building with a grass roof, the Skellig Experience Centre (open Jul & Aug: daily; Mar, Apr & Oct–Nov: Mon–Fri) has displays on every facet of Skellig Michael (Sceiig Mhichil), which is now a UNESCO World Heritage Site. This remote and rocky outcrop contains one of the best-preserved early Christian monastic sites in the world. The audiovisual presentation is full of fascinating detail on the centuries in which the monastery thrived on the island and on the way of life of its remarkably resilient monks. There are also displays on the bird and underwater life of the island. The Centre is able to arrange boat trips to Skellig Michael.

🚗 *On leaving the parking lot, turn left up the hill. At the first junction turn left again, following the signs for Skellig Drive, and continue to a fork in the road. To access the path to Bray Tower, fork left and drive until a turnout at the end of the road is reached. Park here.*

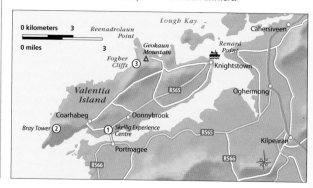

② Bray Tower

Bray Tower is an 18th-century signal tower standing on the promontory of Bray Head. It is thought originally to have been a Martello lookout tower, many of which were built around Ireland in response to the threat of an invasion by Napoleon. From the parking lot, head out on foot along the track that leads out to the headland and the tower. On a clear day, the sweeping vistas of the surrounding headlands and islands are truly magnificent. Allow an hour for the whole walk.

Return to the fork in the road and this time take the other fork. Continue until you see a left sign for Geokaun Mountain and Fogher Cliffs. Drive to the top or park at the foot of the mountain and walk (20 minutes).

③ Geokaun Mountain and the Fogher Cliffs

These are the highest points on Valentia Island and among the most elevated on the whole Ring of Kerry.

The views from the top are certainly worth the short trek up. On **Geokaun Mountain** there is a viewing platform and 34 information plaques relating to the views of the Skelligs, the Blasket Islands, and Bray Tower among others. Before reaching the top, walk the short path on the left to the **Fogher Cliffs** and take in the panoramic landscape from the viewing deck there.

Continue to Knightstown for the car ferry that runs continuously to Renard Point. From there it is a straight run east to Cahersiveen.

Above Rossbehy Beach at Glenbeigh, on the road from Cahersiveen to Caragh Lake

---

Monastic miracle

In the 6th century, a group of monks established a monastery on the island Skellig Michael – nothing short of a miracle of devotion and ingenuity. Having withstood the forces of the Atlantic for nearly 1,500 years, the chapel and beehive huts are still remarkably preserved. The hardy monastic community remained there for 600 years.

Above View of Bray Head and its steep cliffs, Valentia Island

⑨ Cahersiveen
Co Kerry

Cahersiveen is the main service town for this part of the peninsula. Its chief claim to fame is that Daniel O'Connell, who agitated for Catholic emancipation, was born here. The Heritage Centre has displays covering the life of O'Connell and the ill-fated Fenian uprising of 1867.

Take the N70 north. It dips down to sea level at Glenbeigh. Beyond this, turn right for Glencar and Caragh Lake. Turn right over a bridge and drive round the lake to Blackstone Bridge over the River Caragh, a picturesque picnic spot.

⑩ Ballaghbeama Gap
Co Kerry

From Blackstone Bridge, a narrow road winds its way up in the shadow of the Magillicuddy Reeks to Ballaghbeama Gap. On a clear day there are sweeping views across the lonely, windswept landscape. Take a right fork half a mile (1 km) after the bridge to a T-junction (1 mile/2 km), then turn right toward Cahersiveen, past the Climber's Inn, then sharp left at the sign for Ballaghbeama Gap. From the top, the road descends to join the R568, skirting the southern flanks of the Reeks.

On the R568 turn left to Moll's Gap.

EAT AND DRINK

SKELLIG RING DRIVE

The Moorings *moderate*
Looking out over the harbor, this guesthouse, restaurant, and bar caters for all needs. The award-winning Bridge Bar is ideal for a light lunch before venturing onto Valentia Island. Both restaurant and bar take full advantage of the area's abundant seafood.
Harbour Front, Portmagee; 066 947 7108; www.moorings.ie; closed Mon

VALENTIA ISLAND

Knightstown Coffee Shop *inexpensive*
This charming coffee shop offers a selection of wraps, croissants, and baguettes, as well as a range of more substantial meals. It doubles up as a second-hand bookstore and offers Internet access.
Market Street; 066 947 6373; www.knightstowncoffee.com

CAHERSIVEEN

The Point Bar *moderate*
Near to where the ferry disembarks from Valentia Island, this place is an institution and a great spot for a pint outdoors on a summer's evening, watching harbor life. However, the real draw here is the fresh seafood, which is very reasonably priced. Food is served during the summer months only.
Renard Point, Cahersiveen; 087 259 5345

Eat and Drink: inexpensive, under €25; moderate, €25–€50; expensive, over €50

VISITING KILLARNEY

Tourist Information
Beech Road, Killarney; 064 663 1633;
www.killarney.ie

Killarney National Park Information
Muckross House; 064 667 0144;
www.killarneynationalpark.ie

Parking
There is a parking lot next to the Tourist
Information center, but this may be full
in high season. An alternative is Glebe
parking lot on College Road.

WHERE TO STAY

KILLARNEY

Killarney Lodge *moderate*
Just a stroll from the town center yet
beautifully secluded in its own walled
garden, this family-run guesthouse
offers excellent accommodation.
Countess Road; 064 663 6499;
www.killarneylodge.net

KILLARNEY NATIONAL PARK

Cahernane House Hotel *moderate*
Set in its own parklands on the edge of
the national park, this has a charming
old-world atmosphere and open fires.
Muckross Road (off N71); 064 663
1895; www.cahernane.com; closed
Nov–Jan

Coolclogher House *moderate*
This early Victorian house on a working
farm is a haven of tranquillity. Four
rooms have mountain and sea views.
Mill Road (third left off N71 from
Killarney); 064 663 5996;
www.coolclogherhouse.com

Muckross Park Hotel
moderate–expensive
Dating from 1795, this is Killarney's
most beautifully located hotel, opposite
Muckross Abbey. Elegant bedrooms.
Muckross Village; 064 662 3400;
www.muckrosspark.com

Below Lovely Muckross House, in the heart of
Killarney National Park

Above Majestic Upper and Muckross lakes and Lough Leane, seen from Ladies' View

⑪ Moll's Gap
Co Kerry
Moll's Gap is where the R568 meets
the N71, which runs between
Killarney and Kenmare. There are
several spectacular vistas from here,
but sadly many of the best places
for viewing have been fenced off.

🚗 *Continue on the N71 to Ladies'*
View, pausing at the turnout just
before it for more splendid views.

⑫ Ladies' View
Killarney, Co Kerry
Ladies' View takes its name from one
of Queen Victoria's ladies-in-waiting
who, accompanying the monarch on
a visit to Killarney in 1861, pronounced
it "the finest view in the realm." It

would be hard to disagree with her.
From here it seems as if the whole of
Kerry is laid out directly below. Upper
Lake stretches away to link up with
the two lower lakes, Muckross and
Leane. On the far side is the dramatic
Carrauntoohil massif.

🚗 *Continue on the N71 to Killarney*
National Park and Muckross.

The Liberator
Daniel O'Connell (1775–1847), "The
Liberator," campaigned for equal
rights and religious tolerance. His
goal was partially achieved in 1829,
when Catholics were at last admitted
to Parliament in Westminster, and
he became the first Irish Catholic
MP in the House of Commons.

⑬ Killarney National Park
Co Kerry
Killarney National Park covers approximately 25,000 acres (10,000 ha)
and encompasses three lakes – Upper, Muckross, and Leane – and the
surrounding mountains. It contains Ireland's largest area of ancient
oak forest and its only remaining herd of indigenous red deer.

A two-hour walking tour
This circular tour, known as the
Dinis Walk, is a delightful stroll
around Muckross Lake, through
ancient woodlands of oak and
mountain ash. The walk starts at
Muckross House *(open daily)* ①,
next to the parking lot. The focal
point of the park, the house is a
fine Victorian residence, completed
in 1843 to designs by Scottish
architect William Burn. Queen
Victoria herself visited in 1861 as a
guest of the Herbert family, who
landscaped the gardens in her
honor, planting them with azaleas
and rhododendrons. Today, the

main rooms have been renovated in
period style. Next door, the working
farm project at the Traditional Farms
(open May–Aug: daily; Apr & Sep–Oct:
weekends) has recreated Irish rural life
of the 1930s, before electrification.
Mucros Pottery and Weaving can
be seen in action next to the craft
shop in the Walled Garden Centre.
From the house there are several
alternative walks around the lakes
and through the woods or, for a
different touring experience, trips
in a horse-drawn jaunting car are
also possible *(pick one up outside the*
house). To continue the Dinis Walk,
follow the marked trail down to

Where to Stay: inexpensive, under €100; moderate, €100–€200; expensive, over €200

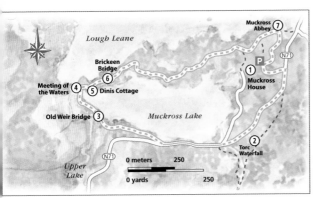

Above Riding in a traditional jaunting car through the woods in Killarney National Park

the spectacular 60 ft (20 m) **Torc Waterfall** ② – a 30-minute walk. From here, follow the Torc Trail along the base of Torc Mountain to the **Old Weir Bridge** ③, where Muckross Lake and the Upper Lake first meet. Soon afterward the path arrives at the thrilling **Meeting of the Waters** ④, where the Upper Lake actually flows into Muckross Lake. It's worth pausing here to watch the boatmen negotiate the turbulent flow of water. A little way further along on the right is **Dinis (Dinish) Cottage** ⑤ (*open May–Sep daily*), an 18th-century hunting lodge, now an eco-friendly tearoom. Continue along the narrow stretch of land between Muckross Lake and Lough Leane to the picturesque arches of **Brickeen (Bricin) Bridge** ⑥. Cross the bridge and carry on past Colleen Bawn Rock, following the path along Lough Leane to **Muckross Abbey** ⑦,

Stained-glass pub window

founded in 1448. Return to the parking lot, completing the circuit. Back in the car, turn left out of the main entrance onto the N71. Turn left before Killarney to the 15th-century Ross Castle, on a peninsula in Lough Leane. From here boats cross to Innisfallen Isle, home to the ruins of another abbey.

> 🚗 **Return to the N71 and continue to Killarney.**

⑭ Killarney
Co Kerry
Killarney is a convenient base from which to explore the natural splendors of the national park. **St. Mary's Cathedral**, designed by Pugin and built in 1842, is considered Ireland's finest example of High Gothic, and is worth a visit. The little Victorian lanes that branch off the main street are also enjoyable to wander. There are lively pubs – many playing live music – and restaurants in the town, and a good choice of accommodation.

EAT AND DRINK IN KILLARNEY

Bricin *inexpensive*
Bricin is Gaelic for small trout, so it's no surprise that fish dishes feature in this family-run restaurant and high-quality craft store. Also worth trying is *boxty*, a traditional potato pancake.
26 High Street; 064 663 4902; www.bricin.com

Gaby's Seafood Restaurant *moderate*
At this excellent seafood restaurant you can choose from a wide selection of fish, cooked in a variety of ways. The lobster and wild Atlantic salmon steaks are particularly succulent. Cozy, rustic decor, with an open fire.
27 High Street; 064 663 2519; www.gabysireland.com

DAY TRIP OPTIONS
Killarney and the area around Valentia Island are ideal bases from which to explore the glorious Kerry landscape.

Lakes and abbeys
Stroll around Killarney ⑭ and have a look at the cathedral, then head to Killarney National Park ⑬. After doing the Dinis Walk, take a jaunting-car trip up to Muckross Abbey and on to the pier at Ross Castle, where boat trips set off across Lough Leane to visit the

lovely 6th-century ruined abbey on the heavily wooded island of Inisfallen.

From Killarney, take N71 to the Killarney National Park and park in Muckross House or Muckross Abbey parking lot (just before house on the right).

Islands and monasteries
Explore Valentia Island ⑧, starting the day at the Skellig Experience Centre to find out about the Skellig Michael UNESCO World Heritage

Site – a monastery established in the 6th century on the remote island of Great Skellig. The drystone beehive huts built by the monks can be seen on a cruise from the center or on an independent boat trip from Valentia Island or Portmagee. Back on dry land, continue to Bray Tower or Geokaun Mountain and the Fogher Cliffs for bracing clifftop walks.

Follow the drive instructions from Ballinskelligs and Valentia Island.

Eat and Drink: inexpensive, under €25; moderate, €25–€50; expensive, over €50

The Dingle Peninsula

Tralee to the Maharees Peninsula

Highlights

- **Lively musical town**
  Discover the vibrant, colorful harbor town of Dingle, situated in the heart of an Irish-speaking region

- **Culinary delights**
  Sample the freshest seafood and other produce to see why the local cuisine is held in such high regard

- **Dramatic headland**
  Explore the wild scenery of Slea Head, one of Europe's most westerly fringes

- **Historic landscapes**
  Delve into countryside rich in atmosphere and studded with Neolithic and early Christian sites

Rocky cliffs on the northern coastline of the Dingle Peninsula

The Dingle Peninsula

Of the five peninsulas in southwest Ireland, the Dingle is perhaps the connoisseur's choice. This is a drive through an ancient landscape, dotted with remnants of early Christian churches, monastic settlements, and Neolithic structures. It runs through the most westerly landscape in Europe, and the dramatic scenery of Slea Head, the brooding presence of Mount Brandon, and the marvelous chain of precipitous cliffs and sandy beaches will remain etched in the memory. Food-lovers will enjoy the famed seafood of Dingle, part of the burgeoning culinary scene that has seen its reputation soar in recent years.

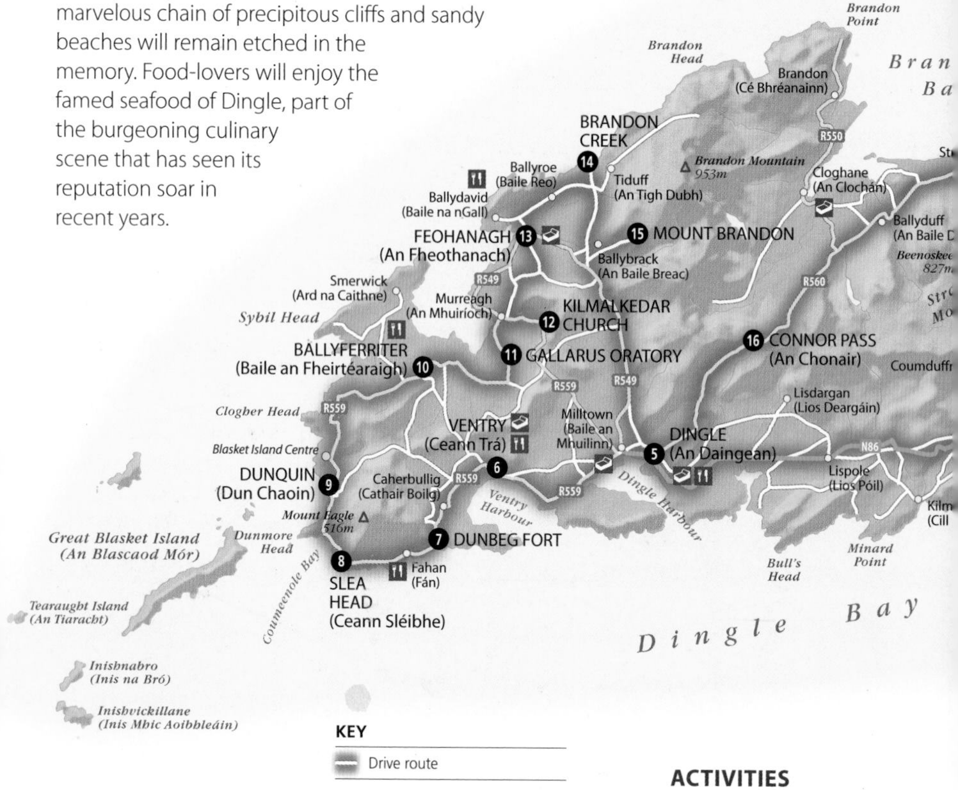

KEY

Drive route

Below A prehistoric beehive hut, or *clochan*, in the Fahan Group near Dunbeg Iron Age Fort, overlooking Dingle Bay, *see p66*

ACTIVITIES

Savor delicious seafood chowder in Dingle and finish off with a gourmet Irish whiskey ice-cream

Stroll along a white sandy beach at Ventry Bay and take a refreshing dip in its clear waters

Walk among prehistoric homes – the *clochans*, or beehive huts, of Fahan

Take a ferry ride out to Great Blasket Island and spend time exploring this lovely, now-uninhabited island

Cross the Connor Pass, Ireland's highest, and enjoy splendid views over the Brandon and Tralee bays

PLAN YOUR DRIVE

Start/finish: Tralee to the Maharees Peninsula.

Number of days: 2, allowing half a day for a trip to Great Blasket Island.

Distance: 110 miles (180 km).

Road conditions: Roads are well paved and marked but, in places, narrow with some steep inclines.

When to go: April to October are the best months to explore the Dingle Peninsula, when hedgerows and fields glow with wild fuchsias and montbretia. Many places close in winter. In peak season, be sure to book accommodation well in advance.

Opening times: Most shops and attractions open from 9 or 10am to 5 or 6pm. Shops are usually open Mon–Sat and from 12 to 6pm on Sun. In most villages there are convenience stores, open from 7 or 8am until late.

Main market days: Tralee: Sat; Dingle: Fri.

Shopping: Dingle has delightful little shops selling lovely artisan jewelry, crystalware, pottery, and other crafts. Traditional Blasket Islands weaving can be seen, and items bought, on Great Blasket in summer, or articles woven on the islands can be bought in Dingle year-round.

Major festivals: Tralee: Rose of Tralee Festival, Aug; Dingle: Regatta, Aug; Dingle Races, Aug; International Film Festival, Sep; Food and Wine Festival, Oct; Other Voices Festival, Nov.

DAY TRIP OPTIONS

Families might enjoy a day of **water-based activities**, starting with an early morning **dolphin-swim** at Dingle, then **kayaking** or **windsurfing** at Ventry or Sandy Bay and **bodyboarding** at Coumeenole Bay. A visit to the Blasket Islands Centre in Dunquin, followed by a trip out to Great Blasket, will appeal to **history enthusiasts**, and **movie-lovers** may spot locations used in the David Lean film *Ryan's Daughter*. For full details, *see p69*.

Above Vivid orange swathes of montbretia flowers lining the quiet country roads of the Dingle Peninsula

Above Steam train that once ran from Tralee

VISITING DINGLE

Parking
There is a pay-and-display parking lot on the waterfront, adjacent to the pier.

Tourist Information
Strand Street; 066 915 1188; www.dingle-peninsula.ie; open May–Sep: daily; Apr & Oct: Mon–Sat

WHERE TO STAY

AROUND TRALEE

Camp Junction *inexpensive*
This B&B is 5 minutes' walk from the beach. Eight bedrooms, all ensuite. Rooms at the front overlook Tralee Bay; those at the back have views of the Slieve Mish mountains.
Camp; 066 713 0848; www.campjunctionhouse.com

INCH POINT

Inch Beach Guest House *inexpensive*
Stylish B&B in a lovely scenic location only 3 minutes from Inch Beach, with spectacular views across the bay.
Inch Beach, Dingle; 066 915 8118; www.inchbeachguesthouse.com

DINGLE (AN DAINGEAN)

The Hide Out Hostel *inexpensive*
Located in the heart of Dingle, this friendly, well-run hostel caters for the independent traveler and for families. There is a mix of private and dormitory rooms. Michael, the owner, is a fount of wisdom on the whole area.
Dykegate St; 066 915 0559; www.thehideouthostel.com

Ballintaggart Manor House *moderate*
Affording beautiful views across the harbor, Ballintaggart House is an ideal base from which to explore the peninsula. This family-run manor house manages to combine boutique hotel style with homey charm.
Race Course Road; 066 915 1333; www.ballintaggarthouse.com

❶ Tralee
Co Kerry
Tralee (Trá Lí) is the administrative capital of County Kerry. A busy market town, it is probably best known for the international pageant, the Rose of Tralee, celebrating Irish womanhood, which takes place here each August. Though the town is principally 19th-century in character, there are some fine Georgian buildings. For a pleasant family outing, visit the Tralee Bay Wetland Centre, which offers an Activity Zone (with canoeing and cycle paths) and a Nature Zone (with viewing towers and safari tours).

🚗 *From Tralee take the N86 along the northern flank of the peninsula. Cross the stone bridge by the Blennerville Windmill, follow the undulating road and fork left after Camp. On reaching a farm building, head up the narrow road to its left. At the next junction turn left, which leads over the Pass of Caherconree.*

❷ Pass of Caherconree
Co Kerry
This is a little-known pass through the Slieve Mish Mountains to the southern flank of the peninsula. Near the summit of the pass is a sign for the Caherconree Iron Age Fort. It's worth a scramble up a boggy path to see it on a fine day. At the brow of the pass there are fantastic views over Castlemaine Harbour to the south.

🚗 *Descend into Aughils and turn right on the R561 for Inch.*

❸ Inch Point
Co Kerry
The setting for much of David Lean's 1970 movie *Ryan's Daughter*, Inch (Inse) Point is a splendid sand and dune spit that curves out into Dingle Bay – popular for water sports and swimming. When the tide is out, it is the perfect place for a bracing walk along its 4-mile (6-km) strand. Look out for sea otters, seals, and dolphins in the bay. There are splendid views across the bay to the Macgillycuddy Reeks, the highest mountain range in Ireland (*see p57*).

🚗 *From Inch Point, continue west on R561 toward Anascaul. Soon after leaving Inch, look out for a rest area from which there are great views of Dingle Bay. Further along, there will be a T-junction. Turn right here onto the N86 for Anascaul.*

❹ Anascaul
Co Kerry
In Anascaul is a pub called the South Pole Inn. Its former owner was Tom Crean, a member of both Scott's and Shackleton's expeditions to the Antarctic, known to locals as "Tom the Pole." The pub is full of memorabilia, as well as photographs of visiting dignitaries. There is a Memorial Garden, with a bronze statue of Crean holding the sled dog puppies of which he was so fond.

🚗 *Return to the main road and turn right, following the N86 to Dingle. Park in waterfront lot by pier.*

South Pole Inn pub sign

Below Fishing boats moored in front of St. Mary's Church in Dingle's pretty harbor, seen from the bay

⑤ Dingle (An Daingean)

Co Kerry

Dingle, the westernmost town in Europe, is located in the heart of a Gaeltacht – an Irish-speaking area (see p178). Though hardly undiscovered, it is nonetheless a gem. Probably just as popular with tourists as Killarney, it never seems overrun, and many visitors are seduced as much by its charm as by its "star" – the friendly dolphin, Fungi, who lives in the harbor. The town's characteristic features are brightly painted houses, traditional storefronts, and tightly bunched, narrow streets, all of which run down to the harbor. Good restaurants and traditional pubs tempt visitors to linger.

A one-hour walking tour

From the parking lot, turn right along Quay Street, with the harbor on your right. The Visitor Centre **Tourist Office** ① is at the foot of the pier. Continue into Strand Street and up the hill into Green Street, lined with shops, restaurants, pubs, and cafés. On the left is **St. Mary's Church** ②, and in its grounds is the Diseart Cultural Centre, housed in an old convent. Here in the chapel there are 12 stained-glass windows by the celebrated stained-glass artist Harry Clarke. Opposite is the famous pub **Dick Mack's** ③, which doubles up as a hardware store. Only a few of these store-cum-pubs now remain in Dingle. At the top of Green Street you come to Main Street, with its many traditional pubs and restaurants. To the right on Main St is **Lord Baker's Restaurant** ④ (see right),

Live music sign written in Irish

which has a cozy dining area around a turf fire. Turn right into Lower Main St, past **Ashes pub** ⑤, which allegedly serves the best seafood chowder on the planet. Turn right again down Dykegate Lane, looking for **An Café Liteartha** ⑥ on the left, a café-bookshop specializing in books of local interest. Continuing further on, turn left into Bridge Street for **O'Flaherty's Pub** ⑦. Here, a lively musical session usually commences when the landlord picks up his accordion. Retrace your steps and turn left into Strand Street to return to the parking lot. Stop in at the turquoise building on the left for at least one scoop of **Murphy's** ⑧ delicious, award-winning ice cream.

🚗 **Leave Dingle with the harbor on your left and follow signs for Ventry, heading due west on the R559, to the start of the drive around Slea Head.**

EAT AND DRINK

INCH POINT

Sammy's *inexpensive*
A popular seafront restaurant, which looks out across Inch Beach. Casual dining with a wide range of dishes.
Inch Beach; 066 915 8118

ANASCAUL

The South Pole Inn *inexpensive*
This historic, family-run pub serves excellent home-cooked food.
Main Street; 066 915 7388

DINGLE (AN DAINGEAN)

Garden Café *inexpensive*
Come to this café for home-cooked soups, sandwiches, and baked potatoes.
Green Street; 087 781 5126;
www.thegardencafedingle.eu

John Benny Moriarty's Pub *inexpensive*
A traditional Irish music pub, serving good food in a friendly atmosphere.
Strand Street; 066 915 1215;
www.johnbennyspub.com

Ashes Bar and Restaurant *moderate*
Ashes is famed for its seafood chowder, but it also serves hearty meat dishes.
Lower Main Street; 066 915 0989;
www.ashesbar.ie

Goat Street Café *moderate*
This small restaurant aspires to slow food with fast service and has been praised for its culinary acumen.
Goat Street; 066 915 2770;
www.thegoatstreetcafe.com

Lord Baker's Restaurant *moderate*
This well-known Dingle venue serves mainly seafood – lobster often features.
Main Street; 066 915 1277;
www.lordbakers.ie

Global Village *expensive*
Outstanding seafood restaurant offering one of the best dining experiences in town.
Upper Main Street; 066 915 2325;
www.globalvillagedingle.com;
open Mar–mid-Nov

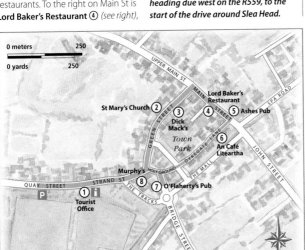

Eat and Drink: inexpensive, under €25; moderate, €25–€50; expensive, over €50

Above Rocky headland overlooking Dingle Bay, site of the Iron-Age fort of Dunbeg

VISITING THE BLASKETS

Blasket Island Ferries cross from Dunquin Harbour roughly every half hour from 10am to dusk Easter-end Sep. *066 915 6422; www.blasketislands.ie*

WHERE TO STAY AROUND VENTRY (CEANN TRÁ)

Moriarty's Farmhouse *inexpensive*
This friendly guesthouse is set on a working farm in an idyllic location near Ventry. Its six ensuite rooms have stunning views over Ventry Harbour. Owners Ted and Brid Moriarty are experts on the history of the region. *Rahanane (1 km/2 miles from Ventry at the start of the Slea Head Drive); 066 915 9037; www.dinglevacation.com*

Torann Na Dtonn *inexpensive*
The gentle wash of the sea lulls guests to sleep in this B&B overlooking Ventry Harbour and Dingle Bay. All five ensuite bedrooms have excellent views. *Slea Head Drive (5 minutes' drive from Ventry); 066 915 9952; www.dingle-peninsula.com*

Milltown House *moderate*
Robert Mitchum stayed in this award-winning period guesthouse during the filming of *Ryan's Daughter*. The 10 rooms are furnished to a high standard. *Ventry Road, Milltown (at the start of the Slea Head Drive between Dingle and Ventry); 066 915 1372; www.milltownhousedingle.com*

⑥ Ventry (Ceann Trá)
Co Kerry

Cushioned up against the slopes of Mount Eagle, Ventry perches alongside a wonderful crescent of white sandy beach, backed by sand dunes and hills. Here, upturned *currachs* (traditional Irish fishing boats of black-tarred canvas) are a common sight. The beach, one of the safest in the region, is popular with water sports enthusiasts and is ideal for swimming. On hot summer days, the pier at Ventry is also a popular swimming spot.
🚗 *Continue along the R559 to Dunbeg Fort.*

⑦ Dunbeg Fort
Fahan, Co Kerry

Just beyond Ventry, on a promontory looking out across Dingle Bay, is the Iron Age fort of Dunbeg. Surrounded by sea on three sides, this fortress has walls 23 ft (7 m) thick, surrounded by earthen trenches. Though much of the original construction has long since tumbled into the sea, it still presents an imposing sight. Opposite is the **Visitor Centre** (*open Mar–Nov: daily*), where there is a parking lot.

A little further along the R559 is the first set of *clochans*, or beehive huts, with the **Fahan Group** a short walk or drive away (there is ample parking at the site). It is estimated there are up to 400 of these huts scattered on the southern slopes of Mount Eagle. Many of these prehistoric dwellings, constructed in unmortared stone, are still in good condition and remain watertight.

Quite a few of them are on private land, and farmers may charge a small entry fee to view them.
🚗 *Continue west on the R559 to Slea Head and round into Coumeenole Bay. This is an exhilarating stretch of cliff-hugging road, high above Dingle Bay. On the right, the western flanks of Mount Eagle slope down to the sea, on the left you can see the Blaskets.*

The Blasket Islands

Once the most westerly settlement in Europe, Great Blasket was finally abandoned in 1953, when its dwindling population could no longer be sustained. Nevertheless, the Blasket Islands remain, for many Irish people, a potent symbol of an ancient Irish-speaking culture. Three books by islanders recount a lost way of life: Muiris O'Suilleabhan's *Twenty Years a' Growing*; Peig Sayer's *A Woman's Reflections*; and Tomas O'Criomhthain's *The Island Man*. English translations retain much of the local flavor and evocative phrasing of the original Irish.

⑧ Slea Head (Ceann Sléibhe)
Co Kerry

Offering exhilarating views across Dingle Bay and over to Great Blasket Island, **Slea Head** is the westernmost point in Europe, and the focal point of the Dingle drive. The sweep of sea, craggy coves, and outlying islands that come into view as you round the headland is a spectacular sight. The dramatic confluence of sea and land can be appreciated from the viewing point – a much photographed scene. A short

Below Road curving down from Dunmore Head, with views over Blasket Sound to the Blaskets

distance further on, the road sweeps around to **Coumeenoole Bay** (Trá an Choma) popular with surfers and bathers. The bay has an organized picnic area which affords breathtaking vistas across the bay. Behind the picnic area is a stone stile. On the other side of it is a grassy path leading out to Dunmore Head, which overlooks the Blasket Sound.

Stay on the R559, which now begins to turn north as it rounds the peninsula's headland and heads slightly inland for Dunquin.

Above Looking across Smerwick Harbour between Ballyferriter and Ballydavid

9 Dunquin (Dun Chaoin)
Slea Head, Co Kerry

Dunquin is famous as the setting for David Lean's epic drama *Ryan's Daughter*. While the film was not a critical success upon release – though acclaimed today – the breathtaking scenery certainly did wonders for regional tourism.

Dunquin was also the place where the Blasket Islanders came ashore to trade or buy provisions, which is why it has a certain historical resonance with local people. Some still speak of the crossing from Dunquin to the Blaskets as the "authentic one" – the one from Dingle to Great Blasket actually takes longer. In Dunquin, the **Blasket Islands Centre** (open Easter–Oct: daily) has exhibitions and audiovisual displays that show life as it was once lived on the Blaskets.

Here also is Kruger's pub, a popular landmark, and the last pub this side of the Atlantic. From the bar can be seen the island known as Skellig Michael (see p57) in the distance.

Follow the R559 north, then east, toward Ballyferriter.

10 Ballyferriter (Baile an Fheirtéaraigh)
Slea Head, Co Kerry

In the middle of Ballyferriter is O'Cathain's pub, a good lunch and music stop. On the first Wednesday of each month, traditional *Sean-nós* sessions take place here, at which singers perform unaccompanied by any musical instruments. At the end of the village, on the left, is the **Chorca Dhuibhne Museum** (open Easter–Sep: daily), dedicated to the peninsula's archeology. The area between Ballyferriter and **Ballydavid** (Baile na nGall) has retained its traditional way of life. Here, and in the villages around Smerwick Harbour, *Gaelige* (Irish) is spoken.

Continue on the R559 which turns sharply left after the Smerwick Hotel. Further along, turn right at the signpost for Gallarus Oratory.

11 Gallarus Oratory
Slea Head, Co Kerry

Often compared to an upturned boat in appearance, the Gallarus Oratory is one of the best-preserved early Christian churches in Ireland. Just as impressive are the dry-stone corbelling techniques that meant it has been able to withstand the elements for nearly 1,300 years. There is a **Visitor Centre** (open Jun–Aug) with a café and an audiovisual exhibition on the Oratory. The center also provides information on Kilmalkedar Church (see p68), the other important early Christian site in the area.

Leaving the Oratory, retrace your steps to the R559 and turn right in the direction of Murreagh (An Mhuirioch). From here, turn sharp right, at the sign for Kilmalkedar Church.

Above The simple but stunning early Christian Gallarus Oratory, whose dry-stone walls have survived 1,300 years

EAT AND DRINK

VENTRY (CEANN TRÁ)

Skipper Restaurant *inexpensive*
This atmospheric restaurant offers French food at affordable prices. The emphasis is on seafood.
Ventry; 066 915 9853

DUNBEG FORT

Stone House Restaurant *inexpensive*
Husband-and-wife team Paul and Deirdre run this lovely family restaurant located opposite Dunbeg Fort.
Fahan, Ventry; 066 915 9970; www.stonehouseventry.com

BALLYFERRITER

Tigh Uí Chathain *moderate*
A restaurant brimming with local character, this offers excellent value for money. With some of the best produce in Ireland on their doorstep, they cook simply, seasonally, and extremely well.
Ballyferriter; 066 915 6359

Eat and Drink: inexpensive, under €25; moderate, €25–€50; expensive, over €50

WHERE TO STAY

FEOHANAGH (AN FEOTHANACH)

An Riasc Guest House *moderate*
This charming stone farmhouse is located just outside Feohanagh amid breathtaking scenery. Denise, the owner, places a strong emphasis on using fresh and local produce. Short courses in Irish available as well as cooking demos and walking tours. Evening meals available on request.
Feohanagh; 066 915 5446; www.anriasc.ie

AROUND CONNOR PASS (AN CHONAIR)

O'Connor's Guesthouse *inexpensive*
In a stunning location at the foot of Mount Brandon, overlooking Brandon Bay, this family-run guesthouse in the village of Cloghane is popular with walkers. Breakfast, evening meals, and packed lunches are available, as well as a pint in the bar.
Cloghane (turn left on R585 as you descend the Connor Pass); 066 713 8113; www.cloghane.com

THE MAHAREES PENINSULA

Tigh Beagh *moderate*
This compact, beautifully restored farmhouse – the "small house" – is set in 17 acres of native woodland, and comes with its own mountain river and waterfall. It should appeal to those seeking peace and solitude. The house is fully equipped with all mod cons and has a geothermally heated tiled floor, as well as a wood-burning stove. Two large bedrooms.
Glanteenassig, Castlegregory (take R560 from Castlegregory and right turn uphill to Glanteenassig); 087 779 3126; www.tighbeag.com

Below Ancient crosses near the Irish Romanesque Kilmalkedar Church

⑫ Kilmalkedar Church
Slea Head, Co Kerry

This early Christian and medieval site is spread over 10 acres (4 ha) and is associated with St. Brendan. At the center is the 12th-century Kilmalkedar Church, an excellent example of Irish Romanesque style. Near the chancel door is an early Christian Alphabet Stone, and there are several ancient crosses here, as well as an Ogham Stone (marked with ancient script). The Pilgrim's Way walk to the top of Mount Brandon starts behind the church. Even a short 20-minute stretch of the walk is rewarded with fine views across Smerwick Harbour.

🚗 *Return on R559 toward Murreagh. Before the village is a school house. Turn right here, but, if the turning is missed there is another right turn onto the R549 in Murreagh itself. Either road will take you into Feohanagh.*

Local Flavors

In the last 10 years a culinary renaissance has taken place on the Dingle Peninsula. Some of the local delicacies worth sampling are Blasket Island lamb, highly regarded for its fine flavor; black (blood) and white pudding made in Anascaul; award-winning Dingle Peninsula seaweed-flavored cheese from Castlegregory; Dingle's smoked fish; and Murphy's ice cream *(see p65).*

⑬ Feohanagh (An Feothanach)
Slea Head, Co Kerry

As you arrive in Feohanagh, pull into the parking lot to admire stupendous views across Smerwick Harbour and the ragged headland of Ballydavid. Below you is Dooneen pier, which is accessible on foot. There you may see the remains of old *currachs*, once the main fishing vessels here. Though they are still built on the peninsula, their use has declined.

🚗 *Just past Feohanagh, turn sharp left and take the minor road marked for Ballyroe and Tiduff.*

Above Steep-sided cliff walls form a sheltering harbor at lovely Brandon Creek

⑭ Brandon Creek
Slea head, Co Kerry

Brandon Creek is believed to be the spot from which St. Brendan the Navigator set out on his epic voyage to Newfoundland in the 6th century. His journey is recounted in *Navigato Brendan*, the earliest copies of which in Latin and dating from the 11th century, were once housed in medieval libraries across Europe.

It is not advisable to drive down to the pier at Brandon Creek. Leave the car in the small parking area above, and walk the short distance. At the end of the pier is a rock within which is a large crevice. This creates an air pocket that, depending on the roll of the tide, makes a booming sound when trapped air is released.

Brandon Creek nestles in the shadows of imposing Mount Brandon, the second-highest mountain in Ireland and one of the country's holiest places.

🚗 *From Brandon Creek, drive due south on a minor road which eventually joins the main R549 road back toward Dingle. Just before it joins the main road there is a sign pointing left for Mount Brandon parking lot. Take this narrow road.*

⑮ Mount Brandon
Co Kerry

According to legend, St. Brendan climbed to the top of this mountain to view the Americas before starting out on his voyage. Near the Mount Brandon parking lot, a gateway, a grotto and a stream mark the starting point for the annual pilgrimage to the summit, which takes place on the nearest Sunday to June 29. On this day a special mass is celebrated on top of the mountain. A well-trodden path, punctuated by the Stations of the Cross, winds its way to the summit. It's well worth walking at least as far as the early markers for panoramic views of Dingle Harbour.

🚗 *Return to the R549, turn left, and follow the road back to Dingle. On leaving Dingle, turn first left at the first roundabout for the Connor Pass.*

⑯ Connor Pass (An Chonair)
Co Kerry

Ireland's highest route, the Connor Pass road rises quickly, winding its way to the summit at 1,500 ft (460 m). On a clear day there is a view of some of the most spectacular scenery in Ireland, with a panorama of mountains, sea, lakes, and boulder-strewn valleys. The whole of Ireland seems to be laid out below. To the south is Dingle Bay, while to the north are sweeping views over the Maharees Peninsula to Tralee Bay (on the right), and across Brandon Bay to Brandon Point (to the left).

🚗 *From the summit, the road winds down between Brandon and Stradbally mountains to the coast. It is narrow in places, so exercise caution, especially in poor weather. At Stradbally, turn left onto a minor road toward Killiney and go on from there to Castlegregory.*

⑰ The Maharees Peninsula
Co Kerry

Castlegregory is the gateway to the Maharees Peninsula, a sandy spit that divides Brandon and Tralee bays. It is a pretty village with narrow streets and gaily colored little houses. The Maharees itself has mile upon mile of sandy beaches, and is one of Ireland's main water sports centers. Birdwatchers may want to stop at Lough Gill, outside Castlegregory, which is famed for the variety of bird species.

From Castlegregory, follow the main road along the central spine of the spit to the village of **Fahamore**. This is one of the few places in which *currachs* are still made. Continue to **Scraggane Bay**, at the tip of the peninsula. It is popular with windsurfers, and its harbor is home to a small fishing fleet. From the pier there are views across to the **Magharee Islands**, known as the Seven Hogs. On the largest, Illauntannig, there are three stone huts and two oratories, the remnants of an early Christian monastery. Occasionally, local fishermen will ferry people across.

Above Road leading to Brandon Creek, in the shadow of Mount Brandon

EAT AND DRINK

AROUND FEOHANAGH (AN FEOTHANACH)
Gorman's Clifftop House and Restaurant *moderate*
A top-notch restaurant with an emphasis on local produce, organic when possible, and robust Irish cooking. The owners are very knowledgeable about the local area.
Glashabeg (just outside Feohanagh); 066 915 5162; www.gormans-clifftophouse.com

THE MAHAREES PENINSULA
Spillane's *moderate*
Run by Marilyn and Michael Spillane, this popular bar and restaurant is one of the landmark eating houses on the Maharees Peninsula. It has a wide-ranging menu, designed to suit all tastes. Specials usually include two meat and two fish dishes. Also offers self-catering accommodation.
Fahamore; 066 713 9125; www.spillanesbar.com

DAY TRIP OPTIONS
This drive never strays far from the sea or from history, so make the most of both. One day trip links up a range of water-based activities, while, for those caught up in the romance of Irish history and culture, there's a chance to step back in time.

Watery wonders
Start the day in Dingle ⑤ with a boat trip or swimming safari to see Fungi the dolphin, then head out to Ventry ⑥ and try windsurfing or kayaking on the Blue Flag beach. After lunch, join the surfers at Coumeenoole Bay ⑧ and stay for a fabulous sunset view over the Blasket Islands.

Follow the itinerary from Dingle to Ventry. From Ventry, take the coastal R559 to Coumeenoole, and use the same road to return to Dingle.

Irish history
With Dunquin ⑨ as the base, first visit the Blasket Islands Centre to learn about the unique history of the Islands, then take the boat to Great Blasket to explore this lonely place. On returning, head to Ballyferriter ⑩ for a lively pub music session. Movie fans will feel they have stepped right into *Ryan's Daughter*.

Follow the drive instructions.

Eat and Drink: inexpensive, under €25; moderate, €25–€50; expensive, over €50

Viking Country

Waterford City to Ballymacarbry

Highlights

- **Viking city**
  See Waterford glass being made and walk in the footsteps of the Vikings in Waterford City

- **The colorful Copper Coast**
  Find out about the fascinating geology of the coast between Tramore and Bunmahon

- **Fairytale castle**
  Visit Lismore Castle, the Duke of Devonshire's Irish retreat in the Blackwater Valley

- **Exhilarating pass**
  Tackle the exhilarating Vee, a dramatic high pass through the Knockmealdown Mountains

The dramatic coastline at Great Newtown Head, near Tramore

Viking Country

The large county of Waterford in southeast Ireland has fine stretches of coastline, gently indented with small coves, the big strand and holiday resort of Tramore, the beautiful Copper Coast beyond, and the stirring seascapes of Helvick Head. At the eastern end of the county is Waterford City, founded by the Vikings in the 10th century. Inland are the pretty towns of Lismore and Cappoquin in the languid Blackwater Valley. Two wild mountain ranges stretch north to the borders of Tipperary – the Knockmealdown Mountains, with their dramatic high passes, and the Comeragh Mountains, accessed along the beautiful Nire Valley Drive.

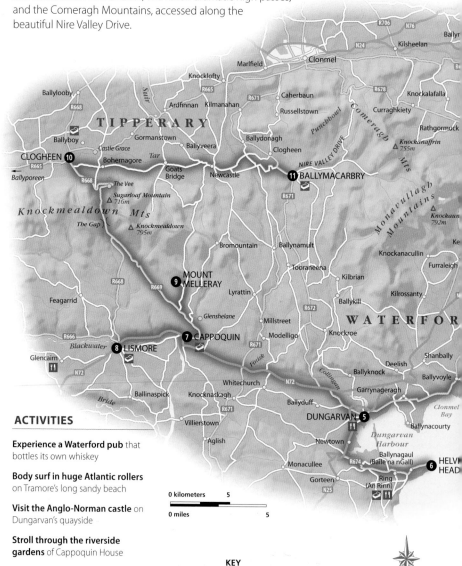

ACTIVITIES

Experience a Waterford pub that bottles its own whiskey

Body surf in huge Atlantic rollers on Tramore's long sandy beach

Visit the Anglo-Norman castle on Dungarvan's quayside

Stroll through the riverside gardens of Cappoquin House

Enjoy afternoon tea in the peaceful setting of Mount Melleray Abbey

KEY

⬛ Drive route

Left The Anglo-Norman fortress of Dungarvan Castle, *see p76*

PLAN YOUR DRIVE

Start/finish: Waterford to Ballymacarbry.

Number of days: 3.

Distance: 109 miles (175 km).

Road conditions: Generally well paved and well marked. Steep inclines and hairpin bends through the Knockmealdown Mountains.

When to go: Spring and summer are warm, autumn is bright and colorful, winter is mild. Southeast Ireland is sunnier than other regions.

Opening times: Most shops and attractions open from 9 or 10am to 5 or 6pm. In towns shops stay open late on Thu and 12–6pm on Sun.

Main market days: Waterford City: Sat; Dungarvan: Thu; Lismore: Sun (Jun–Sep).

Shopping: Waterford City is the main shopping center. World-famous hand-cut Waterford Crystal can be bought at shops and the visitor center there.

Major festivals: Waterford City: Waterford New Music Week, Feb; Spraoi, Aug; **Tramore:** Horse Racing Festival, Aug; **Dungarvan:** Waterford Festival of Food, Apr; **Lismore:** Immrama Festival of Travel Writing, Jun.

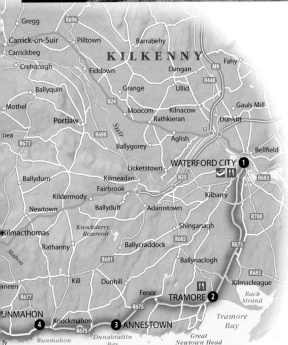

DAY TRIP OPTIONS

Explore the Copper Coast, which combines fine **beaches** and unusual **geology**. For contrasting **scenery** visit the idyllic towns of Cappoquin and Lismore, with their **stately homes** and **riverside gardens**, then take a **rollercoaster ride** through the Knockmealdown mountains. For full details, *see p77*.

Left Yachts, fishing trawlers, and pleasure craft moored in Waterford marina, *see p74*

Above Reginald's Tower, a 13th-century landmark on Waterford's riverfront

❶ Waterford City
Co Waterford

The capital of County Waterford is a handsome cathedral city set on the estuary of the River Suir. Founded by the Vikings in 914, by the 18th century it was southeast Ireland's main port as well as a center for glass-making. The Mall, with its elegant Georgian buildings, is testament to this period, while the old quays are now part of a revitalized historic quarter.

A one-hour walking tour

Start at **Reginald's Tower** ① *(open summer: daily; mid-Sep–Easter: Wed–Sun)*. This squat 13th-century tower forms the east corner of the Norse and medieval city – a rough triangle of streets between The Mall, Garden Alley, Michael Street, Broad Street, Barronstrand Street, and the Quays. A stronghold of the Anglo-Norman kings, the tower is said to be the first Irish building to use mortar, at the time a mixture of blood, lime, fur, and mud.

From the tower, turn right onto The Mall. Here is the **City Hall** ②, incorporating the Theatre Royal, designed in 1788 by John Roberts, a local man, and remodeled in the 19th century. Turn right on Palace Lane, leading into Cathedral Square. On the right, the 13th-century **Chorister's Hall** ③ incorporates two medieval buildings housing Waterford's Medieval Collection. To the left stands the Protestant **Christ Church Cathedral** ④ *(open daily)*, also designed by Roberts and built on the site of a 12th-century church. Its medieval remnants include a crypt containing the 1481 cadaver tomb of James Rice, a former mayor of Waterford. Depicting a badly decayed corpse

Waterford city coat of arms

crawling with worms, it is inscribed: "I am what you will be; I was what you are now."

From the cathedral, go back down Palace Lane, then turn right onto The Mall. On the right is the **Bishop's Palace** ⑤, an 18th-century building housing the Waterford Treasure and the world's largest collection of historic Waterford glass. From here, turn right up Colbeck Street, then up Henrietta Street, and finally left into High Street and **John Roberts Square** ⑥, named after the architect whose influence is everywhere in the city. One of his last works was the intimate **Catholic Cathedral** ⑦ *(open daily)* on Barronstrand Street, which has a rich Neo-Classical interior. From here, return to John Roberts Square and turn right into Great George's Street. On the left a palatial townhouse built in 1795 for the Morris family, also by Roberts, now contains the **Waterford Chamber of Commerce** ⑧. Head along O'Connell Street and left into Thomas Street to **Henry Downes** ⑨, a famous pub *(see right)*. Walk down to Merchants Quay and along the river back to the start.

🚗 *Leaving the city, take the R675 to Tramore. Park near the Lifeguard Station by Tramore Strand.*

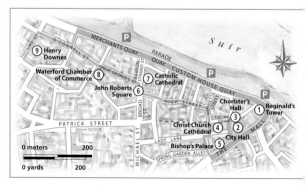

Far left Waterford City Hall and Christ Church Cathedral **Left** Boats in Waterford Marina

EAT AND DRINK

WATERFORD CITY

Henry Downes *inexpensive*
This atmospheric old pub has been in the same family since 1797. Try the whiskey Downes No. 9, which is blended on the premises.
Thomas St; 051 874 118

Bodéga! *moderate*
Bright and lively with a varied menu – chargrilled Cajun chicken salad, organic Irish lamb burger, Kilmore Quay fish cakes.
John St; 051 844 177;
www.bodegawaterford.com

La Bohème *moderate–expensive*
Stylish restaurant in the basement of one of the city's finest buildings. Dishes include quail with foie gras, pan-fried sea scallops, Dunmore East monkfish, and saddle of rabbit.
2 George's St; 051 875 645;
www.labohemerestaurant.ie

TRAMORE

Rockett's of the Metal Man
inexpensive
Famous for its *crubeens* (pig's trotters) served with *colcannon* (mashed potato, kale, and onion) with pints of stout and an open fire. On the west side of Tramore Bay.
Westown, Tramore; 051 381 496

Below Secluded cove near Bunmahon on County Waterford's Copper Coast

② Tramore
Co Waterford

Due to its long sandy beach, Tramore has been a popular holiday resort for generations. There is a lively seafront, with an amusement park, miniature railway, and other attractions, plus good swimming and surfing. Its Horse Racing Festival in August is a fashionable four-day event.

On the east side of town, a 5-mile (8-km) circular walk passes along the **Cush Sandspit** to **The Burrow** and back along the beach. It is a lovely stretch with opportunities to see a large variety of birds on the **Back Strand**'s mudflats, including Brent geese, golden plover, black-tailed godwit, red-throated diver, little egret, kingfisher, and fulmar.

Accessible by car on the west side of the bay is **Great Newtown Head** (leaving Tramore, take the first left after 2 miles (4 km), along the coast, then marked) where the **Metal Man** can be seen pointing shipping safely through the sand bars. Park at Newtown Cove for a short, tricky walk to the headland.

🚗 *Carry on, turning left onto the R675 to Annestown. Park by the beach.*

Heart of Glass

Waterford has been famous for its delicate cut glass since 1783, when George and William Penrose started the crystal manufacturing business. The industry prospered until 1851, when a lack of capital and crippling taxes caused business to fail. In 1947 a new factory opened, with craftsmen brought in from Europe to teach what had become a lost art. In 2009, the factory closed again, a victim of the credit crunch, but a major visitor center, factory and shop have now opened on the historic Mall.

The Metal Man

High on the cliffs on the west side of Tramore Bay are three pillars, one topped by the Metal Man, a 61-ft (19-m) high figure dressed in the colorful uniform of a 19th-century petty officer. The Metal Man's outstretched right arm points to the safe channel for ships. He is one of four such figures cast in London in 1819 following a shipping disaster in the bay; another is in Sligo Bay *(see p204)*.

③ Annestown
Co Waterford

The cluster of houses at Annestown lies on the so-called **Copper Coast** between Tramore and Dungarvan, an area known for its copper mining in the 19th century. It is a beautiful drive past unspoiled beaches, coves and grassy headlands. Annestown has a good **beach**, popular with surfers.

🚗 *Continue along R675 to Bunmahon. Park in town center parking lot.*

④ Bunmahon
Co Waterford

Waterford's Copper Coast has been designated a European Geopark on account of its extraordinary geological heritage. Bunmahon's **Geological Garden** *(www.coppercoastgeopark.com; open daily)* explains the volcanic and sedimentary rock that remains after two continents collided, creating Ireland. There is also a standing stone inscribed with ogham, an early Irish script in use from the 3rd century. Some 19th-century copper mine workings are still visible in the area.

🚗 *Leaving Bunmahon, take a left turn off the R675 and follow the coast road to Stradbally, which has a good beach. Stay on the road as far as Ballyvoyle crossroads (looking out for neolithic remains), then rejoin the R675 left to Dungarvan. Park on the street.*

Above Boats at Helvick Head pier **Above top right** Brightly painted shopfront in Lismore **Above right** Barrels outside a pub in Dungarvan

WHERE TO STAY

HELVICK HEAD

Gortnadiha Lodge *moderate*
Family farm with views of Dungarvan Harbour. Serves exceptional breakfasts.
Ring (An Rinn); 058 46142;
www.gortnadihalodge.com

CAPPOQUIN

Richmond House *expensive*
Built by the Earl of Cork in 1704, this charming country house offers exceptional comfort and fine food.
Cappoquin (just east of town); 058 54278; www.richmondhouse.net

LISMORE

Ballyrafter Country House Hotel
moderate
Small hotel built in the1800s for the Duke of Devonshire's estate manager.
Lismore; 058 54002;
www.waterfordhotel.com

AROUND CLOGHEEN

Ballyboy House *inexpensive*
Georgian farmhouse just out of town, with antique furniture and log fires.
Ballyboy, Clogheen Road, Cahir (on R665 between Clogheen and Castle Grace); 052 746 5297, www.ballyboyhouse.net

AROUND BALLYMACARBRY

Hanora's Cottage *moderate*
Country house hotel known for its food.
Nire Valley (a short drive east of Ballymacarbry on a minor road); 052 613 6134; www.hanorascottage.com

⑤ Dungarvan
Co Waterford

Set around a large harbor and looking out to Helvick Head, this old market town retains much of its original charm. For centuries it was protected by its Anglo-Norman **castle** (1186), the history of which is told in its 18th-century **barracks** *(open daily)*. Dungarvan blossomed in the early 19th century when the 5th and 6th dukes of Devonshire modernized its center. In the Old Town Hall on Augustine Street, **Waterford County Museum** *(open Mon–Fri)* charts its maritime history.
🚗 *Take the N25 south from Dungarvan and then the first left onto the R674 to Helvick Head. There are parking lots at the end of the head.*

⑥ Helvick Head
Co Waterford

The road to Helvick Head passes through Ring (An Rinn), in Waterford's Gaeltacht (Irish-speaking) area. Rising 230 ft (70 m) above a harbor, the headland has fine views.
🚗 *Return inland to Dungarvan and turn left on the N72 to Cappoquin, which has ample street parking.*

⑦ Cappoquin
Co Waterford

This pretty town on the River Blackwater is famous for fly fishing and has a salmon and trout run. Day tickets issued by Cappoquin Salmon and Trout Anglers' Association can be bought from Titelines tackle shop on Main Street *(www.fishcappoquin.com)*.

The town's other attraction is **Cappoquin House** *(open Apr–Jul: Mon–Sat)*, an 18th-century mansion. Following a fire in 1923, the house was rebuilt back to front so as to take better advantage of its riverside location. The lovely gardens are particularly notable for their rhododendrons in May.
🚗 *Continue on the N72 to Lismore. There is pay parking on the street.*

Local Specialties

Dungarvan's market is a good place to find local produce and specialties. These include Knockanore farmhouse cheese and Knockalara sheep's milk cheese. Also look for Gallwey's chocolates, handmade in Waterford. Ardkeen Quality Food Store, on Dunmore Road in Waterford, is a source of artisan food from all over Ireland.

⑧ Lismore
Co Waterford

Situated in the Blackwater valley beneath the Knockmealdown Mountains, Lismore was once famous for its double monastery (housing both nuns and monks), founded in the 7th century by St. Carthage. It was a world-renowned center of learning. Its **castle**, dominating the approach to the town, is the Irish seat of the Duke of Devonshire. It is largely 19th-century,

Below Lismore Castle, the Irish seat of the Duke of Devonshire

hough there has been a castle on his spot since the 12th century. Fred Astaire's sister Adele, who married he second son of the 9th Duke of Devonshire, lived here for some years. The gardens *(open daily)* contain a collection of modern sculpture and a lovely riverside walk.

The town has two cathedrals dedicated to St. Carthage, the late 19th-century **Catholic Cathedral**, and the Protestant **Cathedral of St. Carthage** (1633), which has Gothic vaulting and a stained-glass window by the Pre-Raphaelite artist Edward Burne-Jones.

Return to Cappoquin and take the R669 toward Tipperary. Turn right at the Cats Bar to Mount Melleray.

9 Mount Melleray
Co Waterford

Set on the bare slopes of the Knockmealdown Mountains, the Cistercian abbey at **Mount Melleray** *(open daily)* was founded in 1832 by Irish monks expelled from France. The monks observe a rule of silence but keep a tradition of hospitality; it is usual to make an offering. Visitors can view most areas in the abbey and have tea in the restaurant.

On leaving Mount Melleray, return to the R669 and turn right to join the R668 for an exhilarating drive through the **Gap**, the road's highest point, and the **Vee**, a series of hairpin bends, to Clogheen. On the way, look out for the beehive-shaped tomb of Samuel Grubb (1750–1815) on Sugarloaf Mountain. One-time owner of Castle Grace, near Clogheen, Grubb was buried upright in order, it is said, to overlook his land.

Carry on to Clogheen and park on the street.

Above Mount Melleray abbey at the foot of the Knockmealdown Mountains

10 Clogheen
Co Tipperary

A small market town on the River Tar, Clogheen was a prosperous mill town in the 18th and 19th centuries, as a smattering of fine Georgian townhouses testifies. Two miles (3 km) east of town, off the R665, are the remains of **Castle Grace**, an Anglo-Norman castle with a tower at each corner; 5 miles (8 km) west, also on the R665, is **Ballyporeen**, where former US president Ronald Reagan came to celebrate his Irish roots in 1984.

From Clogheen, go back along the R668 and take the first left, following signs to Newcastle. Pass through Goats Bridge and Newcastle to Ballymacarbry.

11 Ballymacarbry
Co Waterford

This village is an ideal base for exploring the majestic **Comeragh Mountains**, either on foot or by car. The **Nire Valley Drive** (marked off the R671 east of town) into the mountains is a spectacular route flanked by the Comeragh range to the right and the dramatic Punchbowl formation to the left.

EAT AND DRINK

DUNGARVAN

Quealy's *moderate*
A busy and friendly café bar in the center of town with daily specials such as a seafood platter.
O'Connell St; 058 24555

The Tannery *expensive*
This is regarded as one of the country's finest restaurants, reinventing many Irish classics using the best local produce. Reservations advisable.
Quay St; 058 45420; www.tannery.ie

HELVICK HEAD
An Seanachaí *moderate*
A thatched cottage has been converted to a cozy bar, with good food, on the road from Dungarvan.
Pulla Cross, An Rinn (Ring); 058 46755; www.seanachai.ie

LISMORE
O'Brien Chop House
moderate–expensive
This traditional Victorian pub delivers robust Irish recipes, including West Cork garlic and herb sausages.
Main Street; 058 53810; www.obrienchophouse.ie

DAY TRIP OPTIONS
Spend a day on the coast or in Waterford's inland valleys.

Tramore and the Copper Coast
Begin at Tramore ❷, taking in the beach and seafront attractions, and a walk along the sandspit east of town. Afterward head along the Copper Coast to Dungarvan ❺ via Annestown ❸ and Bunmahon ❹,

stopping at the Geological Garden. In the late afternoon, the sun brings out the colors of the cliff face.

Leaving Waterford City take the R675 all the way to Dungarvan. Return by the same route or cut inland along the N25.

Mountains and valleys
Combine a gentle drive along the lovely Blackwater Valley, stopping in

picturesque Cappoquin ❼ and Lismore ❽, with an exciting ride through the Knockmealdown Mountains to Clogheen ❿.

From Cappoquin take the N72 to Lismore. From there take the R668 to join the R669 and head north through the Knockmealdown Mountains to Clogheen. Return to Cappoquin on the R669, making a detour to Mount Melleray if there is time.

Eat and Drink: inexpensive, under €25; moderate, €25–€50; expensive, over €50

Kilkenny's Medieval Treasures

Kilkenny City to Carlow Town

Highlights

- **Kilkenny's commanding castle**
  Explore the interior of Kilkenny's magnificent castle and stroll through its grounds

- **Rural Kells**
  Walk through the haunting ruins of Kells fortified priory

- **Delightful details**
  Discover the elaborate carvings adorning the cloister of Jerpoint Abbey, a Cistercian masterpiece

- **Granary of the Monks**
  Visit the ecclesiastical center of Graiguenamanagh, for centuries dominated by Duiske Abbey

The market town of Graiguenamanagh on the banks of the lovely River Barrow

Kilkenny's Medieval Treasures

On the fringes of well-heeled Leinster, beyond the gravitational pull of Dublin, Kilkenny City has a keen sense of its own worth. For 500 years the powerful Earls of Ormonde held sway here, and for a time in the 17th century it even challenged Dublin as the center of power in Ireland. Running through the city and County Kilkenny is the River Nore, a lovely waterway that laps ivy-clad priories, stone castles, round towers, and picturesque villages such as Inistioge and Thomastown on its course south. This route stops off at many of the Kilkenny's medieval treasures, from Dominican Black Abbey in the county capital to Cistercian Jerpoint Abbey and Duiske Abbey in Graiguenamanagh, the "Granary of the Monks."

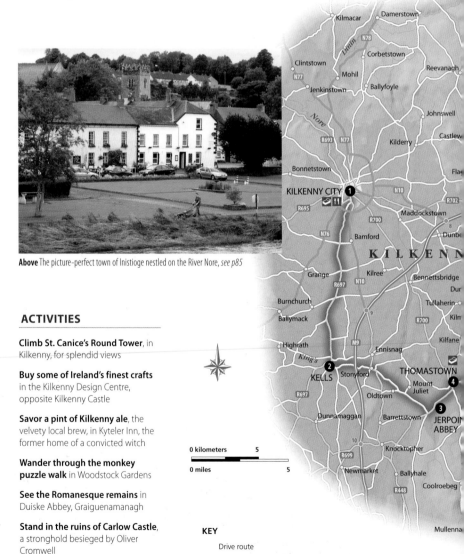

Above The picture-perfect town of Inistioge nestled on the River Nore, *see p85*

ACTIVITIES

Climb St. Canice's Round Tower, in Kilkenny, for splendid views

Buy some of Ireland's finest crafts in the Kilkenny Design Centre, opposite Kilkenny Castle

Savor a pint of Kilkenny ale, the velvety local brew, in Kyteler Inn, the former home of a convicted witch

Wander through the monkey puzzle walk in Woodstock Gardens

See the Romanesque remains in Duiske Abbey, Graiguenamanagh

Stand in the ruins of Carlow Castle, a stronghold besieged by Oliver Cromwell

KEY

Drive route

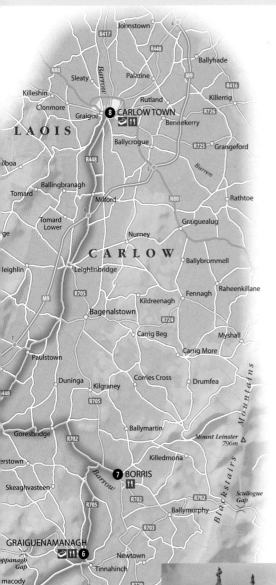

PLAN YOUR DRIVE

Start/finish: Kilkenny City to Carlow Town.

Number of days: 1–2 days.

Distance: 91 miles (170 km).

Road conditions: Well paved and well marked.

When to go: The weather is better in summer, and some places are closed Nov–Feb. There is plenty to see and do all year, especially in Kilkenny City.

Opening times: Shops and attractions are open from 9am to 6pm, Mon–Fri, and shorter hours on Sunday.

Main market days: Kilkenny City: Farmers' Market, Thu am; **Carlow Town:** Sat.

Shopping: Visit the Kilkenny Design Studio for high-quality crafts.

Major festivals: Kilkenny City: Rhythm and Roots Music Festival, May; The Cats Laugh Comedy Festival, Jun; Kilkenny Arts Festival, Aug; Celtic Festival, Sep/Oct.

DAY TRIP OPTIONS

Art and architecture buffs are richly served by Kilkenny City's **medieval heritage**. For **12th-century ruins** nestling in **lush river valleys**, head for Kells Priory and Jerpoint Abbey, and then relax in the **romantic gardens** at Inistioge. For full details, *see p85*.

Below The 13th-century early English Gothic-style St. Canice's Cathedral, Kilkenny City, *see p82*

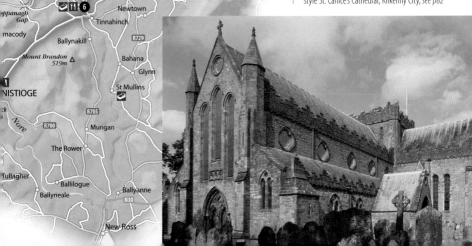

VISITING KILKENNY CITY

Parking
Park in Market Yard off Bateman's Quay, or in one of the central parking lots on Ormonde Street or James Street.

Tourist Information
*Rose Inn St; 056 775 1500;
www.discoverireland.ie/kilkenny;
open daily year-round.*

Shopping
Kilkenny Design Centre stocks a superb range of high-quality crafts. The Crafts Council of Ireland is in the same complex.
*Castle Yard, The Parade; 056 772 2118;
open daily, closed Sun and public
holidays Jan–Apr*

WHERE TO STAY IN KILKENNY CITY

Laragh House *inexpensive*
Modern, family-run guesthouse within walking distance of the city center.
*Waterford Rd; 056 776 4674;
www.laraghhouse.com*

Butler House *moderate*
Comfortable Georgian townhouse that is part of the castle estate. Breakfast is served at the Kilkenny Design Centre.
*16 Patrick St; 056 7722 828;
www.butler.ie*

Kilkenny Hibernian Hotel *moderate*
Housed in a former bank. This hotel has spacious rooms mixing traditional and modern styles.
*Ormonde St; 056 777 1888;
www.kilkennyhibernianhotel.com*

Kilkenny River Court Hotel *moderate*
Comfortable hotel with lovely riverside terrace and pool.
*The Bridge, John St; 056 772 3388;
www.rivercourthotel.com*

① Kilkenny City
Co Kilkenny

Ireland's only inland city, Kilkenny is also one of its finest. It brims with medieval treasures and has narrow alleyways, gaily colored storefronts, and a vibrant atmosphere. Set on the west bank of the River Nore, the historic center is book-ended by its two main landmarks, St. Canice's Cathedral and Kilkenny Castle.

A two-hour walking tour

From Market Yard **parking lot** ① follow the walkway onto St. Kieran's Street and then Parliament Street. On the right, in the yard of **Kilkenny Brewery** ②, are the ruins of 13th-century St. Francis' Abbey (*closed to public*). Leaving the yard, turn right onto Irish Town. Ahead is **St. Canice's Cathedral** (*open daily*) ③, a 13th-century Protestant cathedral in the Early English Gothic style; it sits on the site of a pre-Norman church dedicated to St. Canice – *Cill Chainnigh* (Church of

Canice), from which Kilkenny derives its name. Inside, look out for the 16th-century carved effigies of Kilkenny's powerful Butler family (*see box*), a model of the town in its Elizabethan heyday, and the 13th-century east window. Climb the cathedral's round tower (847) for far-reaching views.

Leaving the cathedral, turn right down Dean Street. After 656 ft (200 m) cross the road and turn left, following signs for **Black Abbey** (*open daily*) ④, a 13th-century Dominican Friary with

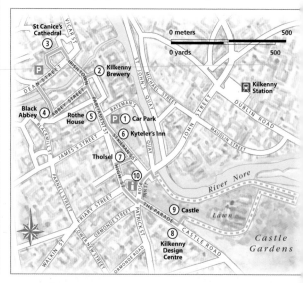

Dukes of Ormonde

In 1391 Edmund Butler, the third Earl of Ormonde, bought Kilkenny Castle, a move designed to consolidate the family's power in Kilkenny and Tipperary. Butlers of various branches influenced life in the region for nearly 500 years. Their strength lay in their loyalty to the English Crown, their disdain of Irish ways, and their success in dismantling the power of the Catholic Geraldines.

ine stained-glass windows. From here, nead down Abbey Lane, through Black Freren Gate. On the right are remnants of the city walls. Turn right onto Parliament Street to arcaded **Rothe House** (open daily) ⑤, a medieval merchant's house. Continuing up Parliament Street, veer left down St. Kieran's Street, past **Kyteler's Inn** ⑥, a good place to enjoy a pint of ale. It was once the home of Alice Kyteler, convicted of witchcraft in the 14th century. Kyteler fled the country, but her maid was sent to the stake. The presiding judge, Bishop Ledrede, is buried in St. Canice's graveyard.

Continue along St. Kieran's Street and turn right up the Butter Slip, the old butter market, to Main Street. On the left is the **Tholsel** ⑦, a Georgian remodeling of the medieval exchequer and subsequent Town Hall. Turn left up High Street and fork left up the Parade to the castle, stopping to look at Irish crafts in the **Kilkenny Design Centre** ⑧, (open daily; closed Sun and public holidays Jan–Apr) in the castle's stable block. The **Castle** (open daily) ⑨ was the seat of the Dukes of Ormonde for 500 years. Inside, the Long Gallery (1820s) has a hammer beam roof painted with motifs from the Book of Kells. From the castle gates, follow the path around the lawn,

turning right at the end. Turn down a slipway and through a gate in the castle walls. Turn left to follow the canal (which merges with the river) to St. John's Bridge. Turn left up Rose Inn Street, where the **Tourist Information Office** (open daily) ⑩ occupies a medieval almshouse, and take St. Kieran's Street to the parking lot.

🚗 *Leave the city center by Patrick Street (N10) and turn right at Kells Road (R697). In Kells, drive to top of village and turn left to Kells Priory.*

② Kells

Not to be confused with the more famous Kells Monastery in Meath, 13th-century **Kells Priory** lies at the end of a sloping field, accessed through a kissing gate. Its fortified towers and connecting walls date from the 15th century.

🚗 *Turn left from the priory. After 2 miles (3 km) turn right at a T-junction, marked for Mount Juliet. At the junction with the R448, turn left. Jerpoint Abbey is just before Thomastown.*

③ Jerpoint Abbey

Founded in 1180, this Cistercian abbey is a daughter house of Mellifont Abbey (see p159). Its tower and battlements stand out proudly, and there is still a sense of its former grandeur. Most of the buildings still standing date from the 15th century, but the abbey's principal attraction lies in its details. The carvings in the cloister are the most ornate of any religious building in Ireland, with knights, courtly ladies, bishops, and dragons. Enjoy a scone at Jerpoint Park, a heritage site that is only a few minutes away by car.

🚗 *Turn right on leaving the abbey and drive into Thomastown.*

Above The 15th-century cloisters of Jerpoint Abbey, one of Ireland's finest Cistercian ruins

EAT AND DRINK IN KILKENNY CITY

Kyteler's Inn *inexpensive*
The former home of convicted witch Alice Kyteler in the 14th century, this historic inn serves Smithwick's beer, brewed in Kilkenny since 1710.
Kieran's St; 056 776 1064; www.kytelersinn.com

Chez Pierre *moderate*
Popular well-established restaurant with robust, bistro-style cooking.
17 Parliament St; 056 776 4655

Kilkenny Design Centre *moderate*
Self-service restaurant in the castle's former dairy and stables, overlooking the craft courtyard. Consistently good food at reasonable prices.
The Parade; 056 772 2118; www.kilkennydesign.com

Rinuccini *moderate*
Bustling Italian restaurant with an extensive menu, conveniently located opposite Kilkenny Castle. Offers good quality and outstanding value.
Parade; 056 776 1575; www.rinuccini.com

La Campagne *expensive*
This restaurant delivers seriously good modern French food in a relaxed setting.
5 Gashouse Lane; 056 777 2858; www.campagne.ie

Far left Mullins Mill Museum, next to Kells Priory **Left** The 15th-century fortified towers of Kells Priory

Above View over the small market town of Graiguenamanagh

WHERE TO STAY

THOMASTOWN

Ballyduff House
inexpensive–moderate
Handsome and elegant 18th-century house overlooking the River Suir. Elegant but relaxed.
Thomastown; 056 775 8488; www.ballyduffhouse.ie

AROUND GRAIGUENAMANAGH

Ballyogan House *inexpensive*
Period farmhouse with views of the Blackstairs Mountains. Situated 3 miles (5 km) from Graiguenamanagh, on the road to New Ross (turn right opposite Duiske Abbey).
Graiguenamanagh; 059 972 5969; www.ballyoganhouse.com

Mulvarra House *inexpensive*
On a hill overlooking picturesque St. Mullins village, 4 miles (6 km) south of Graiguenamanagh. Breakfast and dinner are impressive. Some rooms have a balcony view over the valley.
St. Mullins, Co Carlow; 051 424 936; www.mulvarra.com

CARLOW TOWN

Barrowville Townhouse *inexpensive*
Period house near the town center. Serves hearty breakfasts.
Kilkenny Rd; 059 914 3324; www.barrowville.com

Right Riverside garden in the attractive village of Inistioge

❹ Thomastown
Co Kilkenny

Strategically important in medieval times, this market town gives few hints of the walled town it once was, save for its old stone bridge over the River Nore and the 13th-century ruins of **St. Mary's Church**. A pleasant, 1 mile (2 km) walk along the river leads to the 13th-century shell of **Grennan Castle**.

🚗 *Turn left onto The Quay and follow signs for the R700 toward New Ross and Inistioge.*

Statutes of Kilkenny

In 1366 the English Crown decided that the Anglo-Norman rulers of Ireland were becoming too enamored of Irish ways and customs. Fearful of losing its grip, it enacted the much-hated "Statutes of Kilkenny." Under the new laws, intermarriage between Anglo-Normans and Irish was an act of high treason, and Norman settlers speaking Irish, adopting Irish dress, or wearing their hair long in the Irish style risked forfeiting their lands.

❺ Inistioge
Co Kilkenny

Picture-perfect Inistioge sits elegantly on the River Nore, the ideal setting for an Irish country drama. It's no surprise then that *Circle of Friends* (1995), starring Minnie Driver, and *Widow's Peak* (1994), with Mia Farrow, were both filmed here. There is a lovely riverside walk, and the nine-arch stone bridge – the largest in Ireland – is a source of local pride. Unusually in Ireland, the Catholic and Anglican churches stand side by side.

Just above the town are **Woodstock Gardens** *(open daily)*, which are being

meticulously restored and feature an arboretum, a monkey puzzle walk, dovecote, and grotto. Derelict Woodstock House, burnt down in the civil war of 1922, gives an extra poignancy to the garden.

🚗 *Leaving Inistioge, cross the arched bridge and take the first left to Graiguenamanagh (7 miles/11 km) almost immediately after the bridge. Arriving in Graiguenamanagh, drive up the hill, past Duiske Abbey, to the parking lot on the right.*

❻ Graiguenamanagh
Co Carlow

Once a place of significant ecclesiastical importance, Graiguenamanagh (Granary of the Monks) is a small market town on the River Barrow. Occupying center stage is **Duiske Abbey** *(open Mon–Fri)*, founded in 1204 by Cistercian monks. After the Dissolution of the Monasteries in 1536, it was abandoned and fell into gradual decline, the tower finally collapsing in 1774. In the early 19th century, parts of the church were roofed and mass was celebrated here once again. Most of the present building dates from this period. However, it retains some original features, in particular a Romanesque doorway, an effigy of a Norman knight, and by the main entrance the original fleur-de-lis paving stones. A second restoration was undertaken in the 1970s, and the abbey is now a working parish church.

🚗 *Exiting the abbey's parking lot, drive uphill to the roundabout. Take the third exit onto Borris Road. At the junction with the R702 turn right for Borris (1 mile/2 km).*

⑦ Borris
Co Carlow

Nestling in the Barrow valley below
the Blackstairs Mountains, this is a
pretty village with a cluster of
Georgian houses. Its two main
landmarks are the Regency-styled
Borris House (group tours by
appointment; www.borrishouse.com),
ancestral home of the High Kings of
Leinster, and the 16-arch **viaduct** at
the bottom of the town. In the 1800s
Borris experienced a period of
prosperity, thanks to its sawmills and
lace industry. For a time Borris lace
enjoyed an international reputation.

Above Borris House, ancestral home of the
High Kings of Leinster

*🚗 Exiting Borris, follow the R702 as
far as Gowran. Just before the village,
turn right onto the R448 toward
Carlow (12 miles/19 km).*

⑧ Carlow Town
Co Carlow

The county town of Ireland's second-
smallest county, Carlow was an
Anglo-Norman stronghold guarding
the River Barrow. Its position on the
fringes of the English Pale, the
protected area around Dublin, gave
it a significant role in the history of
Ireland. During the 1798 rebellion
600 rebels were massacred here after
attempting to take the town. The
Liberty Tree sculpture off Hanover
Street commemorates this event.

Standing next to the River Barrow
are the ruins of **Carlow Castle**. It
survived many sieges, including one
by Oliver Cromwell, but was finally
laid to waste by a Dr. Middleton in
1814. Determined to convert the
castle into an asylum, he set about
reducing the thickness of its walls
with explosives, eventually causing
their demolition. Other buildings of
note are the Neo-Gothic Catholic
Cathedral and **St. Mary's Church of
Ireland**, both dating from the early
19th century.

Above left Traditional bar at
Graiguenamanagh **Above right** Colorful
narrow boats moored on the River Barrow
at Graiguenamanagh

EAT AND DRINK

INISTIOGE

Footlights *inexpensive*
A riverside bistro offering pretty views,
light dining, and evening meals.
*The Square; 086 361 9411;
www.footlights.ie*

The Motte Restaurant *moderate*
Small country restaurant. Menu
includes beef with brandy sauce and
crispy stuffed duckling.
Plas Newydd Lodge; 056 775 8655

GRAIGUENAMANAGH

**Waterside Restaurant and
Guesthouse** *inexpensive*
Stone warehouse on the bank of the
River Barrow. Smoked eel from the
river is a signature dish.
*The Quay; 059 972 4246;
www.watersideguesthouse.com*

BORRIS

The Stephouse Hotel *moderate*
Classic Irish cooking with a modern twist.
*66 Main St; 059 0773209;
www.thestephousehotel.com*

CARLOW TOWN

Pompei Ristorante *moderate*
Rustic Italian and French cuisine.
Centaur St; 059 917 9717

DAY TRIP OPTIONS

Kilkenny City is a good base to
explore the area. Kilkenny City can
be quickly accessed along the M9
from Waterford City and the M7
(then N8 and N77) from Dublin.

Kilkenny's Castle and Cathedral
The highlights of Kilkenny City ①
can easily fill a whole day. Climb the
cathedral's round tower, find the

grave of the judge who convicted
Alice Kyteler of witchcraft in the
14th century, and admire the 13th-
century east window. Afterward
head for the castle, seat of the
Butler family for 500 years.

Kilkenny City can be explored on foot.

Abbeys and gardens
Just a few kilometers apart are Kells
Priory ② and Jerpoint Abbey ③, set

in countryside south of Kilkenny City.
Kells has fortified walls and towers;
Jerpoint is known for its carvings.
Afterward head to Inistioge ⑤ to
see Woodstock Gardens and have
lunch overlooking the River Nore.

*From Kilkenny City, head south along
the R697 Kells Road (or faster N10 to
Stonyford and turn right), then cut east
to Jerpoint via Mount Juliet, and then
south along the R700 to Inistioge.*

Eat and Drink: inexpensive, under €25; moderate, €25–€50; expensive, over €50

Tipperary's Holy Glen

Cashel to Clonmel

Highlights

- **The Ancient Rock of Cashel**
  Marvel at the solitary glory of
  Ireland's finest ecclesiastical site

- **Tranquil Athassel Priory**
  Discover this hidden Augustinian
  priory on the banks of the River Suir

- **The verdant Glen of Aherlow**
  Strike out on one of the many hiking
  trails or explore the leafy lanes of this
  resplendent river valley in the shadow
  of the Galtee Mountains

- **Stronghold of Cahir**
  Explore the formidable castle of the
  medieval dukes of Ormonde, and
  their *cottage ornée* from a gentler era

The peaceful rural setting of 12th-century
Athassel Priory

Tipperary's Holy Glen

Bordered by the Galtee and Knockmealdown mountains to the south, this fertile, landlocked county is often overlooked by visitors, eager to move on to the more dramatic landscape of the western coastal counties. This is a pity, as Tipperary's many captivating sights warrant far more than a cursory glance. Chief among them is the resplendent Glen of Aherlow, studded with holy wells and ruined abbeys. Also here is Ireland's most fascinating ecclesiastical site – the totemic Rock of Cashel, a lofty citadel that soars above the surrounding vale. To the east are the vibrant former Anglo-Norman strongholds of Cahir and Clonmel, quintessential Irish market towns that are ideal for a leisurely stroll.

KEY

▬▬ Drive route

Map labels:

Clonkelly
Dundrum
Ballym
Newtown
Knockavilla
R505
Donohill
Ballyn
Moanmore
R497
Gorteen
Mulleen
R661
Donaskeagh
Cullen
Monara
Thomastown
N24
Kilfeakle
ATHASSEL PRIORY ❷
Tipperary
N74
Lattin
R515
Shronell
Bawnbrack
Lagganstov
Ballinleenty
R664
Bansha
R662
Brookville
Rathdermot
Glen of Aherlow
Kilross
GLEN OF AHERLOW NATURE PARK ❸
Foxfort
Ballygorteen
N24
R663
Ab
Newtown
Lisvernane
CLONBEG CHURCH ❹
Rossadrehid
THE KYLE ❻
Galbally ❺
MOORE ABBEY
Bally
R663
Spittle
Barna
Galty Mountains
R662
△ Galtymore 920m
△ Greenane 804m
Clonmor

ACTIVITIES

Walk out to Hore Abbey for an outstanding view of the soaring Rock of Cashel

See red squirrels and spring flowers on the Bianconi Forest Walk in the Glen of Aherlow

Climb up to Darby's Bed, a megalithic passage tomb on a hillside near Galbally

Visit Cahir's curious Swiss Cottage, a *cottage ornée* designed by Georgian architect John Nash

Left Celtic cross in Cashel's broad Main Street, *see p90*

Above The town of Cashel, below the famous Rock, *see p90*

PLAN YOUR DRIVE

Start/finish: Cashel to Clonmel.

Number of days: 2–3.

Distance: 154 miles (240 km).

Road conditions: Well paved and marked.

When to go: Mar–Oct is best. Many of the holy wells and monastic sites are wet and boggy in winter.

Opening times: Shops are generally open 9 or 10am to 5 or 6pm, but closed Sun. Sights may be closed in winter.

Main market days: Cahir: Farmers' Market, Sat am (parking lot beside Craft Granary on Church Street).

Major festivals: Cashel: Art Festival, mid-Nov; **Glen of Aherlow:** Walking Festival, end of Jan and beginning of Jun; **Clonmel:** National Coursing Meeting, Feb; Junction Festival (art festival), Jul.

DAY TRIP OPTIONS

For fascinating insights into Irish **history and culture**, dramatic **views**, and outstanding **Romanesque architecture**, head to the Rock of Cashel, Cahir Castle and the old market town of Clonmel. Keen walkers can explore the many **hiking trails** in the Glen of Aherlow, taking in the **wooded hillsides**, **ruined abbeys**, and **holy wells**. For full details, *see p91*.

Below the Glen of Aherlow, ideal walking country, *see p91*

Above The dramatic Rock of Cashel tops a craggy limestone outcrop

① Cashel
Co Tipperary

All royal and ecclesiastical ruins in Ireland fade into insignificance when compared with the **Rock of Cashel** *(closed Dec 24–26)*. Visible from afar, this tight cluster of turrets and towers soars majestically above the vales of Tipperary. From the 4th or 5th century it was the seat of the Kings of Munster, whose kingdom extended over much of southern Ireland. Legend has it that St. Patrick baptized Aengus, King of Munster, here in AD 448. In 1101, Cashel was handed over to the Church. It flourished as a religious center until Cromwell's army sacked it in 1647.

From the parking lot, Bishop's Walk leads to the 15th-century **Hall of the Vicar's Choral**, built for Cashel's top choristers. It now houses the ticket office and an audiovisual presentation on the site. In the museum on the lower floor, look out for **St. Patrick's Cross**; its base is believed to be the coronation stone of the Munster kings, and the carving on the east face depict St. Patrick on his visit to Cashel in 450. Opposite the **Dormitory of the Vicar's Choral** is **St. Cormac's Chapel**, a Romanesque masterpiece with superb carvings on the tympanum, containing the sarcophagus of Cormac the Bishop, a 12th-century King of Munster.

The largest building on the Rock is **St. Patrick's Cathedral**, burned in 1495 by the Earl of Kildare and again by a Cromwellian army, when 3,000 townfolk seeking sanctuary were roasted to death by Lord Inchoquin, one of Cromwell's generals. Look out for the panels of three 16th-century tombs in the north transept of the cathedral, decorated with intricate carvings of vine-leaf designs and stylized beasts. Next to the cathedral, the 92-ft (28-m) **Round Tower** dates from the early 12th century.

Beyond the ramparts of the Rock (a 1-mile/2-km walk across the fields) is **Hore Abbey**, which affords one of the best views of the Rock.

In Cashel itself, in the grounds of the Protestant cathedral on John's Street, **Bolton Library** *(open Mon–Thu)* contains Ireland's most important collection of antiquarian books outside Dublin. Among the 12,000 volumes is Geoffrey Chaucer's *Book of Fame*, printed by William Caxton.

Back in the parking lot at the foot of the rock, the **Brú Ború Cultural Centre** – named after Brian Ború, a 10th-century king of Munster – charts the history of Irish culture, and holds traditional music, song and dance performances.

🚗 *From the parking lot, turn left, then left again onto the main Dublin–Cork road. Turn right and drive through Cashel. At the end of the High Street turn right and left onto R505. At the first round-about turn left onto N74. After 4 miles (6 km), past the village of Golden, turn left after Bridge House pub. After the priory comes into view, 1 mile (1.5 km) from the turning, pull into a rest area on the left, past some stone pillars.*

② Athassel Priory
Co Tipperary

From the stone pillars a path leads over a bridge and through the old gate lodge of the priory. Founded in 1192 by the Anglo-Norman knight William de Burgh, this Augustinian priory *(open daily)* was once the largest in Ireland. Its walls still stand, and the church has an aisled nave, a choir, and transepts with a 15th-century tower over the crossing. Look for a carved face protruding from the tower.

🚗 *From the stone pillars, retrace the route to Golden and then take a left turn onto the N74, following signs toward Tipperary. Once in Tipperary, take the R664 off Main Street. Follow the road for a short distance, then turn right at a traffic island, following signs for the Tipperary Golf Club. Continue to the Christ the King statue and the entrance to the Glen of Aherlow Nature Park. Park at the foot of the statue.*

Below The ruined 15th-century tower, nave and choir of Athassel Priory

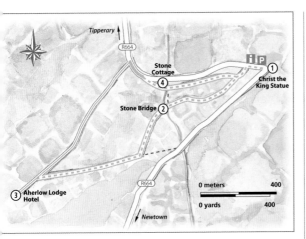

VISITING GLEN OF AHERLOW NATURE PARK

Parking
There is a parking lot at the Christ the King Statue, the entrance to the Glen of Aherlow Nature Park.

Glen of Aherlow Information Centre
Maps and information on the Glen.
Glen of Aherlow Fáilte Society, Coach Road; 062 56331; www.aherlow.com; open Jun–Sep.

③ Glen of Aherlow Nature Park

The Glen of Aherlow, a 15-mile (25-km) long valley dotted with megalithic and early Christian sites, runs from Galbally in the west to Bansha in the east. Within the valley, the Christ the King statue is a major landmark and the starting point for a network of hiking trails in the Glen of Aherlow Nature Park. It is said that the statue's raised hand bestows a blessing on all who pass.

One- to two-hour walk

One of several trails in the nature park, Bianconi Forest Walk is a 4-mile (7-km) loop. It is glorious at all times of the year, but especially in spring, when the woods – a habitat for red squirrels – are filled with bluebells and primroses.

From the parking lot near the **Christ the King statue** ①, walk up to the display board above the picnic area. The Bianconi Walk is marked by a blue arrow. Entering the forest, follow the path down stone steps, over a wooden bridge, and turn right. When the path divides after about 984 ft (300 m), veer left, pausing to read the first of a series of poems on a tree trunk.

Continue along the path to a stone stile. Cross this and turn left along a broad path, shaded by oak and ash trees – once part of the old Bianconi coach route from Tipperary to Limerick, named after Charles Bianconi, who founded public transport in Ireland with a carriage service from Clonmel to Cahir in 1815. Walk down the hill to

The Christ the King statue

a beautiful forest glade, mountain stream, and **stone bridge** ②. Cross the bridge and follow the wide track as it snakes to a T-junction. Turn right and follow the path to a paved road. To the left is the **Aherlow Lodge Hotel** ③, a good stop for refreshments. Turn right, follow the road up a steady rise for half a mile (1 km), taking in the views of the glen. At the T-junction turn right and walk downhill, with a clear view of Galtymore, the highest peak in the Galtee Mountains. Leave the road and re-enter the forest. The path leads down to a crossroads. On the left, stone steps lead up to the ruins of an old **stone cottage** ④ from the famine era (1845–70). Follow the path back to the start.

🚗 *From the Christ the King statue follow the R664 to Newtown (2 miles/3 km). At the T-junction, turn right onto the R663, toward Galbally. Just outside Newtown, after the Glen Hotel, follow the left sign for Clonbeg Church.*

EAT AND DRINK IN CASHEL

The Bakehouse *inexpensive*
A bakery with a café upstairs, opposite the Tourist Information Office. Offers well-prepared, unfussy food.
Main St; 062 61680; closes 5:30pm

Feehan's Bar *inexpensive*
This pleasant pub serves up home-made soups, steak sandwiches, and more from noon to 6pm daily. Take-out service is also available.
Main St; 062 61929

Chez Hans *expensive*
Fine food served in the unusual setting of an old church. A signature dish is the cassoulet of seafood. Next door, Café Hans offers more informal dining.
Moore Lane; 062 61177; www.chezhans.net

Below View over the glorious Glen of Aherlow with the Galtee Mountains in the background

Eat and Drink: inexpensive, under €25; moderate, €25–€50; expensive, over €50

Above The Swiss Cottage at Cahir, a *cottage ornée* designed by John Nash

WHERE TO STAY

AROUND CLONBEG CHURCH

Ballinacourty House and Restaurant
inexpensive
Eighteenth-century building with rooms and restaurant overlooking an inner courtyard. Camping and self-catering cottages attached. Located a short distance north of Lisvernane on a minor road.
Glen of Aherlow; 062 56000; www.ballinacourtyhse.com

Aherlow House Hotel *moderate*
Former hunting lodge set in acres of woodland. Elegant and comfortable with beautiful views over the Galtee mountains. Frequently has special offers. Situated just off the R663, a short distance west of Newtown.
Glen of Aherlow; 062 56153; www.aherlowhouse.ie

CAHIR

Cahir House Hotel *moderate*
The former home of the Butler family, this is a popular hotel complete with a landscaped garden in the middle of Cahir. Lively music session on Friday evenings.
The Square; 052 744 3000; www.cahirhousehotel.ie

④ Clonbeg Church
Co Tipperary
This 18th-century Church of Ireland chapel is unusual in having both a Catholic and Anglican burial ground. It is built on the site of a church founded by St. Sedan – the ivy-clad remains of an earlier church can still be seen – and is notable for **St. Sedan's Well**, situated in the far right-hand corner of the graveyard. The water from the well is noted for its healing properties, in particular for treating eye ailments. People visiting the well tie "clooties" – pieces of clothing belonging to the sick – to the birch tree behind the well.

🚗 *Return to main road (R663) and turn left toward Galbally and Lisvernane. Moore Abbey is 2 miles (4 km) beyond Lisvernane. As the road approaches the abbey it swings right over a stone bridge. There is a small parking bay on the right-hand side just past the abbey.*

Above The cemetery of the 18th-century Clonbeg church

⑤ Moore Abbey
Co Tipperary
On the western end of the Aherlow Valley, **Moore Abbey** was founded in 1204 by Donough O'Brien, King of Thomond (North Munster). Repeatedly destroyed by the Desmond and Ormonde dynasties, it took 300 years to build. The remains date mainly from the 15th century.

Continue on along the R663 to **Galbally**, a quiet town centering on a large square with a statue commemorating republican heroes. Just outside town on Duntryleague Hill is **Darby's Bed**, a megalithic passage tomb. To get there, take the narrow road (behind the statue) off Galbally's main square. The tomb is a 15-minute walk from the parking lot.

🚗 *From Galbally, return to Newtown and continue east toward Bansha. After 2 miles (3 km) turn right onto an unclassified road marked for Rossadrehid (4 miles/7 km). Immediately after the first crossroads, pull in and park in front of cottage on the right-hand side of the road. To find the Kyle, follow the path to the right of the cottage, climb over a stile and follow a rough path across the field.*

Holy Wells
The Glen of Aherlow has some holy wells, many of them pre-dating Christianity in Ireland. Druids were said to draw their power from them. They continue to be considered holy and to possess miraculous healing powers. Pilgrims often use a piece of cloth to wash the afflicted part of their body and then tie it to the tree overhanging the well – usually an ash or whitethorn – as a prayer offering.

⑥ The Kyle
Co Tipperary
The oval enclosure known as the **Kyle** was created to preserve a collection of Celtic relics – grinding stones, fragments of a cross and carvings – found on the site here. It has also been used as a burial place for unbaptized children.

To reach **St. Berrihert's Well**, walk past the Kyle, through the wooden gate and along a causeway over marshy ground. Follow the path to some wooden steps and a bridge,

bove The Main Guard in Clonmel, built as a ourthouse by the Earl of Ormonde

nd turn left toward a second gate. Through the gate veer right. The well s marked by a "rag tree." According to ocal legend, water from the well will not boil; it also protects from fire.

🚗 *Continue in the same direction to the N24. Turn right for Cahir. Park just ast Cahir Castle, across the bridge.*

❼ Cahir
Co Tipperary

The main attraction of this market town is **Cahir Castle** *(open daily)*, an Anglo-Norman stronghold of the Butler dynasty, Earls of Ormonde. It was a formidable defense, although Cromwell's army breached its walls in 1650. The foundations, curtain walls, and keep are 13th-century; much of the rest dates from the 15th and 16th centuries. Don't miss the magnificent Great Hall and the ramparts.

A 1-mile (2-km) walk along the River Suir (marked from the back of the parking lot) leads to the **Swiss Cottage** *(open Mar–Nov)* a *cottage ornée* designed by Regency architect John Nash for Richard Butler in 1810, and conceived as an ornamental retreat where the earl could entertain guests. By the parking lot, **Inch Field** has a fine view of the castle.

From the parking lot turn right along Castle Street to the main square, designed by the Victorian architect William Tinsley, and turn left along **Church Street** for a medley of shops and cafés. At its end is **St. Paul's**, a Church of Ireland chapel also designed by John Nash in the early 1800s.

🚗 *Turn right from the parking lot and drive to the top of Castle Street and the main square. Turn left at the junction, following signs for Clonmel (10 miles/16 km).*

❽ Clonmel
Co Tipperary

This is Tipperary's most important market town and its bustling atmosphere makes it a pleasant place to stroll around. Like many towns in the area, it was besieged by Cromwell in 1650, but was one of the few places that put up serious resistance. The medieval **West Gate** (rebuilt in 1831) leads to **O'Connell Street**, the main thoroughfare. A stone plaque in the gate commemorates Laurence Sterne, author of the early comic novel *Tristram Shandy*, who was born in Clonmel in 1713. Halfway down O'Connell Street, in Mary Street, **St. Mary's Church** contains one of the oldest organs in Ireland, stained-glass windows by William Tinsley and remnants of the original city walls.

At the east end of O'Connell Street, **Main Guard**, built as a courthouse in 1675, houses the **Tourist Information Centre** *(open Mon–Fri)*. Nearby, off pedestrianized Mitchell Street, Abbey Street leads to the **Old Quay**, where the **Franciscan Friary** retains a 15th-century tower. At the end of Mitchell Street, Emmet Street leads to Mick Delahunty Square, with a statue of Clonmel's favorite son, the tenor Frank Patterson (1938–2000), and the **County Museum** *(open Tue–Sat)*.

EAT AND DRINK

CAHIR

The River House
inexpensive–moderate
Opposite the castle, this restaurant offers breakfast and lunch in a relaxing setting. Good for homemade soups and salads. View of castle from the upper floor.
1 Castle St; 052 744 1951; closes 5pm; www.riverhouse.ie

Galtee Inn *moderate*
Highly regarded pub, run by the same family for three generations. Famous for its large succulent steaks. Log fires in winter.
The Square; 052 744 1247; www.galteeinn.com

CLONMEL

Befani's Mediterranean & Tapas Restaurant *moderate*
Stylish restaurant that is popular with locals and discerning diners. The food is bold and flavorsome with such mainstays as cassoulet sausage and duck confit. Also provides accommodation.
6 Sarsfield St; 052 617 7893; www.befani.com

Below Quayside walk in Clonmel, a lively market town on the River Suir

DAY TRIP OPTIONS
Cashel is the ideal base to explore the area's two highlights.

Fortified rock
One of Ireland's top attractions, the Rock of Cashel ❶ is a fortified cathedral with towers, turrets, and a round tower rising straight out of the rock. Be sure to get there early to avoid the crowds. Afterwards take in Cahir ❼, a market town with a superb castle, or historical Clonmel ❽.

From Cashel take the M8 to Cahir and then the N24 to Clonmel.

The Glen and holy wells
Combine a walk through the Glen of Aherlow Nature Park ❸ with a drive through its main valley, stopping at ruined abbeys, holy wells, villages, and megalithic tombs.

Follow driving instructions from Cashel.

The Sunny Southeast

Enniscorthy to the Saltees

Highlights

- **Miles of beach**
  Wander Curracloe's uncrowded sandy beach, the longest in Ireland, keeping an eye out for seals

- **Rebel town**
  Explore the rebellious history of Wexford, a handsome town now famed for its opera festival

- **Wildlife havens**
  Go bird-watching at Lady's Island and Tacumshane lakes, and on rugged Great Saltee Island

Atlantic Puffin perched, on a rock, on Great Saltee Island

The Sunny Southeast

Wexford's mild maritime climate yields Ireland's best strawberries and potatoes and has made the county a favourite haunt of Dubliners who want a retreat away from home. This drive includes a good stretch of the coastline, with long and unspoiled beaches and two world-class sites for birdwatchers. There are many links along the route with the 1798 Rebellion, which took place largely in Wexford (*see p106*). The southern end of the county is very rural, with thatched cottages and one of the last original windmills in Ireland.

Above Tacumshane's lovingly preserved windmill, dating from 1846, *see p101*

ACTIVITIES

Walk the ridge of Oulart Hill, site of an important rebel victory in 1798

Have a go at bodyboarding on Curracloe, Ireland's longest beach

Listen to uplifting music during the Wexford Opera Festival

Take a short boat ride to Great Saltee Island to see its colony of puffins

KEY

 Drive route

0 kilometers 4

0 miles 4

- Kilcormick
- OULART HILL **3**
- Oulart
- Derry
- R744
- Ballymurry
- Courtclogh
- R742
- Ballyvaldon
- R744
- Ballynamona
- **4** BLACKWATER
- Ballymurn
- Monroe
- R741
- Ballyconnigar
- Movilla
- Ballina
- R742
- Curracloe
- Castlebridge
- **5** CURRACLOE BEACH
- Ardcavan
- *Wexford Wildfowl Reserve*
- R741
- Crosstown
- *The Raven Point*
- **7** WEXFORD TOWN
- *Rosslare Point*
- *Wexford Harbour*
- Drinagh
- Killmacree
- Rosslare
- N25
- Killnick
- Tagoat
- Rosslare Harbour
- Kilrane
- Twelveacre
- Tenacre
- *Greenore Point*
- R736
- Broadway
- Ballyhitt
- TACUMSHANE **9**
- **8** LADY'S ISLAND LAKE
- *Tacumshane Lake*
- *Lady's Island Lake*
- Churchtown
- *Carnsore Point*
- *ltic Sea*

Fishguard, Pembroke →

Cherbourg, Roscoff

PLAN YOUR DRIVE

Start/finish: Enniscorthy to Kilmore Quay for the Saltee Islands.

Number of days: 3, allowing half a day for a visit to the Saltee Islands.

Distance: 47 miles (75 km).

Road conditions: Larger roads are in good condition and well marked. Smaller roads are often winding, so take care on bends.

When to go: All year round – Wexford is famous for its mild climate. Opera-lovers should go in October for the Wexford Festival Opera.

Opening times: Shops open Mon–Sat from 9 or 10am to 5 or 6pm.

Main market days: Enniscorthy: Sat; Wexford Town: Fri.

Shopping: Fresh produce such as artisan cheeses, hand-pressed apple juice, and dry-cured bacon are widely available. Wexford Town's shops include a craftsman silver- and gold-smiths established in 1647.

Major festivals: Enniscorthy: Strawberry Festival, Jun; Celtic Roots Folkdance Festival, Aug; **Wexford Town**: Book Festival, Apr; Wexford Festival Opera, Oct.

DAY TRIP OPTIONS

Fans of **Irish history** will want to visit Vinegar and Oulart hills, important sites of the 1798 rebellion; while **bird-watchers** and **nature lovers** should not miss the chance to visit Lady's Island and Tacumshane lakes. For full details, see p101.

Below Wexford Town Harbour, bustling with fishing boats and pleasure craft, see p100

Above Enniscorthy, with the spire of its magnificent cathedral **Above top right** Pastoral landscape near Curracloe **Above right** Enniscorthy's 13th-century castle

② Vinegar Hill
Enniscorthy, Co Wexford

This was the principal camp for the insurgents who took the town of Enniscorthy in May 1798. In June, they were surrounded by 20,000 troops; many were massacred, and the rest escaped through a gap in the British lines. The windmill used as a fort still stands, and there are great views across the country, to Enniscorthy and over to Oulart Hill.

Return toward Enniscorthy and take the R744 in the direction of Blackwater. When the road veers right, take the fork to the left, toward Oulart. The narrow road passes through pleasant farming country to the village of Oulart. Turn left, then left again before the church, then up a long straight road to the top of the hill, where there is a parking lot.

① Enniscorthy
Co Wexford

An attractive market town on the hilly west bank of the River Slaney, Enniscorthy was a focal point of the 1798 Rebellion. After a victory against the British here, insurgency spread through the region. **St. Aidan's Cathedral** *(open daily)*, by Augustus Welby Pugin, is a mid-19th-century Gothic Revival building of superb quality. The 13th-century castle on which the town was founded has been restored as a local history **museum** *(open daily)*.

Leaving Enniscorthy, cross the river to the eastern side and follow the signs for Vinegar Hill, which overlooks the town.

Artisan food

Enniscorthy and Wexford markets are the best places to find artisan produce from the county's farmers. Carrigbyrne's St. Killian (voted Best Irish Cheese at the 2007 World Cheese Awards) and Irish Brie, made in Adamstown west of Wexford Town, are excellent, as are the juices from Ballycross Apple Farm, in Bridgetown near Kilmore Quay.

③ Oulart Hill
Oulart, Co Wexford

In May 1798, the day before the rebel stormed Enniscorthy, a small insurgent force under Father John Murphy defeated the British on Oulart Hill. A short walk from the parking lot

WHERE TO STAY AROUND ENNISCORTHY

Ballinkeele House *moderate*
A stately Italianate country house, 10 miles (16 km) southeast of Enniscorthy, which has been home to the same family since it was built in 1840. Wonderful parkland and woods, fabulous food, and warm hospitality. *Enniscorthy; 053 913 8105; www.ballinkeele.ie*

Monart *expensive*
A most luxurious destination spa, set in 100 acres (40 ha) just northwest of Enniscorthy, Monart encourages its guests to connect with themselves and the landscape by immersion in relaxation therapy, wandering in the gardens and eating sumptuous meals. *The Still, Enniscorthy; 053 923 8999; www.monart.ie*

Below View over Enniscorthy toward Oulart Hill from Vinegar Hill

Where to Stay: inexpensive, under €100; moderate, €100–€200; expensive, over €200

passes along the brow of the hill, on a path marked with stones engraved with the names of people and places associated with the 1798 Rebellion in Wexford. At the end is *Tulach a' Solais* (meaning "mound of light"), a grassy mound bisected by a striking and austere concrete memorial, erected to commemorate the bicentenary of the Rebellion, designed by leading architect Ronald Tallon and enclosing an oak sculpture by Michael Warren. The central shaft of the monument, cut through the hill, is aligned with Vinegar Hill. There are great views of the surrounding countryside and Wexford Bay.

🚗 *Return to Oulart village and turn left. At the junction with the R741 turn right. At the junction with the R744 turn left, heading for Blackwater.*

④ Blackwater
Co Wexford
This village features many of the thatched cottages for which County Wexford is famous, some decorated in patterns with seashells. Turn left, then right, down a pretty road with more thatched cottages, to reach **Ballyconnigar**. The beach here runs all the way to Wexford Town.

🚗 *Return to Blackwater and head south on the R742, toward Curracloe. Take a left turn at the sign for Bently Cottage/Ballinesker down a narrow road through sand dunes to Curracloe Beach.*

Below The dunes behind sandy Curracloe Beach, location for the film *Saving Private Ryan*

Above Typical Wexford-style thatched cottage near Blackwater village

⑤ Curracloe Beach
Co Wexford
The D-Day landing scenes in Steven Spielberg's film *Saving Private Ryan* were shot on Curracloe's 10 miles (16 km) of golden sands. The easy, well-marked **Raven Point Loop** trail here passes through an area that is home to grey seals and wild orchids. Stay on the path and allow at least two hours. The **Wexford Wildfowl Reserve** *(open daily)*, where thousands of birds winter, is nearby.

NEW POTATOES HOME GROWN
Curracloe village farm sign

🚗 *Take the R742 to the junction with the R741 (signs point left to the Wildfowl Reserve). Cross the bridge at Wexford, turn right onto the R730 towards the N11, then take the left turn at the sign for the Irish National Heritage Park.*

⑥ Irish National Heritage Park
Ferrycarrig, Co Wexford
A trail within the 35 acres (14 ha) of the park *(open daily)* takes visitors through superb reconstructions of Irish settlements dating from the Stone Age to the arrival of the Normans in the 12th century.

🚗 *Return to the R730 towards Wexford Town. Turn left for Wexford Town and park on the quayside.*

Wexford Wildfowl
Around 10,000 Greenland white-fronted geese winter here, but others to look out for in the marshes and grasslands include dunlins, godwits, plovers, scoters, pochards, and shovelers, and listen out for warblers and cuckoos in season.

EAT AND DRINK IN ENNISCORTHY

Toffee and Thyme *inexpensive*
A busy, bright lunch place serving wholesome, home-cooked food.
24 Rafter St; 053 923 7144

Via Veneto *moderate*
A good, authentic Italian restaurant offering fish and rice dishes, polenta, broths, and stews, as well as pasta. Stylish and informal.
58 Weafer St; 053 923 6929; www.viaveneto.ie

Eat and Drink: inexpensive, under €25; moderate, €25–€50; expensive, over €50

Above Striking statue of a Pikeman of the 1798 Rebellion, Wexford Town

VISITING WEXFORD TOWN

Parking
Paid parking on Paul Quay near the Tourist Office.

Tourist information
Crescent Quay; 053 912 3111;
www.wexfordtourism.ie

VISITING GREAT SALTEE ISLAND

Boats to Great Saltee leave Kilmore Quay mid-morning in fine weather.

WHERE TO STAY

WEXFORD TOWN

Whites *expensive*
This well-loved hotel has been renovated and modernized, with first-class facilities such as a tranquility spa.
Abbey St; 053 912 2311;
www.whitesofwexford.ie

AROUND WEXFORD TOWN

Killiane Castle *moderate*
At this stunning castle and working farm guests can watch cows being milked, lambs being born, and even use the golf driving range. Lovely rooms. Excellent breakfasts are served.
Drinagh, Wexford; 053 915 8885;
www.killianecastle.com

KILMORE QUAY

Quay House *inexpensive*
This pleasant, bright B&B is especially popular with fishermen.
053 912 9988; www.quayhouse.net

Hotel Saltees *moderate*
A modern hotel with its own restaurant (open Jun–Sep only) and a nice bar.
053 912 9601; www.hotelsaltees.ie

❼ **Wexford Town**
Co Wexford

This handsome walled town at the mouth of the River Slaney was founded by the Norsemen in the 9th or 10th century and, in the 12th century, it was the first Irish town to be captured by the Anglo-Normans. The charming quays of Wexford's once-thriving port are now given over to recreation, and the pretty, narrow streets tucked behind it are full of shops, museums, and sights of historic interest.

A one-hour walking tour

From the **Tourist Office** ① walk along Crescent Quay to the statue of Commodore John Barry, father of the US Navy, who was born near here in 1745. Go back to the tourist office, turn up Oyster Lane and then right, left and right again, onto High Street. On the right is the **Opera House** ②, *(see box)* hidden behind a facade of town houses. Turn back to the first corner, then right into Mary Street and up to School Street, where the mainly 18th-century **Franciscan Friary** ③ holds a relic of St. Adjutor, the Roman boy-martyr. Walk along School Street and turn right onto Rowe Street. The **Church of the Immaculate Conception** ④ was built in1858 to a design by architect Robert Pierce, a pupil of Pugin. Walk down Rowe Street to North Main Street and turn left. At the junction of North Main, Abbey, and Common Quay streets is the **Bullring** ⑤, scene of bull-baiting in Roman times, and of a massacre in 1649 by Cromwell's men. The impressive figure of a 1798 **Pikeman** ⑥,

erected in 1905, is by Oliver Sheppard. Carry on up North Main and Selskar streets into Westgate to the **Abbey of the Holy Sepulchre** ⑦ *(open daily)*, the remains of a 14th- century church of the Augustinian Priory. It was here that the English king Henry II is said to have spent Lent of 1172 doing penance for the murder of Thomas à Becket. To return to the parking lot, walk down Westgate to Wellington Place, and along the quays, pausing to admire the striking modern bridge on the way.

🚗 *Leave Wexford on the R730, then take the N25 south to Tagoat, then turn right and follow the signs to Lady's Island Lake.*

Wexford Opera Festival

Each autumn, Wexford Town's streets are packed with opera fans from around the world. Founded in 1951, the Festival often showcases little-known or neglected works. In 2008, a superb new dedicated opera house opened, reinforcing the Festival's status as a musical event of global stature and importance.

Below View of Wexford Town's quays from across the estuary of the River Slaney

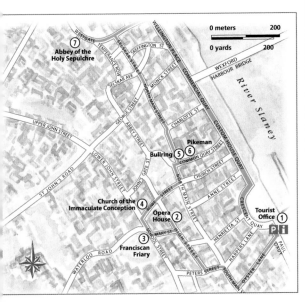

Above The Gothic Revival mansion of Johnstown Castle, with its glorious gardens

EAT AND DRINK

WEXFORD TOWN

Westgate Design *inexpensive*
The restaurant in this superb crafts and design center serves tasty, generous, home-cooked local dishes.
22 North Main Street; 053 912 3787; www.westgatedesign.ie

La Dolce Vita *moderate*
Italian restaurant said to be the best in Ireland. Great care goes into every detail, from homemade bread to Italian wine imported by the owners.
6/7 Trimmers Lane; 053 917 0806

TACUMSHANE

The Millhouse *inexpensive*
They serve good, hearty fare in this family-run pub beside the windmill.
053 53 913 1700; www.millhousebar.ie

KILMORE QUAY

Crazy Crab *moderate*
Family-owned café/bistro serving the freshest locally caught seafood.
053 914 8848; www.crazycrab.ie; open Mar–Sep

Silver Fox Seafood Restaurant *moderate*
This restaurant serves a wide range of locally caught fish.
053 912 9888; www.thesilverfox.ie

⑧ Lady's Island Lake
Co Wexford

Lady's Island Lake is a saltwater lagoon, separated from the sea by a barrier of sand and shingles. It is an internationally important site for breeding terns, including the rare roseate tern, and home to many species of migrating birds. The island, linked to the mainland by a causeway, is named for an abbey dedicated to the Virgin Mary. Now in ruins, it has for centuries been a place of pilgrimage. Off the coast to the east is Tuskar Rock, with its 19th-century lighthouse.
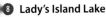 *The roads are narrow, winding, and rarely marked. To avoid getting lost, return to Tagoat, turn left on R736, left again at the sign for Tacumshane.*

⑨ Tacumshane
Co Wexford

Tacumshane Lake is another salt-water lagoon, cut off from the sea by a storm beach. The exceptionally diverse waterfowl population includes vagrant American waders, and rare breeds can be seen all year. In Tacumshane village there is a fine windmill, dating from 1846 and one of the last in Ireland. Ask for the key to see inside it at the friendly pub, the Millhouse, nearby.
Return to the R736 and turn left onto it, then left onto the R739 signposted for Kilmore Quay.

⑩ Kilmore Quay
Co Wexford

This pretty seaside village, with many old thatched cottages, is an important fishing port and holiday resort. It is also the departure point for **Great Saltee Island**, Ireland's most important bird sanctuary, just off the coast. The Saltees are home to important colonies of gannet, guillemot, puffin, razorbill, and fulmar. There is also a breeding colony of around 120 grey seals. The islands are privately owned but day visitors are welcome on Great Saltee, and boat trips run daily in good weather from Kilmore Quay.

DAY TRIP OPTIONS
This is a region of great significance in Irish history. It also offers the country's best birdwatching opportunities.

Rebel views
From a base in Enniscorthy ①, Vinegar Hill ②, and Oulart Hill ③, two important sites of the 1798 Rebellion, are close together, and offer panoramic views. The drive between them is on pretty country roads. Pack a picnic of great local fare.
Follow the directions in the itinerary.

Birders' paradise
For rich wildlife, visit Lady's Island Lake ⑧, Tacumshane ⑨, and then Kilamare Quay ⑩ for a trip to Great Saltees.
Follow the directions in the itinerary from Wexford Town to Kilmore Quay.

Eat and Drink: inexpensive, under €25; moderate, €25–€50; expensive, over €50

Carlow's Hidden Treasures

Tullow to Bagenalstown

Highlights

- **Ancient earthworks**
  Explore atmospheric Rathgall hill fort, burial place of the Kings of Leinster

- **Castle life**
  Step back in time at Clonegal's 17th-century castle

- **Mountain wilderness**
  Drive the narrow mountain road around Mount Leinster and leave the modern world behind

- **Natural wonders**
  Enjoy a woodland walk at Altamont, one of the most magical gardens in Ireland

Slopes of Mount Leinster, covered in lush green pasture and purple heather

Carlow's Hidden Treasures

County Carlow is out of the way of the usual tourist trails and is rarely explored by foreign tourists, or even visitors from elsewhere in Ireland, but there are secrets to be discovered on this drive through lushly wooded countryside. The county is crossed by lovely waterways, including the rivers Barrow, Slaney, and Derry, affording ample opportunities for peaceful walks or even a spot of fishing.

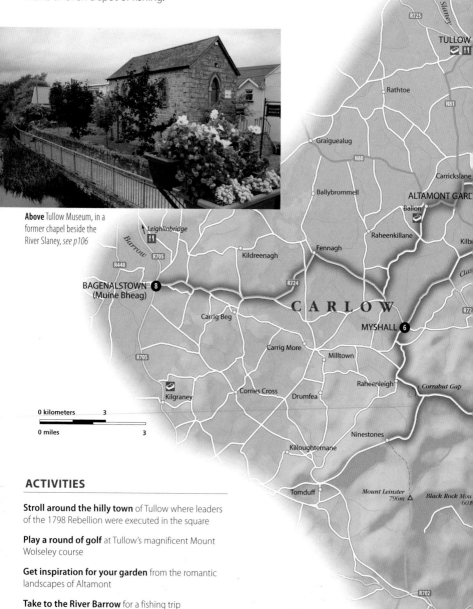

Above Tullow Museum, in a former chapel beside the River Slaney, *see p106*

Map labels: R725, Slaney, TULLOW, Rathtoe, N81, Graiguealug, N80, Carrickslane, Ballybrommell, ALTAMONT GARD, Ballon, Leighlinbridge, Barrow, R705, Raheenkillane, Kilb, R448, Kildreenagh, Fennagh, Cla, BAGENALSTOWN 8 (Muine Bheag), R724, C A R L O W, R72, Carrig Beg, MYSHALL 6, R705, Carrig More, Milltown, Raheenleigh, Corrabut Gap, Kilgraney, Corries Cross, Drumfea, Ninestones, Killoughternane, Tomduff, Mount Leinster 796m, Black Rock Mou 601, R702, Kiltealy

0 kilometers 3
0 miles 3

ACTIVITIES

Stroll around the hilly town of Tullow where leaders of the 1798 Rebellion were executed in the square

Play a round of golf at Tullow's magnificent Mount Wolseley course

Get inspiration for your garden from the romantic landscapes of Altamont

Take to the River Barrow for a fishing trip

KEY

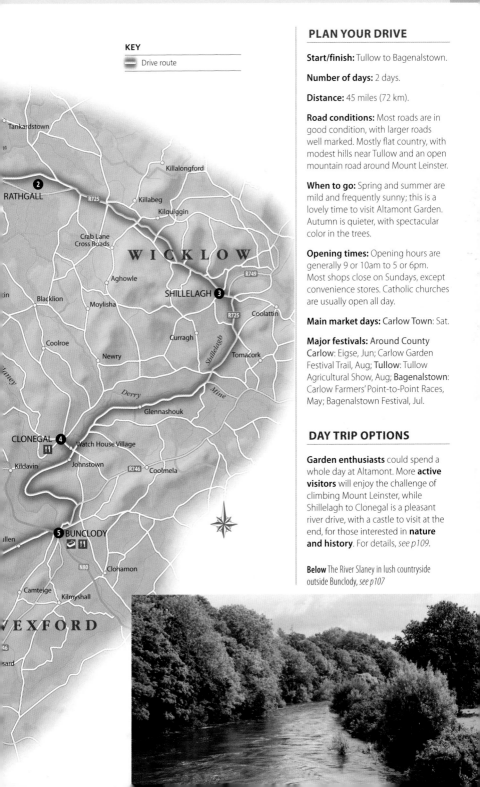

Drive route

WICKLOW

Tankardstown

Killalongford

2
RATHGALL
R725
Killabeg

Kilquiggin

Crab Lane
Cross Roads

Aghowle

R749

Blacklion
Moylisha

SHILLELAGH 3

R725
Coolattin

Coolroe
Curragh

Newry
Tomacork

Derry
Mine

Glennashouk

CLONEGAL 4
Watch House Village

Kildavin
Johnstown
R746
Coolmela

5 BUNCLODY

N80
Clohamon

Camteige
Kilmyshall

WEXFORD

sard

PLAN YOUR DRIVE

Start/finish: Tullow to Bagenalstown.

Number of days: 2 days.

Distance: 45 miles (72 km).

Road conditions: Most roads are in good condition, with larger roads well marked. Mostly flat country, with modest hills near Tullow and an open mountain road around Mount Leinster.

When to go: Spring and summer are mild and frequently sunny; this is a lovely time to visit Altamont Garden. Autumn is quieter, with spectacular color in the trees.

Opening times: Opening hours are generally 9 or 10am to 5 or 6pm. Most shops close on Sundays, except convenience stores. Catholic churches are usually open all day.

Main market days: Carlow Town: Sat.

Major festivals: Around County Carlow: Eigse, Jun; Carlow Garden Festival Trail, Aug; **Tullow:** Tullow Agricultural Show, Aug; **Bagenalstown:** Carlow Farmers' Point-to-Point Races, May; Bagenalstown Festival, Jul.

DAY TRIP OPTIONS

Garden enthusiasts could spend a whole day at Altamont. More **active visitors** will enjoy the challenge of climbing Mount Leinster, while Shillelagh to Clonegal is a pleasant river drive, with a castle to visit at the end, for those interested in **nature and history**. For details, *see p109.*

Below The River Slaney in lush countryside outside Bunclody, *see p107*

Above Tullow Museum, which tells the events of the 1798 Rebellion in Tullow

VISITING CARLOW AND WICKLOW COUNTIES

Tourist Information
www.discoverireland.com

Bicycle Hire
Celtic Cycling rents bikes and arranges itineraries and accommodation in the perfect rolling cycling country of southeast Ireland.
Lorum Old Rectory;
www.celticcycling.com

Shillelagh Sticks
Old Shillelagh Stick Makers, Main Street, Shillelagh; 0 942 9113;
http://misticshillelagh.tripod.com

WHERE TO STAY IN TULLOW

Ballyderrin House *inexpensive*
An old house attractively modernized, this is a charming and comfortable place to stay, just east of Tullow. The six bedrooms offer luxurious facilities. There's a café and cooking school on-site, and breakfasts are outstanding.
Shillelagh Rd, Tullow; 059 915 2742;
www.ballyderrin.com

Mount Wolseley Hilton Hotel
expensive
A luxury hotel with spa, to the southeast of Tullow, popular with golfers who play the adjoining 18-hole championship course.
Mount Wolseley, Tullow; 059 918 0100;
www.mountwolseley.ie

① Tullow
Co Carlow
A handsome small market town by the River Slaney, with some fine old stone town houses and shops, Tullow is known locally as "the granite town." On the hilly main street is a monument in memory of two leaders of the 1798 Rebellion, Father John Murphy and John Gallagher, "most cruelly and barbarously put to death by English soldiers on the square of Tullow." The **museum** *(open Sun afternoon)*, in a former chapel beside the River Slaney, tells their story. The Tullow Agricultural Show, which takes place each August, is a major livestock show, famous for its enormous prize bulls.

🚗 *From Tullow take R725 (Shillelagh Road) east. After 1 mile (2 km) turn left onto a narrow side road. After 1 mile (2 km), Rathgall stone fort is on the right, a short walk across a field. Park at the gate and climb over it. Be careful of cattle and be sure to close any gate that is opened en route.*

② Rathgall
Co Carlow
Unrestored and overgrown with briars, this impressive prehistoric four-ring stone hill fort appears much as it has stood for thousands of years. The medieval outer walls encircle earlier fortifications from the Bronze and Iron Ages, when spears, swords, and shields were fashioned here. North of the fort are the impressive Harolds-town Dolmen, while a stone circle to its east is said to be the birthplace of the 5th-century Kings of Leinster.

🚗 *Carry on along the side road until it rejoins the R725. Continue through lovely wooded country to the estate village of Shillelagh.*

The 1798 Rebellion
The revolutionary United Irishmen planned a national revolt against British power in May 1798, when sporadic uprisings took place in parts of Leinster and Ulster. The only substantial rebellion occurred in Wexford, where the insurgents displayed great fortitude and the fighting lasted until July.

③ Shillelagh
Co Wicklow
Shillelagh is an attractive planned village with stone cottages and a courthouse. **Coolattin Park**, 1 mile (2 km) east, in whose estate Shillelagh was set, was built in 1804 for Earl Fitzwilliam, a former Lord Lieutenant of Ireland. It is now a golf course. In **Tomnafinnoge Wood** (2 miles/3 km northeast on the R749) are remnants of one of the great ancient Irish oak forests, which provided the roof timbers for St. Patrick's Cathedral in Dublin and Westminster Hall in London. Shillelagh gives its name to the famous Irish oak cudgel, now more usually made of blackthorn. It is possible to visit a traditional stickmaker's yard in the village to see how they are made.

🚗 *From Shillelagh take R725 east. Turn right after 2½ miles (4 km) on a minor road along the Derry river valley toward Watchhouse village, where you turn right for Clonegal.*

Above Cycling the peaceful, empty mountain roads that skirts Mount Leinster

Above left Lush watermeadows and woods along the banks of the River Derry **Above** Bicentennial memorial to those who died in the 1798 Rebellion in Bunclody

④ Clonegal
o Carlow

lonegal, a pretty and particularly well-preserved village, marks the end of the Wicklow Way, a mountainous 9-mile (127-km) trail that starts in Dublin. The surrounding countryside of wooded hills is very beautiful, and he banks of the River Derry here are opular for fishing. The 17th-century acobean **Huntington Castle** (open Jun–Aug: daily; Sep: Sun) that adjoins he village can be visited, and is said o be haunted. Within the grounds re a prehistoric megalith, an ancient ew walk, and a temple to Isis.

Go back across the River Derry to Watch House and take the road right along the river through fine wooded country; on reaching the R746, turn ight for Bunclody.

⑤ Bunclody
o Wexford

unclody, site of a bloody battle in he 1798 Rebellion, is a small and harming town situated where the iver Slaney meets the River Clody at he foot of the Blackstairs Mountains. narrow canal from the Clody flows own the middle of its main street. he town is the best base for climbing 610-ft (795-m) **Mount Leinster**. To each Mount Leinster, leave Bunclody eading uphill and turn left opposite he Wexford Farmers' Co-op. After 6 iles (10 km), near Corrabut Gap, urn left for Nine Stones. The road rosses a cattle grid and there is fine cenery on both sides. Park at the ine Stones megalithic alignment for he walk to the top. It's a steep climb, ut the surfaced road goes all the ay, with spectacular views of the

surrounding mountains, valleys, and sea. Watch out for cloud.

From Nine Stones retrace the route and drive back across the cattle grid to the junction with the main road. Turn left and follow the road as it descends. On the descent, take a right turn at the T-junction and continue on to Myshall.

⑥ Myshall
Co Carlow

This little village is noted for the beautiful Adelaide Memorial Church built in 1912 by John Duguid of Dover, around the graves of his wife and daughter. It is designed as a miniature of Salisbury Cathedral and, among the exquisite features of the interior, the design of the floor was taken from St. Mark's in Venice.

Take R724 heading northeast and take the first road left, after 1 mile (2 km). After crossing the N80, Altamont Garden is on the right.

EAT AND DRINK

TULLOW

Rathwood *moderate*
The café-restaurant in this award-winning garden center is a good place to take a break, and the food is wholesome and fresh. Pleasant outside sitting area.
Rath, Tullow; 059 915 6285; closes 5pm; www.rathwood.com

CLONEGAL

Sha-Roe Bistro *expensive*
This small restaurant in a fine 18th-century house in an unspoilt village provides exceptional food and comfort. Imaginative cooking features Wexford lamb, local aged beef, fish, and cheeses. Reservations recommended.
Main Street; 053 937 5636

Above Icons in niches on the pebble-dashed exterior of the Adelaide Memorial Church, Myshall

Eat and Drink: inexpensive, under €25; moderate, €25–€50; expensive, over €50

7 Altamont Garden
Ballon, Co Carlow
Altamont *(open daily)* is a natural
woodland garden of some 40 acres
(16 ha). The woodland walks and
granite steps leading up from the
River Slaney are thought to have been
designed by William Robinson. Called
"the most romantic garden in Ireland,"
it is now managed by the state
according to the principles of Corona
North, the last member of the family
to live there. There are many mature
trees, both native and exotic, and
walks take visitors along the lawns and
paths, by the pond, and down to the
river. A highlight in spring is one of
Ireland's largest snowdrop collections.

🚗 *Continue along the road to the
N81. Turn left, then right at the N80.
Before reaching Ballon, turn left,
heading south. At the R724, turn
right to Bagenalstown.*

Above Entrance of Altamont Garden **Above
right** Colorful herbaceous border in the
Robinsonian garden **Above top right**
Overgrown doorway, Altamont Garden

VISITING BAGENALSTOWN
(MUINE BHEAG)

Parking
There is ample parking in town.

Tourist Information
www.discoverireland.com

WHERE TO STAY

AROUND ALTAMONT GARDEN

Sherwood Park House *inexpensive*
A short way northeast of Ballon, this is
a beautiful Georgian farmhouse.
*Kilbride, Ballon; 059 915 9117;
www.sherwoodparkhouse.ie*

Ballykealey Manor Hotel *moderate*
This grand Gothic hotel, just southwest
of Ballon, also has a good restaurant.
*Ballon, 059 915 9288;
www.ballykealeymanorhotel.com*

**AROUND BAGENALSTOWN
(MUINE BHEAG)**

Kilgraney House *moderate*
A charming Georgian house
overlooking the Barrow valley.
*Kilgraney (4 miles/6 km on the R705
from Bagenalstown); 059 977 5283;
www.kilgraneyhouse.com*

Lorum Old Rectory *moderate*
A former Victorian rectory with elegant
rooms and a warm welcome.
*Kilgraney; 059 977 5282;
www.lorum.com*

8 Bagenalstown (Muine Bheag)
Co Carlow
This pretty market town on the River Barrow is now officially called
Muine Bheag, meaning "small thorn tree," but is still widely known
by its old name. It was founded in the 18th century by Walter, Lord
Bagenal, who intended it to bear the name New Versailles. While not
achieving this level of magnificence, the town does have notable
buildings, including a courthouse modeled on the Parthenon in
Athens – the only part of Bagenal's grand plans to be realized – and
a handsome 19th-century Neo-Classical railway station.

A two-hour walking tour
This 5-mile (8-km) walk from
Bagenalstown to Leighlinbridge
(pronounced "lock-lin-bridge") and
back is along a stretch of the Barrow
Way, a walk trail that covers 65 miles
(114 km) in total, following the canal
and river towpaths of the Barrow,

Above Picturesque ruins of medieval Ballymoon Castle, with its thick granite walls, standing majestically
in fields to the east of Bagenalstown

he second-longest river in Ireland.
he walk is best enjoyed in the
arly morning or at dusk. Be sure
o look out for herons and
ingfishers along the tranquil
vaterway. Follow Barrow Way signs
orth out of **Bagenalstown** ①. Pass
he charming "lifting bridge" linking
he quayside with a wooded island
ird sanctuary and ruined watermill.
he river sweeps on round to
icturesque **Rathellin Lock** ② and,
urther along, a brick-arched bridge
eads to another island. The path then
ollows the side of the canal until a
veir where the route rejoins the river.
   Approaching Leighlinbridge there
re views of Mount Leinster to the
ght. By the splendid seven-arched
ridge in Leighlinbridge, the **Black
astle** ③ is a 14th-century tower,
ll that remains of a castle built to
ommand the river crossing.
   Return to Bagenalstown, along
he same river- and canal-side route,

The Barrow Way

The Barrow Way extends from
Lowtown near Dublin in the north to
St. Mullins near Wexford in the south.
At its southern end it rejoins the
even longer and more mountainous
Wicklow Way *(see p135)*. An easy, well-
marked walk through the counties
of Carlow and Kildare in the eastern
region of Leinster, the Barrow Way
wends its way from start to finish
along the banks of canals and rivers
through this largely flat region. Its
charms are both natural – walkers
may well spot hawks and hares as
they meander through fields of
daisies, yarrow, and mint – and man-
made as the towpath skirts pretty
Georgian towns and mansions,
Norman castles, and Cromwellian
battle sites. Waymarked Ways of
Ireland (www.irishtrails.ie) lists
suggestions for day- and half-day-
long walks along the route.

Above Typically pretty local granite cottage at
Fennagh, between Ballon and Bagenalstown

and finish the walk with the finest
view of the Grecian courthouse,
along with the town's church spire
and tower.
   In the fields east
of Bagenalstown
are the ruins of
Ballymoon Castle
(a 2-mile/3-km
drive along the
R724 toward
Fenagh), thought
to have been built
around 1300 by
Roger Bigod, one
of the 12th–13th-
century Earls of
Norfolk, and later
occupied by the
Knights Templar.
Thick granite
walls, two storys
high, surround
a huge courtyard
80-ft (25-m)
square.

EAT AND DRINK

AROUND ALTAMONT GARDEN

The Forge *inexpensive*
A landmark stone building on the N80
near the turn-off for Altamont, this is a
good place to stop for homemade
soup, sandwiches, scones, and tea.
Kilbride Cross, Ballon; 059 915 9939

**AROUND BAGENALSTOWN
(MUIN BHEAG)**

Lord Bagenal Hotel *expensive*
This well-known pub (3 miles/4.5 km
on the R705 from Bagenalstown) has
expanded into a chic, modern hotel,
but retains its original, cozy wood-
paneled bar, complete with open fires.
Hearty pub food is available, but there
is also a more formal restaurant in a
lovely setting beside the River Barrow.
*Main Street, Leighlinbridge; 059 977
4000; www.lordbagenal.com*

DAY TRIP OPTIONS

Tullow, Bunclody, and Ballon are ideal
bases to visit the highlights of this area.

Romantic gardens

Explore the delights of Altamont
Garden ⑦, with a break for a
delicious, home-cooked lunch at
the nearby Forge *(see right)*.

Altamont is marked from the N81 *(left
from Tullow, right from Ballon)* and the
N80 *(right from Bunclody)*.

Mount Leinster

See Bunclody ⑤, then make the steep
but exhilarating climb to the top of
Mount Leinster for spectacular views of
the surrounding mountains, the valleys
below, and the sea in the distance.

From Bunclody, follow the itinerary to
Nine Stones, then park and walk.

Derry valley drive

The road from Shillelagh ③ to
Clonegal ④ runs through gorgeous
scenery. End the day with a visit to
fascinating Huntington Castle.

Follow the directions in the itinerary.

Eat and Drink: inexpensive, under €25; moderate, €25–€50; expensive, over €50

Loughs and Lighthouses

Portumna to Tarbert

Highlights

- **Formidable Norman fortress**
  Climb the battlements of King John's Castle in Limerick, Ireland's finest Norman fortress

- **Treasure island**
  Follow in the footsteps of pilgrims and plunderers on a boat trip to Lough Derg's Holy Island

- **Megalithic mysteries**
  Visit Grange Stone Circle and the banks of Lough Gur, the source of important archaeological finds

- **Pioneering flights**
  Recapture the excitement of early transatlantic air travel at the Foynes Flying Boat Museum

The stone mill at Bruree, near the old school of Irish leader Eamon de Valera

Loughs and Lighthouses

Follow the majestic Shannon as it snakes toward the ocean, from the jagged shores of Lough Derg to the broad estuary that opens out at Limerick. This is an extraordinarily rich region, with pretty lakeside villages, smart marinas, a splendid city with medieval and Georgian quarters, and grand 18th-century country estates. This fertile valley has a long and illustrious history; it was widely settled in megalithic times; the base of Brian Boru, King of Ireland, in the 10th century; and in modern times the birthplace of Eamon de Valera, the founder of the Irish Free State.

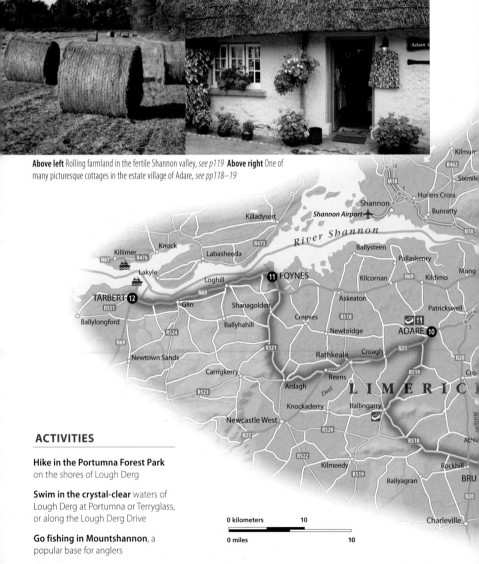

Above left Rolling farmland in the fertile Shannon valley, see p119 **Above right** One of many picturesque cottages in the estate village of Adare, see pp118–19

ACTIVITIES

Hike in the Portumna Forest Park on the shores of Lough Derg

Swim in the crystal-clear waters of Lough Derg at Portumna or Terryglass, or along the Lough Derg Drive

Go fishing in Mountshannon, a popular base for anglers

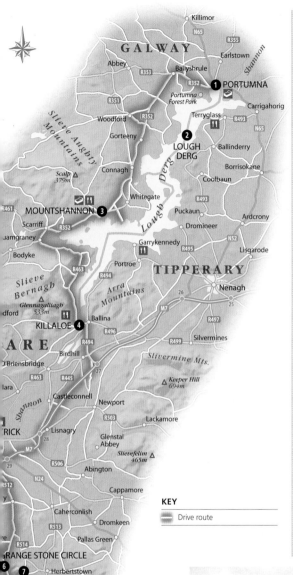

PLAN YOUR DRIVE

Start/finish: Portumna to Tarbert.

Number of days: 2–3.

Distance: 188 miles (302 km).

Road conditions: Main roads are well paved and well marked. Some smaller roads are potholed.

When to go: Although winters are mild in southwest Ireland, May–Oct is the best time to visit. To swim in Lough Derg, visit in Jun–Aug.

Opening times: Most sights and attractions are open from 9 or 10am to 5 or 6pm, or dusk if earlier.

Main market days: Limerick: Riverside Market, Sun noon–3pm, Bedford Row; Milk Market, Sat am, Cornmarket Row.

Major festivals: Limerick: River Fest, 1st week May; Adare: Village Festival, mid-May.

DAY TRIP OPTIONS

Enjoy a lazy day **swimming** and **boating** in Portumna. **Families** can take in a **forest walk** or view the **lakeside gardens** at Portumna Castle. For **history and culture**, spend a morning in **medieval and Georgian** Limerick, and the afternoon seeing the **megalithic sites** around Lough Gur. For a scenic drive, focus on the Shannon's south bank from Foynes to Tarbert. Take a **picnic** and visit two **museums**. For full details, *see p119.*

Below A roadside sculpture forms part of the scenery near Adare, *see pp118–19*

Above Portumna Friary, a Dominican Friary built over a Cistercian chapel

VISITING MOUNTSHANNON

Boat Trips to Holy Island
Boat trips to Holy Island are operated by Ger Maddan and leave from Mountshannon Harbour. Tickets can be bought from a kiosk on the pier.
Ger Madden; 061 921 615;
www.eastclareheritage.com

VISITING KILLALOE
AND BALLINA

Tourist Information
Brian Boru Heritage Centre,
Killaloe; 061 376 866;
www.shannonheritage.ie

WHERE TO STAY

MOUNTSHANNON

Mountshannon Hotel *inexpensive*
A stone's throw from the harbor, this modest family-run hotel has a popular restaurant and a cozy bar with an open fire in winter.
Main St; 061 927 162; www.
mountshannon-hotel.ie

KILLALOE

Lakeside Hotel *moderate*
Popular for its location beside the lake, this hotel features an indoor pool, steam room, and sauna.
061 376 122; www.lakesidehotel.ie

❶ Portumna
Co Galway
Surrounded by open farmland and forests, Portumna lies at the head of Lough Derg, its bridge straddling the Tipperary and Galway banks of the Shannon. In summer, it plays host to small groups of vacationers cruising on the river. It has a **lakeside bathing spot**, with picnic tables and a lifeguard *(Jun–Aug)*, less than half a mile (1 km) from the center (marked "Swimming Area" from the Bank of Ireland).

Portumna's main sight is **Portumna Castle and Gardens** *(open Apr–Sep)*, reached by turning left opposite Portumna Catholic Church in the center of town (the entrance to the castle is 984 ft (300 m) along on the right; fork right after the Gate Lodge). A fortified mansion built in the early 17th century for the De Burgo family, the castle is undergoing continual restoration, but the ground floor is open to visitors. The gardens are known for the Renaissance Sun Garden, laid out in a geometric design in front of the house, a rare 17th-century rose, and a fully restored kitchen garden.

Return to the Gate Lodge and this time take the left fork to the **marina** where there are picnic tables looking across Lough Derg. Nearby are the ruins of **Portumna Friary**, a Cistercian chapel extended by the Dominican order in the 15th century.

From the marina, it is possible to continue on foot to **Portumna Forest Park** *(open daily)*, a public forest park along the shore of Lough Derg.

Alternatively drive there (1 mile/ 2 km) along the Gort Road (R353). Maps of its marked trails can be picked up at the entrance. There is a wide variety of birdlife in the park, as well as red squirrels and fallow deer.

While visiting Portumna, it is also worth taking a look at **Terryglass**, a pretty boating village with a couple of good restaurants *(see right)*, just around the bay, off the N65.

🚗 *Exit Portumna on Shannon Road, then follow R352 along the lakeshore.*

❷ Lough Derg
Co Galway and Co Clare
The section of Lough Derg between Portumna and Mountshannon (around 21 miles/40 km) is sparsely populated. Views of the lake are largely obscured by trees, but two scenic detours off the R352 make the drive worthwhile. Six miles (10 km) from Portumna, at a crossroads, turn right at the sign for **Lough Derg Drive**, leading to higher ground away from the lake but offering better views. It reaches the quaint village of Woodford before returning to the R352.

Continue through Gorteeny and 1 mile (2 km) before Whitegate, where the road bends sharply left, leave the main road by veering right onto a narrow country lane. Drive straight for 1 mile (2 km) and turn left at a cottage, crossing the R352 again. Continue to the shore of the lake, where there is a shallow area that is good for swimming.

🚗 *Return to the R352 , turn left, and drive on to Mountshannon.*

Above The quay at Killaloe, a pleasant town on the banks of Lough Derg

Where to Stay: inexpensive, under €100; moderate, €100–€200; expensive, over €200

❸ Mountshannon
Co Clare

Picturesque Mountshannon has an elevated position overlooking Lough Derg. Long and linear, it was conceived as a plantation town, intended for Protestant settlers; even by the 1830s it didn't have a single Catholic resident. Today it is a good base for exploring the surrounding area and is popular with anglers. Solid 18th-century cottages line the harbor, and it has several good pubs, including Cois na h'Abhna bar on Main Street (see right), which sometimes holds traditional music sessions in summer. Information on angling can be obtained in any of the town's tackle shops.

Boats to **Holy Island**, just 1 mile (2 km) offshore, in Scarriff Bay, leave from the pier (see left). St. Caimin founded a monastery on the island in the 7th century. The ruins include monastic cells, five churches, and 80 marked graves pre-dating the 12th century. Dominating the island is an 260-ft (80-m) high round tower.

The island has been a draw for both pilgrims and plunderers through the centuries. Lured by the prospect of monastic wealth, the Vikings ransacked the island in 836 and again in 922. It is also associated with Brian Boru, the powerful High King of Ireland ("Ard Ria"). His brother Marcan, an abbot, is said to have rebuilt one of the island's churches on the orders of Boru.

🚗 *Follow the R352 along the lakeshore as far as Tuamgraney, bypassing Scarriff, and carry on along the lake, now on the R463, into Killaloe. It is possible to swim in the lough at Two Mile Gate, and walk in Cragg Wood. In Killaloe, park on the street.*

Brian Boru

King of Munster and High King of Ireland, Brian Boru is credited with uniting Ireland's clans and routing the Vikings. Born in Killaloe, he earned his nickname Brian of the Tribute (Boru), for the tributes he exacted, used mainly to rebuild monasteries ransacked by the Vikings. In 1014 – at the ripe old age of 74 – the great warrior was slain by a Viking as he prayed in his tent at the Battle of Clontarf.

❹ Killaloe
Co Clare and Co Tipperary

The twin towns of Killaloe and Ballina are actually in different counties, but they face one another on opposite banks of the River Shannon, linked by a 17th-century bridge. **Killaloe** is the more interesting of the two. Brian Boru, the High King of Ireland, was born here and built his palace, Kincora, on the site of the Catholic church at the top of the hill. It was the center of power in Ireland until his death at the Battle of Clontarf in 1014. Learn more about this totemic figure in Irish history at the **Brian Boru Heritage Centre** (see left) on the bridge over the Shannon.

The other building of note is **Flannan's Cathedral**, dating from around 1182, on Royal Parade at the bottom of the hill. Inside, look for the Romanesque doorway, the Thorgrim Stone, a bilingual rarity inscribed with both Nordic runes and Ogham markings, and the 13th-century font.

Ballina has less to offer in the way of historical sites, but has a pleasant riverside and a lively pub scene.

🚗 *From Killaloe, cross the bridge into Ballina and take the R494 south until it meets the M7. Turn right onto the M7 and leave at junction 29, following the signs to Limerick.*

Above left Motor cruisers in Portumna Marina, a popular springboard for boating on the Shannon **Above** The 17th-century bridge linking the twin towns of Ballina and Killaloe

EAT AND DRINK

AROUND PORTUMNA

Derg Inn *inexpensive*
Laid-back bar with good food in the pretty village of Terryglass, 7 miles (12 km) from Portumna (head south on the N65 and turn right onto the R493). *Terryglass; 067 22037; www.derginn.ie*

Paddy's Bar *inexpensive*
Congenial spot for good steaks, burgers, lasagna, wraps, and salads. See website for directions. *Terryglass; 067 22147; www.paddysbar.ie*

MOUNTSHANNON

Cois na h'Abhna *inexpensive*
Popular local pub known for its music sessions (Sat & Sun eves). Sit in the beer garden in summer or by an open fire in winter. *Main St; 061 927 189*

KILLALOE AND BALLINA

Ponte Vecchio *inexpensive*
Italian deli and wine store. Eat in or stock up for a picnic. *Royal Parade House, Killaloe; 061 622 845; closed Mon*

Wooden Spoon Café *inexpensive*
Offers a wide selection of freshly baked foods. Take-out bakery upstairs. *5 Abbey St, Killaloe; 061 622 2415*

AROUND KILLALOE

Larkin's Lakeside Pub and Restaurant *inexpensive*
Landmark pub on the Tipperary shore of Lough Derg. Wide choice of dishes, from fish chowders to T-bone steaks. Renowned for its music sessions. *Garrykennedy (turn left at Portroe, 8 miles/13 km north of Ballina on the R494); 067 23232; www.larkinspub.com*

Eat and Drink: inexpensive, under €25; moderate, €25–€50; expensive, over €50

Above The medieval tollgate on Thomond Bridge in Limerick

VISITING LIMERICK

Tourist Information
Arthur's Quay; 061 317 522;
www.limerick.ie; open Mon–Sat
year-round

Parking
The best place to park in is in **Arthur's Quay Centre**, a multistory parking lot near the Tourist Information Centre on Arthur's Quay, just off Patrick Street. For on-street parking, discs are available from shops and service stations.

WHERE TO STAY IN LIMERICK CITY

Railway Hotel *inexpensive*
Traditional family-run hotel opposite the railway station. Comfortable standard accommodation and friendly atmosphere. All rooms ensuite.
Parnell St; 061 413 653;
www.railwayhotel.ie

Absolute Hotel *moderate*
Overlooking the confluence of the Abbey and Shannon rivers, this stylish modern hotel has a waterside bar and restaurant with an outside terrace. For a small premium, guests have access to the spa.
Sir Harry's Mall; 061 463 600;
www.absolutehotel.com

No. 1 Pery Square Hotel and Spa
moderate–expensive
Luxurious boutique hotel (20 rooms) in an immaculately restored 18th-century property on one of Limerick's finest squares. On-site parking.
1 Pery Square; 061 402 402;
www.oneperysquare.com

---

⑤ Limerick City

Co Limerick

Limerick city center has two distinct areas, divided by the Abbey River. North of the river is King's Island, the medieval quarter clustered around the 12th-century castle, and south is the Georgian development of Newtown Pery, laid out in the 18th century on a grid plan by the Italian architect Davis Ducart.

A two-hour walking tour

Start at the **Tourist Information Centre** ①, where you can pick up maps and details of events in the city. Walk down Arthur's Quay and turn left into Patrick Street to the **Limerick Museum** *(open Tue–Sat)* ②, which relates Limerick's history. Continue along Rutland Street to the **Hunt Museum** *(open daily)* ③. Occupying the 18th-century Customs House, this private museum is crammed with antiquities and art, from Neolithic bronze artifacts to works by Picasso. From the museum, turn left across Matthew Bridge, over the Abbey River, and left into Merchant's Quay. Further along the quay is the glass-and-steel **City Hall and Civic Centre** ④. Walk through its foyer to the courtyard, which leads onto an embankment with river views.

Return to Merchant's Quay and turn left up St. Augustine's Place. On the right the 12th-century **St. Mary's Cathedral** *(open Jun–Aug: daily; Sep–May: am only)* ⑤ has exquisite barrel-vaulted ceilings, fine stained-glass windows and, in the Jebb Chapel, Ireland's only surviving misericords.

Continue to Nicholas Street and turn left into it, passing **King John's Castle** *(open daily)* ⑥ on the left. Dating from 1210, this is one of Ireland's most impressive Anglo-Norman castles. Guided tours take in the extant walls and towers. Cross Castle Street onto the Parade. On the left corner is the Neo-Classical facade of the old **Bishop's Palace** *(open daily)* ⑦. Visitors are free to enter. Adjacent is **St. Munchin's Garden** ⑧ (part of St. Munchin's Protestant Church), the picturesque graveyard of Church of Ireland St. Munchin's church, with some very old tombstones. It has fine views down to Villiner's Alms Houses below.

Leaving the palace, turn right down Castle Street, cross Thomond Bridge to the west bank, and turn left onto Clancy's Strand and the riverside walkway. On the corner of the bridge is Catholic **St. Munchin's Church** ⑨. Further along the walkway is the prodigious bulk of the **Treaty Stone** ⑩, on which the treaty that ended the Second Siege of Limerick was signed in 1691. It promised religious freedom to the Irish Catholics, but within two months England had

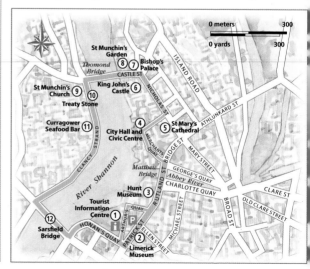

St Munchin's Garden ⑧ ⑦ Bishop's Palace
Thomond Bridge
CASTLE ST
ISLAND ROAD
St Munchin's Church ⑨ ⑩ King John's Castle ⑥
Treaty Stone
NICHOLAS ST
ATHLUNKARD ST
Curragower Seafood Bar ⑪
④ ⑤ St Mary's Cathedral
City Hall and Civic Centre
ATHLUNKARD ST
CLANCY'S STRAND
River Shannon
Matthew Bridge
MERCHANT'S QUAY
RUTLAND ST
BRIDGE ST
GEORGE'S QUAY
Abbey River
CHARLOTTE QUAY
MARY STREET
BROAD ST
CLARE ST
OLD CLARE STREET
Hunt Museum ③
Tourist Information Centre ①
⑫ Sarsfield Bridge
HONAN'S QUAY
ARTHUR'S QUAY
PATRICK STREET
ELLEN STREET
MICHAEL STREET
② Limerick Museum

0 meters 300
0 yards 300

Where to Stay: inexpensive, under €100; moderate, €100–€200; expensive, over €200

eneged on the treaty – the stone came to symbolize hatred of English rule. Further along on the right is **Curragower Seafood Bar** ⑪, renowned for its Irish oysters. Continue along the river as far as **Sarsfield Bridge** ⑫ and cross back to the east bank. Go down the first set of steps on the left to Honan's Quay, leading to Arthur's Quay Park, which has a great view of the castle. Follow Arthur's Quay back to the parking lot.

🚗 *From the parking lot, turn right onto Patrick Street, left up William Street and Upper William Street, and veer right along Roborough Street. Take the first exit off the roundabout, and at the next roundabout take the R512 for Lough Gur and Killmallock. Grange Stone Circle is 12 miles (20 km) from Limerick. Park in the turnout in front of the entrance.*

Above A sheltered backwater on Lough Gur, an area rich in archeological sites

⑥ Grange Stone Circle
Co Limerick
Though not as imposing as Stonehenge in the UK, Grange Stone Circle packs a significant punch, not least because of its isolation. Dating from 2000 BC, the ring consists of 113 standing stones and has an internal diameter of 150 ft (46 m), making it Ireland's largest stone circle. In Irish it is called *Lios na Grainsi* (Stones of the Sun), suggesting that it had a ritualistic function. The largest stone, the Rounach Croim Dubh (Prominent Black Stone), is over 6 ft (2 m) high and weighs 40 tons. Entrance to the site is free, but visitors are asked to leave a small contribution in the donation box.

🚗 *Continue in same direction on the R512 and turn left at Holycross, where Lough Gur is marked (3 miles/5 km) left. On the left immediately after the turn*

are the ruins of the old church of Tempall Nua (New Church), and farther along on the right is Giant's Grave, a megalithic wedge tomb. Follow signs to Lough Gur and the visitor center.

⑦ Lough Gur
Co Limerick
Horseshoe-shaped and cupped in the limestone hills, Lough Gur is one of Ireland's richest archeological sites. The whole area is dotted with megalithic remains, including burial chambers and ring forts. When the lough was partially drained in the 19th century, many artifacts were revealed, the most significant of which was the magnificent Lough Gur Shield, dating from 700 BC (now in the National Museum in Dublin). Many other finds are in the Hunt Museum in Limerick *(see left)*.

On the shores of the lake are the ruins of two castles, both of which once stood on islands in the lake: 15th-century **Bourchier's Castle**, near the parking lot, and on the far side of the lake, ivy-mantled **Black Castle**, dating from the 13th century, where the Earls of Desmond periodically resided. (It can be reached along a path on the east side of the lake.)

Overlooking the lake, in two replica Neolithic huts, the **Interpretive Centre** *(open May–Sep)* sheds light on the history of the area with exhibits and information boards. It also sells light refreshments.

🚗 *Return to Holycross and rejoin the R512, following signs to Kilmallock (9 miles/15 km). On reaching Kilmallock, take an immediate right after John's Gate and park in the public parking lot.*

Above Grange Stone Circle, a remote and atmospheric spot shaded by oak trees

Above The old stone mill in the market town of Bruree, near Kilmallock

EAT AND DRINK IN LIMERICK CITY

Curragower Seafood Bar *inexpensive*
Cozy, unpretentious seafood bar with a loyal following. Choose from chowder, crab claws, sea bass, salmon, oysters, and much more. Winter months: weekends only.
Clancy's Strand; 061 321 788

The French Table
inexpensive–moderate
This riverside restaurant produces tasty rustic French cooking. Some items on the menu offer excellent value.
Steamboat Quay; 061 609 274; www.frenchtable.ie

The Locke Bar *inexpensive–moderate*
Reputedly Limerick's oldest pub (1724), Locke's has a lovely location overlooking the Abbey River. During the summer a barbecue is served on the terrace out front. Also worth a try is the Oyster House and Seafood Bar. Relaxed and informal.
3 George's Quay; 061 413 733; www.lockebar.com

Eat and Drink: inexpensive, under €25; moderate, €25–€50; expensive, over €50

Above Kilmallock's Dominican Friary, a testament to the town's medieval prosperity

WHERE TO STAY

KILMALLOCK

Flemingstone House *moderate*
Award-winning farmhouse accommodation at the base of the Ballyhoura Mountains, on the R512 about 2 miles (3 km) south of Kilmalock, in an elegant house with period furnishings and five bedrooms overlooking the surrounding countryside. Sumptuous breakfasts. Dinner on request. Complimentary scones, tea, and coffee on arrival.
Kilmallock; 063 98093;
www.flemingstown.com

AROUND KILMALLOCK

Old Bank House *inexpensive*
Pleasant family-run B&B in a former bank building in the village of Bruff, just off the R512 between Lough Gur and Kilmallock. Two rooms have four-poster beds.
Bruff; 061 389 969; www.theoldbank.ie

AROUND BRUREE

Echo Lodge *moderate–expensive*
This is a spacious Victorian country residence that was converted from a 19th-century convent. Set in extensive gardens, it is also home to the highly acclaimed Mustard Seed Restaurant. Nonresidents welcome to dine by reservation. Overlooks Ballingarry, on the R519, 8 miles (13 km) south of Adare.
Ballingarry; 069 68508;
www.mustardseed.ie

ADARE

Dunraven Arms Hotel *expensive*
Established in 1792 and still retaining the ambience of a country inn. Though luxurious, it has a lovely informal elegance.
Main St; 061 605 900;
www.dunravenhotel.com

8 Kilmallock
Co Limerick
In medieval times Kilmallock was one of the most important towns in Munster. But from the mid-17th century, having suffered badly in the confederation wars of 1641, it went into decline, and it never really recovered. Nevertheless, it is one of the most intact medieval towns in Ireland. A substantial portion of the old walls survive, as well as **John's Gate** and **Blossom Gate**. Notable buildings include the 13th-century **Collegiate Church of Saints Peter and Paul**, and down by the river the **Dominican Friary**, attacked and destroyed by Cromwellian forces under Lord Inchiquin in 1648. The **Ballyhoura Heritage Centre** *(open Mon–Fri)* near the Friary is home to the Friar's Gate Theatre and **Kilmallock Museum** *(open Mon–Fri)*, which traces the history of the town during the 19th and 20th centuries. Daily tours of Kilmallock leave from outside the museum at 2pm.

From Kilmallock drive to the top of the town and turn right onto the R518 toward Bruree (4 miles/6 km). Drive through the center of Bruree and just before the road swings left over a stone bridge veer right and park across the road from an old school house.

9 Bruree
Co Limerick
The market town of Bruree has two main attractions, both on the outskirts of town, facing one another off the road to Ballingarry. They are the **Eamon de Valera Museum** *(closed Mon)*, in the school where de Valera was educated, and the **Genesius Theatrical Museum** *(visits by appointment, 087 926 8481)* dedicated to Vic Loving. They were two very different figures in

Irish history. Eamon de Valera, one of the leaders of the 1916 uprising, founder of the Irish Free State, and keen advocate of Catholic values, was a colossal figure in post-independent Ireland. Vic Loving, performer, actress, and impresario, was also a famous male impersonator. The de Valera Museum is also home to the **Bruree Heritage Centre** recounting the town's history. Across the road, the Genesius Theatrical Museum – a hidden gem – includes costumes from 1860, posters, old programs, photographs, and other memorabilia. Vic Loving's granddaughter runs the museum; entry is free but donations are gratefully accepted.

Return to the stone bridge and turn right, follow the R518 to Ballingarry (11 miles/18 km) and then turn right onto the R519 for Adare. Park by the village green.

Irish Coffee
Irish coffee, almost as symbolic of Ireland as a shamrock or harp, was invented in the 1940s by Joseph Sheridan, head chef at Foynes International Airport, forerunner of Shannon Airport. During World War II all transatlantic flights flew under the cover of darkness, and this invigorating concoction of black coffee, cream, and Irish whiskey warmed up chilly passengers before they set off. The drink gained further favor in 1950s Los Angeles.

Above Kilmallock's beautifully kept 13th-century Collegiate Church of Saints Peter and Paul

10 Adare
Co Limerick
With its thatched cottages and spruce green, Adare prides itself on

being Ireland's prettiest village. In fact, the beautification of this estate village was the personal project of the third Earl of Dunraven. An "improving landlord," he wished to create a bucolic haven and indulge his passion for early Irish architecture.

For a village intended to be an Irish idyll, it feels quite English. Nonetheless, it is hard to resist its quaint charm. It has an array of medieval buildings, including three monasteries, two in use and the third a ruin. In the middle of the village the **Heritage Centre** (open daily) runs guided tours of 15th-century **Desmond Castle**. Next to the center is the 15th-century **Catholic parish church**, once part of the Trinitarian Abbey, which has an unusual stone dovecote.

Just south of the river, an **Augustinian Friary** is now an Anglican church and school (limited access after 3pm). On the golf course beyond the castle, the **Franciscan Friary** has a fine cloister and the tombs of the Desmonds (permission to visit from the clubhouse). **Adare Manor**, ancestral home of the Earls of Dunraven, is now a luxury hotel.

🚗 *Take the N21 west toward Newcastle West. Two miles (4 km) after the turn for Rathkeale take the R523 to Ardagh and then the R521 for Foynes (9 miles/14 km). Park at the Flying Boat Museum in the center.*

Thatched cottage in picture-perfect Adare

⓫ Foynes
Co Limerick

During the late 1930s and early 1940s this sleepy port overlooking the Shannon estuary was the focal point of transatlantic air travel. On July 9, 1939, Pan Am's luxury flying boat, the *Yankee Clipper*, landed at Foynes, the first direct commercial passenger flight between the United States and Europe. In the center of town, the **Flying Boat Museum** (open daily Apr–mid-Nov) re-creates these pioneering days. See the original terminal building, the radio and weather room, an early commercial passenger plane, and a 1940s tea room. Foynes is also where Irish coffee was invented.

🚗 *Turn left from the parking lot and drive along the N69 to Tarbert. A roadside picnic spot near Foynes offers good views of the estuary and access to a forest walk.*

⓬ Tarbert
Co Limerick

The N69 between Foynes and Tarbert is one of the best riverside drives in Ireland, with sweeping views of the estuary and **Tarbert Lighthouse**. In Tarbert itself, the **Tarbert Bridewell Courthouse and Jail** (open daily) re-creates the plight of early 19th-century convicts. The town also operates regular **car ferries** across the Shannon to Killimer in County Clare.

Above The Blue Door Restaurant in Adare, a village beautified by the Earl of Dunraven

EAT AND DRINK IN ADARE

Blue Door Restaurant *moderate*
Bistro-style restaurant in archetypal thatched cottage. Also serves morning coffee and, in summer, afternoon tea in the pretty cottage garden.
Church View; 061 396 481; www.bluedooradare.com

The Wild Geese Restaurant *moderate*
Acclaimed restaurant in cottage setting. Uses locally sourced meat, fish, and cheese and organic vegetables. Renowned for its seafood.
Rose Cottage, Main St; 061 396 451; www.thewild-geese.com

DAY TRIP OPTIONS

Spend a leisurely day on Lough Derg enjoying simple lakeside pleasures, explore the many sites around Limerick, or take the lovely drive along the River Shannon.

Messing about on the lake
For boating, swimming, and riverside drinking and eating, concentrate on Portumna ❶ at the northern tip of Lough Derg. There are bathing spots and a marina, as well as forest walks and Portumna Castle and Gardens to explore. At the end of the day, drive to Garrykennedy for dinner in lakeside Larkin's (see p115).

Portumna and Limerick are ideal bases for these day trips.

Limerick Loop
Spend a morning exploring medieval and Georgian Limerick ❺, visiting the eclectic Hunt Museum, the Cathedral, and King John's Castle, then have lunch at Curragower Seafood Bar (see p117). Afterward head out to Grange Stone Circle ❻ and Lough Gur ❼, a peaceful lake and valley packed with megalithic sites. From there, drive on to Kilmallock ❽, a medieval gem, and then to Adare ❿, Ireland's prettiest village, stopping for afternoon tea at

the Blue Door (see above), before returning to Limerick.

Follow the drive instructions from Limerick to Adare and return to the city on the N21.

Foynes to Tarbert
Combine a lovely riverside drive with a picnic, a forest walk, and visits to two museums – the Flying Boat Museum at Foynes ⓫ and the Tarbert Bridewell Courthouse and Jail in Tarbert ⓬.

From Limerick take the N69 direct to Foynes, then follow the drive instructions to Tarbert.

Eat and Drink: inexpensive, under €25; moderate, €25–€50; expensive, over €50

Lyrical Clare

Ennis to the Burren

Highlights

- **Musical Ennis**
  Soak up the atmosphere of this vibrant medieval market town, famous for its folk music

- **Lovely Shannon Estuary**
  Savor the rolling pastoral land where the gentle waters of the Shannon meet the driving force of the Atlantic

- **Dramatic Cliffs of Moher**
  Experience the Atlantic Edge, where the plateau plunges into the sea, at the Cliffs of Moher Visitor Experience

- **The Stony District**
  Survey the wild beauty of the Burren's unusual limestone landscape, with its flagstones fissured by grikes

View over the Burren from Corkscrew Hill, south of Ballyvaughan

Lyrical Clare

County Clare can be broadly separated into two geographical regions: in the south, the gently rolling countryside along the course of the River Shannon; and in the north, a rugged and stony land with vertiginous coastal cliffs. Cutting across the county, northwest to southeast, is the magical region of the Burren, a limestone plateau crisscrossed by deep fissures sprouting a dizzying array of plant life. Then there is the music. Many of the towns on the coast and around the edges of the Burren live and breathe traditional music, perhaps more than any other county.

Above The soaring Cliffs of Moher, where the limestone plateau of the Burren meets the sea, *see p126*

ACTIVITIES

Spot bottlenose dolphins in the Shannon Estuary

Tune in to Clare's music scene, which takes place in characterful pubs all over the county

Follow the exhilarating coast road around Black Head

Delight in the wildflowers of the Burren landscape

Visit one of the megalithic tombs and 5th-century ring forts that pepper the Burren

KEY

⊂⊃ Drive route

0 kilometers 5

0 miles 5

Galway Bay

ACK
EAD 7
Aghaglinny North
Finavarra
Burren
Ballyvaughan Bay
Caherloughlin
Corranroo
Belaclugga
Cappaghmore

Fanore
Formoyle
8 BALLYVAUGHAN

Ailwee Cave
St Colman's Well
Slieveelarran 334m

e Elva 345m
Corkscrew Hill
9 THE BURREN

Poulnabrone Dolmen

omaghera
Caherconnell Stone Fort
Carran

Lisdoonvarna
Castletown
Knockans
Aughrim

Noughaval
Mullaghmore

Father Ted's House
Lough George

Kilfenora
Lough Cullaun
Lough Atedaun
Ruan

Lickeen Lough
Killinaboy
Inchiquin Lough
Corrofin

Ennistimon
Drinagh
Dromore Lough

C L A R E
Mauricesmills
Barefield
14

Inagh
Kilnamona
Fountain Cross
13

Bauntlieve
Slievecallen 391m
Kilmaley
ENNIS 1
M18
12

Shanavogh
Kilmurry
Carncreagh
Clarecastle
R458

Darragh
Caherea
Ballyveskil

ermurphy
Lissycasey
Lisheen

ilhil
Ballynacally
Deer I. Coney I.

Knocklough
Lisnafaha
Horse I.

Cranny
Killadysert
Canon I.

Kilmurry
Effernan
Inishcorker

Labasheeda
Shannakea

kerin
River Shannon

PLAN YOUR DRIVE

Start/finish: Ennis to the Burren.

Number of days: 2–3 days.

Distance: 121 miles (195 km).

Road conditions: Well paved and well marked except on some unclassified roads.

When to go: May–Oct are the best months to visit, but May, when the flowers on the Burren are in bloom, is particularly lovely.

Opening times: Pubs and music venues stay open until 11pm or later.

Main market days: Ennis: Fri/Sat; Kilrush: Thu.

Shopping: Ennis has a variety of small independent shops – from fashion boutiques to antiques and specialist food shops – while Doolin is known for its music shops, selling traditional Irish instruments and music. Burren Perfumery sells lotions inspired by the wildflowers.

Major festivals: Ennis: Fleadh Nua (folk music), 3rd week May.

DAY TRIP OPTIONS

Walkers will love the spectacular north coast of Clare, with the **cliff path** at the vertiginous Cliffs of Moher; finish with a visit to the **music village** of Doolin or head up the coast to Black Head. Alternatively, devote a whole day to exploring the Burren's **landscape, villages, ring forts** and **megalithic sites**. For full details, *see p127*.

Below The lighthouse at Loop Head, on the southwest tip of County Clare, *see p125*

Below The creeper-clad ruins of Ennis Friary, dating from the 14th century

Above Vandeleur Walled Garden, the last remnant of Kilrush House

❶ Ennis
Co Clare
This is Clare's largest town, located midway between the Shannon Estuary and the Burren. Straddling the River Fergus, it retains a winding medieval street pattern either side of O'Connell Street, named after Daniel O'Connell, the first Catholic MP to sit in Westminster, in 1828. His statue stands in O'Connell Square.

The ruins of 14th–15th-century Franciscan **Ennis Friary** *(open May–Oct)* on Abbey Street are noted for their

Colourful mural on a pub in Ennis

rich carvings and decorated tombs – above all, the alabaster panels of the McMahon tomb. On the corner of Francis Street, is the Queen's Hotel, featured in James Joyce's *Ulysses*. The town is also renowned for its painted storefronts and folk music festivals or *fleadhs*. To find out more drop into the **Glór Music Centre**, on Friar's Walk, or the **Tourist Information Centre** and **Clare Museum** *(open Tue–Sat).*

🚗 *Take the R473 toward Clarecastle, turning right 1 mile (2 km) before the town. Follow signs for Ballynacally along the Shannon Estuary. Continue on the R473, through Labasheeda, Kilmurry and Knock, until Killimer, then join the N67 to Kilrush.*

❷ Kilrush
Co Clare
Cill Rois ("church of the promontory") is a designated Heritage Town, in recognition of its legacy as an 18th-century estate town with strong

maritime traditions. Its **Heritage Centre** *(open May–Sep: daily)* has an exhibition about the Great Famine.
Vandeleur Walled Garden *(open Oct–Mar: Mon–Fri)*, just outside the town (drive clockwise around the main square and turn right off Moore Street, following signs for the garden) was once part of Kilrush House, seat of the Vandeleur family. The house was demolished in 1973. Enclosed by lovely old stone walls, the garden was restored to its former glory in the 1990s and is now noted for its tropical plants.

Drive back to the main square in Kilrush and take Frances Street off the square. This long broad street leads down to **Kilrush Creek Marina**, from where there are boat trips on the Shannon Estuary to see Ireland's only resident bottlenose dolphins and excursions to Scattery Island, 1 mile (2 km) offshore.

🚗 *Board a boat at the marina (see left).*

❸ Scattery Island
Co Clare
This tiny island boasts a 6th-century monastery, founded by St. Senan, five churches and a 100-ft (300-m) high round tower, still relatively intact (unusually, its main door is at ground level). On the north of the island are the remains of a gun rampart from the Napoleonic Wars (1799–1815).

🚗 *Return to Kilrush. From the town's square, take the N67 west, toward Kilkee (14 miles/23 km).*

④ Kilkee

Co Clare

In summer, Kilkee is popular with out-of-towners, mostly from Limerick, who come for its splendid crescent-shaped beach. When the tide is fully out, deep rock pools known as the Pollock Holes can be explored at the southern end of the sands; they are favorite swimming and snorkeling spots. The cliffs on either side of the beach offer good walks with stunning views.

A 45-minute cliff walk

The cliffs above Kilkee offer scenery almost as dramatic as that of the Cliffs of Moher *(see p126)*, but are less visited. This walk begins to the left of Kilkee beach in the so-called West End. From the public parking lot next to the **Diamond Rock Café** ①, where there is a life size statue of the actor Richard Harris, who was a frequent visitor to Kilkee as a child, a paved path gently ascends to the top of the cliffs. To the right, just beyond the café, are flat, limestone slabs known as the **Diamond Rocks** ②, a natural amphitheater used for musical and theatrical events in summer. About 164 ft (50 m) further on is a shelter with seating and a look out. On a clear day, the hazy silhouettes of the three Aran Islands are visible to the north, and the outline of the Kerry coastline can be discerned to the south. To the west is the tapering finger of Loop Head.

The paved path continues for about 1 mile (1.5 km) to **Foohagh Point** ③, where it curves left, away from the cliff edge. The final section, which gets progressively steeper, overlooks Intrinsic Bay, named after a Liverpool-bound cargo ship that sank in a gale here in 1830.

Heading away from the cliff edge, take the first left down Dunlicky Road and into Kilkee. Along the way are views across Kilkee and over the bay. For a longer walk, adding a further 2 miles (4 km), turn right instead of left on Dunlicky Road and follow it to Goleen Bay.

Back in the West End, explore the delights of Kilkee's beach. If the tide is out, scramble over the rocks in front of the parking lot to the three **Pollock Holes** ④, deep tidal pools popular with snorkelers. For snacks or lunch, the Diamond Rock Café has a terrace with views to George's Head. In summer, vendors on the seafront sell periwinkles and dillish – an edible sea grass gathered from the rock pools.

🚗 *From Kilkee, either take a scenic drive around Loop Head (15 miles/23 km) on the R487, or head direct to Milltown Malbay on the coastal N67. From there it is possible to continue toward Ennistimon (an attractive market town with painted storefronts), which offers an alternative inland route to the Burren continuing on the N67 via Lisdoonvarna. To experience the full drama of Clare's coastline, however, turn left off the N67 at Lehinch, taking the R478 to the Cliffs of Moher.*

Above The cliffs at Loop Head, along the scenic drive from Kilkee

VISITING KILKEE

Parking
Park by the beach in the town's West End, next to the Diamond Rock Café.

EAT AND DRINK

ENNIS

Rowan Tree Café Bar *moderate*
Mediterranean-style food is on offer at this café in a lovely old manor house with an outdoor terrace. Accommodation is available next door. *Harmony Row; 065 686 8669; www.rowantreecafebar.ie*

Town Hall Bistro *moderate*
Part of the Old Ground Hotel, but with a separate entrance. The restaurant offers a contemporary dining experience with an emphasis on bistro-style dishes. *O'Connell St; 065 682 8127; www.flynnhotels.com*

KILKEE

The Strand Restaurant and Guesthouse *moderate*
Family-run restaurant and guesthouse on the seafront overlooking Kilkee Bay. The menu leans toward seafood but also includes mainstays such as rack of lamb and fillet steak. Has six ensuite rooms above the restaurant. *Strand Line; 065 905 6177; www.thestrandkillkee.com*

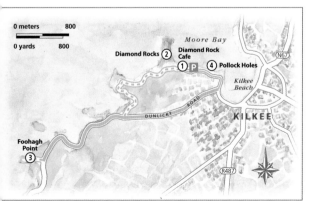

Eat and Drink: inexpensive, under €25; moderate, €25–€50; expensive, over €50

Above The majestic Cliffs of Moher rising from the Atlantic Ocean

SHOPPING IN DOOLIN

The **Traditional Music Shop** on Fisher Street sells recordings of musicians from the area, sheet music and locally made musical instruments *(065 707 4407; www.irishmusicdoolin.com)*.

WHERE TO STAY

DOOLIN

Ballinalacken Castle Country House and Restaurant *moderate–expensive*
This manor house is the perfect retreat, with views of the Aran Islands. *Doolin; 065 707 4025; www.ballinalackencastle.com*

BALLYVAUGHAN

Hyland's Burren Hotel *inexpensive*
18th-century hotel with 30 ensuite rooms and turf fires in the public area. *Ballyvaughan; 065 707 7037; www.hylandsburren.com*

Rusheen Lodge *inexpensive–moderate*
Family-run guesthouse offering good food and a warm welcome. *Ballyvaughan; 065 707 7092*

THE BURREN

Fergus View *inexpensive*
Neat farmhouse well located for exploring the surrounding area. *Killinaboy, Corrofin; 065 683 7606; www.fergusview.com*

Gregan's Castle Hotel *expensive*
A charming manor house hotel. Turf fires and sweeping views of the Burren. *Corkscrew Hill, 2 miles (4 km) south of Ballyvaughan; closed Dec–mid Feb; 065 707 7005; www.gregans.ie*

⑤ Cliffs of Moher
Co Clare

One of Ireland's most remarkable natural features, the Cliffs of Moher are where the limestone plateau of the Burren plunges 1,000 ft (300 m) into the sea. They stretch for 5 miles (8 km) along the coast of Clare. Park at the northern end, by the **Cliffs of Moher Visitor Experience** *(open daily)*. The state-of-the-art visitor center offers interactive exhibits and virtual experiences, including the Atlantic Edge, which simulates the sensation of stepping onto the cliff edge.

To view the cliffs in relative isolation, take the cliff path to the southern extremity of **Hag's Head**. On a clear day there are views of the Aran Islands and the mountains of Connemara.

🚗 *From the Cliffs of Moher, a winding coastal road leads to Doolin. However, this gets congested, especially in summer, so take the R478 north and turn left at the sign for Doolin.*

⑥ Doolin
Co Clare

If County Clare is the heartland of traditional Irish music, the village of Doolin is its music capital, brimming with music pubs and shops. These days some of them cater more to the tourist industry than for genuine music lovers, but there are several authentic music pubs where visitors can still pull up a seat and experience the full force of a rousing session.

Below Stunning views over Galway Bay from Black Head Lighthouse

McGann's, McDermott's, and **Gus O'Connors**, are highly recommended, the last especially for rollicking ballads.
🚗 *Take the R479 north and then turn left at the junction with the R477. This rejoins the coast, eventually rounding Black Head.*

⑦ Black Head
Co Clare

The drive around Black Head to Ballyvaughan is thrilling, sweeping close to the shore with a succession of glorious views. Pull in and stretch your legs on **Fanore Beach** or stop at the **lighthouse**, from where there are far-reaching views across Galway Bay.
🚗 *Continue along the R477 to Ballyvaughan.*

⑧ Ballyvaughan
Co Clare

A fishing village dotted with slate-roofed cottages, Ballyvaughan bustles with visitors in summer. It is often described as the gateway to the Burren, for this is where the limestone plateau at the heart of the Burren begins. The town has a range of good hotels, pubs, and restaurants. Bicycle rental and guided walks to view the area's geology and botany can be arranged through the **Tourist Information Centre** *(see right*
🚗 *Take the N67 inland toward Lisdoonvarna, famous for its match-making competition. Look back for stunning views over Galway Bay. After 1 mile (1.5 km), turn left onto the R480 for the heart of the Burren.*

⑨ The Burren

Co Clare

This massive plateau covers the whole of northwest Clare. Its name derives from the Irish *An Bhoieann*, meaning "The Stony District," for it is covered with huge flagstones called clints broken by deep fissures called grikes, through which millennia of rainfall have drained to form underground caves and rivers. One of Cromwell's surveyors declared it a savage land, yielding little. In fact, it is astonishingly rich in plant life, and it abounds in stone forts and megalithic tombs.

Above Poulnabrone Dolmen, one of many megalithic portal tombs on the Burren

Heart of the Burren

The characteristic karst landscape of the Burren unfolds as the R480 heads south. On the left is the western flank of **Aillwee Rock** and **Aillwee Cave**, a series of spectacular showcaves (*www.aillweecave.ie; open daily*).

Go south for 4 miles (7 km) to **Poulnabrone Dolmen**, a large portal tomb dating from 2500–2000 BC and one of some 70 in the area. A further 1 mile (2 km) south is **Caherconnell Stone Fort** (*www.burrenforts.ie; open Mar–Oct*). Such ring forts were common from the 5th century.

Turn right on leaving the fort and then left at the next junction, up **Magga Hill** and down into **Carran** (3 miles/5 km). Turn left after Cassidy's pub and then right, toward Boston Gort. After half a mile (1 km) turn left for **Burren Perfumery** (*open daily;*

www.burrenperfumery.com), an artisan perfumery inspired by the local flora.

Leaving here, continue in the same direction. After about 2 miles (4 km) the road descends steeply. After it levels out, look on the left for the entrance to **St. Colman's Well**, a 20-minute walk along a path. This healing well is overhung by an ash tree strung with "clooties," rags tied for a wish or a blessing.

After 2 miles (4 km), turn right on the Kinvarra road, then left at the next junction (2 miles/4 km). After a further 1 mile (2 km) turn right for Killinaboy and Corrofin, staying left when the road forks. After 2 miles (4 km), a large grey house with bay windows was the location for the popular TV sitcom *Father Ted*, and serves tea and cakes by appointment. Leaving here, turn right and at the next junction turn left to skirt the southern flank of **Mullaghmore**. This area is rich in plants and a short walk is recommended (a full circuit of the mountain will take about 2 hours). Afterward return to the first junction after Father Ted's and turn left to **Killinaboy** (2 miles/4 km), with a round tower and church. From here, turn left onto the R476 to **Corrofin**, for the 9-mile (14-km) drive to Ennis.

Above Sign at the Burren Perfumery

The Burren

The vast limestone pavement of the Burren – what Cromwell's surveyor described as "yielding neither water enough to drown a man, nor tree to hang him in, nor soil enough to bury" – extends across the whole of northwest Clare until it gives way to the black shale and sandstone of the Cliffs of Moher in the southwest.

VISITING THE BURREN

Tourist Information
Village Stores, Main Street, Ballyvaughan; www.ballyvaughantourism.com

The Burren Centre
Kilfenora, 065 708 8030; www.theburrencentre.ie; open Mar–Oct

EAT AND DRINK

BALLYVAUGHAN

Monk's Bar and Restaurant *inexpensive*
A cozy place with several small bars. Has a well deserved reputation for seafood. Great views over Galway Bay. *Old Pier, Ballyvaughan; 065 7077059*

THE BURREN

Vaughan's Pub *moderate*
Landmark pub known for its music in Kilfenora. Traditional menu featuring seafood chowder, bacon, and cabbage. *Main Street, Kilfenora; 065 708 8004; www.vaughanspub.ie*

An Fulacht Fia *moderate–expensive*
Gaelic for "cooking pot," *Fulacht fia* showcases local produce. *Coast road to Ballyvaughan; 065 707 7300; www.anfulachtfia.ie*

DAY TRIP OPTIONS

Ennis or Ballyvaughan make ideal bases to explore the dramatic north coast and rocky land of the Burren.

Coastal drama
Head to the northeast tip of Clare's coastline for a bracing walk at the Cliffs of Moher ❺, then stop in Doolin ❻ for traditional music or continue to Black Head ❼ for stunning views.

Take the N85 from Ennis and follow the drive's instructions around the coast.

A day in the Burren
Ballyvaughan ❽ is the gateway to the Burren ❾, and it is possible to hire a bike, walk or drive through the stark scenery, prehistoric remains, and unusual geological features of the region from the town. Stop off at Aillwee Rock and the showcaves at

Aillwee Cave, then head on to the 5th-century ring fort at Caherconell. Pause at the Burren Perfumery for restorative floral scents and make a wish at St Colman's Well. Then take tea at Father Ted's house to gain energy for a walk on Mullaghmore – a chance to appreciate the flora.

From Ballyvaughan take the R480 and R476 to reach the heart of the Burren.

Eat and Drink: inexpensive, under €25; moderate, €25–€50; expensive, over €50

Through the Sally Gap

Enniskerry to Mount Usher Gardens

Highlights

- **Great gardens**
  Admire two of Ireland's finest gardens – formal Powerscourt and romantic Mount Usher

- **The Wicklow Mountains**
  Explore spectacular high passes, deep wooded valleys, and rolling foothills

- **Monastic serenity**
  Contemplate the tranquillity of lakeside Glendalough and the ruins of its 6th-century monastery

- **Great statesmanship**
  Discover more about Irish political history at Avondale House, home of statesman Charles Stewart Parnell

- **Superb beaches**
  Stride along dune-backed Brittas Bay, Wicklow's loveliest stretch of coast

Wicklow Mountains near the Sally Gap

Through the Sally Gap

County Wicklow is known as the Garden of Ireland, and with its forests, lakes, and waterfalls, and its country estates, it lives up to its reputation. As you enter the county from Dublin to the north, abundant trees give way to the rolling Wicklow Mountains. Two notable valleys – Glendalough, one of the loveliest in the country, and the Sally Gap, a remote pass flanked by heather and blanket bog – are wildly beautiful. In contrast are the formal gardens of Powerscourt, the romantic gardens of Mount Usher beside the River Vartry, and the lush farmland in the Vale of Avoca. The coastal part of the drive takes in the sweeping beaches of Brittas Bay and rugged Wicklow Head topped by its three lighthouses.

Above Powerscourt House, a Palladian mansion famous for its garden, see p132

ACTIVITIES

Picnic by Powerscourt Waterfall, the highest waterfall in Ireland

Trek through the foothills of the Wicklow Mountains on horseback

Hike into the hills above Glendalough or walk beside its lakes

Let the kids run wild at the Clara Lara Funpark, an outdoor adventure center for under-12s

Tee off at Woodenbridge Golf Course, noted for its scenic setting

KEY

 Drive route

PLAN YOUR DRIVE

Start/finish Enniskerry to Mount Usher Gardens.

Number of days: 3–4 days.

Distance: 62 miles (100 km).

Road conditions: Roads are mostly good although unclassified roads are narrow and have no central markings. Mountain roads may be impassable in bad weather; check the forecast and make sure you have enough fuel.

When to go: Spring, summer, and autumn are the best times to visit.

Opening times: Most shops and attractions open 9 or 10am–5 or 6pm. Shops open Mon–Sat; in large towns also noon–6pm on Sun. Convenience stores in villages open 8am until late.

Main market days: Enniskerry: 2nd and 4th Sun; **Glendalough:** Crafts and Country Market, 2nd Sun; **Arklow:** Sat am; **Aughrim:** Farmers' Market, Sat.

Shopping: Buy colorful woolen scarves, throws, and rugs at Avoca Handweavers, or browse Enniskerry's quaint crafts and antiques shops.

Major festivals: County Wicklow: Gardens Festival, May–Sep; **Wicklow Town:** Regatta Festival, Jul–Aug; Arts Festival, May.

DAY TRIP OPTIONS

Take the R115 over the dramatic **Wicklow Mountains** or down the lush **Vale of Avoca. Gardeners** may want to focus on **Powerscourt** and **Mount Usher. Beach lovers** should head for **Brittas Bay.** For full details, *see p137.*

Below Monument to Wicklow's lost seafarers, Wicklow Harbour, *see p137*

Above Clocktower in the main square of the picture-postcard estate village of Enniskerry

① Enniskerry
Co Wicklow

Set around a square in the foothills of the Wicklow Mountains, this picture-postcard estate village is a good starting point for exploring the northern reaches of the hills. In summer it bustles with tourists, who come to visit nearby Powerscourt

House and linger in Enniskerry to browse its crafts, design, and antiques shops, or sample gourmet delights from Emilia's Fine Food and Wine.

🚗 *Head uphill from the village square, taking the road (R760) on the left-hand side of the square. Powerscourt House and Gardens are a short way up on the right-hand side.*

② Powerscourt House and Gardens
Enniskerry, Co Wicklow

Approached along an avenue lined with more than 2,000 beech trees, this Palladian house is set in magnificent formal gardens below the Great Sugar Loaf Mountain. An exhibition inside the house reveals its origins as a 13th-century Anglo-Norman castle, but the current house was commissioned by Richard Wingfield, the 1st Viscount Powerscourt, in the 1730s and designed by architect Richard Cassels. Gutted by fire in 1974, the renovated building now houses an upmarket shop with an excellent café and restaurant – all part of the Avoca Handweavers enterprise *(see p137).*

VISITING THE WICKLOW MOUNTAINS

Parking in Enniskerry
Park in or around the main square.

Powerscourt House and Gardens
Enniskerry; 01 204 6000;
www.powerscourt.ie; house, gardens,
and waterfall open daily

Trekking and Horseback Riding
Several companies offer guided trekking and horseback riding in the foothills of the Wicklow Mountains. For details visit *www.visitwicklow.ie.* One alternative is **Clissmann Donkey Walking Holidays**, from Rathdrum or Avoca *(Cornyberne Farm; 0404 46920; www.clissmann.com/wicklow)*.

WHERE TO STAY IN ENNISKERRY

Ferndale *inexpensive*
This is a charming Victorian House, furnished in period style and located right in Enniskerry village. Scrambled eggs and smoked salmon with home-made breads for breakfast.
Enniskerry; 01 286 3518;
www.ferndalehouse.com; closed Dec–Jan

Summerhill House Hotel *moderate*
This beautiful period house in its own wooded grounds has great views. It is located right opposite the entrance to the Powerscourt Estate. New courtyard rooms available.
Enniskerry; 01 286 7928;
www.summerhillhousehotel.com

The gardens at Powerscourt are probably the finest in Ireland, both for their design and for their dramatic setting. The grounds were remodeled along with the house in the mid-18th century, in a design created to blend into the landscape. A century later the 6th Viscount asked architect Daniel Robertson to draw up new designs for the gardens. He redesigned them – from a wheelbarrow, fortified by sherry to relieve his gout – in an Italian style, adding the terraces leading down from the house. The new ornamental gardens were finally completed in 1858–75 by the 7th Viscount, who added gates, urns, and statues collected during his travels in Europe. He brought back the gilded wrought-iron **Bamberg Gate** from a church in Bavaria.

The centerpiece of the garden today is the **Triton Lake**, dug out for the first garden, which takes its name from the central fountain – modeled on a 17th-century work by Bernini in Rome. The **Perron**, a beautiful Italianate stairway added in 1874 and flanked on either side by the terraced **Italian Garden**, leads down to the lake. It is guarded by two **statues of Pegasus**, the mythical winged horse and emblem of the Wingfield family. A **mosaic** at the top was made of pebbles from nearby Bray beach.

Next to the secluded **Dolphin Pond** is a **Pets' Cemetery** containing the graves of Wingfield family cats, dogs, and even horse and cattle.

Powerscourt Waterfall is a 2-mile (3-km) drive from the house (turn right onto the R760 and, after a humpback bridge, sharp right). Cascading into the River Dargle from a height of 400 ft (122 m), it is Ireland's highest waterfall and a popular picnic spot.

Below Italianate statues and urns added to Powerscourt Gardens by the 7th Viscount

📷 **Return to Enniskerry and take the right-hand road uphill from the square. Continue past Kilgarron Cottages and Glen View and follow the road to Glencree.**

The Wicklow Mountains

Wicklow Mountains National Park extends over 50,000 acres (20,000 ha) of upland mountain scenery southwest of Enniskerry. The product of the interaction of man and nature through turf-cutting over thousands of years, it is a rugged wilderness of unpopulated heath and extensive bogland. Although no peak exceeds 3,000 ft (915 m), the mountains can be dangerous in bad weather, and the roads are narrow, winding, and bumpy in summer, and may be impassable after snow in winter.

❸ Glencree

Co Wicklow

The Valley of Glencree is home to the **Glencree Centre for Peace and Reconciliation**, established in the 1970s in response to the Northern Ireland conflict, but now concerned with global peace-building. It is housed in an 18th-century British barracks. There is a **Visitor Centre** (open daily) and café. Further along the valley is the **German Cemetery** containing graves of servicemen killed in the world wars.

📷 **Leaving Glencree visitor center, turn left onto the R115 and drive south through the Sally Gap.**

❹ Sally Gap

Co Wicklow

One of the most spectacular drives in Wicklow, this remote mountain pass is surrounded by blanket bog and

heather, dotted with pools and streams. It follows the Military Road, built through the mountains to flush out rebels after the 1798 Rebellion. Now the road provides easy access to the Wicklow Mountains National Park, which has open access for walkers. The landscape changes color with the seasons, from bright green in spring to purple in summer, russet-brown in autumn, and snow-white in winter. Look out for stacks of freshly-cut peat. Toward the end of the pass there is a viewpoint over the Wicklow Gap, another scenic route.

📷 **Continue south on the R115 and turn right at Laragh onto the R755. After the sign for Wicklow Gap, turn left into the parking lot at Glendalough Visitor Centre.**

Below Powerscourt Waterfall cascades into the River Dargle from a height of 400 ft (122 m)

Above left Patchwork fields in the foothills of the Wicklow Mountains **Above** Johnnie Fox's, a pub with plenty of character and good food

EAT AND DRINK

ENNISKERRY

Poppies *inexpensive*
With wholesome country cooking, this friendly and cozy café is always buzzing and is a great place to stop for breakfast, morning coffee, or lunch. Plenty of choice for vegetarians.
The Square; 01 282 8869; www.poppies.ie; open daytime only

Emilia's Ristorante *moderate*
This friendly Italian restaurant has a sister shop below, **Emilia's Fine Food and Wine**, which is a good lunch stop.
Enniskerry; 01 276 1834; www.emilias.ie

AROUND ENNISKERRY

Johnnie Fox's *moderate–expensive*
From Enniskerry, drive toward Dublin through the Scalp (R117 north) to reach Johnnie Fox's, Ireland's highest pub, with nightly music, crackling turf fires, and excellent steaks and seafood.
Glencullen; 01 295 5647; www.jfp.ie

POWERSCOURT HOUSE AND GARDENS

The Terrace Café *moderate*
Run by Avoca (see pp136–7), typical fare includes imaginative salads, Mediterranean tarts, and hearty casseroles (beef and Guinness a specialty). Views over the gardens and Sugar Loaf mountain.
Powerscourt House; 01 204 6070; www.avoca.ie

Eat and Drink: inexpensive, under €25; moderate, €25–€50; expensive, over €50

Above The two granite arches of the gatehouse at Glendalough

❺ Glendalough
Co Wicklow

Glendalough (*Gleann Da Locha* in Irish), or "valley of the two lakes," was carved out by glaciers during the Ice Age. A place of great beauty and tranquility, it is the setting for a monastic settlement founded in the 6th century by St. Kevin, a descendant of the royal house of Leinster who rejected his privileged life to become a hermit in a cave in this valley. It would be easy to spend half a day here, exploring the monastery ruins and walking around the two lakes, perhaps stopping to picnic. There are two information points – the Glendalough Visitor Centre, which tells the story of the monastery, and the Wicklow Mountains National Park Information Office, at the Upper Lake, where visitors can find out more about the park, valley, and walking trails in the area.

A two-hour walking tour

Most of the monastic ruins (*open daily*) lie between the entrance and the Lower Lake. From the **Visitor Centre** ① follow the path behind the center and cross the bridge. Turn right onto the Green Road, which leads around the complex, and walk through the **main gateway** ② – originally two storys – with two granite arches. To the right is the landmark Round Tower, one of the finest towers of its type: 100 ft (30 m) high and with its entrance 11 ft (3.5 m) from the ground (it would have been reached by ladders that could be hauled up from inside),

Round Tower at Glendalough

it served as a belfry and a beacon for approaching visitors, and was a place of security for the monks during times of attack.

Straight ahead are the **monastic buildings** ③, including the Cathedral, dating from the 12th century and the largest building in the complex; just to the south is St. Kevin's Cross. Behind these is The Priest's House, reconstructed from the original stones, which was a place of burial for local clergy. Further along the path is St. Kevin's Church, known as St. Kevin's Kitchen, as well as the remains of St. Kieran's Church, commemorating the founder of

Below The tranquility of Glendalough, which attracted the 6th-century hermit St. Kevin

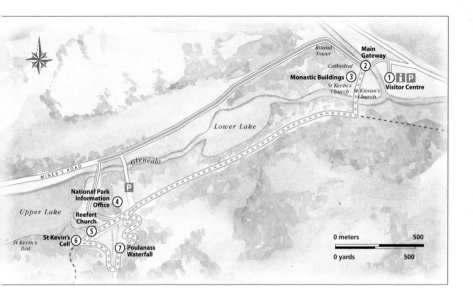

Clonmacnoise. From here, take the path back across the river and turn right toward the Lower Lake.

Walk along the Green Road, leaving the Lower Lake on the right. Just before the Upper Lake is the **National Park Information Office ④**.

From here, follow the Poulanass Walk to **Reefert Church ⑤**, dating from 1100. A little further on, up some steps, is **St. Kevin's Cell ⑥**, a beehive-shaped hut where the saint is said to have lived and prayed. Little is known about the saint, but legend has it that he lived to the age of 120, and that a blackbird once laid an egg in the saint's outstretched hands as he prayed, which he held until it hatched. Further along the lake is a small cave known as St Kevin's Bed. It is not accessible, but can be seen from Miner's Road on the far shore.

From the hermit's cell follow the Poulanass Walk to the **Poulanass Waterfall ⑦** – a steep climb through woodland – and views over the Upper Lake. Descend from the waterfall to the information office and return to the parking lot along the far side of the Lower Lake.

🚗 *From the parking lot bear right onto the R756, passing through Laragh. Turn right onto the R755 to Rathdrum and then right onto the R752 for Avoca. After 1 mile (1.5 km) take left and next left at the sign for Avondale House. Park in the parking lot.*

The Wicklow Way

This is a self-guided walking trail running 79 miles (127 km) from Marlay Park in South Dublin to the village of Clonegal in County Carlow, taking in mountains, lakes, rivers, forests, and farmland on the way. The entire trail takes 7–10 days and requires a good level of fitness, equipment, and a proper map. Alternatively it is possible to walk short segments of the trail. For more information on the trail, visit *www.wicklowway.com*.

⑥ Avondale House and Forest Park

Rathdrum, Co Wicklow

The birthplace and home of Charles Stewart Parnell (1846–91), one of Ireland's greatest political leaders, Avondale House (*open mid-Apr–Oct; house closed Mon except Bank Holidays*) has an important place in Irish history. Tours of its impressive interior recount the tale of Parnell's fight for Home Rule and the founding of the Irish Parliamentary Party. The house, built in 1179 by Samuel Hayes, is set in an extensive forest park (*www.coillte.ie*) along the west bank of the Avonmore River with marked trails, picnic spots, and children's play areas. There is also a restaurant and shop.

🚗 *Leaving Avondale, return to the R752 toward Avoca, stopping at the Meeting of the Waters.*

EAT AND DRINK AROUND GLENDALOUGH

Glendalough Green Café *inexpensive*
Come to this café for a great selection of freshly baked breads, soups, and hotpots, as well as artisan chocolates. There are also outdoor tables for al fresco dining.
Laragh; 0404 45151

Wicklow Heather Restaurant *moderate*
This fully licensed restaurant has a selection of meat and seafood dishes.
Glendalough Road, Laragh; 0404 45157; www.thewicklowheather.com

Below Avondale House, birthplace of the Irish nationalist leader Charles Stewart Parnell

Eat and Drink: inexpensive, under €25; moderate, €25–€50; expensive, over €50

Above Pretty garden at Hunter's Hotel, a former coaching inn, Rathnew

WHERE TO STAY

VALE OF AVOCA

Woodenbridge Hotel and Lodge
moderate
Established in 1608 as a coaching inn, this is Ireland's oldest hotel and a charming and intimate place to stay.
Arklow, Vale of Avoca; 0402 35146; www.woodenbridgehotel.com

WICKLOW HEAD

Wicklow Head Lighthouse *expensive*
This restored lighthouse, originally built in 1781, is now run by The Irish Landmark Trust and can be hired on a self-catering basis. It has six octagonal rooms and stunning views of the Irish Sea. A special place to stay.
Dunbur Head; 01 670 4733; www.irishlandmark.com

AROUND WICKLOW TOWN

Ballyknocken House *moderate*
This 19th-century country house is a guesthouse, farm, cooking school and restaurant (for residents only), overseen by chef Catherine Fulvio and her Italian husband. It is 1 mile (1.5 km) from Glenealy on the road to Ashford.
Glenealy, Ashford; 0404 44627; www.ballyknocken.com

Hunter's Hotel *moderate*
A romantic 18th-century coaching inn (on R761 to Newcastle) combining old-style elegance with modern comforts. Run by the same family since 1820.
Newrath Bridge, Rathnew; 0404 40106; www.hunters.ie

Tinakilly Country House *moderate*
An old-fashioned country house set in elegant gardens. Some period rooms with four-poster beds and sea views.
Main Street, Rathnew; 0404 69274; www.tinakilly.ie

⑦ Vale of Avoca
Avoca, Co Wicklow

The **Meeting of the Waters** is a tranquil spot where the Avonmore ("large river" in Irish) and Avonbeg ("small river") merge to form the River Avoca. The poem "The Meeting of The Waters" by Thomas Moore (1779–1852) commemorates "that vale in whose bosom the bright waters meet." The Avoca eventually flows into the Irish Sea at Arklow. Continue on the R752 to Avoca and the Vale of Avoca.

Nestling in the wooded Vale of Avoca, an area that once had gold, copper, lead, and zinc mines – dating back to 1720 – is the village of **Avoca**. The last mine closed in the early 1980s, but Avoca Handweavers has the oldest working woollen mill in Ireland, established in 1723, and is still thriving, with stylish modern designs to buy *(see right)*. To see the weaving process, drive through the village, pass the church and go down the hill; it is on the left-hand side. From Avoca, continue south along the R752, bearing right onto the R747 for Aughrim.

At the meeting point of the Avoca and Aughrim rivers, **Woodenbridge** is the scenic setting for the Woodenbridge Golf Course *(0402 35202; www. woodenbridgegolfclub. com)*, and Ireland's oldest hotel, the Woodenbridge Hotel and Lodge

Bearnas na Diallaite
SALLY GAP
↑ **Bealach Mileata**
MILITARY ROAD 17 90
← **Gleann Life**
LIFFEY VALLEY
↗ **Bealach Fheartire** →
VARTRY DRIVE

Many options in the Wicklow Mountains

(see left), founded in 1608. Trout fishing is popular in the River Aughrim

🚗 *After Woodenbridge, take the R747 toward Arklow. Entering Arklow, take first exit at roundabout and follow signs toward N11/Dublin. Leave the N11 at Jack White's Cross Roads, turning right for Brittas Bay.*

⑧ Brittas Bay
Co Wicklow

Running for 3 miles (5 km) and backed by rolling sand dunes, Brittas Bay is a stunning beach with Blue Flag status, ideal for swimming. In summer, it is busy with day-trippers and second-home-owners from Dublin, but there is enough space to absorb the crowds. Lifeguards are on duty from mid-June through August. Out of season it is ideal for bracing walks along the sand, which provide a chance to spot some of the rare wildlife in the dunes backed by extensive marsh and fen. Wild asparagus, sea rocket and sea parsley grow among the marram grass, where dune rabbits may be seen. At different times of year it is possible to spot little tern and ringed plover, sedge warbler and reed bunting, dunlin and sanderling.

🚗 *Drive north along Brittas Bay, following the R750, which runs parallel to the beach, passing bathing beaches at Jack's Hole and Silver Strand, to Wicklow Head.*

Below Glorious expanse of Brittas Bay, fringed by dunes that are a haven for wildlife

9 Wicklow Head
Co Wicklow

This headland, rising 276 ft (84 m) above the sea, has been watched over by two lighthouses since 1781, when they were built to aid ships' navigation through channels between the sand banks in the Irish Sea. The rear lighthouse on Long Hill remains intact, and has been restored as holiday accommodation, while the front one was rebuilt in 1816. The third lighthouse, the only one currently in use, was built further down the cliff for greater visibility.

Follow the R750 into Wicklow Town and park near the Gaol.

10 Wicklow Town
Co Wicklow

The main attraction of Wicklow Town is its **Historic Gaol** *(open Apr–Oct: daily; www.wicklowshistoricgaol.com).* Built in 1702 and now a museum, it details important episodes in Irish history, such as the 1798 Rebellion and the Great Famine. Visitors can climb aboard a reconstructed prison ship and learn about prisoners' harsh

conditions inside the dungeon. The building is supposed to be haunted, so brave souls could try a night tour, held on the last Friday of every month.

Follow the R750 out of Wicklow to Rathnew and pass two roundabouts, following signs for Ashford. Mount Usher Gardens are on the right-hand side on entering Ashford.

11 Mount Usher Gardens
Ashford, Co Wicklow

Beautifully set along the River Vartry, these gardens *(open Mar–Nov daily; www.mountushergardens.ie)* were designed in 1868 by Edward Walpole in the Robinsonian informal style made famous by the Irish gardener William Robinson (1838–1935). Meandering walks and pretty bridges afford romantic views framed by rare shrubs and trees, from Chinese conifers and bamboos to Mexican pines and pampas grass. Seasonal highlights include crocuses, bluebells, and magnolias in spring, azaleas and rhododendrons in early summer, and the glorious Maple Walk in autumn.

Above left The River Vartry cascading through Mount Usher gardens **Above** Ruins perched on the clifftop at Wicklow Head

SHOPPING IN THE VALE OF AVOCA

Avoca Handweavers
Brightly colored handwoven woollen scarves and throws can be bought at the original Avoca mill. The **Avoca Café** serves delicious homemade baked beans with garlic and rosemary on toasted ciabatta, pancakes with fresh berries, and similar delicacies. *The Mill, Avoca; 0402 35105; www.avoca.ie*

EAT AND DRINK

AROUND THE VALE OF AVOCA
The Strawberry Tree *expensive*
Award-winning organic restaurant in an upmarket resort hotel, 11 miles (15 km) from Woodenbridge. Tasty dishes using locally sourced produce. *Brooklodge Hotel, Macreddin; 0402 36444; www.brooklodge.com*

AROUND WICKLOW TOWN
Ballyknocken House and Cookery School *moderate*
See "Where to Stay," left

DAY TRIP OPTIONS
Mountains, coast, vale, or gardens, there are plenty of day trips that can be taken from Enniskerry or Wicklow.

Dip into the mountains
To sample the Wicklow Mountains, follow the Military Road, the R115, from Glencree ③ to Laragh, turning off at Glendalough ⑤ to picnic by the lakes and see the ruins.

From Enniskerry, follow signs to Glencree and then join the R115

toward Laragh. Return on the R755 via Roundwood and Vartry reservoir.

The Vale of Avoca
This valley has several interesting stops, including Avondale House ⑥, the Meeting of the Waters, and Avoca Handweavers in the Vale of Avoca ⑦.

Take the R750 from Wicklow, then the R752 toward Avoca.

For gardeners
Compare and contrast two gardens by combining a morning at Powerscourt

House and Gardens ② with an afternoon at Mount Usher Gardens ⑪.

Follow directions to Powerscourt from Enniskerry. Mount Usher is 16 miles (26 km) along the scenic coastal R761.

The Wicklow coast
Drive around Wicklow Head ⑨ to spend the day at Brittas Bay ⑧, the finest beach on the east coast.

Take the R750 from Wicklow Town, avoiding holidays when roads are busy.

Eat and Drink: inexpensive, under €25; moderate, €25–€50; expensive, over €50

The Plains of Kildare

Celbridge to Kilcullen

Highlights

- **Georgian splendor**
  Take a tour of Castletown House, the grandest Georgian house in Ireland

- **Walk in the woods**
  Wander the trails of Donadea Forest Park, a delightful old woodland estate

- **Kildare Town**
  Explore the wealth of historic monuments in this charming town

- **Sport of kings**
  See how some of the world's finest bloodstock is raised, at the Irish National Stud

Heading for the winning post at the Curragh Racecourse

The Plains of Kildare

The county of Kildare is within easy reach of Dublin but still retains its traditional rural character. Ireland's world-famous bloodstock industry is largely based here, on some of the best grassland in the country. This drive follows the leafy roads beside the River Liffey and the Grand Canal, past such diverse attractions as writer James Joyce's boarding school, a prehistoric hill fort, a great Irish Palladian house, and one of the world's most prestigious racecourses.

Above The Japanese Gardens at the Irish National Stud, *see p45*

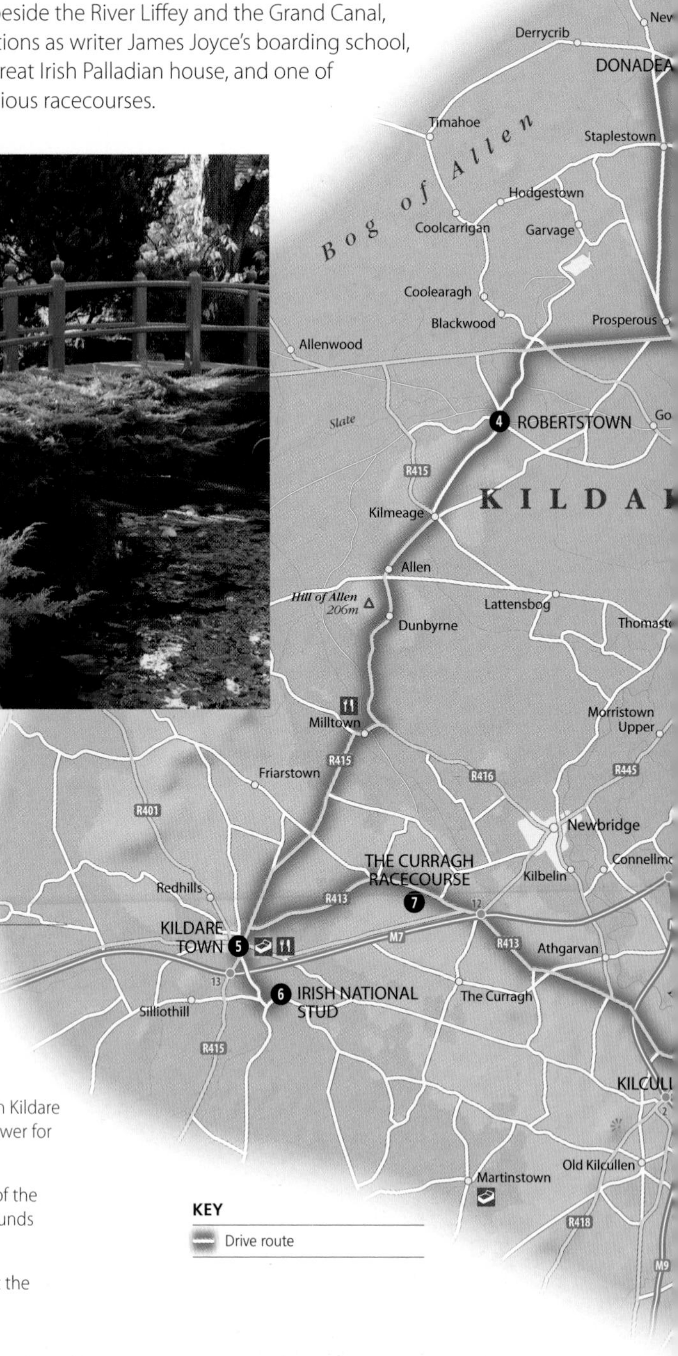

ACTIVITIES

Listen to a recital of chamber music in a great 18th-century house

Savour a pint on a peaceful stretch of the Grand Canal

Visit St. Brigid's Cathedral in Kildare Town and climb the round tower for spectacular views

Unwind in the tranquillity of the Japanese Gardens, in the grounds of the Irish National Stud

Place a bet on the horses at the Curragh Racecourse

KEY

Drive route

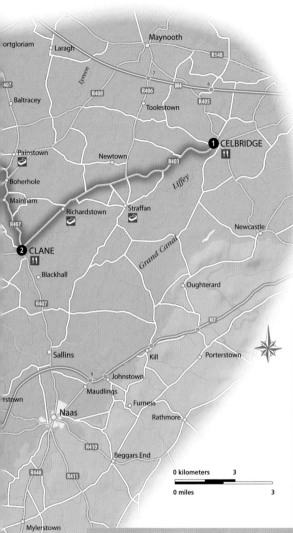

PLAN YOUR DRIVE

Start/finish: Celbridge to Kilcullen.

Number of days: 2.

Distance: 37 miles (60 km).

Road conditions: The roads are in good condition, larger roads well marked.

When to go: Summer is the best time for horse-racing and musical events. The autumn colors of the county's woodlands are spectacular.

Opening times: Shops and attractions open 9am–6pm. Shops open Mon–Sat; also 12–6pm on Sun. Convenience stores in villages open 8am until late.

Main market days: Celbridge: Sat; Kildare Town: Fri.

Major festivals: Celbridge: Castletown Concerts (Castletown House), summer; **The Curragh:** Irish Derby, Jun; **Punchestown:** National Hunt Festival, Apr–May.

DAY TRIP OPTIONS

Lovers of **history and nature** could combine a visit to Castletown House with a stroll in Donadea Forest Park. **Walkers** might prefer to walk a stretch of the Grand Canal and climb the Hill of Allen. And, if the timing is right, a **day at the races** at The Curragh is unmissable. *For details, see p145.*

Below St. Brigid's Cathedral in Kildare Town, with its striking 9th-century Round Tower, *see p144*

Above The 13th-century fortified tower of Barberstown Castle

WHERE TO STAY AROUND CLANE

Ashley *inexpensive*
A comfortable bed-and-breakfast in a bungalow with a pleasant garden.
Richardstown, Clane (north of Clane on the R403); 045 868 533

Laurels B&B *inexpensive*
This long-established family-run B&B is located close to Clane and Donadea Forest Park.
Dublin Rd, Clane; 045 868 274

Barberstown Castle *expensive*
This long-established country house hotel, the oldest part of which dates from the 13th century, is set in its own extensive grounds, with lovely gardens; rooms furnished with antiques; a fine-dining restaurant and comfortable public areas with log fires in winter.
Straffan, Clane (located off the R403 between Celbridge and Clane, 7 km/4 miles from Clane – well signposted); 01 628 8157; www.barberstowncastle.ie

① Celbridge
Co Kildare

This well-preserved village on the Liffey has long associations with the author and Dean of St. Patrick's, Dublin, Jonathan Swift (1667–1745). His beloved Esther Van Homrigh, whom he immortalized as "Vanessa," lived at Celbridge Abbey. At the end of the Main Street, the gates of **Castletown House** *(open Mar–Oct: Tue–Sun; Nov–Dec: weekends)* open onto a long driveway to the house, now accessible only on foot (cars must turn left at the gate and follow the signs around to the right and find the back entrance and parking lot). The house was built in 1722 for William Conolly, the Speaker of the Irish House of Commons, and is the largest private house in Ireland. It is a masterpiece of Georgian architecture in the Palladian style. The interiors were created by Lady Louisa Lennox, wife of Conolly's great-nephew, and include the only intact 18th-century print room in Ireland. A portrait of Lady Louisa can be seen in the superb stuccowork on the staircase. Castletown is set in a stately park of mature trees. Also within the park is Conolly's Folly, built by Richard Castle, commissioned by Conolly's widow, Katherine, in 1740 as a memorial to him and to provide employment on the estate after a harsh winter.

Conolly family crest, Castletown House

🚗 *Leaving Celbridge, take the R403 to Clane.*

② Clane
Co Kildare

The Neo-Gothic **Protestant church** (1884) on elegant Main Street stands on the site of one of the earliest monasteries in Ireland. Founded around the 5th century, it predated the arrival of St. Patrick. Nothing of it remains today. Just outside the village, on the R407 heading north, is **Clongowes Wood College**, a long-established Jesuit boarding school, set in a beautiful estate of ancient woods and playing fields, the latter evoked by former student James Joyce in the opening pages of *A Portrait of the Artist as a Young Man*. The main building is Castle Browne, which was a border fort of the Pale, that part of Ireland around Dublin controled by the English until the 17th century.

🚗 *Continue along the R407; take the side road to the left marked for Donadea, follow the signs to Donadea Forest Park and park in the parking lot.*

③ Donadea
Co Kildare

The Aylmer family lived at **Donadea Castle** from the 15th to the 20th century. The property is now owned by the state. The imposing castle still stands but is derelict. Visitors can walk on marked trails of varying lengths around the 590-acre (240-ha) **Donadea Forest Park** *(open daily)* with its mixed woodland, walled garden, streams, lake, and boathouse. In a grove of oak sapling

Below left Interior of Castletown House, Celbridge, decorated in the Pompeiian style
Below right Exquisite mahogany bureau flanked by 18th-century portraits in Castletown House

below The impressive former Grand Canal Hotel in Robertstown, at the centre of lively canalside activity

a limestone replica of the World Trade Center's twin towers commemorates members of the American emergency services who died in the attacks of September 11 2001, including Sean Tallon, a young firefighter whose family was from Donadea. In the nearby **St. Peter's Church** *(open for services)* is a fine 17th-century canopied tomb with effigies of Sir Gerald Aylmer and his wife Dame Julia Nugent.

🔟 *Leaving Donadea Forest Park, turn left, left, and left again, in the direction of the small village of Prosperous. Turn right on the R403, then take a left turn on to a smaller road for Robertstown.*

④ Robertstown
Co Kildare

The Grand Canal, which links Dublin in the east to the River Shannon in the west of Ireland, is now used only for leisure purposes. The highest point on its route is at picturesque Robertstown at the Hill of Allen. In 1804, the Grand Canal Company built one of its grand hotels here, which is now a **visitor center** *(open daily)*, serving the needs of vacationers who embark on canal trips from the town or call in en route. There are also several good pubs, often with live music in the evenings. A little further to the west is Lowtown, whose marina is one of the most popular mooring spots in Kildare. Here the canal divides, with an offshoot toward Athy and the River Barrow.

🔟 *From Robertstown, follow signs for the pleasant hamlet of Kilmeage.*

Join the R415 and proceed along it with the Hill of Allen on the right-hand side, passing Milltown, on a feeder line to the canal. There is paid parking in and around Kildare's Market Square.

The Grand Canal Way

This marked canalside trail runs for 86 miles (138 km) from Dublin to Shannon Harbour. Robertstown is situated at the 28-mile (45-km) mark. The path is well-maintained along its entire route, making it safe for walkers and cyclists of all ages. Visit the website of the Inland Waterways Association of Ireland *(www.walks.iwai.ie)* for details of this and other marked trails. Alternatively, see Waterways Ireland *(www.waterwaysireland.org)* for information about day trips and boat rental on the canal.

EAT AND DRINK

CELBRIDGE

CHC at the West Wing *inexpensive*
An excellent café based in the high-ceilinged former kitchen of Castletown House, serving lunches of soups, tarts, and salads; a good place in which to start or finish a tour of the house.
Castletown House; 01 627 9498; closed Mon & Tue

CLANE

Zest Cafe *inexpensive*
A popular café which turns into a restaurant at night. Imaginative menus include homemade burgers, and unusual pastas and desserts. A small but good wine list.
Clane Shopping Centre; 045 893 222; www.zestcafeandrestaurant.ie

AROUND ROBERTSTOWN

Hanged Man's *inexpensive*
A traditional country pub and restaurant on the canal at Milltown. The restaurant specializes in fresh food, simply cooked. Live music sessions every Monday.
Milltown (6 miles/9 km from Robertstown on the R415); 045 431 515; www.hangedmans.ie

Below Imposing Donadea Castle, set in its own forest park

Eat and Drink: inexpensive, under €25; moderate, €25–€50; expensive, over €50

Above Kildare Town Heritage Centre, in the fine 18th-century Market House

VISITING KILDARE TOWN

Parking
There is pay-and-display parking in and around Market Square.

Tourist Information
Kildare Town Heritage Centre, Market Square; 045 530 672; open Mon–Sat, 10am–1pm, 2–5pm; www.kildare.ie/kildareheritage/

WHERE TO STAY

KILDARE TOWN

Cherryville House *inexpensive*
Charming bed-and-breakfast with three rooms, two ensuite, in an old farmhouse on a working farm, just off the R445 heading towards Monasterevan from Kildare Town. *Kildare; 045 521 091; www.kildarebedandbreakfast.com*

AROUND THE CURRAGH RACECOURSE

Martinstown House *expensive*
Charming Gothic-style *cottage ornée* designed in the 1830s by the English architect Decimus Burton, set in extensive grounds with wonderful trees and even a rescued donkey, well signposted a few miles (kilometers) south of the Curragh Racecourse on minor roads. Four luxurious bedrooms and a friendly, comfortable ambience. Five-course gourmet dinner (on 24-hour advance notification) and exceptional breakfasts. *Martinstown, The Curragh; 045 441 261; www.martinstownhouse.com*

⑤ Kildare Town
Co Kildare

Kildare is a pretty, well-preserved small cathedral and market town, where St. Brigid, one of the three great Irish saints (the other two were Patrick and Colmcille), founded a monastery in the 6th century. It later became the principal church in Leinster, and was unusual in being a double monastery (for both nuns and monks). A fine Round Tower, built as a place of refuge from the Norse raids of the 9th–10th centuries, stands beside the cathedral. Kildare is the main town serving the army camp and the racecourse, set in the great plain of The Curragh, and is the center of the Irish bloodstock industry.

A one-hour walking tour

Start in the **Market Square** ① in the center of the town, at the Heritage Centre, formerly the Market House. According to the Statutes of Henry VI (1458) a market has been held in Kildare "from time whereof memory runs not," but the present building is from the 18th century. As well as a place of business, the Market Square was a venue for town gatherings, and it is still the social hub, with its bars, restaurants, and shops. In the Heritage Centre *(open daily)*, as well as the tourist office, is a multimedia exhibition recounting the history of the town. Opposite is the St. Brigid's Flame monument, by Alex Pentek, unveiled in 2006 as a memorial to the sacred flame kept alive by St. Brigid as a perpetual fire of Christianity, which burned until the suppression of the monasteries in the 16th century. At the top of Market Square is **St. Brigid's Cathedral** ② *(open May–Sep: daily)*. There has been a church on the site since the 6th century; it may have been a pagan sanctuary before that. The present building, dating from the 13th century, has undergone much destruction and restoration, but contains some interesting medieval relics and modern stained-glass windows. On the north side of the cathedral are the restored foundations of St. Brigid's Fire Temple, where a small fire is still lit on the saint's feast day (Feb 1). Behind the cathedral, is the 106-ft (32-m) **Round Tower** ③. It is possible to climb to the top, for wonderful views. To the east of the Market Square, behind the Silken Thomas pub, is a remaining 15th-century tower from **Kildare Castle** ④. Lord Edward Fitzgerald (1763–98), leader of the United Irishmen, lived in an adjoining house, now gone. Walk up Market Square back to the parking lot.

Lord Edward Fitzgerald statue

🚗 *From Market Square, follow Tully Road over the M7 motorway, then turn left, at the sign for the National Stud.*

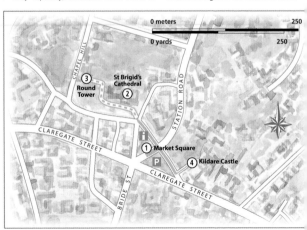

6 Irish National Stud
Co Kildare

Established in 1946 to develop Irish bloodstock, this is the home of some of the finest thoroughbred horses in the country *(open Feb–Dec: daily)*. The guided tour includes a visit to the stableyard to see mares and foals, as well as some retired champions. The **Horse Museum** tells the history of Irish horses, shows films of some classic races, and exhibits include the skeleton of the great Arkle.

Above St. Fiachra's Garden at the Irish National Stud, a peaceful place of rock and water

In the grounds of the National Stud are two superb gardens. St. Fiachra's Garden *(open daily)*, established in 1999 and named after the patron saint of gardeners, is a spiritual place reflecting the Irish landscape. The beautiful Japanese Gardens *(open Feb–Dec: daily)*, laid out 1906–10, symbolize the Life of Man, and are regarded as the finest such gardens in Europe.

🚗 *Turn right out of the National Stud, then right again, and continue through Kildare Town. Turn right onto R413 to the Curragh Racecourse. Ample parking.*

7 The Curragh Racecourse
Co Kildare

Set in a great plain, where sheep graze freely and horses from the surrounding stud farms are exercised, **The Curragh** *(open race days only)* is where all five Irish Classics are raced – the 2,000 and 1,000 Guineas in May, the Irish Derby in June, the Oaks in July and the St. Leger in September. A place to see Irish racing at its best, there is always a great atmosphere.

🚗 *Leaving the racecourse, turn right onto R413. At the first roundabout take the second exit, toward Newbridge. Follow signs for Kilcullen through two roundabouts, crossing the M9 highway, to the village of Kilcullen.*

Horse Sense

The Curragh is the home of Ireland's best flat racing, while Punchestown, near Naas, is where the National Hunt Festival takes place over the jumps. Ireland is famous for its thoroughbred racehorses, and the bloodstock industry flourished for many years thanks to tax exemption on stallion profits.

---

8 Kilcullen
Co Kildare

This is a winding village on the river Liffey in the midst of horse country, with good restaurants and bars and a pleasant riverside walk. There are many antiquities nearby, including an early monastery at **Old Kilcullen**, where St. Patrick founded a bishopric. The base of a round tower and portions of three carved stone crosses survive. The hill to the northwest, Knockaulin, is topped by an important prehistoric circular hill fort, **Dún Áilinne**. It is on private land, so inquire about visits at the Kildare Town Heritage Centre.

Above Statue of Irish thoroughbred legend Vintage Crop at the Currah Racecourse

EAT AND DRINK

KILDARE TOWN

Silken Thomas
inexpensive–moderate
A refurbished traditional pub in the center of town, a popular place with a bright and busy restaurant or an inexpensive carvery at the bar.
Kildare Town; 045 522 232;
www.silkenthomas.com

L'Officina *moderate*
This Italian restaurant is in the Kildare Village shopping outlet, not far from Kildare Town. Inventive, authentic cooking, and lovely views.
Kildare Village shopping outlet,
Kildare Town; 045 535 850

KILCULLEN

Fallons Bar and Café *moderate*
The owners of this long-established eating house bring a lively atmosphere and excellent food. Try the seafood chowder, special burgers, or tapas, or just enjoy a pint of Guinness by the turf fire.
Main St; 045 481 260; www.fallonb.ie

DAY TRIP OPTIONS

Places of interest are all within easy reach of Celbridge, Robertstown and Kildare Town.

History and nature
Spend the morning exploring lovely Castletown House at Celbridge ①, then continue to Donadea ③ for a meander through the tranquil woodlands of Donadea Forest Park.

Take the R403 from Celbridge toward Clane, then the R407 north and follow signs to Donadea Forest Park. Return along the same route.

Walking trails
Combine a stroll – or a boat trip – along the Grand Canal at Robertstown ④ with a walk up the Hill of Allen, for marvelous views. End the day with a music session.

Follow the route from Robertstown; turn right to the Hill after Barnacrow.

A day at the races
Walk around Kildare Town ⑤ and visit the National Stud ⑥ and The Curragh Racecourse ⑦ for a day of equine action *(see www.curragh.ie for the dates of races)*.

Follow the drive's instructions.

Eat and Drink: inexpensive, under €25; moderate, €25–€50; expensive, over €50

Valley of the Kings

Drogheda to the Hill of Tara

Highlights

- **Cistercian abbey**
  Trace the ruins of tranquil Mellifont Abbey, the first Cistercian monastery to be built in Ireland

- **Ancient tombs**
  Explore Brú na Bóinne, home to the extraordinary 5,000-year-old passage tomb at Newgrange

- **Norman castle**
  Visit Trim to see one of Ireland's most spectacular medieval castles, featured in the film *Braveheart*

- **Seat of the High Kings**
  Climb the Hill of Tara, a site of mythical importance as the political and spiritual center of Ireland

Mellifont Abbey's Romanesque ruins include this octagonal lavabo (washing chamber)

Valley of the Kings

The Boyne Valley is considered to be the cradle of Irish history and civilization. Among the remarkable heritage sites located in this rolling river valley are the medieval monastery of Monasterboice; the Boyne battlefield – setting for the most significant battle in Irish history; the world-famous Stone Age passage tombs of Newgrange; the Hill of Slane where St. Patrick proclaimed the arrival of Christianity, and the Hill of Tara where Ireland's ancient High Kings were crowned. Important in shaping the country's destiny, these ancient sites have become tranquil beauty spots, where history and legend meet.

Above Oldbridge House tells the dramatic story of the Battle of the Boyne, *see p159*

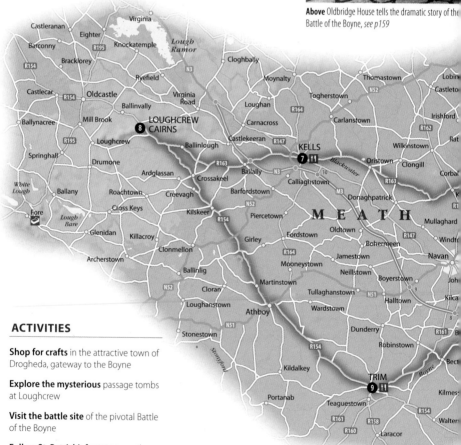

ACTIVITIES

Shop for crafts in the attractive town of Drogheda, gateway to the Boyne

Explore the mysterious passage tombs at Loughcrew

Visit the battle site of the pivotal Battle of the Boyne

Follow St. Patrick's footsteps on the Hill of Slane

Stroll beside the River Boyne at Trim, taking in the majestic castle and ruined abbeys on its banks

Above Trim on the banks of the Boyne. The ruined Belfry Tower on the left-hand side is one of several medieval monuments in the town, *see p161*

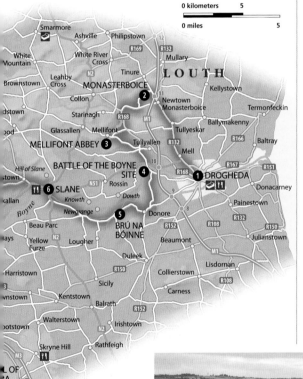

PLAN YOUR DRIVE

Start/finish: Drogheda to the Hill of Tara.

Number of days: 3.

Distance: 85 miles (137 km).

Road conditions: Some surfaces of minor roads are poor and uneven (for example, the road to Mellifont Abbey).

When to go: Most of the main sights on this drive are outdoors, so spring, summer, or autumn are preferable. Whatever the season, rain gear and comfortable walking shoes are a must.

Opening times: Most shops and attractions open 9 or 10am–5 or 6pm. Shops open Mon–Sat; in large towns also 12–6pm on Sun. Convenience stores in villages open 8am until late.

Main market days: Drogheda: Sat; Kells: Farmers' Market Sat am.

Major festivals: Drogheda: Arts Festival, Apr/May; Samba Festival, Jun; Loughcrew: Opera Festival, May/Jun; Trim: Swift Festival, Jul.

DAY TRIP OPTIONS

Visit three of Ireland's **best historical sights**, all within a short distance of each other. Those fascinated by Ireland's Celtic **High Crosses** and **round towers** should head for Monasterboice for impressive examples of both. Romantics can spend a day exploring the **medieval town** of Trim. For full details, *see p161*.

Below The area around Newgrange is dotted with underground passage tombs, *see p160*

KEY

 Drive route

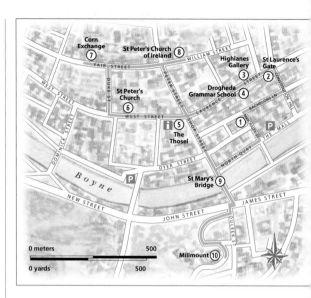

Below The lively and historic town of Drogheda viewed from Millmount

① Drogheda
Co Louth

Near the mouth of the River Boyne, Drogheda is one of Ireland's finest medieval towns and the gateway to the Boyne Valley. A mix of old and new, it has abundant history and color, with quiet lanes and busy shopping streets. High on a hill overlooking the town is Millmount, a former military complex that is now a museum – there are splendid panoramic views from its Martello tower.

A one-hour walking tour

Start at the corner of Mayoralty Street and Bachelor's Lane ①; turn right into Bachelor's Lane, then left onto Constitution Hill. At the top is **St. Laurence's Gate** ②, dating from 1234, the only surviving gate of an original 10. Walk left along Laurence Street to **Highlanes Gallery** ③ *(open daily, Sun pm only)*, once a Franciscan church and now an art gallery with works by eminent 20th-century Irish artists. Note the site of old **Drogheda Grammar School** ④, attended by the first Duke of Wellington.

At the intersection with Shop Street, **The Thosel** ⑤ is a pretty tower (1770) with a large four-sided clock. Cross over and walk ahead along West Street to Gothic **St. Peter's Church** ⑥, containing the preserved head of the Irish martyr St. Oliver Plunkett, Archbishop of Armagh. Turn right up Duke Street and left onto Fair Street, site of the old **Corn Exchange** ⑦. Return along Fair Street and cross over Peter Street into William Street. **St. Peter's Church of Ireland** ⑧ has a medieval font and ancient grave stones. From the church, turn left down Peter Street, becoming Shop Street, and cross the river at **St. Mary's Bridge** ⑨ for a view of the impressive Boyne Viaduct (1855), with its 18 arches. Across the road an alley leads up to **Millmount** ⑩, the 18th-century military barracks, now a museum *(open daily, Sun pm only)*. The Martello Tower (1808) is built over a Norman motte.

To return to the start, cross the bridge, turn right for North Quay and The Mall, and left to Mayoralty Street.

Leave Drogheda from South Quay, turn right for M1/Belfast. Cross the river, follow signs for R132. At the roundabout take R132 for Dunleer, follow for 3 miles (5 km). At the roundabout turn left, then after half a mile (1 km) turn left again to Monasterboice. Park by the round tower

Monasterboice
Drogheda, Co Louth

Founded by St. Buite in the 6th century, this monastic settlement is one of Ireland's most famous religious sites. It includes two churches and one of Ireland's tallest round towers at 110 ft (33 m) high, but its greatest treasure is the three 10th-century Celtic High Crosses. **Muiredach's Cross**, carved with biblical scenes, is the finest of its kind in Ireland.

Turn left from the parking lot and at the T-junction turn right. At the R168 turn left and then take the second right for Mellifont Abbey. Go over the small crossroads and into the parking lot.

Mellifont Abbey
Tullyallen, Drogheda, Co Louth

The first Cistercian abbey in Ireland, Mellifont *(open site)* was founded by St. Malachy, Archbishop of Armagh, in 1142. He introduced the formal style of architecture used in Europe, and Mellifont became a model for other Cistercian centers in Ireland. It is now a ruin, but it is possible to trace the original ground plan, including the octagonal lavabo (washing house) with four of its Romanesque arches intact. The visitor center *(open May–Sep daily)* has a display on medieval masonry.

Return to the main road, turn right (marked Newgrange), then turn right at the end of the road. At the crossroads, go straight over, down the hill, and over the main road. Cross the river, drive alongside the canal, and after a small bridge turn right for the Battle of the Boyne site at Oldbridge.

④ Battle of the Boyne site
Oldbridge Estate, Drogheda, Co Meath

Oldbridge, on the banks of the River Boyne, is the site of the most iconic battle in Irish history– the Battle of the Boyne in 1690 – between the Protestant King William of Orange and the deposed Catholic King James II of England, who sought to regain his Crown by enlisting Catholic support in Ireland. Over 61,000 troops took part. William's victory led to Protestant ascendancy in Ireland and became the source of bitter religious divisions for more than 300 years. The visitor center *(open daily)* in **Oldbridge House** has multimedia presentations, and living history displays take place on weekends in summer.

🚗 *Turn right on leaving Oldbridge and then right again for Donore village. In Donore, turn right for Newgrange. After 1 mile (2 km), turn right for Brú na Bóinne Visitor Centre.*

Above left A 12th-century Romanesque arch, Mellifont Abbey **Above** The entrance to the main burial chamber at Newgrange

SHOPPING IN DROGHEDA

As well as being a light and contemporary space for Drogheda's municipal art collection and temporary exhibitions, **Highlanes Gallery** also houses the **Louth Craftmark**, selling ceramics, jewelry, leatherware, candles, and textiles by over 50 craftworkers. **Millmount** incorporates a Design Store, which sells the work of a silversmith, knitwear designer, quilter, and glass designer who have studios in Millmount.

EAT AND DRINK IN DROGHEDA

Borzalino Restaurant *inexpensive*
Lively and popular pizzeria serving a variety of traditional Italian dishes.
20 Lough boy, Mell; 041 984 5444; closed Tue; www.borzalinorestaurant. com

Brú Bar Bistro *moderate*
This contemporary building beside the River Boyne has a good bistro on the ground floor and a stylish cocktail bar on the first floor. Its floor-to-ceiling windows offer great riverside views.
Unit 8, Haymarket Northbank; 041 987 2784; www.bru.ie

Eastern Seaboard Bar & Grill *moderate*
This restaurant serves up a mixture of traditional and modern cuisines. Dishes include grilled lamb chops, a wide range of salads, and *moules frites*.
Dublin Road; 041 980 2570; www.easternseaboard.ie

Above The River Boyne, near the site of the Battle of the Boyne of 1690

Eat and Drink: inexpensive, under €25; moderate, €25–€50; expensive, over €50

Above Slane Castle, where Irish rock band U2 recorded the *Unforgettable Fire* album

VISITING BRÚ NA BÓINNE

Access to Newgrange and Knowth is by guided tour only (2 hours), from the **Brú na Bóinne Visitor Centre** *(open daily; 041 988 0300; www. newgrange.com)*. There is no advance booking, so arrive early to be sure of a place on a tour, especially during the summer. There is no access to Dowth.

WHERE TO STAY

AROUND SLANE

Smarmore Castle *moderate*
Dating back more than 700 years, Smarmore has everything from towers to four-poster beds. A courtyard restaurant serves delicious Italian dishes made with fresh local produce. It is 9 miles (15 km) north of Slane, off the N2.
Smarmore, Ardee; 041 685 7167; www.smarmorecastle.com; closed mid-Dec–mid-Jan

AROUND LOUGHCREW CAIRNS

Hounslow House *inexpensive*
This large, relaxed farmhouse is around 10 miles (16 km) west of Kells, on the R195 south of the cairns, and has lovely views down to the Fore Valley. Visitors are greeted with tea and home baking.
Fore, Castlepollard; 044 966 1144; http://hounslowhouse.com; open Apr–Sep only

AROUND HILL OF TARA

Bellinter House *moderate*
An elegant and comfortable Georgian country house in extensive grounds a mile (2 km) from the Hill of Tara. Restaurant, pool, and spa.
Bellinter, Navan; 046 903 0900; www.bellinterhouse.com

⑤ Brú na Bóinne
Donore, Co Meath
This incredible archeological landscape, comprising Newgrange, Dowth, and Knowth, is a UNESCO World Heritage Site. As well as its famous prehistoric passage tombs, it has 49 burial mounds and many other examples of megalithic art. The focal point is **Newgrange**, a passage tomb and temple dating back to 5000 BC. It is supported by 97 large curbstones, including an elaborately carved stone in front of the entrance. Inside the mound, a 60-ft (19-m) long passage leads to a cross-shaped chamber which is penetrated by sunlight during the winter solstice.

🚗 *Leaving Brú na Bóinne, turn right. After 1 mile (2 km), look to the right for a view of the outside of the Newgrange mound. At the next Y-junction, turn right for Slane/N2, then right again for Slane.*

⑥ Slane
Co Meath
The village of Slane has many attractive features including a bridge over the River Boyne and fine 18th-century buildings. **Slane Castle** *(open Jun–Aug: Sun–Thu pm)* can be viewed on a guided tour. Highlights include the Neo-Gothic ballroom, hallway, and bedrooms. Rock concerts are often staged in the Capability Brown grounds, where U2 recorded the *Unforgettable Fire* album.

Head up to the **Hill of Slane**, just north of the village. It was here that St. Patrick, Ireland's patron saint, is reputed to have lit a Paschal (Easter) fire as a challenge to the pagan High King, symbolizing Christianity's triumph over paganism.

🚗 *From Slane, drive down the hill and turn right onto the N51. After a few kilometers turn right onto the R163 for Kells and take the next left. At the junction in Kilberry turn right, then left to stay on the R163.*

⑦ Kells
Co Meath
A center of Christian settlement since the earliest years of Christianity in Ireland, Kells is famous for the *Book of Kells*, an illuminated manuscript produced by the monks of **Kells Monastery** in around 800. The original is in Trinity College, Dublin

(see pp150–51), but there is a copy in **Kells' Heritage Centre** *(open daily, Sun pm only)*. The monastery also has a 82-ft (25-m) high round tower surrounded by carved High Crosses. Just outside the Heritage Centre is the **Market Cross**, dating from the 9th century and used as a gallows during the 1798 uprising.

🚗 *Drive up through the town and turn left and then right into Cannon Street for the round tower. Take the R163 for Loughcrew (marked Oldcastle). After 9 miles (15 km) turn right for Loughcrew Passage Tombs.*

⑧ Loughcrew Cairns
Loughcrew, Oldcastle, Co Meath
This group of 25 passage tombs, spread over three hills, dates from around 3000 BC. According to one legend, they were created by a witch, hence the Irish name *Slieve na Calliagh* (Mountain of the Witch) for the highest hill. To enter Cairn T, Loughcrew's largest passage tomb, pick up the key from the visitor center at **Loughcrew Gardens** *(open mid-Mar–Sep: daily; Oct–mid-Mar: Sun only; call in advance; 049 854 1060; www.loughcrew com)*, half a mile (1 km) further along the Oldcastle road. Take a torch and prepare for a steep walk up to the cairns from the parking lot. The gardens are known for their yew walk.

🚗 *From Loughcrew, drive back along R163 and turn right onto R154, following signs for Trim through Athboy. In Trim, park at the visitor center near the castle.*

Above The round tower and one of several High Crosses on the grounds of Kells Monastery

9 Trim
Co Meath

This pretty, historical town hugs the River Boyne and is dominated by **Trim Castle** *(open Easter–Oct daily; Nov–Easter weekends only)*, Ireland's largest Anglo-Norman castle, founded by Hugh de Lacy in 1173. Extensively restored, the castle is a breathtaking sight and was used as the set for the 1995 film *Braveheart.*

Across the Millennium footbridge over the Boyne stands the **Belfry Tower** (125 ft/38 m high), which is also known as the Yellow Steeple. Built in 1368 for the original Augustinian Abbey, it later served as a watchtower. Beside the steeple is **Talbot Castle** or St. Mary's Abbey, built in 1415 over the original abbey. In the 18th century, it became an exclusive Protestant school. **Sheep Gate** is the last surviving gateway of the medieval town, and further east along the river are the remains of the 13th-century Gothic cathedral, **Newtown Abbey**.

St. Peter's Bridge, thought to be the second oldest bridge in Ireland, leads to the ruins of the **Hospital of St. John the Baptist**, founded by monks in the 13th century.

Trim Visitor Centre *(open Mon–Sat; Sun pm only)* is on Castle Street. Nearby **St. Patrick's Cathedral** on Loman Street is built on the site of a medieval church reputedly founded by St. Patrick. The stained glass in the west window is the first ever designed by Pre-Raphaelite artist Edward Burne-Jones.

🚗 *Take R154 (for Athboy), then turn right onto R161. After 3 miles (5 km), turn right at the crossroads for Bective. About half a mile (1 km) past the abbey turn left, then right after another 3 miles (5 km), and left after a further half a mile (1 km). Turn right for the Hill of Tara after 750 yards (700 m).*

10 Hill of Tara
Co Meath

The **Hill of Tara** *(guided tours May–Sep daily)* was, according to tradition, the seat of Ireland's High Kings, who ruled until the Norman takeover in the 12th century. Some 142 kings were supposedly crowned here. The tour explains the myths and legends around the hilltop enclosure and its Stone of Destiny, said to cry out when touched by the new king. The hill offers outstanding views and it is said that on a clear day 23 of Ireland's 32 counties can be seen from here.

Above left Cairn T, Loughcrew's largest cairn
Above center View of Trim across the Boyne
Above right Ruins of 12th-century Bective Abbey, visible on the way to the Hill of Tara

EAT AND DRINK

SLANE

The Poet's Rest *moderate*
Customers cook their own steak and seafood at their table at this unique restaurant.
Chapel Street; 041 982 0738

KELLS

The Ground Floor Restaurant *moderate*
Colorful paintings, tasty daily specials, and a central location keep this place buzzing.
Bective Square; 046 924 9688

TRIM

Marcie Regan's
Well-known pub beside one of the oldest bridges in the country. Traditional music on Friday evenings.
Lackanash Rd, Newtown; no phone; open from 9pm, closed Wed

HILL OF TARA

O'Connells Pub
Characterful pub in tiny village.
Skryne Hill, near Tara; 046 902 5122; open from 4pm, Sun also lunch

---

DAY TRIP OPTIONS
Drogheda is a good base for these excursions into the Boyne Valley.

Historical trio
Combine three sites charting key periods in Ireland's history – the Battle of the Boyne site ④, the passage tombs at Brú na Bóinne ⑤ and the Hill of Slane ⑥, where St. Patrick challenged the High Kings.

Take R132, then N51 to the Boyne battle site. Next follow the drive instructions to Brú na Bóinne, then on to Slane, and return to Drogheda on the N51.

High Crosses and round towers
Monasterboice ② has one of Ireland's tallest round towers and its finest High Cross: 18 ft (5.5 m) high and richly carved with biblical scenes.

Follow drive instructions there and back.

Medieval Trim
Explore Trim's ⑨ splendid medieval churches, castle, and monastic hospital.

Take R132 and N51 to Navan, then R161 to Trim. Retrace route to Drogheda.

Eat and Drink: inexpensive, under €25; moderate, €25–€50; expensive, over €50

Heart of the Lakelands

Athlone to Strokestown Park House

Highlights

- **Spiritual Clonmacnoise**
  Experience the ethereal beauty of this great 6th-century religious site

- **Scenic walks**
  Hike into the foothills and forests of the Slieve Bloom Mountains in the south of the region

- **Ancient peat bogs**
  Discover the magic of the bogs, their flora and fauna and the archeological remains preserved within them

- **Stately homes and gardens**
  Explore the grounds of Birr Castle Demesne, Belvedere House, and Strokestown Park House

The round tower at Clonmacnoise, overlooking the tranquil Shannon

Heart of the Lakelands

Though often overlooked by visitors to Ireland, the Lakelands has plenty of history, scenery, and character, its special highlight being the medieval monastic settlement of Clonmacnoise, a European center of trade and learning founded in 545. It also has bustling heritage towns containing age-old whiskey distilleries, Norman castles, and grand Georgian estates. Its landscapes include ancient boglands, rich in wildlife and archeological finds, and the Slieve Bloom Mountains, undulating wooded hills crisscrossed with hiking trails.

Above The Jealous Wall, a folly with an intriguing history, in the grounds of Belvedere House, *see pp168–9*

ACTIVITIES

Take a boat trip from Athlone and listen to tales of Nordic valor

Explore seven ruined temples at the ancient monastic complex of Clonmacnoise

See the Great Telescope in the grounds of Birr Castle

Tour haunted corridors at Charleville Forest Castle, near Tullamore

Taste fine Irish whiskey at Tullamore Dew Visitor Centre

Stroll down the longest herbaceous border in all of Britain and Ireland in the grounds of Strokestown Park House

KEY

⬭ Drive route

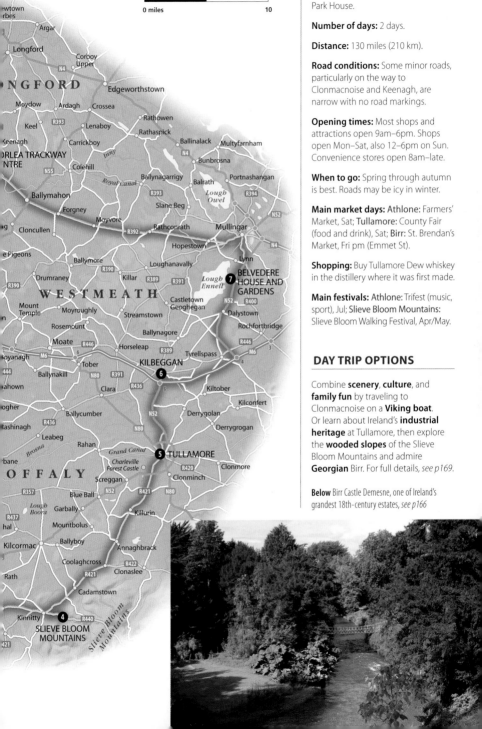

0 kilometers 10

0 miles 10

PLAN YOUR DRIVE

Start/finish: Athlone to Strokestown Park House.

Number of days: 2 days.

Distance: 130 miles (210 km).

Road conditions: Some minor roads, particularly on the way to Clonmacnoise and Keenagh, are narrow with no road markings.

Opening times: Most shops and attractions open 9am–6pm. Shops open Mon–Sat, also 12–6pm on Sun. Convenience stores open 8am–late.

When to go: Spring through autumn is best. Roads may be icy in winter.

Main market days: Athlone: Farmers' Market, Sat; **Tullamore:** County Fair (food and drink), Sat; **Birr:** St. Brendan's Market, Fri pm (Emmet St).

Shopping: Buy Tullamore Dew whiskey in the distillery where it was first made.

Main festivals: Athlone: Trifest (music, sport), Jul; **Slieve Bloom Mountains:** Slieve Bloom Walking Festival, Apr/May.

DAY TRIP OPTIONS

Combine **scenery**, **culture**, and **family fun** by traveling to Clonmacnoise on a **Viking boat**. Or learn about Ireland's **industrial heritage** at Tullamore, then explore the **wooded slopes** of the Slieve Bloom Mountains and admire **Georgian** Birr. For full details, *see p169.*

Below Birr Castle Demesne, one of Ireland's grandest 18th-century estates, *see p166*

Right The Grand Canal, a tranquil waterway that crosses County Offaly

WHERE TO STAY

ATHLONE

Bastion Townhouse *inexpensive*
A former draper's shop, this charming townhouse offers simple rooms and buffet breakfasts.
2 Bastion St; 090 649 4954;
www.thebastion.net

AROUND ATHLONE

Wineport Lodge *moderate–expensive*
Lodge on Lough Ree with good food, lake views, and a rooftop hot-tub. From Athlone, take the N55 to Ballykeeran and fork left at the Dog & Duck pub.
Glasson, Athlone; 090 643 9010;
www.wineport.ie

BIRR

Townsend House *inexpensive*
Guesthouse in a 19th-century townhouse in the center of Birr.
Townsend St; 057 912 1276;
www.townsendhouseguesthouse.com

AROUND BIRR

Charlotte's Way *inexpensive*
This restored 17th-century townhouse on Banagher Hill in the Lakelands, has associations with 19th-century writer Charlotte Brontë, who stayed here and whose husband lived here after her death. There are great views of the surrounding countryside.
The Hill, Banagher (take R439 from Birr), Co Offaly; 057 915 3864;
www.charlottesway.com

Below The terraced gardens at Birr Castle
Below right Clonmacnoise's 9th-century round tower on the banks of the Shannon

① Athlone
Co Westmeath
Situated on a ford on the River Shannon, **Athlone Castle** *(open Easter–Sep)* was built in 1210 for King John of England. An important military barracks, it twice came under siege from Williamite troops after the Battle of the Boyne *(see page 159)*, falling in the second siege of 1691.

Athlone is a departure point for boat trips on the Shannon and Lough Ree. The company Adventure Viking Cruise offers boat trips to Clonmacnoise aboard a Viking-style boat, accompanied by tales of Viking battles and buried treasure.

🚗 *From Athlone, take the N6 (Dublin) road and then the N62 toward Birr. At Ballynahown, turn right onto the R444 to Clonmacnoise.*

② Clonmacnoise
Shannonbridge, Co Offaly
Founded by St. Ciarán around AD 549, this monastic complex *(open daily)* lies on an important medieval crossroads. With the Shannon flowing north–south and a glacial ridge forming the main road east–west, it became a hub of scholarship and trade, and many kings of Tara and of Connaught were buried here. Plundered by Vikings and Anglo-Normans, it was finally devastated by the English in 1552.

The ruins comprise two **round towers**, a **cathedral**, and seven **churches** (temples). Look for the carvings of saints Francis, Patrick, and Dominic above the cathedral's north doorway, known as the **Whispering Door** on account of its acoustics. The **visitor center** contains early grave slabs and crosses, including the **Cross of the Scriptures**, a 9th-century high cross carved with biblical scenes.

🚗 *Take the R444 to Shannonbridge and then turn left onto the R357 to Cloghan. Here, turn right onto the N62 for Birr. The entrance to Birr Castle Demesne is in the center of Birr.*

③ Birr
Co Offaly
This handsome estate town retains its original Georgian layout and architectural details. **Birr Castle Demesne** *(open daily)*, seat of the Earls of Rosse, is famous for its gardens and grounds, containing 5 miles (8 km) of footpaths and thousands of rare trees and plants. Also in the grounds are the **Great Telescope**, the largest in the world when it was built in the 1840s, and the **Historic Science Centre**, devoted to engineering, astronomy, botany, and photography, passions of the 19th-century earls.

🚗 *From Birr, take the R440 to Kinnitty. Drive 2 miles (3 km) beyond Kinnitty for the entrance to Kinnitty Forest in the Slieve Bloom Mountains.*

④ Slieve Bloom Mountains
Co Westmeath

The Slieve Bloom Mountains rise unexpectedly from the flat landscape of Offaly. Crisscrossed with walking trails and dotted with picnic areas and viewpoints, they include blanket boglands, forests, and farmland, and are rich in wildlife. Kinnitty Forest offers a variety of signposted walks from the entrance in the northern foothills.

Above Kinnitty Castle, a Gothic Revival mansion in Kinnitty Forest

A two- to three-hour walk in Kinnitty Forest

From the **parking lot** ① at the entrance, follow the path into the forest. At the Y-junction keep left, following the Glinsk Castle Loop Walk, the trail marked with the blue arrow (the green arrow is for the shorter Kinnitty Castle Loop and the yellow arrow marks the Slieve Bloom Way, a 52-mile/84-km loop). After about half a mile (1 km), the trail reaches a three-way junction with a wooden gate to the left. Pass through the gate and into the grounds of **Kinnitty Castle** ②, a Gothic Revival castle in extensive parkland, for a long time run as a luxury hotel.

Returning to the gate, follow the trail right, walking uphill along a forest track for half a mile (1 km) to a right bend and then to a Y-junction. Keep right, following the green and blue arrows.

Turn left after a short distance, heading uphill through mature woodland, following the blue arrow and the Slieve Bloom Way.

On reaching a forestry road, turn right and after 656 ft (200 m) turn left at a three-way junction, veering left almost immediately afterwards, still following the Slieve Bloom Way.

Climb the hill and turn right at the track junction. After another 1,968 ft (600 m) leave the Slieve Bloom Way and turn right onto a woodland trail leading to **Glinsk Castle** ③, now little more than stone pillars and walls.

Follow the trail through the pillars and over the hill, and keep on downhill through the trees, rejoining the Slieve Bloom Way at a forest track. Turn right here and, after a short distance, turn left onto a forestry trail. Follow the track downhill, through mature trees, and cross two forestry tracks back to the starting point.

🔲 *Return to Kinnitty and turn right onto the R421 for Tullamore, passing through Cadamstown.*

The stables at Kinnitty Castle

VISITING ATHLONE

Parking
Plentiful pay-and-display on-street parking is available.

Tourist Information
Athlone Castle; 090 649 4630; open Easter–Oct

River Cruises
Adventure Viking Cruise, 7 St Mary's Place; 090 647 3383

EAT AND DRINK IN ATHLONE

Sean's Bar *inexpensive*
Dating back to 900 AD, this is the oldest pub in Ireland. It has a cozy atmosphere and lots of interesting features, including a sloping floor in case of flooding from the river. *13 Main St; 090 649 2358; www.seansbar.ie*

The Olive Grove *moderate*
A vibrant restaurant on the banks of the River Shannon right in the heart of Athlone. Great views of the castle, and tasty modern, European food. *Custume Pier; 090 647 6946; www.theolivegrove.ie*

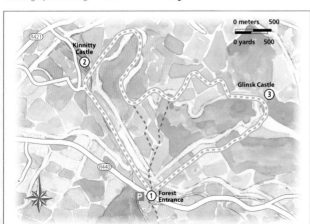

Eat and Drink: inexpensive, under €25; moderate, €25–€50; expensive, over €50

Above left Iron-studded portal, Charleville Forest Castle **Above right** Gothic-style crenellations, Charleville Forest Castle

⑤ Tullamore
Co Offaly

On the outskirts of Tullamore, a gate lodge on the left marks the entrance to **Charleville Forest Castle**, a Gothic-style mansion that is said to be haunted. Ring the bell for guided tours *(on the hour in summer; pre-book by email the rest of the year: info@ charlevillecastle.com)*.

This Lakelands town is also the birthplace of Tullamore Dew Irish whiskey. The **Tullamore Dew Visitor Centre** *(open daily)* on Bury Quay (in the center of town) offers guided tours and tastings in the old distillery buildings. It also explains the role played by the Grand Canal, running alongside the distillery and connecting Tullamore with Dublin.

🚗 *Take the N52 north to Kilbeggan. Locke's Distillery is in the center.*

⑥ Kilbeggan
Co Westmeath

Established in 1757, **Locke's Distillery** *(open daily)* in Kilbeggan is thought to be the oldest pot-still distillery in the world. Harnessing local resources – pure water, grain, and turf (used for power), it produced malt whiskey for 200 years until, unable to compete with Scottish whiskey manufacturers, it went bankrupt in 1954. The aroma of whiskey – the small percentage that evaporates from the barrels as it matures and is known as the angels' share – hung around for years. The distillery museum now offers guided tours of the grain grinding and casking equipment and the steam engine and waterwheel that powered the mill.

🚗 *Take the M6 toward Mullingar. At Tyrellspass, turn left onto the N52 for Mullingar. Belvedere House is on the left, 3 miles (5 km) before Mullingar.*

⑦ Belvedere House and Gardens
Mullingar, Co Westmeath

The Palladian villa *(open daily)*, built in 1740 by Richard Castle for the Earl of Belvedere, is set in extensive grounds beside Lough Ennell. The interior is known for its Rococo plasterwork,

---

Peat Bogs

The Lakelands has an abundance of peat bogs, formed up to 10,000 years ago from compressed vegetation in waterlogged ground. Some have yielded amazing archeological finds, such as the Corlea Trackway. Long harvested for fuel, some are now protected habitats for flora and fauna.

WHERE TO STAY AROUND STROKESTOWN PARK HOUSE

Gleesons Townhouse *moderate*
Pretty 19th-century townhouse in the center of Roscommon, with a popular restaurant and café. Situated 12 miles (20 km) south of Strokestown (take the R368 south and turn left at the junction with the N61).
Market Square, Roscommon; 090 662 6954; www.gleesonstownhouse.com

Castlecoote House
moderate–expensive
Romantic and luxurious Georgian house with four-poster beds, roll-top baths, tennis courts, a croquet lawn, and an orchard. Situated 17 miles (28 km) southwest of Strokestown.
Castlecoote, Co Roscommon; 090 666 3794; www.castlecootehouse.com; closed Nov–mid-Apr

Right Copper pot-still at Locke's Distillery, Kilbeggan, established in 1757

Where to Stay: inexpensive, under €100; moderate, €100–€200; expensive, over €200

while exterior highlights include a Victorian walled garden and the Jealous Wall folly – built to block the view of a more opulent mansion belonging to the Earl's brother. The Earl believed his brother was conducting an affair with his wife, whom he punished by imprisoning in her own home for 31 years.

🚗 *From Belvedere, take the R400 to Mullingar and then the R392 to Ballymahon. Corlea is 4 miles (6 km) after Ballymahon. The Corlea Trackway Centre is to the right.*

8 Corlea Trackway Centre
Keenagh, Co Longford
An Iron Age timber bog road believed to have been constructed in 148 BC, the Corlea Trackway is the largest example of its kind to be uncovered in Europe. Its remarkable state of preservation is due to the anaerobic conditions of the bog in which it eventually sank. The Centre *(open Apr–Sep)* has a 60-ft (18-m) stretch of road on display.

🚗 *From Corlea, turn right onto the R392, taking the R371 for Strokestown after Lanesborough and then turning left at the N5. At the roundabout take the third exit onto Bawn Street and drive into Strokestown Park House.*

9 Strokestown Park House
Strokestown, Co Roscommon
The splendid Palladian mansion of **Strokestown Park House** *(open mid-Mar–Oct)*, the finest in County Roscommon, was built in the 1730s. The original furnishings can be seen on guided tours of the interior, while the stable block houses the **Famine Museum**, telling the story of the 1840s Great Famine through documents of the time. The **Garden** includes the longest herbaceous border in Britain and Ireland, and a Georgian fruit and vegetable garden.

Above The gently rolling parkland surrounding Belvedere House

Above left Pergola over the long herbaceous border in Strokestown Park Gardens
Above Strokestown Park House, the finest Palladian mansion in Co Roscommon

EAT AND DRINK AROUND STROKESTOWN PARK HOUSE

Keenans *moderate*
Modern restaurant built onto a traditional bar in the tiny village of Termonbarry on the River Shannon, 8 miles (13 km) along the N5 east of Strokestown. Serves good modern European dishes.
Termonbarry, Co Roscommon; 043 332 6098; www.keenans.ie

The Purple Onion *moderate*
Good food using locally sourced ingredients, and cozy booths for discreet dining. There is also an art gallery above the bar. In Termonbarry, 8 miles (13 km) east of Strokestown.
Termonbarry, Co Roscommon; 043 335 9919; www.purpleonion.ie

DAY TRIP OPTIONS
Athlone is an ideal base from which to visit the religious and historic sites of the Lakelands.

The Shannon river
From Athlone ❶, follow the Shannon to Clonmacnoise ❷, an important monastic site, bristling with crosses, a round tower, and churches. One of the nicest ways of getting there is on a Viking-wstyle boat. Trips depart from Athlone.
Take a boat from Athlone or follow the drive instructions.

Look and learn
Find out about the industrial history of the Lakelands in Tullamore ❺, then drive to Kinnitty for a walk in the Slieve Bloom Mountains ❹. Next, head to Georgian Birr ❸ and Birr Castle Demesne with its Historic Science Centre and Great Telescope.
From Athlone, take the M6/N52 to Tullamore, then the R421 to the Slieve Bloom Mountains. Take the R440 to Birr, returning to Athlone on the N62.

Eat and Drink: inexpensive, under €25; moderate, €25–€50; expensive, over €50

Connemara and its Loughs

Clifden to Cong

Highlights

- **Bustling Clifden**
  Stroll around the delightful harbor town and "capital" of Connemara

- **Coastal beauty**
  Explore the glorious coastline and take a boat out to Inishbofin Island

- **Mountain valleys**
  Experience the magical atmosphere and sublime beauty of empty valleys and mountain passes

- **Lakeland splendor**
  Drive around, swim in, or picnic on the shores of the some the largest and most spectacular loughs in Ireland

View across the vast expanse of Lough Mask from Mauntrasna

Connemara and its Loughs

It is said that "for every star God put in the sky, he laid a million stones on Connemara." An exaggeration, yes, but this rocky, mostly treeless terrain is part of what makes up the enigmatic beauty of the region. This drive takes on several facets of Connemara: the bog-mantled moorland and sea-bitten western coastline around Clifden; the dramatic, mountainous landscapes of the north; and, to the southeast, a place of tranquil, watery vistas – for all this wild and hilly terrain drains into some of the most beautiful and majestic loughs in Ireland.

ACTIVITIES

Try some of the finest seafood in the vibrant fishing port of Clifden

Take an exhilarating drive along the Sky Road to the western tip of Connemara

Walk around lovely Diamond Hill in the Connemara National Park

Go on a boat trip out into fjord-like Killary Harbour, or to Inishbofin Island, a center for traditional Irish music

Picnic, swim, walk, or drive along the shores of any of the region's lovely loughs

Below River valley at Delphi, named after Grecian Delphi by the Marquis of Sligo, see p177

KEY

🔲 Drive route

PLAN YOUR DRIVE

Start/finish: Clifden to Cong.

Number of days: 3–4.

Distance: 137 miles (220 km).

Road conditions: Roads are generally in good condition, well paved and marked. Mountain passes are steep and winding, so take extra care.

When to go: March to October is the best time for good weather on the coast and lakes, and in the mountains.

Opening times: Most shops and attractions open 9 or 10am–5 or 6pm. Shops open Mon–Sat; in large towns also 12–6pm on Sun. Convenience stores in villages open 8am until late.

Main market days: Inishbofin: Farmers' Market, Mon pm.

Shopping: Connemara is famous for its fine tweed and green marble.

Major festivals: Clifden: Arts Week, Sep; Connemara Pony Show, Aug; **Omey Island:** Omey Races, Jul/Aug; **Inishbofin:** Arts Festival, May; **Around Connemara:** Connemara Walking Festival, Mar; **Leenane:** Curragh Racing, Jun.

DAY TRIP OPTIONS

For **a taste of traditional Irish life** visit Inishbofin Island, or **to explore Irish history** visit the poignant Doolough and Delphi valleys. To experience the **Connemara lakelands**, spend a day driving along the shores of four loughs. For full details, see p179.

Below left Stately Ashford Castle in Cong, on the shores of Lough Corrib, see p179 **Below** View of Lough Corrib from Cornamona, see p179

0 kilometers 6

0 miles 6

Above Clifden, nestled below the imposing Twelve Bens range

VISITING CLIFDEN

Parking
There is a free public parking lot immediately behind the Tourist Office.

Tourist Information
Galway Road; 095 21163; www.discover ireland.ie/connemara; open Mar–Oct

Shopping
Whitethorn Gallery on Galway Road showcases local artists. **O'Dalaigh Jewellers** on Main Street *(www. celticimpressions.com)* sells Celtic-inspired jewelry. **Millars** on Main Street stocks Irish fashion designers.

VISITING INISHBOFIN ISLAND

Inishbofin Island Discovery makes the 30-minute crossing from Cleggan at least once daily all year *(095 44878; www.inishbofinislanddiscovery.com)*.

WHERE TO STAY IN CLIFDEN

Foyle's Hotel *inexpensive*
Old-fashioned, quirky hotel run by the Foyle family for generations. Attached is Marconi's seafood restaurant.
Main St; 095 21801;
www.foyleshotel.com

The Quay House *moderate*
A charming, award-winning guest-house with views across the water. Once the harbor master's residence, this is the oldest building in Clifden.
Clifden Harbour; 095 21369;
www.thequayhouse.com

Abbeyglen Castle Hotel *expensive*
A 10-minute walk from the center of town. Views over the Bay and Twelve Bens Mountains and gourmet dining at the hotel restaurant.
Sky Road; 095 21201; www.abbeyglen.ie

❶ Clifden
Co Galway

Situated on a hillside between the Twelve Bens mountain range and the Atlantic, and nestling at the head of a broad bay, Clifden (An Clochán) is blessed with a wonderful setting. Compact and picturesque, it is Connemara's largest town and effectively its capital. It was founded in the early 19th century by John D'Arcy, a Galway sheriff, and still retains much of its Georgian architecture. Boasting a healthy number of good restaurants, pubs and shops, and a bustling atmosphere, this vibrant town deserves more than a cursory glance.

A one-hour walking tour

Begin the walk at the **Tourist Office** ①. Turn uphill on Galway Road and then right into Westport Road and right again, where Clifden's Catholic **Church of St. Joseph** ② can be seen. It is from the site of this church that Clifden derives its name, built as it was upon the site of an early Christian monastic beehive hut or *cloghan*. Turn left up Church Hill and, a little further up on the left, the Protestant **Christ Church** ③, built in 1820, holds a silver replica of the Cross of Cong *(see p179)* and has better views than St. Joseph's. Carry on along Church Hill, which becomes the beginning of the **Sky Road** ④. From this vantage point visitors can look down and fully appreciate Clifden's majestic setting, with the lofty spires of its churches elegantly set against the looming presence of the Twelve Bens. Continue on Sky Road past the Abbeyglen Castle. A path to the left is the start of a steep, 15-minute climb up to the **D'Arcy Monument** ⑤, which offers spectacular views.

Return by the same route until reaching a right turn down Church Street to Main St and Market Square. **Mullarkey's Bar** ⑥, at the back of Foyle's on the square, often has evening open mic sessions with an eclectic range of music, from Irish traditional to modern folk. From Market Square, follow Beach Road down to the pretty **Harbour** ⑦ – one of Ireland's safest. Look back for a good view of the town and its twin spires. Return to Market Square and turn right down Market Street, lined with interesting shops, restaurants, bars, and pubs including **Lowry's** ⑧, another great place to catch live music. Turn left onto Bridge Street and then right back onto Galway Road. Next to the Tourist Office, don't miss the **Station House Museum** ⑨ *(open May–Oct: daily)* whose varied exhibitions tell the tale of aviators Alcock and Brown – who ended their transatlantic flight near here in 1919 – and the Connemara pony.

🚗 *From the tourist office parking lot, turn right up Wesport Road, left up Church Hill, and follow Sky Road signs.*

Below View across the green countryside of the Sky Road toward Cleggan

Where to Stay: inexpensive, under €100; moderate, €100–€200; expensive, over €200

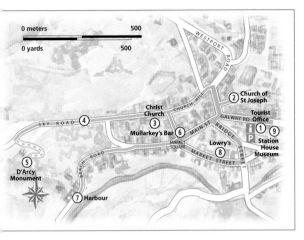

Above Ferry to Inishbofin Island from Cleggan Harbour near Claddaghduff

② Sky Road
Co Galway

A rollercoaster of a drive skirting the northern flank of Streamstown Bay, at its summit the Sky Road reaches a height of 500 ft (152 m), affording breathtaking sea views across the islands of Turbot and Inishturk. At the top there is a lay-by, ideal for pausing to take in the sweeping views. Follow the road back to the N59 and turn left, then take the next left, toward **Claddaghduff**. Having safely descended again to sea level at this little village, there may be time to unwind with a drink while waiting for the tide to recede, making it possible to cross the causeway to Omey Island.

🚗 *Drive across the short, sandy causeway via Star of the Sea Church at low tide, following the markers with great care.*

③ Omey Island
Co Galway

For one day each year, in August, this peaceful spot becomes the center of attention, for the Omey Races, and the beach makes a spectacular setting for a horse race. The rest of the year, the most important site is a 6th-century monastic graveyard and a holy well and chapel dedicated to St. Fechin. In the center of the island is the reedy **Fahy Lough**, around which there are good walking and birdwatching opportunities. Keep an eye on the time, though, in order not to misjudge the tide, which would mean an enforced wait of six hours.

🚗 *From Claddaghduff it is a half-mile (1-km) drive north to Cleggan Harbour for ferries to Inishbofin Island.*

④ Inishbofin Island
Co Galway

Inishbofin is a small island with cliffs and sandy beaches, blessed with crystal-clear waters great for swimming, snorkeling and excellent shore angling. At the island's center is peaceful **Lough Boffin**, home to a range of wading and migrant birds; on its western side are rocky outcrops known as "The Stags," with impressive sea stacks and blow-holes.

Inishbofin ("island of the white cow") is also a center for traditional Irish music. As well as having its own famous *ceilidh* band, the island plays host to visiting musicians and artists. The shell of a 14th-century chapel – the last vestiges of a monastic settlement established by St. Colman in the 7th century – and the remains of a Cromwellian barracks, used to house captured Catholic clergy from all over the country, can be visited too. Near the pier is the small but interesting **Heritage Museum**, dedicated to island history and life.

🚗 *From Cleggan, drive southeast on the R379 to the N59. Turn left onto the N59 to Letterfrack for access to the Connemara National Park.*

Rollercoaster Sky Road

EAT AND DRINK

CLIFDEN

Cullens Café Bistro *inexpensive*
Simple dishes prepared extremely well. This is a lovely restaurant with a cozy, welcoming ambience, offering very good value.
Market Street

Connemara Hamper *moderate*
This deli is perfect when stocking up for a picnic, with a superb range of cheeses and cold meats. It specializes in local produce such as Connemara smoked salmon and artisan chocolates.
Main Street, Clifden; closed Sun; www.connemarahamper.com

Mitchell's Restaurant
moderate–expensive
Clifden's premier eating-place; a great dining experience with beautifully presented food. The menu is especially strong on seafood dishes. Good value lunchtime menu.
Market Street; 095 21867

AROUND INISHBOFIN ISLAND

Oliver's Seafood Bar and Restaurant
inexpensive–moderate
Overlooking the harbor in Cleggan, Oliver's is a handy spot for a quick bite while waiting for the ferry to Inishbofin. Unsurprisingly, it specializes in fish and seafood – particularly flatfish, Connemara smoked salmon, and Cleggan scallops. The bar serves local oysters. Also has six ensuite rooms.
Cleggan Harbour; 095 44640; www.oliversbar.com

Eat and Drink: inexpensive, under €25; moderate, €25–€50; expensive, over €50

Above Diamond Hill, in Connemara National Park, seen from the Visitor Centre

VISITING CONNEMARA NATIONAL PARK

Parking
Park at the National Park Visitor Centre.

National Park Visitor Centre
Letterfrack, Co Galway; 095 41323; www.connemaranationalpark.ie; open Mar–Oct daily

Shopping
Cottage Handcrafts at Moyard by park entrance stocks green marble, tweeds, and knits.

VISITING KILLARY HARBOUR AND LEENANE

Killary Harbour Boat Trips
Cruises up the fjord depart several times daily Apr–Oct.
Leenane, Co Galway; 091 566 736; www.killarycruises.com

WHERE TO STAY

KILLARY HARBOUR AND LEENANE

Leenane Hotel *moderate*
A former coaching station, this family-run hotel offers beautiful views over Killary Harbour. Now refurbished, it retains its old-world character and has a warm, welcoming ambience.
Clifden Road; closed mid-Nov to mid-Mar; 095 42249; www.leenanehotel.com

DELPHI VALLEY

Delphi Lodge *expensive*
Set in a beautiful secluded location on the shores of Lough Finny and facing the graceful slopes of the Mweelrea mountains, the lodge also offers superb dining in the evening around a communal table.
Delphi Valley; closed mid-Oct to mid-Feb; 095 42222; www.delphilodge.ie

⑤ Connemara National Park
Co Galway
This protected parkland spreads over 6,000 acres (3,000 ha) of mountains, bogs, heaths, and grasslands. The 19th-century Quaker-founded village of **Letterfrack** offers the best access to the park, and is a good opportunity for visitors to leave the car for a while and experience at first hand the unique terrain of Connemara. The excellent **Visitor Centre** *(open mid-Mar–mid-Oct)* provides general information on fauna and wildlife in the park, and maps of the walking trails. One of the best is the circular **Diamond Hill Walk** which offers rewarding views of Kylemore Abbey and its surrounding bays and mountains. It is a looped walk taking about 2–3 hours. For something less strenuous and shorter, there are also three less demanding trails that skirt the lower slopes of Diamond Hill. All routes are clearly marked. Along the way, walkers may well glimpse red deer and Connemara ponies, and hear a wide variety of songbirds.

🚗 *From Letterfrack, continue east on the N59, along the shores of Lake Pollacappull, to Kylemore Abbey.*

⑥ Kylemore Abbey
Co Galway
One of the most photographed vistas in Connemara is from the shores of Lake Pollacappull. Across this tranquil stretch of water, nestling at the foot of Duchruach Hill, is the castellated form of **Kylemore Abbey** *(open daily)*.

Below Spectacular Kylemore Abbey, perched on the shoreline of Lake Pollacappull

Built in the 19th century, since 1922 the abbey has been home to a semi-enclosed order of Benedictine nuns who, until recently, ran a boarding school for girls. Part of the abbey is open to visitors, who can view the dining rooms, library, and main hall. The visitor center recounts the history of the building and the order, and the craft shop sells delicious jams made by the nuns, as well as local pottery. But perhaps the biggest attraction here is the **walled garden** *(open mid-Mar–Oct)*, originally laid out in 1860 with no fewer than 21 glass-houses. There is a shuttle bus to the gardens from the abbey.

🚗 *Leaving the abbey, turn left onto the N59 to Leenane for Killary Harbour*

Above View of the lovely winding fjord of Killary Harbour

⑦ Killary Harbour and Leenane
Co Galway
Killary Harbour is Ireland's only fjord and the small, picturesque village of Leenane sits at its head. The best view of the fjord is a little way before

the village, to the left, as the N59 slopes down toward it. There are several off-road viewpoints for exhilarating panoramas of the glacial valley and, on the opposite shore, the vertiginous dark slopes of Mweelrea mountain plunging into the blue waters. From Leenane, a 90-minute cruise sails the length of the 9-mile (14-km) fjord, offering excellent views. As the waters of the harbor are exceptionally calm, it is rare for passengers to suffer seasickness.

🚗 *Head northeast on the N59. At Aasleagh, turn left onto the R335, through the Doolough Pass between the Sheeffry Hills and Mweelrea to the Delphi Valley.*

❽ Delphi Valley
Co Mayo

The Delphi Valley was given its name by the Marquis of Sligo who, on his return from Delphi in Greece in the 1830s, built his country home, Delphi Lodge, on the shores of beautiful Lough Finny, opposite the lower slopes of Mweelrea. It is said that the Grecian landscape reminded him so much of home that he pined for this corner of Mayo.

🚗 *Follow the R335 to Doolough and the Famine Walk Memorial.*

Traditional local road signs

Above View over the surrounding hills from the Tawnyard Pass

Nestled in the midst of the Murrisk Mountains, its enigmatic beauty is further enhanced by the total peace and solitude of its setting. Even in high summer, visitors are few. At the far end of the lake, the small stone **Famine Walk Memorial**, inscribed with a quote from Bishop Desmond Tutu, is on the right. The view back across the lake and the surrounding hills is sublime. For some, the terrible event that took place in this valley in March 1849 to this day reverberates in its somber beauty.

🚗 *Retrace the route back to the Delphi side of the lake. At the first junction, turn left up the hill, signed Liscarney and Drummin, to reach the Tawnyard Pass.*

❿ Tawnyard Pass
Co Mayo

This mountain road cuts through a remote forested area of the Sheefry. Park at the sign for Tawnyard Forests for superb views over Tawnyard Lough and its surrounding hills as well as the Ben Gorm and Mweelrea mountains. A walking trail leads down to the lough. Once it has reached the head of the pass, the road hairpins down to a stone bridge and levels out on the flatter, fertile plains of South Mayo. At the start of this descent is a small lay-by where, on a clear day, the peak of Croagh Patrick, Ireland's holiest mountain, can be seen (*see p195*).

🚗 *Stay on this road as far as the junction with the R330, turning right onto it. At Killavally, turn left for Ballintubber Abbey.*

The Famine Walk

During the Great Famine in Ireland (1845–51) a million people died and a further million emigrated. In March 1849, hundreds of starving people walked over the Doolough Pass from Louisburg to Delphi House, where a party of famine relief commissioners were staying, hoping to get food for their families. They were made to wait overnight in harsh conditions before being turned away. Around 400 people died on the trek back. A memorial stone on the shores of Doolough commemorates the tragedy.

❾ Doolough
Co Mayo

Beyond the Delphi Valley, the road skirts the lake of Doolough ("Black Lake" in Irish), reputed to be the second deepest lake in Ireland.

EAT AND DRINK IN KILLARY HARBOUR AND LEENANE

Gaynor's *inexpensive*
This pub's claim to fame is that many scenes in Jim Sheridan's movie *The Field*, starring Richard Harris, were shot here. It's a very popular and friendly place, serving a good range of food, well prepared. They will also make up a packed lunch on request.
Leenane; 095 42261

Blackberry Café *moderate*
This family-run restaurant serves reliably good food and takes pride in all its dishes being freshly cooked. Delicious homemade soups and chowders, fish cakes, and mussels.
Leenane; 095 42240

Eat and Drink: inexpensive, under €25; moderate, €25–€50; expensive, over €50

Above One of the many little islands that dot the tranquil surface of Lough Corrib

⓫ Ballintubber Abbey
Co Mayo

Founded in 1216 by Cathal O'Conner, the King of Connaught, **Ballintubber Abbey** *(open daily)* is often spoken of as "the abbey that refused to die." Remarkably, it is the only church in Ireland where, for nearly 800 years, Mass has been celebrated without a break and today is still a place of daily worship.

An audiovisual display takes visitors on a journey through Cromwellian burnings, religious persecution, and the actitivies of the notorious "priest hunter" Sean na Sagart ("John of the Priests") who is actually buried in the graveyard. His body was laid facing north instead of the usual practice of burying the dead facing the rising sun. Every year, hundreds of people walk *Tochar Phadraig* ("Pilgrim's Path") from the abbey to Croagh Patrick, and up to the summit of the holy mountain *(see p195)*.

🚗 *Join the N84 at Ballintubber and drive south towards Partry. Turn right onto the R330 (marked for Lough Mask Drive) and then left for the tiny hamlet of Srah (An tSraith). Veer left and follow the road that hugs the northern shore of Lough Mask.*

⓬ Loughs Mask and Nafooey
Co Mayo

Lough Mask is a vast limestone lake, etched by rain and river water out of the porous rock, and one of the best spots in Ireland for brown-trout angling. For almost its whole length the road hugs the shoreline, offering lovely lake vistas. The little town of Tourmakeady (Tuar Mhic Éadaigh)

marks the start of the Gaeltacht. From here, the road veers away from the lough and climbs upwards. Stop and look back for a fabulous view. Soon the road dips down into the valley of **Lough Nafooey**. At the end of the lough is a secluded, sandy beach, from where long-abandoned cultivation ridges called "lazy beds," used for growing potatoes until the Famine of 1845–51, can be seen.

🚗 *Follow the road up over Al Dubh Pass to join the R336, turning left toward Maum.*

The Galway Gaeltacht

The Gaeltacht are regions where the Irish language still holds sway. They are found mainly in the more remote communities of western Ireland. The Galway Gaeltacht in Connemara is the most extensive in Ireland, and even the road signs here may be in Irish only. The government actively supports and promotes its continued use, and schoolchildren from other areas often holiday in the Gaeltacht to improve their Irish.

⓭ Maum (An Mám)
Co Galway

The Irish-speaking area around **Maum** is known for the venerable local Joyce family – it is often referred to as "Joyce Country." The village itself makes a pleasant stop, with Keane's, an ivy-clad pub, opposite the small bridge spanning the River Joyce. From the bridge there are fine views of the Maumturk Mountains.

🚗 *Continue east, taking the R345 along Lough Corrib toward Clonbur and Cong.*

WHERE TO STAY

AROUND BALLINTUBBER ABBEY

Moher House *inexpensive*
This homey bed and breakfast is in the capable hands of owner Marian O'Malley, who ensures all guests are given a warm welcome. Open peat fires and views of Croagh Patrick and Moher Lake add to the friendly, open ambience. Wide choice of breakfasts, and evening meals by arrangement.
Near village of Drummin on the main Leenane–Westport Road (N59); 098 21360; www.moherhousewestport.com

LOUGH CORRIB

Fairhill House Hotel *moderate*
This refurbished Victorian hotel offers simple but very comfortable country-style accommodation.
Main Street, Clonbur; 094 954 6176; www.fairhillhouse.com

CONG

Ashford Castle Hotel
moderate–expensive
For those who want a truly memorable stay, this charming and dignified hotel is one of Ireland's plushest addresses.
095 9544 6003; www.ashford.ie

Below Regional architecture of a stone farmhouse on Lough Mask

Where to Stay: inexpensive, under €100; moderate, €100–€200; expensive, over €200

Above Magnificent mountain scenery between Loughs Mask and Nafooey

⑭ Lough Corrib
Co Mayo and Co Galway

The largest lake in the Republic of Ireland, Lough Corrib is reputed to have an island for every day of the year. One of the largest is **Inchagoil**, which has an important monastic settlement *(see p186)*. Many are wooded, and the dawn chorus in early spring on Lough Corrib is a spectacular natural event.

From Maum to Clonbur there are almost uninterrupted views of this beautiful, island-studded lake. There is a viewing point just before Cornamona (Corr Na Mona). From here it is possible to make a detour onto a tiny peninsula that affords closer views of the Isle of Inchagoil. **Clonbur** (An Fhairche) is a picturesque village on the broad neck of land between Loughs Mask and Corrib. There are forest and lakeside walks in the vicinity and Clonbur Woods are renowned for the variety of butterflies found there. The upper-floor balcony of Burke's pub-restaurant has great views of Mount Gable and the landscape. Its owners also provide maps and advice on local walking trails. One is to the top of Mount Gable, from where the whole of Connemara is spread out below. It is a 3-hour return trek, but it is also possible to drive to within 40 minutes' walk of the summit (ask at Burke's).

🚗 *Take the R346 east to Cong.*

⑮ Cong
Co Mayo

Cong was the location for John Ford's 1951 film *The Quiet Man*, starring John Wayne. Movie buffs should head for the **Quiet Man Museum** *(open Easter–mid-Oct daily)*. Nearby, ruined **Cong Abbey** was founded in the 7th century and rebuilt in the 12th and 13th by the last kings of Connaught: Turlough, Rory, and Cathal O'Connor. The splendid, ornamented 12th-century Cross of Cong once resided here (it is now in the National Museum of Ireland in Dublin, *see p150*). Behind the abbey, a path leads to **Ashford Castle**, once the home of Arthur Guinness, founder of the Guinness stout brewery in 1756, and now one of Ireland's most luxurious hotels. Take tea here to enjoy the lovely ornamental gardens that sweep down to the shores of Lough Corrib.

Cong Abbey's 12th-century arched doorway

EAT AND DRINK

LOUGHS MASK AND NAFOOEY

Maire Lukes *inexpensive*
From the garden at the rear of this landmark pub there are sweeping views of Lough Mask. It serves good light lunches, and helpful staff are knowledgeable about the area. *Toormakeady, Lough Mask; 094 9544080*

LOUGH CORRIB

Burke's *inexpensive*
This family-run pub and restaurant offers wonderful views of Mount Gable as well as a good variety of meat and fish dishes for hungry walkers. *Clonbur; 094 9546175; www.burkes-clonbur.com*

CONG

Hungry Monk Café *inexpensive*
A great place to indulge in freshly ground coffee and homemade desserts and cakes. *Abbey Street, Cong; 094 9545842*

DAY TRIP OPTIONS
Clifden, Killary Harbour and Cong are all good bases from which to explore the coastline, history and loughs of Connemara.

Island life
From picturesque Clifden ❶ take the lovely drive out on the Sky Road ❷ to Cleggan for the ferry to Inishbofin Island ❹, where traditional Irish music and crafts are still a way of life.

Follow the drive instructions out to Cleggan for the ferry to the island.

History trail
From lovely Killary Harbour ❼, the spectacular, steep and winding route over Bengorm Pass leads to poignant Delphi Valley ❽ and Doolough ❾, the site of a moving monument to Ireland's tragic Famine Trail.

Follow the drive instructions over the pass and through the valley along the lough, continuing to the end of the descent from Tawnyard Pass ❿. When the road reaches the N59, turn right to return to Killary Harbour/Leenane.

Connemara's lakelands
From either Clonbur or Cong ⑮ four lovely loughs – Carra, Mask, Nafooey ⑫, and Corrib ⑭ – can be linked in a delightful day's driving tour that also runs through Irish-speaking Joyce Country around Maum ⑬.

Head north to Barna, Ballinchalla, and Ballinrobe, then turn left onto the N84 to the shores of Lough Carra. Continue on the N84 up to Partry, then turn left onto the R300 to Srah, and from there follow the drive instructions back to Clonbur or Cong.

Eat and Drink: inexpensive, under €25; moderate, €25–€50; expensive, over €50

Connemara's Coast

Galway to Spiddal

Highlights

- **Vibrant Galway**
  Join in the "craic" in this fun-loving maritime city

- **Island-studded lake**
  Cruise on lovely Lough Corrib, stopping to visit Inchagoill Island

- **The heart of Connemara**
  Explore two achingly beautiful valleys, set against the Maumturks and Twelve Bens mountain ranges

- **Dramatic coastline**
  Be thrilled by the rugged, island-strewn coast of Connemara

- **Outposts of Irish culture**
  Visit the Aran Islands, Irish bastions, and experience a unique way of life

The vertiginous Dun Aengus cliffs on Inishmore, one of the Aran Islands

Connemara's Coast

When W. B. Yeats coined the phrase "A terrible beauty" he was describing the whole of Ireland, but it was probably the "water and the wilds" of Connemara that he had in his mind's eye. The name alone conjures up romantic notions of the west of Ireland – a harsh yet utterly entrancing landscape of blanket bogs, lakes, and mountains, and a deeply indented coastline strewn with small islands. The region is fringed by the broad sweep of Lough Corrib to the east and the Atlantic to the west, while its northern boundary is defined by Killary Harbour. Dominating the landscape and rarely out of view are the majestic Twelve Bens and Maumturks mountain ranges, whose looming presence lends extra drama to this stunningly beautiful region.

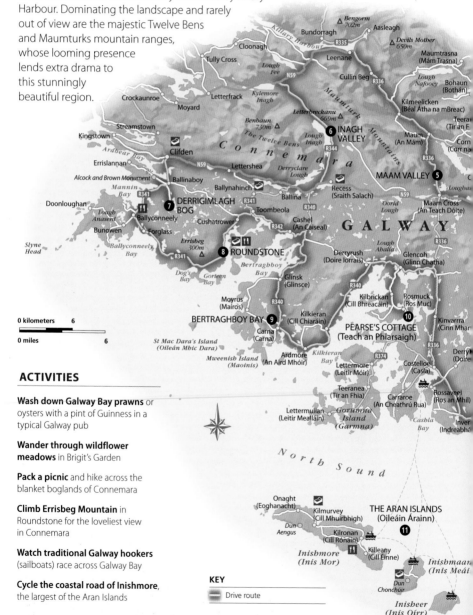

ACTIVITIES

Wash down Galway Bay prawns or oysters with a pint of Guinness in a typical Galway pub

Wander through wildflower meadows in Brigit's Garden

Pack a picnic and hike across the blanket boglands of Connemara

Climb Errisbeg Mountain in Roundstone for the loveliest view in Connemara

Watch traditional Galway hookers (sailboats) race across Galway Bay

Cycle the coastal road of Inishmore, the largest of the Aran Islands

KEY

Drive route

Above Maze-like drystone walls on Inishmore, the most visited of the Aran Islands, see pp188–9

PLAN YOUR DRIVE

Start/finish: Galway to Spiddal (An Spiddéal).

Number of days: 3–4, allowing one day on the Aran Islands.

Distance: 150 miles (240 km).

Road conditions: Coastal roads are often narrow and uneven, and signs can be erratic.

When to go: Mar–Oct is preferable. Most festivals take place in summer, and regional tourist offices are closed Nov–early Mar.

Main market days: Galway: food and craft market (behind St. Nicholas Church), all day Sat & Sun pm.

Shopping: Buy a genuine hand-knitted Aran sweater from the Aran Islands or a traditional Claddagh ring.

Major festivals: Galway: Arts Festival, Jul; Galway Races, late Jul/early Aug; Film Fleadh, early Jul; Galway Oyster Festival, end Sep.

DAY TRIP OPTIONS

Have fun in Galway, with its busy **waterfront**, historic **pubs**, and great **restaurants**. For **coastal scenery** and **beaches**, head for Roundstone and follow the **spectacular drive** around Betraghboy Bay. Alternatively, **leave the car behind** and **escape** to Inishmore, the largest of the Aran Islands, and **cycle** around the coast or take in the sights from a **pony and trap**. For full details, see p189.

Below A view toward the Twelve Bens across Lough Connemara, see p187

Above Galway's brightly painted storefronts are a feature of the city **Below** Swans by the quayside, Claddagh harbor

VISITING GALWAY

Parking
Most of the city center is pedestrianized, so it is best to park in the Eyre Square Centre or Forster Street parking lot opposite St. Patrick's Church. There is also a multistory parking lot off Quay Street, next to Wolfe Tone Bridge. Parking discs for on-street parking can be bought at shops, newsagents, and the tourist office.

Tourist Information
Aras Failte, Forster St; 091 537 700;
www.discoverireland.ie/galway;
open year-round

WHERE TO STAY IN GALWAY

Heron's Rest *inexpensive*
The owner of this boutique B&B near the Spanish Arch has brought the village to the city with her careful attention to detail, individually styled rooms, and gourmet breakfasts. She is also a mine of information on events in Galway and its history.
16a The Longwalk, Spanish Arch; 091 539 574; www.theheronsrest.com; open May–Sep

The House Hotel *moderate*
Fashionable boutique hotel. Rooms are beautifully appointed and have all the comforts of a top-range hotel. Central location.
Lower Merchants Rd; 091 538 900; www.thehousehotel.ie

The Meyrick *moderate*
Formerly a traditional Victorian railway hotel, the Meyrick has been given a contemporary facelift but retains its large, graceful bedrooms. Weekend deals are available.
Eyre Square; 091 564 041; www.hotelmeyrick.ie

❶ Galway
Co Galway

Situated on a narrow neck of land between Galway Bay and Lough Corrib, Galway is the only maritime city in Ireland that actually looks out across the sea and has a tang of salt about it. Despite being the fastest growing city in Europe, it has a village atmosphere and is famous for its summer festivals, thriving arts scene, historic pubs, and painted storefronts. It is also where Irish is most widely spoken – a reminder that it is the cultural hub for the broader hinterland of Connemara and the Aran Islands, Ireland's largest Gaeltacht. From Eyre Square, the main drag leads to the riverfront, a Continental-style promenade where locals come to enjoy the "craic" – fun.

A two-hour walking tour

From Eyre Square Centre parking lot exit onto **Eyre Square** ①, a former market square and jousting ground, once located outside the old city walls, and now a pleasant green space. In the fountain in the center, Galway's maritime traditions are celebrated by the sculpture of a hooker – the traditional Galway fishing boat, examples of which can be seen sailing in Galway's harbor.

Lynch family crest, Lynch Castle

Leaving the square, stroll down William Street and Shop Street, Galway's main drag. On the right is **Lynch's Castle** ②, the home of one of Galway's ruling families in the 16th century. Further down Shop Street, fork left for High Street. On the corner of Cross and Quay streets is **Dillon's Jewellers** ③, which has a quaint museum *(open daily; pm only Sun)* dedicated to the history of the Claddagh ring *(see box)*. Continue down to the river and turn left to the **Spanish Arch** ④, the remnants of the city wall extension (1584), built to protect the river

quays, and a reminder of Galway's once extensive trading links with the rest of Europe. Behind the arch is the glass-fronted **Galway City Museum** ⑤ *(open Jun–Sep: daily; Oct–May: Tue–Sat)*, which has exhibitions on Galway themes, an eclectic permanent collection – a Victorian child's tricycle, an 18th-century reliquary of St. Ursula – and good views over the river. Under the arch is Nimmo's *(see right)*, a good spot for lunch. Look across to the far bank of the River Corrib at this point to see Claddagh, the oldest fishing village in Galway, which gives its name to the Claddagh ring.

From the Spanish Arch, follow **Fishery Walk** ⑥ – the wooden walkway is clearly marked – upstream. Continue past Wolfe Tone Bridge towards the Salmon Weir Bridge, following the river as it curves right onto Waterside. On the opposite bank is the Roman Catholic Cathedral of St. Nicholas, an imposing modern structure built of local limestone and Connemara

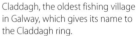

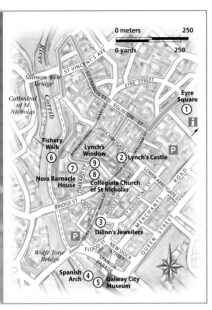

marble, and beyond that the spires of Galway University, which has an 1849 Gothic Revival quad. In summer, look out for salmon ascending to their spawning grounds upstream. At Waterside, the River Corrib, opens out into Lough Corrib – the largest lake in the Republic of Ireland. Beyond the weir are the remaining stanchions of the Galway–Clifden railway bridge.

Just past a slipway on Waterside, turn right down St. Francis Street and walk back toward the center. At the junction with Eglinton Street, turn right and follow Mary Street into Bowling Green. Here is **Nora Barnacle House** *(open summer for guided tours)* ⑦, the family home of Nora Barnacle, muse and long-suffering spouse of the writer James Joyce, who visited Nora here. Now a museum, it houses Joycean memorabilia and holds readings of Joyce's work.

Around the corner, on Lombard Street, is the **Collegiate Church of St. Nicholas** ⑧. Founded in 1320, it is the largest functioning medieval church in Ireland. Legend has it that Christopher Columbus prayed here prior to his voyage to the New World. Behind the church, in Church Lane, is

Lynch's Window ⑨, carved with a skull and crossbones, from which James Lynch, nobleman and mayor, reputedly hanged his own son, Nicholas Lynch, for murdering a Spanish guest in a pique of jealousy. The official executioner had refused to carry out the deed, no doubt heeding the people's pleas for clemency. Galwegians claim this event gave rise to the term "'lynching." From here, return to the main drag of Shop Street and turn left back to Eyre Square.

🚗 *Leaving Galway, cross Wolfe Tone Bridge and follow the signs for Salthill, a resort suburb half a mile (1 km) southwest. With Galway Bay on the left, follow the promenade. Just before the Black Rock diving board, turn right at a mini roundabout. Drive up the hill and through a series of roundabouts, eventually descending to the N59. Turn left here onto it. After 6 miles (10 km), turn right to the Connemara Marble Visitor Centre in Moycullen.*

Traditional Claddagh wedding ring

The Claddagh Ring

A traditional wedding ring featuring two hands holding a heart with a crown on top, the Claddagh ring takes its name from the oldest fishing village in Galway, on the west bank of the River Corrib. It is said to have been designed in the 1730s by goldsmith Richard Joyce, who presented it to William III as a mark of gratitude for securing his release from Moorish pirates. If the heart on the ring is pointing towards the body, it means the wearer's heart is taken; if it points outwards, the heart is open. Internationally famous, the Claddagh ring has been worn by such diverse figures as John Wayne and Queen Victoria.

EAT AND DRINK IN GALWAY

Corrib House Tea Rooms & Guesthouse *inexpensive*
This charmingly restored Georgian townhouse with views over the river offers breakfast and lunch, as well as teas and coffees. Meals include wraps, pies, and soups.
3 Waterside, Woodquay; 091 446 753; www.corribhouse.com

Goya's *inexpensive*
Great place for coffee and cakes. Vibrant and friendly atmosphere.
2–3 Kirwan's Lane; 091 567 010; www.goyas.ie

McDonaghs Seafood House *inexpensive*
Busy eatery on Quay Street. Famed for its chowders – the measure of a good restaurant on the western seaboard – it is everything from a carry-out fish bar to a boulevard seafood café.
22 Quay St; 091 565 001; www.mcdonaghs.net

Tigh Neachtain *inexpensive*
A landmark pub, reputed to be Galway's oldest (the interior has barely changed since 1890). Open fires create a warm, inviting atmosphere, and there is often impromptu live music. Artisan restaurant upstairs.
Quay St; 091 568 820; www.tighneachtain.com

Ard Bia *moderate*
Top-drawer cooking and great atmosphere. Popular with local foodies. Particular favorites are the Galway mussels and haddock chowder. More informal dining available downstairs in the daytime.
Spanish Arch; 091 539 897; www.ardbia.com

Below A *curragh*, or traditional sail boat, in Galway City Museum

Above Fishing boat on lovely Lough Corrib
Above right Brigit's Celtic-inspired garden

WHERE TO STAY

AROUND OUGHTERARD

Camillaun Lodge and Angling Centre *inexpensive*
Family-run guesthouse on the banks of the River Owenriff, with direct access to Lough Corrib. Facilities include a garden hot tub.
Oughterard (turn right down Camp Street at the Boat Inn); 091 552 678; www.camillaun.com; closed Nov–Jan

Currarevagh House *moderate*
Country house from 1842, set in beautiful woodland. Good restaurant (open to nonresidents for dinner).
Oughterard (4 miles/7 km outside the town on the Glann road); 091 552 312; www.currarevagh.com; closed Nov–Feb

AROUND INAGH VALLEY

Ballynahinch Castle Hotel *expensive*
Sumptuous 4-star hotel in extensive woodland. Lunch is available to non-residents in the bar.
Recess (on the R341 to Toombeola); 095 31006; www.ballynahinch-castle.com

Lough Inagh Lodge *expensive*
This former hunting lodge with a lakeside setting is a perfect retreat.
Recess (on the R344 towards Leenane and Letterfrack); 095 34706; www.loughinaghlodgehotel.ie; closed mid-Dec–mid-Mar

AROUND DERRIGIMLAGH BOG

Ardagh Hotel *moderate*
Family-run hotel overlooking Ardbear Bay. The restaurant specializes in locally caught seafood.
Ballyconneely Rd, Clifden (just south of town); 095 21384; www.ardaghhotel.com

ROUNDSTONE

St. Josephs B&B *inexpensive*
Cozy and welcoming with good breakfasts, in the heart of the village.
Roundstone; 095 35865; www.bandbireland.com/stjosephs

② **Connemara Marble Visitor Centre**
Moycullen, Co Galway
Connemara is famous for its marble. Sometimes referred to as Irish jade, it is valued for its subtle shades of green, resulting from the large copper deposits in the Connemara area. The process of turning it into jewelry, ashtrays and chess sets can be seen at the Connemara Marble Visitor Centre *(open daily)*. Items can be bought in the showroom.

🚗 *Take Chapel Road out of Moycullen and turn right onto the N59 toward Oughterard. After 4 miles (7 km), turn right at a sign pointing to Brigit's Garden (1 mile/2 km off the N59).*

③ **Brigit's Garden**
Rosscahill, Co Galway
This is a contemporary garden *(open mid-Feb–Sep)* dedicated to the four seasonal Celtic festivals. Cynics might find it a bit new-agey but there is a real sense of wonderment here and children generally love it. The large grounds feature sculptures, standing stones, ring forts, nature trails, and pools, and the excellent café uses produce from the garden. Particularly attractive are the ancient woodland and wild flower meadows.

🚗 *Return to the N59, turn right, and continue northwest to Oughterard (4 miles/7 km). There is a large parking lot on the right on the way into town.*

④ **Oughterard**
Co Galway
The gateway to Connemara, this is a lively town and an important angling center. Its main attraction is **Lough Corrib**, Ireland's second largest lake, 1 mile (2 km) north of the town itself.

In spring, when the mayfly hatches, Oughterard becomes a magnet for trout fishermen. The best way to see the lake is to take a cruise on the *Corrib Queen*, which leaves from the lake's pier (tickets from the pier or from the tourist office in town). The boat drops passengers on beautiful **Inchagoill Island**, the site of a ruined monastery and Romanesque church.

For information on fishing, call by Thomas Tuck's tackle shop on Main Street. Next door is the Yew Tree Bakery and Café, a good place to stock up for a picnic.

🚗 *From Oughterard, continue north along the N59, and turn right onto the R336 at Maam Cross.*

⑤ **Maam Valley**
Co Galway
This scenic drive along the R336 through the Maam Valley is an opportunity to enjoy the splendors of Connemara in relative isolation. The blanket bog (thinner and flatter than the raised bog of the Midlands) imbues the area with a desolate beauty, and if the light is right, the vivid yellow gorse and pale green reeds yield a rich palette of colors. It is worth stopping the car for a closer look and a walk. Eventually the road skirts the billowing curves of the **Maumturk Mountains** and enters the village of **Leenane**. Follow the road uphill onto the N59 west to Clifden. Look out for splendid views of **Killary Harbour** *(see pp176–7)* on the right.

🚗 *Continue on the N59 toward Clifden. Just before Kylemore Abbey turn left onto the R344, toward Recess (Sraith Salach; 10 miles/16 km). The sign is tucked in tight on a sharp corner, so be careful not to miss it.*

Where to Stay: inexpensive, under €100; moderate, €100–€200; expensive, over €200

⑥ Inagh Valley
Co Galway

This stretch of the route passes through one of the most scenic valleys in Connemara, with broad swaths of blanket bogland on either side of the road. It eventually squeezes through the Maumturk and Twelve Bens mountains. There are wonderful views of Lough Inagh to the right.

🚗 *Regaining the N59, turn right and drive into Clifden (13 miles/21 km). Entering Clifden (see p174), turn left onto the R341 coast road, toward Ballinaboy and Ballyconneely. In Ballinaboy, ignore the left turn for Toombeola and instead take the next left, a narrow road leading through Derrigimlagh Bog for 1 mile (2 km) and ending in a cul de sac.*

Above The pretty fishing village of Roundstone, clustered around its harbor

⑦ Derrigimlagh Bog
Co Galway

This area of bogland on the western fringes of Europe was once at the forefront of modern technology, for it is the site of the world's first transatlantic radio station, built by Guglielmo Marconi and opened with a staff of 150 in 1907. The concrete block and rusty chain by the small lough at the end of the road are the remains. Nearby, a white cairn marks another historic event. On June 15 1919 John Alcock and Arthur Whitten Brown crash-landed their Vickers Vimy bomber biplane here after completing the first non-stop flight across the Atlantic.

🚗 *Return to the R341 and cut straight across onto a narrow well-paved road. Drive up the hill and pull into the parking lot (half a mile/1 km). Below is the official Alcock and Brown Monument. There are also wonderful views across the broad sweep of Mannin Bay. Return to the R341, turn right, following the signs for Ballyconneely and Roundstone.*

⑧ Roundstone
Co Galway

Eventually the coast road loops around to Roundstone (Cloch na Ron – "Seal Rock"). Perched high above the fishing harbor and looking out across island-studded Bertraghboy Bay, this is the most picturesque village on the Connemara coast. In the distance, framing the expanse of water, are the Twelve Bens and Maumturks; behind the village, Errisbeg (984 ft/300 m), a 2-hour hike (follow the road past O'Dowd's pub), affords some of the finest views in all Connemara.

Culturally vibrant, Roundstone has become a magnet for craftsmen and artists, and in summer holds a regatta of traditional Galway hookers. It also has a couple of good bars and restaurants, including O'Dowd's *(see right)*. Two miles (3 kilometers) southwest of town, off the R341, the beautiful white sandy coves of **Gorteen Bay** and **Dog's Bay**, lie back-to-back on a headland.

🚗 *Follow the R341 coastal road to Toombeola (4 miles/7 km) and turn right onto the R342. Continue past Cashel and take the first right onto the R340, toward Glinsce and Carna, skirting Bertraghboy Bay.*

Above A Connemara pony, a sturdy breed suited to the rugged landscape

EAT AND DRINK

OUGHTERARD

Breathnach's Bar *inexpensive*
Country pub with good home cooking and live music.
Camp St; 091 552 2818;
www.breathnachs.com

AROUND DERRIGIMLAGH BOG

Keoghs Bar *moderate*
Popular family-run bar/restaurant. Wide range of dishes, from sirloin steak to warm crab claws with lemon butter. On the R341 south of Clifden.
Ballyconneely; 095 23522

ROUNDSTONE

O'Dowd's *inexpensive–moderate*
In business since 1906, this harborfront pub has superb food, wood-paneled walls, and open fires.
Harbor; 095 35809;
www.odowdsrestaurant.com

Below Gorteen Bay, one of two idyllic beaches near Roundstone

Above Pearse's Cottage, the summer home of the revolutionary Pádraig Pearse

WHERE TO STAY

THE ARAN ISLANDS (OILEÁIN ARANN)

An Dún Guest House *inexpensive*
Welcoming guesthouse at the foot of Connor's Fort on Inishmaan. Ensuite rooms with lovely views, and a mini-spa offering aromatherapy massage.
Inishmaan; 099 73047

Kilmurvey House *inexpensive*
Situated between Kilronan and Bun Gowla on the west side of the island, at the foot of Dun Aengus, this 150-year-old stone house has ensuite bedrooms with fine views. Dinner served in summer.
Kilmurvey, Inishmore; 099 61218; www.kilmurveyhouse.com

Man of Aran Cottage *inexpensive*
Delightful cottage offering limited but good accommodation beside Kilmurvey beach on the west side of Inishmore. Only one room is ensuite. Evening meals available on request.
Kilmurvey, Inishmore; 099 61301; www.manofarancottage.com; Mar–Oct only

SPIDDAL (AN SPIDÉAL)

An Cruiscin Lan Hotel and Restaurant *inexpensive*
Popular, modern hotel in the middle of Spiddal. Rooms are spacious and ensuite. Restaurant attached.
Spiddal; 091 553148; www.ancruiscinlanhotel.com

Right The blanket bogland of Connemara, long harvested for peat

9 Bertraghboy Bay
Co Galway

Rugged and windswept, and littered with tiny islands, Bertraghboy Bay is breathtakingly beautiful. On the far side of the bay is **Carna**, an important lobster fishing center, from where it is a short hop of 3 miles (5 km) to **Mweenish** (Maoinis), an island linked by bridge to the mainland and with beautiful sandy beaches. Due west of Maoinis is isolated **St. Mac Dara's Island** (Oileán Mhic Dara), one of the many uninhabited islands in this area. It has the remains of a church and the bed (grave) of St. Mac Dara. The island is so sacred that fishermen used to dip their sails three times as a mark of respect when passing.

🚗 *From Carna turn right onto the coastal R340 and follow it around the headland, with views of Kilkieran Bay on the right. Pass through the village of Kilkieran and, just before Glinn Chatha, turn right, following the sign for Ros Muc and Pearse's Cottage.*

10 Pearse's Cottage (Teach an Phiarsaigh)
Rosmuck Peninsula, Co Galway

Located just off the R340, Pearse's Cottage *(open Easter & May–Sep daily)* was the summer residence of the Dublin school teacher, revolutionary, and writer Pádraig Pearse (1879–1916). Following the collapse of the 1916 Uprising, Pearse and 14 other leaders were executed, thus becoming martyrs to the cause. Pearse used this cottage to run a summer school for his students. It was also where he penned his graveside oration for the nationalist hero Jeremiah O'Donovan Rossa in 1915. The closing words of the speech, "Ireland unfree shall never be at peace" became the rallying cry for many Irish patriots. The cottage contains mementos of Pearse's life.

While here, it is worth exploring the Rosmuck Peninsula on foot to appreciate the fabulous setting.

🚗 *Drive back to the R340 and continue east. Around 3 miles (5 km) past Glencoh turn right onto the R336 for Rossaveel (marked Rós an Mhil), the main port for the Aran Islands. Cars cannot be taken onto the islands, so park in the port.*

Above Traditional red-sailed Galway hookers catch the breeze in Galway Bay

11 The Aran Islands (Oileáin Arann)
Co Galway

This trio of islands on the western fringes of Europe – Inishmore (Inis Mor; Great Island), Inishmaan (Inis Meáin; Middle Island) and Inisheer (Inis Oírr; Eastern Island) – are a continuation of the limestone base of the Burren in North Clare *(see p127)*. Far out in Galway Bay, they act as a bulwark, helping to protect the city of Galway from the driving force of the Atlantic.

For many Irish people, the islands symbolize a Celtic Eden, where Irish traditions, from language to dress, as

well as farming and fishing methods, persist. The playwright J. M. Synge (1871–1909) put the islands on the map with the publication of *Playboy of the Western World* in 1907. A fraught tale of love and murder, it was inspired by time he spent on Inishmaan.

The largest island, **Inishmore** is the most visited. Boats arrive at **Kilronan** (Cill Rónáin), where bicycles can be rented and jaunting cars (pony and traps) wait to give island tours. The **Aran Heritage Centre** *(Apr–Oct)* in Kilronan is worth a visit.

Inishmore's main attraction is **Dun Aengus** (Dun Aonghasa), an Iron Age promontory fort, thrillingly located on the edge of soaring granite cliffs. It has four concentric stone walls and is protected by a *chevaux de frise*, a ring of razor-sharp stone stakes. Further along the coast, **Dún Duchathair**, known as the Black Fort, has dry-stone ramparts.

Other sights include **Teampall Chiaráin**, a ruined 12th-century church with striking doorways, and **Na Seacht d'Teampaill**, the "Seven Churches," a monastery built between the 9th and 15th centuries.

Inishmaan is the chief bastion of Aran culture and is much quieter than the other islands. Among its main sights are **Dún Chonchúir**, a

pre-Christian fort, and **Synge's Cottage**, where the playwright stayed during his time here.

Sights on the smallest of the three islands, **Inisheer**, include the ruined **Church of St. Gobnait** and the 15th-century **O'Brien's Castle**.

🚗 *From Rossaveel, continue along the R336 to Spiddal.*

Aran Sweaters

These thick woollen jumpers with elaborate patterns on the front are traditionally worn by Aran Island fishermen. Knitted from unscoured wool that retains its natural lanolin, they protected the fishermen from the worst of the elements. Each pattern was unique to a family or village, and would help identify the wearer in case of a fatality at sea.

⑫ Spiddal (An Spidéal)
Co Galway

This long coastal village marks the end of the Gaeltacht region. It has a Blue Flag beach (Silver Strand), and curragh races along the shore in summer. Next to the beach, the **Spiddal Craft Village** *(open year-round)*, a complex of small craft studios, sells high quality textiles, musical instruments, ceramics, jewelry and leatherwork.

VISITING THE ARAN ISLANDS (OILEÁIN ARANN)

Tourist Information
For information on accommodation, which is very limited and needs to be booked, contact the tourist board.
Kilronan; 099 61263; open daily

Aran Heritage Centre
Kilronan; 099 61355;
www.visitaranislands.com;
open Apr–Oct

Aran Island Ferries
Aran Island Ferries operates a year-round passenger service to the Aran Islands (cars are not allowed), with several boats a day. The crossing takes about 40 minutes.
4 Forster St, Galway (main office);
Rossaveel (ferry terminal); 091 568 903;
www.aranislandferries.com

EAT AND DRINK ON THE ARAN ISLANDS (OILEÁIN ARANN)

Ti Joe Macs *inexpensive*
Directly opposite the boat jetty, this pub serves soup and sandwiches, as well as beer and stout.
Kilronan, Inishmore; 099 61248

DAY TRIP OPTIONS
Spend a day in Galway, drive around island-studded Betraghboy Bay, or escape to the Aran Islands.

Vibrant Galway
Galway ❶ is a great place to spend a day. Stroll on the waterfront, visit Nora Barnacle's House, and sample some of Ireland's best pubs.

Galway is easily reached from the rest

of Ireland, including the N6 (linking with M4 from Dublin and N18 from Shannon) and the N17 from the north.

Island-studded Betraghboy Bay
Stroll around the picturesque village of Roundstone ❽, then head for rugged Betraghboy Bay ❾ to experience the outstanding beauty of coastal Connemara.

Follow the drive instructions.

Celtic Eden
Take a ferry to the Aran Islands ⓫. At 8 miles (13 km) long and 2 miles (3 km) wide, Inishmore is easy to explore by bike or jaunting car.

Rossaveel is 20 miles (32 km) west of Galway along the R336/R372. The ferry companies operate shuttle buses between Galway and Rossaveel to coincide with ferry crossings.

Eat and Drink: inexpensive, under €25; moderate, €25–€50; expensive, over €50

DRIVE **19**

Mayo's Coastal Splendor

Westport to Doogort

Highlights

- **Georgian elegance**
  Browse the galleries and bookshops of "pretty little" Westport

- **A holy mountain**
  Trek to the summit of Croagh Patrick and be rewarded by stupendous views over Clew Bay

- **Rugged coastline**
  Head along the south coast of Achill Island and be thrilled by dramatic headlands lashed by crashing waves

- **Sandy beaches**
  Escape to one of the county's many idyllic beaches for crystal-clear seas, white sand, and water sports

View over the many islands of Clew Bay from Croagh Patrick

Mayo's Coastal Splendour

Mayo lies in the far west of Connaught. Gloriously beautiful, it has never had it easy. The land here can be grudging and the wild seas unforgiving. During the Great Famine the county experienced the highest levels of emigration and its sense of isolation is a legacy of this. Many visitors bypass Mayo, drawn by the rugged beauty of Connemara or the romance of Sligo. They miss much – heather-mantled bog lands, majestic mountains, and a stunning coastline. If you could eat scenery, a local saying goes, Mayo would be the richest county on earth. Nowhere is this wealth more evident than in the broad sweep around Clew Bay, from Westport to Achill Island.

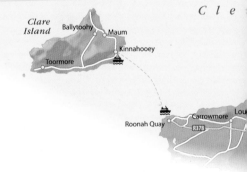

Kinrovar

Srahnamanragh Bridge

Doona — Knock

Ridge Point

Faby Lough — Drumsleed

Dooreel

Ballycroy Pier — Bal

Valley

Inishbiggle

Bell

Saddle Head

Slievemore 672m △

DOOGORT 🛏 11

THE DESERTED VILLAGE **10**

Croaghaun 669m △

Achill Head

DOOAGH 🍴 **8**

KEEL
7

Keel Lough

Bulls Mouth

Annagh Island

Drur

KEEM BAY 9

Keem Strand

R319

Closhreid

Bunacurry (Bun an Churraigh)

Keel Strand

🍴 Dookinelly

Cashel (An Caiseal)

MINAUN HEIGHTS 6

Mweelin △ 466m

R319

Salia (Sáile)

Tonregee (Tóin re Gaoth)

ACHILL SOUND (Gob an Choire)
4

R319

Dooega Head

Dooega (Dumha Éige)

Achill Island (Acaill)

Pollranny (Poll Raithní)

Belfarsad (Béal Feirste)

Curraun Peninsula

△ Corraun Hill 525m

Ma

Portnahally or Ashleam Bay

ATLANTIC DRIVE 5

Carrick Kildavnet

Cloghmore (An Chloich Mhóir)

Achillbeg Island (Acaill Bheag)

Dooghbeg (An Dumhach Bheag)

Bolinglanna (Buaile an Ghleanna)

Achill Sound

C l e

Above The Atlantic Drive through spectacular coastal scenery, on Achill Island, *see p196*

ACTIVITIES

Explore the hundreds of islands in Clew Bay by kayak

See the fortified towers built by a 16th-century pirate queen

Stroll along the sands of Keel beach framed against the dramatic backdrop of Minaun Heights

Visit the Deserted Village at the foot of the Slievemore Mountains

Clare Island

Ballytoohy — Maum

Kinnahooey

Toormore

Roonah Quay

Carrowmore

Lou

R378

KEY

 Drive route

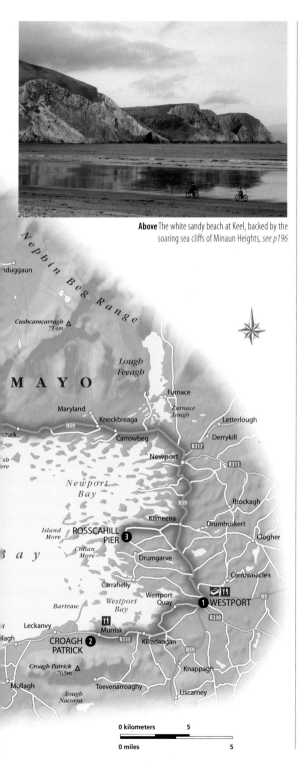

Above The white sandy beach at Keel, backed by the soaring sea cliffs of Minaun Heights, *see p196*

PLAN YOUR DRIVE

Start/finish: Westport to Doogort.

Number of days: 2–3, allowing one day on Clew Bay and two on Achill Island.

Distance: 51 miles (84 km).

Road conditions: Well paved and marked. Some steep terrain with hairpin bends.

When to go: The best time to visit is March to early November. Many tourist facilities are closed in winter.

Opening times: Most shops and attractions are open from 9 or 10am to 5 or 6pm. Shops are usually open from Mon to Sat, however in large towns and shopping centers, shops usually stay open late one night, usually Thu or Fri, and also open from noon to 6pm on Sun. In most villages there are small grocery stores that open from 7 or 8am until late in the evening.

Main market days: Westport: Sat, food and crafts; Thu, Country Market (food).

Shopping: Westport has a couple of good bookstores, craft shops, and galleries selling books and prints on Irish themes.

Major festivals: Westport: Croagh Patrick Pilgrimage, last Sun in July; Arts Festival, Sep/Oct; **Achill Island:** Walking Festival, May; Heinrich Böll Weekend, early May; Yawl Sailing Festival, Aug.

DAY TRIP OPTIONS

For a day of **relaxed wandering**, spend the morning browsing the bookstores and galleries of **Westport**, before an invigorating **hike** up **Croagh Patrick** for the outstanding **views**. For **beach-lovers**, Achill Island is the highlight of Mayo. Follow **Atlantic Drive** around its southern tip to the beaches at **Dooega** and **Keel**. End either day with **live music**, in **Westport** or **Dooagh**. For full details, *see p197*.

Above Westport House, the home of Lord Sligo, who planned the town of Westport

❶ Westport

Co Mayo

Set on the shores of Clew Bay, Westport is one of the prettiest and most congenial towns in Ireland, with an understated Georgian elegance. The English satirist William Thackeray, visiting in 1842, wrote in his book *Irish Sketch Book*: "Nature has done much for the pretty little town of Westport; and after Nature, the traveler ought to be thankful to Lord Sligo, who has done a great deal too." This is a fair appraisal. Sligo commissioned planners and the English architect James Wyatt to design his mansion, its grounds, and the town bordering his estate in the 1770s.

A two-hour walking tour

Westport is one of a handful of planned towns in Ireland, its carefully arranged streets forming a neat square. From the Mall, walk down James Street to the **Octagon** ① for the start of the walk. The town's oldest buildings are arranged around this striking octagonal main square. In the middle, perched on a lofty plinth, is a statue of St. Patrick, under whose benign gaze the town sits.

From the Octagon, walk back down James Street toward the Mall. Opposite the **Tourist Information Office** ② is the **Sea Sky Shore Gallery** ③, featuring local artists' work. The Mall, a popular promenade, flanks the Carrowbeg River, its two sides, South Mall and North Mall, linked by a series of bridges – Wyatt changed the course of the river in order to accommodate his grand designs for the town. Cross the river at James Street and take the

Above Beer barrels stacked up outside a pub

second left by the church onto New Road to the **Linen Mill** ④, which sells homeware made in the adjoining 1960s weaving factory. Trace your steps back to the turn for the North Mall and head down it, taking in the Anglican church. Cross back over the bridge and walk up Bridge Street, the town's other main thoroughfare, with several good restaurants. Halfway up the street is **Matt Molloy's** ⑤, owned by the Chieftains' flautist, Matt Molloy, and the best place for a traditional Irish music session. Westport's music scene really comes alive every year during the 10-day Arts Festival in October (*www.westportartsfestival. com*). Walk back down Bridge Street, to South Mall and the parking lot.

To get to the town's main attraction, Georgian **Westport House and Gardens**, drive down James Street to the Octagon, forking right up Quay Hill, off Peter Street, for 1 mile (2 km). The former home of the

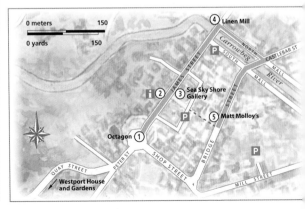

Earls of Altamont *(open Apr–Oct: daily; Mar: Sat & Sun am)* has a sweeping marble staircase and is adorned with family portraits. It has embraced tourism, with swan paddleboats on the lake, a petting zoo, and a minature railroad. The gardens are peaceful and worth a wander. The harborfront near the entrance has restaurants, pubs, and craft shops.

🚗 *Turn right onto Quay Road, marked Louisborough, then R335. Drive 5 miles (8 km) west to Murrisk. Park by the Croagh Patrick Information Centre.*

Mayo's Pirate Queen

In the 16th century, a pirate called Grace O'Malley, or "Granuaile," pretty much ruled the roost from her power base on Clare Island. With her fleet of 20 ships, she belligerently defied Elizabethan forces, eventually gaining the respect of Elizabeth I herself. The remains of her strongholds can be seen around Clew Bay and on Achill Island. She died in Newport in 1603.

② Croagh Patrick
Co Mayo

Ireland's most sacred mountain, Croagh Patrick occupies a peculiar place in the Irish psyche. St. Patrick, who is credited with bringing Christianity to Ireland in the 5th century, is said to have fasted and prayed on its summit for 40 days. Every year on the last Sunday in July – known as Reek Sunday – up to 40,000 pilgrims trek up its rocky slopes, many in bare feet.

The ascent to the 2,510-ft (765-m) summit is steep, with a scramble over loose, shifting scree on the upper half. However, the sweeping view over Clew Bay, with its confetti of islands, is ample reward. Pick up a stout walking stick from the **Croagh**

Patrick Information Centre at the base of the mountain to make the ascent, which takes about two hours, followed by a 90-minute descent.

At the foot of Croagh Patrick, on the other side of the R335, is the **National Famine Memorial**, a harrowing depiction of one of the so-called "coffin ships" that carried Irish emigrants to North America as they fled the Great Famine (1845–52). The terrible conditions on the ships often led to death and disease.

🚗 *Return along the R335 toward Westport. Just before Westport, turn left onto the N59 (north). A few miles (kilometers) after Westport look for a sign pointing left to Rosscahill Pier (4 miles/7 km).*

③ Rosscahill Pier
Co Mayo

A narrow but well-paved road leads to an inlet on Clew Bay. Across the tranquil stretch of water is one of the best views of Croagh Patrick – magical on a clear summer's evening.

🚗 *Return to the N59 and continue north to Mallaranny. Keep left on the R319, marked Achill, passing through Polranny to Achill Sound.*

Above left Matt Molloy's in Westport **Above center** Statue of St. Patrick at the foot of Croagh Patrick overlooking Clew Bay **Above** *Madonna and Child icon on Croagh Patrick*

EAT AND DRINK

WESTPORT

McCormack's at the Andrew Stone Gallery *inexpensive*
Above McCormack's butcher shop. The menu includes quiches, cakes, bacon and cabbage, soups, and Irish stew.
Bridge St; 098 25619

An Port Mór *moderate*
Classy food at affordable prices made by a French-trained patron/chef.
Brewery Place; 098 26730; www.anportmor.com

The Pantry & Corkscrew
moderate–expensive
Run by a husband-and-wife team, The Pantry offers good-value, tasty food.
Peter Street, The Octagon; 098 26977

CROAGH PATRICK

The Tavern Bar and Restaurant
inexpensive–moderate
Family-run restaurant at the foot of Croagh Patrick. Seafood is the specialty.
Murrisk; 098 64060

Below View across Clew Bay toward Clare Island from Atlantic Drive

Eat and Drink: inexpensive, under €25; moderate, €25–€50; expensive over €50

Above Keem Bay, beneath the Croaghaun Heights on the west side of Achill Island

VISITING ACHILL ISLAND

Tourist Information
Cashel; 098 47353;
www.achilltourism.com

WHERE TO STAY

ACHILL SOUND

Achill Island Hotel *inexpensive*
Just before the causeway for Achill Sound. Rooms have good views.
Achill Sound; 098 45138;
www.achillislandhotel.com

ATLANTIC DRIVE

Lavelle's Seaside House *inexpensive*
Good-value B&B. Mickey's, the bar next door, serves sublime crab claws.
Dooega; 098 45116;
www.lavellesseasidehouse.com

KEEL

Achill Cliff House Hotel *moderate*
Family-run hotel with sweeping views and a good restaurant.
Keel; 098 43400; www.achillcliff.com

Bervie *moderate*
Guesthouse in the former coastguard station. Has direct access to the beach.
Keel; 098 43114; www.bervieachill.com

Below Stopping the traffic on the Slievemore Mountain **Below right** The Deserted Village

④ Achill Sound (Gob an Choire)
Co Mayo

Islands in the west of Ireland have a special allure for the Irish. Often seen as the repository of a lost way of life, they remain potent symbols of the past. **Achill Island** is no exception. Ireland's largest island at 15 miles (24 km) long and 12 miles (19 km) wide, it is connected to the mainland by a causeway. It has sandy beaches, dramatic cliffs, boglands, and heathery slopes. Over the years it has inspired artists and writers, including German writer Heinrich Böll, American painter Robert Henri, and painter Paul Henry.

The road bridge spans the narrow, winding strait at **Achill Sound** – a good place to stock up. Facilities here include an ATM, Internet access, a supermarket, hotels, and restaurants.

🚗 *On the island side of Achill Sound, proceed for about 500 yards (500 m), then turn left off the R319, following signs for Atlantic Drive and Cois na Farraige ("Road by the Sea").*

⑤ Atlantic Drive
Achill Island, Co Mayo

After 4 miles (6 km) the road skirts the southern tip of the island and the remains of an 18th-century church and holy well, named after St. Damhnait, an early Christian saint. The graveyard looks across to **Little Achill Island** (Achill Beg). Nearby is **Carrick Kildavnet**, an almost intact example of a 15th-century tower house, built by the O'Malley clan *(see p195)*. From the pier there are fine views across the sound to Corraun Hill.

At **Cloughmore**, as the still waters of Achill Sound give way to Atlantic breakers, some of Ireland's most spectacular coastal scenery unfolds. For 4 miles (6 km) the road rises

steadily to a viewing bay overlooking Ashlean Bay and north to Achill Head, then descends into a series of hairpin bends, looping around the small pebbly beach of **Portnahally** before climbing the other side of the valley. At the next T-junction, turn left to continue along Atlantic Drive and into **Dooega**, a picturesque fishing village with a Blue Flag beach.

🚗 *Minaun Heights loom large above Dooega – to drive to the top, turn left immediately after Mickey's Pub.*

⑥ Minaun Heights
Achill Island, Co Mayo

The road to Minaun Heights climbs steadily. Pass a school, take the next left, and follow the road as it swings right over a small bridge, skirting the slopes of Mweelin Hill. Turn left at the junction and drive up for views of Clare Island to the southwest and Black Sod Bay to the north.

🚗 *Return to junction, turn left, and go along Mweelin road to R319. Follow it to Cashel and Keel 2 miles (3 km) on.*

⑦ Keel
Achill Island, Co Mayo

Keel is known for its white sandy beach, framed by the soaring sea cliffs of Minaun Heights, and is backed by a large lake, popular for water sports.

🚗 *Continue west on the R319 for a couple of miles (kilometers) to Dooagh.*

⑧ Dooagh
Achill Island, Co Mayo

Just west of Keel is the tiny village of Dooagh, which has a nice beach and several good cafés. Gielty's, a popular pub at the west end of the village, hosts traditional music sessions.

🚗 *Continue on the R319 to Keem Bay (2 miles/3 km).*

Left Carrick Kildavnet, a 15th-century base of the pirate Grace O'Malley

9 Keem Bay

Achill Island, Co Mayo

After Dooagh the road rises dramatically. At the peak is a turnout with views of the pincer-shaped beach at Keem Bay, nestling at the foot of the Croaghaun Heights, and across to Achill Head. Descend to the blissfully unspoiled sandy beach – the furthest west you can drive on the island. Bring provisions.

🚗 *Retrace the R319 to Keel. In the village is Minaun View Bar and gas station. Fork left just before here and then left again. Continue for 2 miles (3 km) to the Deserted Village.*

Above The secluded Golden Strand at Bulls Mouth, between Doogort and Bunacurry

10 The Deserted Village

Achill Island, Co Mayo

This is an eerie village, strung along the southern slopes of the Slievemore Mountain. The Great Famine almost certainly played a part in its abandonment, which was hastened when grants for fishing boats became available at the end of the 19th century and its villagers were enticed away from the land to the sea.

🚗 *Retrace the route to the bridge and turn left. Keeping the slopes of Slievemore to the left, follow signs to Doogort (2 miles/4 km).*

11 Doogort

Achill Island, Co Mayo

Nestling in the shadow of Slievemore Mountain, the island's highest point, this tiny village overlooks another fine Blue Flag beach. Opposite the Cottage Coffee Shop, the Red Fox Press sells hand-printed books and prints of Achill Island. Seals can be spotted in the waters around the northern tip of Achill, while amethyst is found in the mountains here. From Doogort, follow signs for Bunacurry but turn left for **Bulls Mouth** 2 miles (3 km) and left it for a secluded beach. From Bunacurry, the R319 leads back to Achill Sound.

OUTDOOR ACTIVITIES

Achill Outdoor Activity Centre provides an extensive program of outdoor activities and water sports, with a strong emphasis on education. It caters for small and large groups, and also provides accommodation (*Cashel-Bunacurry; 098 47253; www.achilloutdoor.com*).

For individuals, **Keel's seasonal tourist information office**, by the beach, can provide information on lake water sports as well as scuba diving, pony trekking and sea kayaking (*contact details as for Cashel tourist information office, see left*).

EAT AND DRINK

KEEL

Beehive Café *inexpensive*
Informal café-cum-craft shop in Keel. Menu includes homemade soups, sandwiches, and seafood. Full license. *Keel; 098 43134; open Mar–Nov*

AROUND KEEL

Black Field Café *inexpensive*
Great coffee and ice cream. Also rents out surfboards, wetsuits, and bicycles. Surfing instruction can be arranged. *Closhreid (1 mile/2 km before Keel); 098 43590; www.blackfield.com*

DOOAGH

Last Drop Coffee Shop *inexpensive*
As the road rises up toward Keem Strand, this is the last opportunity for refreshments. The busy, family-run restaurant is part of Gielty's pub and offers a variety of dishes. *Dooagh; 098 43119; www.gieltys.com*

DOOGORT

The Cottage Coffee Shop *inexpensive*
Just opposite the beach in Doogort, this excellent, family-run café provides inexpensive home cooking. *Doogort; 098 43966; open Easter–Sep*

DAY TRIP OPTIONS

For a gentle day laced with books, art, and music, spend a day in and around Westport. To make the most of Mayo's beaches, spend a day on Achill Island, starting at Achill Sound.

Culture and conviction
Spend a day exploring the perimeter of island-dotted Clew Bay. Start at Westport ❶, where it is easy to while away a morning browsing in bookstores and galleries. After lunch, drive west for an afternoon hike up Croagh Patrick ❷ for views over the bay. Return to Westport for a drink and a traditional music session.

Follow the drive route from Westport to Croagh Patrick and back again.

Beach life
From Achill Sound ❹, take Atlantic Drive ❺ to the beach at Dooega, carrying on via Minaun Heights ❻ to Keel ❼ and its beach, ending up at Dooagh for drinking and music.

Follow the drive route from Achill Sound, taking the R319 along the spine of the island for a direct route back.

Legends and Lakes

Mullaghmore to Lough Key

Highlights

- **Majestic Ben Bulben**
  See the majestic mountain that dominates much of the county, changing mood with the weather

- **Literary landscapes**
  Trace the places mentioned in the poems of Irish poet W. B. Yeats, and visit his grave in Drumcliffe

- **Seaside Sligo**
  Potter around pretty Mullaghmore, surf the waves at Strandhill, and enjoy a walk and pub lunch at Rosses point

- **Legendary burial site**
  Scale the mountain-top burial place at Knocknarea attributed to Celtic warrior Queen Maeve

Shady Drumcliffe churchyard, the burial place of Ireland's greatest poet, W. B. Yeats

Legends and Lakes

County Sligo is an enchanting place to visit, full of stories, poetry, and legend. Two dramatic mountains – mighty Ben Bulben and cairn-topped Knocknarea – overlook much of the county, a landscape that inspired the poetry of William Butler Yeats, who spent his childhood here. Sligo Town is an upbeat city, with a small-town friendliness and a lively river front. South of here are the surfing resorts of Strandhill and Enniscrone, also known for their seaweed baths, and the Ox Mountains, where Lough Easkey and Lough Talt offer good trout fishing and walks. For a feel of ancient Ireland, visit the passage tombs at Carrowmore, the largest megalithic burial site in Ireland, or remote Carrowkeel overlooking Lough Arrow.

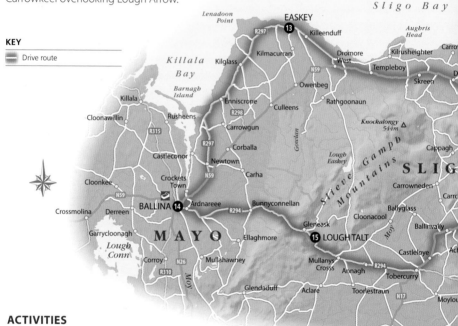

KEY

▬▬ Drive route

ACTIVITIES

Imagine the life of a 17th-century colonist at Parke's Castle on the shore of Lough Gill, then take a boat to Yeats' beloved isle of Innisfree

Read the letters and other writings of W. B. Yeats in Sligo County Library

Relax in a seaweed bath at Enniscrone or Strandhill, perhaps after a round of golf or a surfing lesson

Cast for trout or even salmon in River Ballysadare or Lough Easkey

Pet the equine inmates at a donkey and pony sanctuary at Castlebaldwin or watch a bird-flying display at the Irish Raptor Centre at Ballymote

Above The fishing village of Mullaghmore, a springboard for boat trips to Inishmurray, *see p202*

PLAN YOUR DRIVE

Start/finish: Mullaghmore to Lough Key.

Number of days: 4–5, allowing 1–2 days north of Sligo Town, half a day in the town, and 2 days to its south.

Distance: Approx. 125 miles (200 km).

Road conditions: The drive includes some unclassified roads, which are narrow and may not have markings. Take care on these roads, especially on bends. You may encounter sheep or other wildlife on rural roads.

When to go: Spring to autumn is best, but it can be wet and windy at any time of year. The winter months, when mountain roads may be impassable, are not as suitable for hill walking and other outdoor activities.

Opening times: Most shops and attractions open 9 or 10am–5 or 6pm. Shops open Mon–Sat; in large towns also noon–6pm on Sun.

Main market days: Sligo Town: Fri, Market Yard, (9am–3:30pm); Farmers' Market, Sat, Institute of Technology, (9am–1pm).

Shopping: Sligo Town has a variety of shops on O'Connell Street, Wine Street, and Grattan Street, and The Quayside and Johnston's Court shopping centers.

Major festivals: Sligo Town: Cairde Summer Festival, Jul; Yeats International Summer School, Jul–Aug; Jazz Festival, Jul; Sligo Live, Oct; International Choral Festival, Nov; **Around Carrowkeel Megalithic Cemetery**: Riverstown Vintage Festival, Jun; James Morrison Traditional Music, Riverstown, Aug.

DAY TRIP OPTIONS

Sligo Town makes a good base for day trips to both north and south. **Poetry lovers** might enjoy a trip around **Yeats country**, visiting the places that inspired the poet. To get a feel of **ancient Ireland**, visit the megalithic tombs at Carrowmore and Carrowkeel. For full details, see p209.

Left W. B. Yeats' grave in the churchyard of St. Columba's, Drumcliffe, see p203

Above Lissadell House, once the home of Constance Markeivicz, a leader of the Easter Uprising of 1916

Below A thatched cottage between Bundoran and Mullaghmore **Below center** The Round Tower at Drumcliffe **Below right** Fishing boats in the pretty harbor of Mullaghmore

① Mullaghmore
Co Sligo
The picturesque fishing village of Mullaghmore is pleasant to visit both for its harbor setting and for moody Classiebawn Castle nearby. Both castle and harbor were built from local stone. In the 20th century, the castle was the residence of British earl Lord Louis Mountbatten – killed when his boat was blown up off the coast in 1979. The headland has stunning views and a sandy beach.

The tiny, mystical island of **Inishmurray** lies offshore 4 miles (7 km) northwest of Streedagh Point. Weather permitting, boat trips to the island run from Mullaghmore pier from March to October *(087 667 4522)*. Founded by St Molaise in the 6th century, Inishmurray was a secluded monastic retreat and has remains including cursing stones, beehive cells, and engraved altars. The island is also an important bird and wildlife sanctuary.

🚗 *Take the R279 out of Mullaghmore but follow the Bundoran sign after 1 mile (1.5 km). Go straight across the N15, then straight over a further three small crossroads. Turn left at the sign for the Gleniff Horseshoe Drive, 3 miles (5 km) from the N15.*

The Legend of Diarmuid and Gráinne
Gráinne, daughter of the High King Cormac Mac Airt, was betrothed to the warrior and leader Fionn Mac Cumhaill, but she fell in love and eloped with another warrior called Diarmuid. For years they were pursued around the country by Fionn. While the couple were staying in a cave on Ben Bulben Diarmuid was killed by a boar on the slopes of the mountain and Gráinne died of grief. The cave was their last hiding place and they are said to be buried together inside it.

② Gleniff Horseshoe
Co Sligo
This circular drive through country roads leads to a magical spot behind **Ben Bulben**, the distinctive mountain that rises abruptly out of the plain. This beautifully austere valley is one of the most peaceful places in the county. The dark mouth of a cave

can be seen high up in the mountain-side. According to mythology, this was the last refuge of ill-fated lovers Diarmuid and Gráinne *(see box)*.

🚗 *Follow the drive back to the N15 and turn left onto it, through Mount Temple and Grange. Turn right at a signpost for Carney and follow the road for 3 miles (5 km) to Lissadell village. Follow signs for Lissadell House.*

❸ Lissadell House
Ballinfull, Co Sligo

This early 19th-century estate was the childhood home of Constance Markievicz, the first woman to be elected to the British House of Commons and one of the leaders of the Easter Rising of 1916 by Irish republicans. Her friend W. B. Yeats was a visitor here. The house, which overlooks the ocean, was built in Greek Revival style. Inside there is an eclectic collection of furnishings and paintings. Both the house and grounds have been restored. *(Currently closed due to a legal dispute; info@lissadellhouse.com; 071 916 3150)*

🚗 *Retrace the route to Carney. Head south to Orchard Grove and continue straight ahead. Turn right at the N15 for Drumcliffe, then left onto Drum Road.*

❹ Drumcliffe
Co Sligo

In St. Columba's churchyard in Drumcliffe, below the rocky hulk of Ben Bulben, is the **grave of W. B. Yeats**, one of Ireland's greatest poets *(see box)*. He was laid to rest here in 1948, nearly 10 years after his death, when his body was moved from the South of France. The poet had asked his wife to "dig me up and plant me in Sligo."

The village also has a **round tower**, damaged by lightning in 1396, and a **High Cross**, remnants of a monastic settlement founded in AD 574.

🚗 *Continue south on the N15, then, in Rathcormac, take the second left and immediately left again. Turn left at the N16, then left again for Glencar Lough. There is parking on the right, and a path leads to the waterfall.*

❺ Glencar Lough and Waterfall
Glencar, Co Leitrim

Surrounded by great, sweeping mountains carved out by ancient glaciers, **Glencar Lough** is fed by waterfalls and streams that descend from the slopes behind. These are even more spectacular after heavy rain. In particular, one waterfall sometimes gets blown skyward by the wind, giving the dramatic and unusual appearance that it is actually flowing upward.

The main **Glencar Waterfall** (50 ft/ 15 m high) crashes noisily into a rocky pool. "There is a waterfall ... that my childhood counted dear," wrote W. B. Yeats of Glencar *(Towards the Break of Day,* 1919).

🚗 *Turn right as you exit the parking lot and left onto the N16. Turn right onto the R286 and follow the signs toward Parke's Castle.*

W. B. Yeats (1865–1939)
Although born in Dublin, Nobel Laureate poet William Butler Yeats spent much of his youth in Co Sligo, forming a deep attachment to the county and calling it "The land of heart's desire." He returned many times and is buried in Drumcliffe churchyard. Sligo locations found in his poetry include Glencar, Innisfree (on Lough Gill), Dromahair (Leitrim), Lissadell House, Coole Park, and Ben Bulben. A well-marked tour of Yeats Country features many of these sites. Details are available from the Sligo Town Tourist Information office *(071 916 1201; info@irelandnorthwest.ie).*

Above Yeats Country: the landscape that inspired W. B. Yeats' poetry

Above Glencar Waterfall, one of several waterfalls tumbling into Glencar Lough

EAT AND DRINK

DRUMCLIFFE

Yeats Tavern *inexpensive*
This is a large lively pub with the adjoined Davis's Restaurant offering a variety of seafood, as well as poultry and game. It is popular on weekends for roast lunches and, weather permitting, you can also dine al fresco. *Drumcliffe (5 minutes' walk from the churchyard, along the N15); 071 916 3117; www.yeatstavernrestaurant.com*

AROUND DRUMCLIFFE

Lang's Bar and Restaurant *inexpensive*
As well as offering beautiful views of Ben Bulben, this traditional bar and restaurant incorporates a grocery store. It is a mere 10-minute walk from Streedagh Beach. *Grange; 071 916 3105; www.langs.ie*

Eat and Drink: inexpensive, under €25; moderate, €25–€50; expensive, over €50

Above Parke's Castle, a splendid fortified manor house overlooking Lough Gill

⑥ Parke's Castle and Lough Gill
Co Leitrim

Set on the shore of Lough Gill in spectacular countryside, **Parke's Castle** *(open Apr–Oct)* is a fortified manor house with wide mullioned windows built in 1609 by Captain Robert Parke. The house was built over the site of the original 15th-century castle, home to a prominent local clan, the O'Rourkes (Uí Ruairc). The stones of O'Rourke's tower were used to build the three-story manor on the eastern side. It has been carefully restored using Irish oak and traditional craftsmanship, and is a fine example of the plantation style of architecture favored by the 17th-century settlers.

Boat trips around **Lough Gill** *(Easter–Oct)* leave from a jetty outside the castle walls.

The lake itself is the location of Yeats' beloved **Isle of Innisfree** – "There midnight's all a glimmer, and noon a purple glow." It is possible to visit the tiny island. There is not much to see, though visitors may, like the poet, "hear lake water lapping with low sounds by the shore."

The bell of Sligo Abbey is said to be at the bottom of Lough Gill. According to legend, it was sunk when the abbey was demolished in 1642. It is said that those pure of heart can still hear it tolling.

🚗 *Continue on the R286 to Sligo. On the way there is a viewing point overlooking Lough Colgagh.*

⑦ Sligo Town
Co Sligo

Although technically a city, Sligo is locally referred to as Sligo Town. A gateway to the northwest, it is an attractive blend of quaint charm and modern verve. Striking new buildings like The Glasshouse sit side by side with charming older ones such as the Yeats Memorial Building, both overlooking the Garavogue River, a popular focal point whose banks are lined with shops and restaurants. Sligo's main street is O'Connell Street.

VISITING SLIGO TOWN

Parking
Park in Quay Street parking lot on Lower Quay Street or in the Quayside Shopping Centre underground parking lot, which is just opposite.

Tourist Information
Fáilte Ireland Northwest, Temple St; 071 916 1201; www.discoverireland.ie/ sligo; open Mon–Fri 9am–6pm, Sat 10am–4pm, Sun 11am–3pm; winter closed Sat

WHERE TO STAY IN SLIGO TOWN

The Clarion Hotel *moderate*
Large hotel in a historic building with an Elizabethan facade. Houses a leisure center and spa, as well as a kids' club, making it particularly popular with families. There are also some apartments to rent.
Clarion Road; 071 911 9000; www.clarionhotelsligo.com

The Glasshouse *moderate*
This stunning glass building overlooking the Garavogue River is in an ideal location for exploring the city. Quirky interior in bright colors designed to reflect Sligo's vibrancy.
Swan Point, Hyde Bridge; 071 919 4300; www.theglasshouse.ie

A two-hour walking tour

From the Lower Quay Street parking lot cross to the riverside to see the **Famine Memorial ①**, which commemorates the thousands who died in the Great Famine of 1845. Many others emigrated from Sligo's quays. Turn left into Quay Street for

Above Curiosities in one of the cozy pubs on Sligo Town's Rockwood Parade

City Hall ②, an Italian Renaissance-style building dating from 1865. On the corner is the **Post Office ③** built in 1901 and the traditional storefront of Henry Lyons and Co, a Sligo landmark since 1878.

Across Wine Street, beside Douglas Hyde Bridge, is the **Yeats Memorial Building ④**, erected in 1895 and now home to the Yeats Society and venue for the annual Yeats International Summer School.

Cross five-arched Hyde Bridge onto Stephen Street. In front of the Neo-Classical building commissioned for Ulster Bank in 1863 is a **statue of W. B. Yeats ⑤**. Next door are the **County Library** and **County Museum ⑥** *(both closed Sun and Mon; museum closed lunchtime)*. The museum's Yeats section contains the poet's Nobel Prize medal and letters.

Continue along Stephen Street and into the Mall for the **Model Arts Centre and Niland Gallery ⑦** *(071 914 1405; www.modelart.ie)*. Retrace the route along Stephen

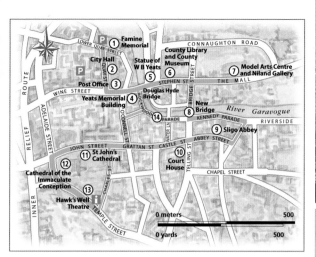

Above Altar by the holy well at Tobernalt on the north shore of Lough Gill

Street and turn left onto Bridge Street to cross **New Bridge** ⑧ – built in 1682 – over the river. Turn left down Kennedy Parade and right into Abbey Street for **Sligo Abbey** ⑨ (open Apr– Oct: daily; Nov: Fri–Sun only) built in 1252, destroyed by fire in 1414, and rebuilt with Gothic and Renaissance carvings and cloisters. It has the only 15th-century high altar to survive in an Irish monastic church.

Pass the sandstone **Court House** ⑩ at the end of Abbey Street, cross over to Castle Street and continue up Grattan Street and John Street to **St. John's Cathedral** ⑪ (closed to visitors), where the parents of W. B. Yeats were married in 1863. Further along John Street is the **Cathedral of the Immaculate**

Yeats statue, Sligo Town

Conception ⑫ (open daily), built in 1858–95 and noted for its fine stained glass.

Turn left onto Temple Street for the **Hawk's Well Theatre** ⑬ and the tourist office. Take a left down "The Lungy" and Charles Street back to John Street and turn right. Take the first left down O'Connell Street and then first right down Tobergal Lane to riverside **Rockwood Parade** ⑭, a bustling hub of cafés, restaurants, and shops. Turn left onto the parade toward Hyde Bridge, left again, then right onto Quay Street to return to the parking lot.

🚗 Take the N15 north, signposted Lifford, and first left onto the R291 for Rosses Point, 5 miles (8 km) from Sligo.

EAT AND DRINK

AROUND PARKE'S CASTLE AND LOUGH GILL

Riverbank Restaurant moderate
Rustic-style restaurant in a picturesque location on the banks of the River Bonet in pretty Dromahair, where the chef serves creative cuisine using fresh local ingredients.
Dromahair (from Parke's Castle return towards Manorhamilton but turn right onto the R288, and follow the road south to Dromahair); 071 91 64934; open Wed–Sun eves and Sun lunch

SLIGO TOWN

Fureys Sheela Na Gig inexpensive
This is an old-style pub with regular traditional music sessions, right in the heart of Sligo Town.
Bridge St; no phone

Bistro Bianconi moderate
Informal Italian restaurant that is popular with locals. Large menu, with pizza, pasta, steak, and seafood.
Tobergall Lane; 071 914 1744; www.bistrobianconi.ie

Coach Lane moderate
Traditional food and a cozy atmosphere in this restaurant above Donaghy's bar. Buffalo wings, seafood, poultry, and organic produce feature on the menu. There is a terrace for outdoor eating, weather permitting.
1–2 Lord Edward Street; 071 916 2417

Fiddlers Creek moderate
Lively pub with food served in the bar or in the more formal restaurant. Options include spicy chicken wings, grilled steak, and tasty seafood bakes.
Rockwood Parade; 071 914 1866; www.fiddlerscreek.ie

Left Five-arched Douglas Hyde Bridge over the River Garavogue in Sligo Town

Eat and Drink: inexpensive, under €25; moderate €25–€50; expensive over €50

Above Fishing at Rosses Point **Above top right** An open fire in the Strand Bar, Strandhill **Above right** Native seaweed, used as a spa treatment at the seaweed baths at Strandhill and Enniscrone

⑧ Rosses Point
Co Sligo

After the bustle of Sligo, drive out to the quiet peninsula of Rosses Point, ideal for a relaxing beach walk. The village has pubs and restaurants and at the end of the peninsula there are beaches, sand dunes, an 18-hole links golf course and a yacht club. In the harbor stands the "Metal Man," a giant statue of a sailor, pointing ships safely into the channel for Sligo. **Oyster Island** and **Coney Island** are both visible from here.

🚗 *Retrace the route back into Sligo. Take the R292 at the bus and train station, for Strandhill, about 5 miles (8 km) from Sligo. In Strandhill, park in the seafront parking lot.*

⑨ Strandhill
Co Sligo

This small seaside resort, overlooked by the brooding Knocknarea Mountain, is a popular surfing destination. The beach is unsafe for swimming (it is prohibited), but the strands are great for leisurely walks in both directions – at low tide it is possible to walk over Dorrin's Strand to **Coney Island**. The village has a surf club, two surf schools, and a challenging 18-hole links golf course. It is also home to the **Voya spa**, which specializes in Ireland's only indigenous therapy – seaweed baths *(open daily; book in advance in summer 071 916 8686; www.voya.ie).*

🚗 *Leaving Strandhill, keep to the right at the Y-junction at the pink church. There is a sign for Ballysadare and Carrowmore. Continue along the R292 until a left turn at the sign for Knocknarea. Park in the parking lot.*

⑩ Knocknarea
Co Sligo

This enormous cairn atop Knocknarea is 180 ft (55 m) in diameter and 33 ft (10 m) high. According to folklore, it was built as a burial place for the legendary Queen Maeve (Medbh in Irish), an Iron Age queen. She is supposed to have been buried standing up, in full battle uniform. Archeologists believe the cairn actually dates from around 3000 BC, much earlier than the legend suggests. Maeve's cairn is a 45-minute walk from the parking lot. On a clear day

WHERE TO STAY AROUND BALLYSADARE

Castle Dargan *expensive*
Set in 170 acres of mature landscape, this hotel also has an 18-hole golf course which was designed by golfer Darren Clarke and a spa with a hydrotherapy pool and oxygen bar. *From the N4, take the R284 exit and follow signs to Ballygawley. Castle Dargan is on Dromahair Road; 071 911 8080; www.castledargan.com*

Above Surfers on the beach at Strandhill, one of Ireland's best beaches for surfing

Where to Stay: inexpensive, under €100; moderate, €100–€200; expensive, over €200

there are fine views over Sligo and the surrounding five counties.

🚌 *Return to the R292 and turn left. Continue straight on at the roundabout to Carrowmore. Park in the parking lot.*

⑪ Carrowmore Megalithic Cemetery
Co Sligo

The largest megalithic burial ground in Ireland, **Carrowmore** is also one of the most significant sites of its kind in Europe. There are in excess of 60 tombs here – a fascinating mixture of small passage-tombs and dolmens (a type of single-chamber tomb enclosed by boulders). Some archeological research suggests that Carrowmore's oldest tombs are more than 5,000 years old. The visitor center *(Apr–Oct daily; last admission 5pm)* offers informative guided tours of the cemetery in season.

🚌 *Turn right out of the parking lot and right again. Return to the R292 and turn left. Turn right onto the N59 and continue straight on into Ballysadare. Park in the center of the village.*

Above View from Knocknarea, the last resting place of the legendary Queen Maeve

⑫ Ballysadare
Co Sligo

This picturesque village, where the River Ballysadare flows into the sea is a prime location for salmon fishing. W. B. Yeats spent a lot of time in this area as a child and it is believed to have inspired his poem *Down by the Sally Gardens.*

Above The River Ballysadare and Lough Easkey are popular with anglers

🚌 *Cross the bridge and turn right onto the N59 for Ballina. Pass a turn for Glen Wood to the left, nice for walks and picnics. Continue on the N59 until a sign for Easkey. Turn right here, onto the R297.*

⑬ Easkey
Co Sligo

The small village of Easkey and the slightly larger seaside resort of **Enniscrone** (also Innishcrone), farther around the coast, are set on a beautiful rocky shoreline. The main attraction here is the **surfing** *(see right)* and the Irish Surfing Association is based here. Enniscrone has a sweeping 2-mile (3-km) Blue Flag beach. Other attractions there include Kilcullen's Seaweed Baths *(www.kilcullenseaweedbaths.com)*, established in 1912, and proud of its Edwardian ambience, and Enniscrone Golf Course.

🚌 *From Easkey or Enniscrone follow the R297 south toward Newtown. After Newtown, turn onto the N59 and continue for Ballina.*

Queen Maeve of Connaught

Maeve (or Medbh), the Celtic warrior Queen of Connaught, was a character in the mythological tale *The Táin*. Although she was powerful, she was jealous of her husband Ailill's white bull. Searching for an equal, she found the Brown Bull of Cooley in Ulster. But its owners refused to lend it to her, so she and her army invaded Ulster and stole it. Legend says that when she got the bull home, it fought and killed her husband's white bull and then died on its way home to Ulster.

SURFING AT EASKEY

Easkey Surf Information Centre is based on Main Street and posts daily surf reports on its noticeboard *(096 49020; easkeyhouse@yahoo.com)*. Lessons are also available from the **Seventh Wave Surf School** in Easkey and Enniscrone *(087 971 6389; www.seventhwavesurfschool.com)*.

EAT AND DRINK AT STRANDHILL

The Venue *inexpensive–moderate*
A traditional-style pub and a large, friendly restaurant, with everything from shrimp to steaks, make this a popular spot in Strandhill.
Top Road; 071 916 8167

The Strand Bar & Restaurant
moderate
A lively bar, popular with surfers, serves bar meals all day and has live music at weekends. Upstairs, a separate restaurant, the Jade Garden serves Chinese and Thai food in elegant surroundings. There is also a seafood restaurant, Trà Ban, on the premises.
Strand Bar: 071 916 8140
Jade Garden: 071 916 8935
Trà Ban: 071 912 8402

Eat and Drink: inexpensive, under €25; moderate, €25–€50; expensive, over €50

Above View from Carrowkeel Megalithic Tombs over Lough Arrow

WHERE TO STAY

BALLINA

The Ice House Hotel *moderate*
This stunning boutique hotel overlooks the River Moy and blends country style and contemporary chic.
The Quay; 096 23 500; www.icehousehotel.ie

AROUND CARROWKEEL MEGALITHIC CEMETERY

Gyreum Ecolodge *inexpensive*
Set in great surroundings near Lough Arrow and the Bricklieve Mountains, Gyreum has small rooms, large dorms, and "tent" capsules in the central hall.
Corlisheen, Riverstown (from Carrowkeel take N4 to Castlebaldwin and turn right, following signs over Bow & Arrow crossroads and through Killadoon crossroads. Take first turn after Killadoon on left (on steep hill) and continue for half a mile (1 km). Entrance to Gyreum is on right); 071 916 5994; www.gyreum.com

Cromleach Lodge
moderate–expensive
This smart, family-run country house hotel has great views over Lough Arrow and the Bricklieve Mountains.
Castlebaldwin, Lough Arrow (4 miles/ 6 km off the N4); 071 916 5155; www.cromleach.com

Coopershill House *expensive*
This beautiful Georgian mansion has been the home of the O'Hara family for seven generations and offers visitors a warm welcome, with open fires, candlelit dinners, acres of lovely grounds, and four-poster beds.
Clearly marked 1 mile (2 km) from Riverstown (from Carrowkeel take N4 to Drumfin and take right turn to Riverstown); 071 916 5108; www.coopershill.com; closed Nov 1–March 31

⑭ Ballina
Co Mayo

The largest town in the county, Ballina is a charming market town, set on the River Moy. It is famous for its hospitality with plenty of shops and cafés, and good fishing along the river. Among Ballina's attractions are the ruins of **Moyne Abbey** and **Rosserk Friary** dating back to the 15th century, and the impressive **St Muredach's Cathedral** (completed in 1831). Every July the town hosts a popular street festival with many events and live music.

🚗 *Take the R294 east toward Gleneask and turn right into the parking lot at Lough Talt.*

⑮ Lough Talt
Co Sligo

This magical place is a favorite spot with trout fishermen. There is an easy walk around the shore (4 miles/6 km) and it is also the start for the much longer Sligo Way walk. Lough Talt has two *crannógs* – small man-made islands inhabited in the Iron Age. Continue along the road through the rolling countryside of the Ox Mountains to reach **Lough Easkey**. With its wide open skies and a spare beauty, it is popular with anglers and walkers. A few miles (kilometers) beyond Lough Easkey, at Mass Hill, is the **Shaking Rock**, a massive boulder that can be rocked by hand, but amazingly, has never fallen.

🚗 *Return to the R294 and continue, signposted Boyle. Carry on into Tobercurry. From here, turn left back onto R294. Just as the R296 is reached there is a left turn for Portinch.*

⑯ Irish Raptor Centre
Portinch, Ballymote

Watch eagles, hawks, and falcons swooping overhead at the center *(071 91 89310; www.eaglesflying.com; open Easter–Nov: daily; closed lunchtime)*, which has two daily flying demonstrations and interactive shows about the lives and habits of the various birds of prey. Visitors are allowed to touch some of the birds. There is also a petting zoo with goats, sheep, rabbits, guinea pigs and donkeys.

🚗 *Return to the R294 and continue on it, following the signs to Boyle. At Tobercurry, turn left onto the N17 toward Sligo, then, after 9 miles (14 km), turn right following the signs for "Eagles flying."*

⑰ Carrowkeel Megalithic Cemetery
Co Sligo

Overlooking Lough Arrow in the scenic Bricklieve Mountains, the remote cemetery at Carrowkeel *(open daily)* dates back to around 3800 BC. The site comprises 14 hill-top passage tombs with an additional six to the west. Excavated in 1911, the tombs, which differ in

Below The 19th-century St. Muredach's cathedral on the banks of the River Moy in the attractive market town of Ballina, seen from one of the town's bridges

Above Ponies enjoy the good life at the Sathya Sai Sanctuary Trust, a charity founded to take care of elderly and abandoned ponies and donkeys

style and size, are particularly good examples of Irish passage tombs. One of them is similar to Newgrange *(see p160)*, except that in Carrowkeel the inner chamber is lit by the sun on the summer solstice (June 21), rather than on the winter solstice as happens at Newgrange.

Children might enjoy a visit to the **Sathya Sai Sanctuary**, a rest home for neglected ponies and donkeys *(www.donkeys.ie; 071 966 6196;*

open Apr–Oct: weekends, Wed–Fri phone ahead for appointment). From Carrowkeel, follow the signs for the equine sanctuary a little farther down the same road.

🚗 *Leaving the sanctuary, head south on the N4. At the first exit for Boyle, continue on the N4 for approximately 5 miles (8 km). The entrance to Lough Key Forest Park is on the left. Go down the driveway to enter the parking lot.*

⑱ Lough Key
Boyle, Co Roscommon

Lough Key Forest Park *(open daily; www.loughkey.ie)* is one of Ireland's most extensive parks. It comprises some 530 acres (350 hectares) of stunning forest and mixed woodland, with walking trails including a tree canopy walk suspended 30 ft (9 m) above the ground. Among the park's lakes and islands, Trinity Island houses the remains of an ancient abbey. Boats are available for rent, and there are also picnic areas, a lakeside visitor's center and a well-equipped children's playground.

Above The entrance to one of the passage tombs at Carrowkeel

EAT AND DRINK AROUND CARROWKEEL MEGALITHIC CEMETERY

Coopershill House
moderate–expensive
Have a drink by the fire before enjoying a superb gourmet meal served in the elegant, authentic Georgian dining room of this country-house hotel.
Clearly marked 1 mile (2 km) from Riverstown; 071 916 5108; www.coopershill.com; closed Nov 1–March 31

DAY TRIP OPTIONS
Sligo Town is an ideal base for exploring Yeats Country and the ancient cemeteries.

Yeats Country
Poetry lovers and romantics could take a trip around the places that inspired W. B. Yeats. In Sligo Town ⑦, pay homage to the poet's statue, and see his Nobel Prize medal in the

County Museum. Drive to Drumcliffe ④, where the poet is buried. Continue to dramatic Glencar Lough and Waterfall ⑤, and return to the town via Lough Gill ⑥, where boat trips to Yeats' beloved Isle of Innisfree are available from Parke's Castle jetty.

Take the N15 to Drumcliffe, then follow the drive's instructions to Glencar Lough and Lough Gill.

Ancient Ireland
Drive south to Carrowmore Megalithic Cemetery ⑪ for a guided tour of the passage tombs. Continue south to Carrowkeel Megalithic Cemetery ⑰.

Follow the drive's instructions to Carrowmore. From there, take the R292 to the N3, then N4, and turn off at Castlebaldwin for Carrowkeel.

Eat and Drink: inexpensive under €25; moderate €25–€50; expensive over €50

Dramatic Donegal

Newmills to Rossnowlagh

Highlights

- **Rugged Glenveagh National Park**
  Spot wild deer and golden eagles and explore mountains, lakes, glens, and Glenveagh Castle

- **Scenic Horn Head**
  Watch puffins, guillemots, and storm petrels, and hike over the headland

- **The rocky Rosses**
  Meander through this pretty corner of Donegal, a landscape dotted with lakes and fringed with secluded bays

- **Old-world Glencolmcille**
  Time travel to 18th-century rural Donegal in the Folk Village Museum

- **Breathtaking Slieve League**
  Brave the sheer drops of Slieve League, some of the highest sea cliffs in Europe

The remains of Donegal's Franciscan Abbey on the mouth of the River Eske

Dramatic Donegal

A rugged hinterland and dramatic headlands give Donegal a fierce beauty. Cliffs battered by fierce Atlantic storms shelter unspoiled coves and beaches; remote inland valleys harbor wild deer and pairs of golden eagles. But the wild is tempered by the human: Glenveagh Castle has one of Ireland's finest gardens and The Rosses is the birthplace of several of Ireland's leading musicians. Everywhere, there's a warm Irish welcome, especially in the good seafood restaurants and pubs. This coastal drive provides a rich and varied experience, from braving the heights of Slieve League to enjoying simple seaside pleasures in Rossnowlagh on Donegal Bay.

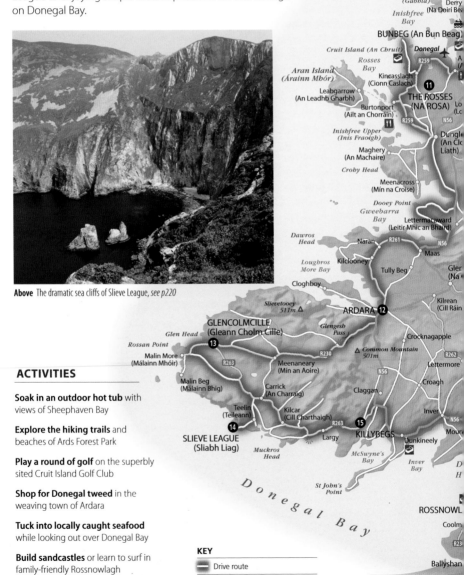

Above The dramatic sea cliffs of Slieve League, *see p220*

ACTIVITIES

Soak in an outdoor hot tub with views of Sheephaven Bay

Explore the hiking trails and beaches of Ards Forest Park

Play a round of golf on the superbly sited Cruit Island Golf Club

Shop for Donegal tweed in the weaving town of Ardara

Tuck into locally caught seafood while looking out over Donegal Bay

Build sandcastles or learn to surf in family-friendly Rossnowlagh

KEY

⊂⊃ Drive route

0 kilometers 8

0 miles 8

Tory Island
(Toraigh)
West Town
(Baile Thiar)

Tory Sound

Inishbofin
(Inis Bó Finne)

Magheraroarty
(Machaire
Rabhartaigh)

Falcarragh
(An Fál Carrach)

Gortahork
(Gort an Choirce)

weedore
aoth Dobhair)

DUNLEWEY
(Dún Lúiche)

Sheephaven
Bay

HORN HEAD **7**

11 DUNFANAGHY

6

Corcreggan

Tramore
Beach

Portnablagh

Carrigart
(Carraig Airt)

11

5 ARDS FOREST PARK

Creeslough

4 DOE CASTLE

Glen

Glen Lough

Drumnaraw
(Droim na Rátha)

Muckish Alt
670m

Glack

GLENVEAGH
NATIONAL PARK
AND CASTLE **3**

Milford

Termon
(An Tearmann)

Errigal
749m

Lough
Beagh

Kilmacrenan

Lough
Fern

Ramelton

Slieve Snaght
683m

THE GLEBE HOUSE
AND GALLERY **2**

Lough
Gartan

Churchill

Dromore

Ellistrin

Glendowan
(Gleann
Domhain)

Corderry

Letterkenny

oocharry
n Dúchoraidh)

Altadush

Breenagh

NEWMILLS **1**

Swilly

Kingarrow
(An Cionn Garbh)

Cark

Bellanamore
(Béal an Átha Móir)

Fintown
na Finne)

Lough
Finn

Cloghan
(An Clochán)

Welchtown

O N E G A L

Commeen
(An Coimín)

Tangaveane
(An tSeanga Mheáin)

b More
676m

Blue Stack
678m

Ardnamona

Friary

Lough
Eske

Barnesmore
Pass

Barnesmore

16 DONEGAL TOWN

Copany

Laghy

Lough
Derg

Bridge Town

Ballintra

angarden

Below Light fades over the Franciscan
abbey on Donegal Bay, *see p221*

PLAN YOUR DRIVE

Start/finish: Newmills to
Rossnowlagh.

Number of days: 4–5 days.

Distance: 157 miles (253 km).

Road conditions: This drive includes
narrow regional and unclassified roads,
which are sometimes single lane – pull
over or reverse into a wide spot to
allow oncoming vehicles to pass.
Watch out for animals on the road.

When to go: Winter can be very wet,
and some hotels and restaurants
close. Jun–Aug is best, but busiest.
Plan carefully around festivals, when
accommodation can get booked up.

Opening times: Shops are usually
open Mon–Sat from 9 or 10am to 5 or
6pm. Attractions are generally open
similar hours, but also Sunday.

Main market days: Donegal: Farmers'
Market, first Sat of month.

Shopping: Ardara is the center for
handwoven Donegal Tweed – from
caps and coats to lengths of cloth.

Major festivals: Dunfanaghy:
Seafood Festival, May; **Dungloe:** Mary
from Dungloe Festival, Jul; **Ardara:**
Cup of Tae Traditional Festival, Apr.

DAY TRIP OPTIONS

Spend a day in **Glenveagh National
Park**, exploring the castle, lake, and
hills; head for **The Rosses**, an area of
small lakes and pretty beaches or focus
on the varied attractions of **Donegal
Bay**, a short hop from Donegal Town.
For full details, *see p221*.

Above Doe Castle, overlooking Sheephaven Bay **Above top right** The waterwheel at Newmills Corn and Flax Mills **Above right** Creeslough, on the road to Dunfanaghy

❶ Newmills
Co Donegal

Newmills Corn and Flax Mills (*open Jun–Sep*), on the banks of the River Swilly, are fine relics of Ireland's industrial heritage, with some parts of the complex dating back 400 years. The corn mill is driven by one of the largest waterwheels in the country, while a smaller wheel powers the machinery for extracting the fiber in flax. There are working models and demonstrations that show how flax is turned into linen cloth.

🚗 *Leaving Newmills, turn left at main road and continue on R250, then on*

R251 to Churchill. Drive on, passing Lough Gartan on the left. Turn left at a sign for Glebe House and Gallery; it is a short distance off the main road.

❷ The Glebe House and Gallery
Churchill, Co Donegal

Once the home of English-born landscape and society portrait artist Derek Hill (1916–2000), this red-brick Regency-style house (*open Easter: daily; Jun–Sep: Sat–Thu*) on the shore of Lough Gartan was built in 1828 as a rectory. Guided tours of the well-preserved interior reveal William Morris wallpapers, Islamic ceramics, paintings by Tory Island artists (*see p217*) and objects collected by Hill over the years – etchings and ceramics by Picasso, and paintings by Renoir, Kokoschka, and Jack B. Yeats. The adjacent Glebe Gallery stages changing exhibitions.

🚗 *Continue on the R251 to Glenveagh National Park Visitor Centre.*

❸ Glenveagh National Park and Castle
Churchill, Co Donegal

This spectacular national park (*open daily*) covers 61 sq. miles (16,000 hectares) of mountains, lakes, bogs, and woodlands, home to red deer and golden eagles – the latter reintroduced to Ireland in 2001. In the center of the park is the castellated **Glenveagh Castle**, a 19th-century structure set beside Lough Veagh, while dome-shaped **Mount Errigal** (2,457 ft/749 m), the highest

Below Moody view of Glenveagh National Park, with Lough Veagh at the center

Above Errigal Mountain, the highest in Donegal, marks the western end of Glenveagh National Park

mountain in Donegal, overlooks the park to the west. The **Visitor Centre** *(open Easter and Jun–Sep)* supplies information, maps, and tickets for the shuttle bus to the castle (every 15 minutes) for guided tours of the late-Victorian interior, walks in the gardens – particularly notable for their rhododendrons from March to May – tearooms, and nature trail leading to a viewpoint over Lough Veagh. It is also possible to walk the 4 miles (7 km) to the castle.

Regular guided walks are offered by park rangers and there are serious walking trails for experienced hikers.

Leaving Glenveagh Visitor Centre, turn right onto the R251 and take the second left onto the R255 toward Termon. Turn left at the N56 for Creeslough and Dunfanaghy. In Creeslough, turn right at the sign for Doe Castle, 2 miles (3 km) off the main road.

④ Doe Castle
Creeslough, Co Donegal
Sixteenth-century Doe Castle *(open daily)* is worth seeing for its lovely setting on a promontory on Sheephaven Bay, with sea on three sides. It was originally the seat of the MacSweeneys, a family of Scottish mercenaries who were outlawed in 1691. Occupied until 1909, it is now run by the state. It is also a venue for traditional music and other events.

Drive back along the same road to the N56 and continue north, turning right at the sign for Ards Forest Park. Park in the marked parking lot.

The Rock of Doon
A right turn off the R255 to Termon from Glenveagh leads to Garton and the **Rock of Doon** (Carraig a Duin), where chieftains of Donegal's leading clan, the O'Donnells, were inaugurated from 1200 until 1603. A path leads up to the rock from a small parking lot, next to which is the **Well of Doon**, one of Ireland's many healing wells. Another path leads to the **Mass Rocks**, where Catholics held Mass in secret after the introduction of anti-Catholic penal laws in 1691.

⑤ Ards Forest Park
Creeslough, Co Donegal
With woodlands, lakes, rivers, bogs, and good sandy beaches, this forest park offers well-marked hiking trails, 2–8 miles (3–13 km) in length. Points of interest include megalithic tombs and four Iron Age ring forts.

Rejoin the N56 and continue north to Dunfanaghy.

⑥ Dunfanaghy
Co Donegal
The gateway to the Horn Head Peninsula, this attractive holiday resort has a fine 18-hole links golf course. Its other attraction is **The Workhouse** *(open Mar–Sep: Mon–Sat)*, once the last refuge of the desperate poor and now a heritage center documenting life in the area during the Great Famine.

Follow Horn Head signs out of town for the scenic drive, and park at Horn Head Bridge for walk to Tramore Beach.

EAT AND DRINK

DUNFANAGHY

Muck and Muffins *inexpensive*
Watch pottery being made in the clay and pottery studio and then enjoy cake and coffee or a glass of wine in this café and wine bar in the center of Dunfanaghy.
The Square, 074 913 6780; www.mucknmuffins.com

AROUND DUNFANAGHY

The Cove *moderate*
This cozy, family-run restaurant overlooking Sheephaven Bay at Rockhill, a couple of miles (kilometers) east of Dunfanaghy (from Dunfanaghy, take the N56 in the direction of Letterkenny), serves contemporary Irish cuisine with an emphasis on fresh seafood.
Rockhill, Port na Blagh; 074 913 6300

Below Heather-strewn hills around the Rock of Doon, beyond Glenveagh National Park

VISITING HORN HEAD

Parking
As you leave Dunfanaghy for the scenic drive around Horn Head you pass Horn Head Bridge half a mile (1 km) west of the town, where you can park for the walk to Tramore Beach.

WHERE TO STAY

AROUND HORN HEAD

The Mill House *inexpensive*
A pretty mill house, dating from 1798, near Tramore Beach, 10 miles (16 km) west of Dunfanaghy. It has ensuite B&B rooms and dormitory rooms, as well as camping facilities.
Corcreggan, Dunfanaghy; 074 913 6409; www.corcreggan.com

Arnold's Hotel *moderate*
This landmark hotel has been in the same family for generations. Some of the well-appointed rooms overlook Sheephaven Bay. Enjoy dinner in the Seascapes Restaurant.
Dunfanaghy; 074 913 6208; www.arnoldshotel.com

BUNBEG

Óstán Gweedore Bunbeg *expensive*
A three-star hotel in a pretty setting overlooking the bay. Has a seafood restaurant, a wine bar, and a leisure complex with heated pool. The sea-facing side of the hotel has outdoor decking on which to have a drink and watch the sunset.
Bunbeg; 074 953 1177; www.ostangweedore.com

⓻ Horn Head
Dunfanaghy, Co Donegal

A scenic 8-mile (13-km) drive around Horn Head offers panoramic views of the northwest coast, from the Rosguill Peninsula off to the east to Tory Island and the Bloody Foreland to the west. The lonely, heather-covered headland rises sheer from the sea, its ledges an ideal habitat for guillemots, gulls, puffins, and storm petrels. At the tip of the headland, walk to the viewpoint at Faugher for the best views of the 600-ft (180-m) high cliffs, as well as the ruins of a 17th-century signal tower. Afterward enjoy a walk to Tramore Beach from Horn Head Bridge.

A two-hour walking tour to Tramore Beach

It is possible to walk all the way round Horn Head (8 miles/13 km), but for a shorter walk (5 miles/8 km), concentrate on the area just north of Tramore Beach, the beautiful dune-fringed arc of sand that stretches along the western side of Horn Head.

The beach can be accessed along a public footpath from **Horn Head Bridge** ①. At the far end of the bridge a public footpath runs for nearly 2 miles (3 km) through the sand dunes. **Tramore Beach** ② has rock pools to explore as well as a Celtic **stone circle** ③ on the hill overlooking the beach – to reach it, follow the sheep track north. Don't miss **McSwine's Gun** ④, near the edge of the cliff – a sea cave with a blow hole which noisily spouts water when the northwesterly winds blow. On a calm day it is possible to peer down the blow hole to the sea, about 100 ft (30 m) below (take extra care around here, especially in inclement weather).

To complete the short walk, retrace the path back to Horn Head Bridge.
🚌 *Continue along the N56 through the Gaeltacht town of Falcarragh, and follow the signs for Bloody Foreland. Keep right on Station Road and turn onto the R257 after Gortahork.*

Flock of sheep clustered on a rugged Donegal hillside

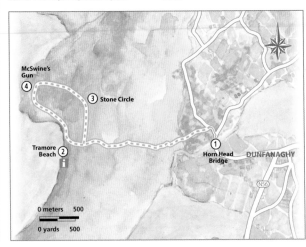

8 Bloody Foreland
Co Donegal

This most northwesterly corner of Ireland is said to have been named for the red glow of its rocks at sunset, though more sinister rumors claim it refers to past battles. Though fairly built up, parts of it remain wild and windswept, and from the north side of the headland there are superb views out to **Tory Island** and back to Horn Head and **Muckish Mountain**. The beaches here attract surfers. As the road turns the corner and heads south to **Bun na Leaca**, there are views to **The Rosses** and **Aran Island**.
🚗 *Continue along the R257 south through Derrybeg to Bunbeg.*

9 Bunbeg (An Bun Beag)

Visitors are likely to hear Irish spoken in this long, narrow village, which has views of the sea on one side and toward conical Mount Errigal on the other. On the way through, take a right turn at the brown "*Trá*" (beach) sign and drive to the tiny harbor. Ferries serve Tory Island year round and nearby **Gola Island** in summer.
🚗 *Leaving Bunbeg, take the R258 to Gweedore, then turn left on the N56. At the junction with the R251, fork right, driving alongside Lough Dunlewey. Dunlewey is at the far end of the lake, below Mount Errigal.*

Visiting Tory Island

Ferries to Tory Island, 9 miles (15 km) off Donegal's coast, leave from **Magheroarty** (which has a good crafts shop) on the road to Bloody Foreland, and the village of **Bunbeg**, and take about an hour (*www.toryislandferry.com*). The island is famous for its artists, drawn here by the quality of its light since the 1950s, and 6th-century **monastic ruins** with a **round tower**. Bikes can be rented to explore the island and coastal paths offer good walking. The main village is **West Town**.

Above left Craggy rock formations on Tory Island **Above** The hilly lanes around the village of Bunbeg

Above Bunbeg's attractive harbor, departure point for ferries to Tory and Gola islands

EAT AND DRINK

AROUND HORN HEAD

The Mill Restaurant *moderate*
Very popular family-run restaurant on the shores of New Lake on the N56 west of Dunfanaghy, soon after the turning for Horn Head. Serves modern Irish cuisine using fresh, local produce. Also has six ensuite guestrooms. Book well in advance, especially in summer. *Figart, Dunfanaghy, Co Donegal; 074 913 6985; www.themillrestaurant.com*

BUNBEG

Ostan Radharc Na Mara (Sea View Hotel) *inexpensive*
Informal bar/restaurant with a great selection of seafood. *Bunbeg; 074 953 1076*

Teach Hiudái Beag *inexpensive*
Traditional pub with a lively folk music session every Monday night. *Bunbeg; 074 953 1016*

Eat and Drink: inexpensive, under €25; moderate, €25–€50; expensive, over €50

Above Isolated cottage near Burtonport in The Rosses **Above top right** Grassy landscape around the village of Ardara, the start of the Glengesh Pass **Above right** Low tide exposes the mudflats at The Rosses

VISITING ARAN ISLAND

Ferries make the 15-minute crossing from Burtonport to Aran (Arranmore) Island frequently in Jun, Jul, and Aug. *Arranmore Fast Ferry; (087) 317 1810; www.arranmorefastferry.com*

WHERE TO STAY

DUNLEWEY

Errigal Youth Hostel *inexpensive*
This hostel enjoys a spectacular location at the foot of Mount Errigal in Dunlewey. It's an ideal base for exploring Glenveagh National Park or Mount Errigal itself.
Dunlewey; 074 953 1180; www.errigalhostel.com

THE ROSSES

Donegal Thatched Cottages *inexpensive–moderate*
A selection of attractive cottages on Cruit Island, set in the midst of some of the most breathtaking scenery in Donegal.
Cruit Island, Kincasslagh; 071 9177197; www.donegalthatchedcottages.com

⑩ Dunlewey (Dún Lúiche)
Dunlewey, Co Donegal

The 100-ft (30-m) high round tower of the Church of the Sacred Heart – a 19th-century take on early Christian forms – signals the approach to Dunlewey, set on the shores of Lough Dunlewey under Donegal's highest mountain, Mount Errigal. The various attractions of **Dunlewey Lakeside Centre** (Ionad Cois Locha), *(open daily)* include a recreated 19th-century weaver's cottage, a small farm with animals to pet, and boat trips on the lake. There is also a crafts shop, which sells Donegal Tweed.

Below The spectacular Glengesh Pass between Glengesh Hill and Common Mountain

🚗 *Drive back to Gweedore, but carry on along the N56 to Crolly, then turn right onto the R259 to Annagry (toward Donegal Airport).*

⑪ The Rosses (Na Rosa)
Co Donegal

This Irish-speaking region is a pretty, hilly corner of Donegal, with a hinterland full of small lake-filled valleys and a jagged coast with sandy coves. Almost every brown sign for a *Trá* (beach) leads to an idyllic stretch of sand, very often deserted. Many well-known musicians have roots in the area, including the popular Irish music group Clannad and the singer Enya.

The famous Irish country singer Daniel O'Donnell is from the small village of **Kincasslagh** (Cionn Caslach). From the village, follow the signs for the airport and head for the parking lot behind the airport; from here a short walk leads to a lovely beach backed by dunes.

Just offshore, joined to the mainland by bridge, is scenic **Cruit Island** (An Chruit), which has one of the most scenic links golf courses in the country. To get to the island, turn right just after Kincasslagh's Viking House Hotel. Drive to the end of the island to take in the outstanding views on all sides.

Ferries for nearby **Aran Island** (Árainn Mhór), a large, populated island, leave from **Burtonport** (Ailt an Chorráin), a small fishing port, which was once one of the most important ports in the country and has a couple of excellent seafood restaurants.

Dungloe (An Clochán Liath), the last stop on the peninsula, is the main town of The Rosses. It has a seasonal tourist office (in the converted church at the top of the village) and is a good place to stock up on provisions. For 10 days every year at the end of July, the Mary From Dungloe Festival takes place, a busy program of music, parades, and children's activities culminating in a beauty pageant to elect the new "Mary from Dungloe" from young contenders representing the counties of Ireland.

Drive straight through Dungloe but instead of turning left with the main road at the top of the hill, keep straight, leaving the church on your left. The road will become narrower and bumpier, but the drive is worth it for the scenery. After rejoining the N56, turn right for a detour to the beach at Dooey Point, then rejoin the N56 and travel south to Ardara.

Above Hand-loom weaver at work on a traditional loom in Ardara

🔟 Ardara
Co Donegal

Ardara is an attractive, hilly village and a good place to buy hand-woven tweeds, handknits, or crafts, with long-established names such as Kennedy of Ardara, John Molloy, Campbells, and Trióna Design for sale. See the weavers' looms in action in some of the larger shops or visit the **Ardara Heritage Centre** *(open Easter–Sep)* on the main street, to learn about the history of the tweed industry in Donegal since the 1900s, from sheep shearing to spinning and weaving.

The drive from Ardara to Glencolmcille west of the town

Above Gweebarra Bay, on the scenic coastal road from Dungloe in The Rosses to Ardara

passes through the spectacular **Glengesh Pass**, a steep mountain road winding between Glengesh Hill and Common Mountain, with viewpoints along the way.

Leaving Ardara take the N56 to Donegal and then turn right onto the R230 for Glencolmcille through the Glengesh Pass. In Glencolmcille drive straight through the village to An Cláchan, the Folk Village Museum. There is a parking lot at the museum.

🔞 Glencolmcille (Gleann Cholm Cille)
Co Donegal

One of the most westerly points of Donegal, on a peninsula reaching far into the Atlantic, the quiet village of Glencolmcille has a remote feel. The area, named after St. Columba (Colm Cille) was hit hard by emigration after the 1950s. The **Folk Village Museum** (An Cláchan) *(open Easter–Sep)* recaptures life in rural Donegal through the centuries, with three cottages representing the 1700s, 1800s, and 1900s. The village is also the base of Oideas Gael, a respected provider of courses in Irish language and culture.

From Glencolmcille take the L1025 to Carrick (7 miles/11 km). Follow signs for Bunglas and Slieve League, turning right at Carrick for Teelin. In Teelin, turn right just before the school. Proceed to the first parking lot and then walk the 1 mile (2 km) to the cliffs (if feeling brave – the road ahead is rough with no barriers and sheer drops – drive on to the top parking lot).

SHOPPING IN ARDARA

The factory shop of **John Molloy** *(07495 41133; www.johnmolloy.com)* sells hand-knitted Aran fisherman's sweaters, contemporary knitwear designs, and classic Donegal tweeds, including traditional caps. **Kennedy of Ardara** *(075 41106)* has been making Aran jumpers in the town for more than 100 years. **Trióna Design** *(07495 41422; www trionadesign. com)*, based in the old Mart building, which used to house one of Donegal's original tweed makers, was reopened by the Mulhern family in the 1980s and now makes stylish handwoven tweed coats and suits.

EAT AND DRINK AROUND THE ROSSES

Danny Minnie's *moderate*
This family-run restaurant in Annagry, The Rosses, serves modern cuisine, with seafood a specialty. Log fires, tapestries and antiques create a cozy atmosphere. Also has a small number of ensuite guestrooms.
Annagry, Co Donegal; 074 954 8201; www.dannyminnies.ie

The Lobster Pot *moderate*
Seafood is a specialty of this pub and restaurant near the pier in Burtonport, with lobster a particular favorite. Open fires and a warm welcome characterize this friendly spot.
Burtonport, Co Donegal; 074 954 2012

Eat and Drink: inexpensive, under €25; moderate, €25–€50; expensive, over €50

Above Killybegs' busy fishing harbor **Above center** Stone-fronted pub in Donegal Town **Above right** Rossnowlagh's wide sandy beach, popular with families and surfers

VISITING DONEGAL TOWN

Parking
Park on the street near the castle.

Tourist Information
The Quay, Donegal Town; 074 972 1148; www.donegaldirect.ie

WHERE TO STAY

AROUND KILLYBEGS

Castle Murray House Hotel *moderate*
Situated on a narrow headland jutting into McSwynes Bay, 5 miles (8 km) east of Killybegs, with views over the bay and the hills. Its French–Irish restaurant specializes in seafood and has a live lobster tank. A romantic treat.
St John's Point, Dunkineely; 074 973 7022; www.castlemurray.com

AROUND DONEGAL TOWN

Harvey's Point *expensive*
A country hotel on the shores of Lough Eske, this is a peaceful haven a few miles north of Donegal Town. Rooms are huge and luxurious, with king-size beds and Italian marble bathrooms.
Lough Eske, Donegal Town; 074 972 2208; www.harveyspoint.com

ROSSNOWLAGH

The Sandhouse Hotel *expensive*
Imposing hotel on the waterfront. Watch the sunset from the deck, fall asleep to the gentle sounds of the Atlantic rolling, and in the morning take in sea views from the hotel's drawing room or outdoor terrace.
Rossnowlagh; 071 985 1777; www.sandhouse.ie

⑭ Slieve League (Sliabh Liag)
Bunglas; Co Donegal
At 2,000 ft (600 m) high, the cliffs at Slieve League are among the highest sea cliffs in Europe. It is possible to walk to their summit, but the walking trail, One Man's Pass, has several narrow ledges and sheer drops and is only suitable for extremely experienced hikers. The full half-day walk has far-reaching views, including to the beautiful crescent-shaped strand at Malin Beg. Perhaps the best way to view the cliffs is to take a boat trip, departing from Teelin pier.
🚗 *Rejoin the R263 and follow signs for Killybegs and Donegal Town.*

⑮ Killybegs
Co Donegal
A major fishing port, Killybegs harbor is always packed with trawlers. It is also home to the **Maritime and Heritage Centre** *(open Mon–Fri; Jul–Aug: daily)*, which tells the story of the area's history. The center has the

longest hand-knitting loom in the world. There are demonstrations of the town's hand-knotted carpet industry, famous since Donegal Carpets was established in Killybegs in 1898. The company's carpets grace some of the world's finest houses, from Dublin Castle to the White House.
🚗 *Continue along the N56 to Donegal Town and park on the street near the castle in the center.*

⑯ Donegal Town
Co Donegal
The county town of Donegal is a good base for exploring the southern part of the county. Its name means "Fort of the Foreigners," possibly after the Vikings, who built a garrison here in the 9th century.

Its main sight is **Donegal Castle** *(open Easter–mid-Sep: daily; mid-Sep–early Apr: Thu–Mon)*, built on a loop in the River Eske in the town center. Restored in the 1990s, it was originally the seat of the O'Donnell clan, rulers of Donegal until 1607

Below The soaring cliffs of Slieve League, among the highest in Europe

Where to Stay: inexpensive, under €100; moderate, €100–€200; expensive, over €200

when they fled Ireland for Spain in the misguided hope of rallying Catholic support against the English. The castle was granted to Sir Basil Brooke, an English captain, who remodeled it in the Jacobean style, retaining the original tower. Guided tours of the castle reveal interiors representative of these two eras.

Brooke also laid out the town's market square, known as the **Diamond**. An obelisk in the center commemorates four Franciscan monks from Donegal Abbey who wrote the *Annals of the Four Masters* (1630s), a history of Gaelic people from 40 days before the Great Flood until the end of the 16th century. The ruins of the **Franciscan Abbey** (1474) – a few cloister arches and Gothic windows – lie on the mouth of the River Eske.

🚗 *From Donegal Town follow the signs for Sligo, turning right onto the N15. At Ballintra, turn right onto the R231 for Rossnowlagh.*

Above Lake in the craggy, boulder-strewn mountains around Slieve League

Lough Derg

Twenty miles (33 kilometers) southeast of Donegal, Lough Derg is the site of an annual pilgrimage known as St. Patrick's Purgatory, marking the 40 days St. Patrick spent in prayer here, trying to rid Ireland of evil spirits. Between June and August, thousands of pilgrims descend on **Station Island** for a three-day fast and 24-hour vigil. Only pilgrims can attend, but it is atmospheric to go to the jetty and view the basilica from the shore. There is also an exhibition in the **visitor center** on the lakeshore.

⑰ Rossnowlagh
Co Donegal

The main attraction here is the long sandy beach. There is a surf school and a surf club, and the gently sloping beach offers suitable conditions for beginners, as well as good swimming. Another attraction is the **Sandhouse Hotel** on the seafront. Dating from the 1830s, it is a nice spot for afternoon tea.

🚗 *Return via the R231 to the main N15 to Sligo.*

Above Teelin Bay, departure point for boat trips around Slieve League

SHOPPING IN KILLYBEGS

Donegal Carpets, next to the Killybegs Maritime and Heritage Centre *(074 9741944; www.visitkillybegs.com),* produces world-famous hand-knotted rugs, many of which grace stately homes across the world. There is also a crafts shop at the center.

EAT AND DRINK

ROSSNOWLAGH

Smugglers Creek *moderate*
Tuck into a selection of bar food or dine in style in the restaurant (Fri–Sun only) at this cozy pub with a lively atmosphere near Rossnowlagh. Accommodation is also available. *Rossnowlagh; 071 985 2366*

AROUND ROSSNOWLAGH

Creevy Pier Hotel *moderate*
Remote location 3 miles (5 km) south of Rossnowlagh on the R231, with superb views of Donegal Bay. Seafood is a specialty and you can either dine in the restaurant or eat in the bar. *Kildoney Glebe, Ballyshannon; 071 985 8355; www.creevy.ie*

DAY TRIP OPTIONS

If time is short, three places are relatively easy to access – Glenveagh National Park, The Rosses and Donegal Bay.

Outdoor activities

Glenveagh National Park ❸ runs a wide program of free events and activities, including ranger-led walks through the park. *For information about events, contact 074 913 7090; www.glenveaghnationalpark.ie.* The gardens at Glenveagh Castle within the park are known for their rhododendrons and walled garden.

Get there on the N56, turning off onto the R255 before Termon.

Rocky coasts and Irish music

A Gaeltacht area, The Rosses ⑪, is one of the loveliest corners of Ireland, with a rocky coast enclosing sandy bays, easily accessed islands such as Aran and Cruit, and a hinterland with many lake-filled valleys. It also has a strong musical tradition, evident in its pubs, and good seafood restaurants.

Access The Rosses on the N56, turning onto the R259 at Crolly.

Clifftop walks and winter woollies

Starting from Donegal, head to the western end of the peninsula for the towering cliffs at Slieve League ⑭, stopping at Killybegs ⑮ for a walk around its busy harbor and to shop for hand knits and tweeds. Returning to Donegal, stop for dinner at Castle Murray Hotel on St John's Point, a slender finger of land with lovely views on all sides.

Donegal is quickly accessed on the N15. From there, the N56 links up with the R263 to Slieve League.

Eat and Drink: inexpensive, under €25; moderate, €25–€50; expensive, over €50

The Fanad Peninsula

Ramelton to Rosguill Peninsula

Highlights

- **Historic departure**
  Learn about the Flight of the Earls, a landmark in Irish history, at the old battery fort in Rathmullan

- **Sweeping bays**
  Discover some of northwest Ireland's loveliest bays, such as Warden Beach and Tranarossan

- **Georgian lighthouse**
  Visit Fanad Head, one of Ireland's most northerly points, for stirring Atlantic views and its lighthouse

- **Scenic Atlantic Drive**
  Take a memorable cliffside drive around the Rossguill Peninsula

The dramatically sited lighthouse on Fanad Head

The Fanad Peninsula

The Fanad (Fanaid) Peninsula and neighboring Rosguill Peninsula feature some of Ireland's finest seascapes. Magnificent golden beaches are backed by a mix of rolling farmland and heathland, threaded by empty roads affording panoramic views over Lough Swilly and Sheephaven Bay. A series of rocky headlands culminate in Fanad Head itself, a dramatic spot topped by a whitewashed lighthouse. Stride or ride along near-deserted beaches, explore heather-lined coastal paths, enjoy fishing, golf, or water sports in Rathmullan or Portsalon, or simply sit on the sands or eat locally caught seafood in the pretty resort towns that dot the coast.

Above The Flight of the Earls Visitors Centre, Rathmullan, *see p226*

ACTIVITIES

Gallop along the shores of Lough Swilly at Rathmullan Strand

Jump on a ferry to Buncrana, a 10-minute trip across Lough Swilly from Rathmullan

Take a walk on the golden sands of Warden Beach

Spin for mackerel off a pier, wrestle with a bluefin tuna, or learn to fly-fish for rainbow trout at Portsalon or Downings

Paddle a kayak or hire a paddleboat from Portsalon Pier

Get into the swing at Portsalon Golf Club or Rosapenna's spectacularly sited 18-hole links courses

KEY

Drive route

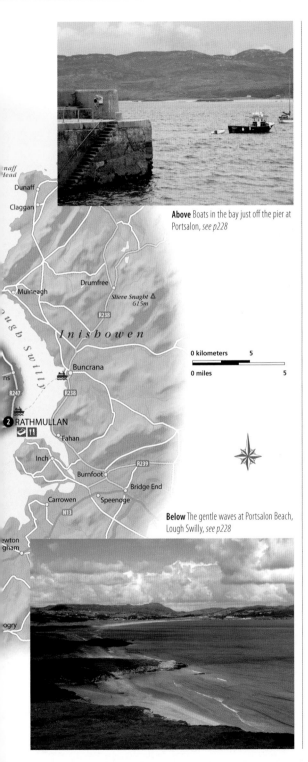

Above Boats in the bay just off the pier at Portsalon, *see p228*

Below The gentle waves at Portsalon Beach, Lough Swilly, *see p228*

PLAN YOUR DRIVE

Start/finish: Ramelton to Rosguill Peninsula.

Number of days: 2 days.

Distance: 72 miles (116 km).

Road conditions: Some regional roads are narrow, and some unclassified roads have no central dividing line, so it is often necessary to slow down when approaching oncoming traffic. On minor roads, watch out for sheep and wildlife.

When to go: The northwest of Ireland can be harsh in winter with cold Atlantic winds, so spring to autumn are the best times to visit. Be prepared for rain at any time of year. Plan carefully around festivals, when accommodation can be hard to find.

Opening times: Most shops and attractions are open from 9 or 10am to 5 or 6pm. Shops are usually open Mon–Sat. In large towns and shopping centers, shops usually stay open late one night on Thu or Fri and open from noon to 6pm on Sundays. In most villages there are small convenience stores which open from 7 or 8am until late.

Main market days: Ramelton: country market (Town Hall), Sun.

Major festivals: Rathmullan: Community Festival, Jul/Aug; Angling Festival, Jun; Earagail Arts Festival (throughout Donegal), Aug; **Rosguill Peninsula:** Downings, Jul/Aug.

DAY TRIP OPTIONS

Families will enjoy a leisurely day in Rathmullan, trying out the **water sports**, **golf courses**, and **horse riding**, just sitting on the **beautiful beach**, or perhaps taking the **ferry to Buncrana** for a change of scene. Alternatively, focus on the Atlantic Drive, a **thrilling ride** round the Rosguill Peninsula with **dramatic views** on all sides. For full details, *see p229*.

Above and **above top right** The old mill buildings and warehouses lining Ramelton's quay **Above right** Brightly painted houses in the seaside resort of Rathmullan

① Ramelton
Co Donegal

Set on the banks of the River Leannan, this pretty heritage town was once a prosperous trading port and linen market. Georgian townhouses and cottages line the streets and stone mills and 19th-century warehouses with red doors create an attractive quayside. The arrival of the railway in Letterkenny led to Ramelton's decline in the 19th century. Rugby Union aficionados might be interested to know that world-famous player Dave Gallaher, captain of New Zealand's All Blacks from 1903 to 1906, was born here.

🚗 *From Ramelton, take the R247 to Rathmullan. Turn right at Pier Road and park in the parking lot by the pier.*

② Rathmullan
Co Donegal

This seaside resort on the shores of Lough Swilly has a magnificent setting, with sweeping views across the lough to Inch Island and Buncrana on the Inishowen Peninsula. It has a pier with a marina and a long sandy beach, backed by trees. The resort offers angling, sailing, kayaking, kite-surfing, pony trekking, and a 9-hole golf course. This circular walk combines historical interest, fine views, a ruined friary, and an invigorating stretch along the beach.

A three-hour walk

From the parking lot by the pier, walk to the **Flight of the Earls Visitor Centre** ① *(open Jun–Sep: daily; Easter–Jun: weekends only)* in the old battery fort (1810). It was from this spot that the earls of Tyrone and Tyrconnell and some 90 supporters fled to France in 1607 with the aim of proceeding to Spain to rally support for the overthrow of the English in Ireland. Their failure led to the confiscation of great tracts of Irish land by the British Crown and the Plantation of Ulster – colonization by English and Scots. The visitor center tells the story of the earls and the events that followed, an important episode in Irish history, which effectively ended its old aristocracy.

Turn north along the beach (with the sea on the right), for a lovely walk along Rathmullan Strand past the rocky outcrop of **Kinnegar Head** ② and carry on along Kinnegar Strand to the end of the beach, where a stream flows under a bridge. Cross Killygarvan Bridge and turn left. To shorten the

VISITING RATHMULLAN

Ferry to Buncrana
In summer (Jun–Sep), a car ferry operates between Rathmullan and Buncrana on the Inishowen Peninsula. A continuous shuttle service, the crossing takes about 20 minutes. *Rathmullan; 074 938 1901; www.loughfoyleferry.com*

WHERE TO STAY IN RATHMULLAN

Fort Royal Hotel *moderate*
Quiet family-run hotel in woodlands on the shores of Lough Swilly. Facilities include a 9-hole pitch-and-putt course and tennis court. *Rathmullan; 074 915 8100; www.fortroyalhotel.com*

Rathmullan House *expensive*
Luxury country house hotel on Lough Swilly, with direct access to the beach. Facilities include tennis courts, a spa with a long list of pampering treatments, a heated indoor pool, log fires in winter, and an excellent restaurant, which uses produce from its own walled garden. *Lough Swilly; 074 915 8188; www.rathmullanhouse.com*

Right the lush green headlands of fjord-like Lough Swilly

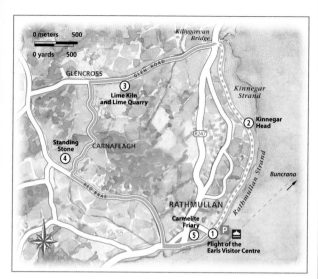

Above Horseback riders on Rathmullan Strand, with the Inishowen Peninsula beyond

walk, return along the road to Rathmullan, through pretty copses, to the friary. For the hardy, continue on Glen Road, a long, steep climb with spectacular views of Lough Swilly. The land on the left is known as The Flats. The route passes between an abandoned **lime kiln and lime quarry** ③, once used to make whitewash for the cottages and farmhouses of the area. Turn left at Glencross, just after the farmhouse, and walk through Carnafeagh, turning sharp right at the top of the hill. Look out for a **Standing Stone** ④ on the right. At the T-junction, turn left down the Red Brae, back to Rathmullan. The route passes the ruins of a 15th-century **Carmelite Friary** ⑤, with a church that was converted to a bishop's private residence in the 17th century. Follow the road along the seafront and back to the pier. In summer, there is a car ferry to Buncrana (*see left*), an attractive resort, with two castles and sandy beaches, on Inishowen Peninsula.

🚗 *From Rathmullan, head north on the R247 toward Portsalon. This becomes the R268, marked Fanad Drive.*

❸ Ballymastocker Bay
Co Donegal

North of Rathmullan, the Fanad Drive coast road becomes progressively more scenic as stunning views across Lough Swilly unfold. A series of viewing points along the way offer opportunities to stop and take in the

glorious panorama. Just after the road starts climbing, look down to the right. The circular cages in the water below are used to farm salmon, an important (though sometimes controversial) industry on Lough Swilly.

A little further on, the slopes of **Knockalla Mountain** rise to the left. 3 miles (5 km) before Portsalon, the road rounds on a view over **Ballymastocker Bay** and its golden strand, **Warden Beach**, one of the best beaches in Ireland. The winding drive down to the bay is one of the prettiest in Donegal.

🚗 *Continue north along the Fanad Drive (R268) to Portsalon.*

Above Spectacular view from the slopes of Knockalla Mountain

HORSE RIDING IN RATHMULLAN

Golden Sands Equestrian Centre
Specializes in beach rides. Half or full-day outings with picnic included, as well as rides by the hour.
Rathmullan; 074 915 8124

EAT AND DRINK IN RATHMULLAN

Belle's Kitchen/Salt 'n' Batter *inexpensive*
A great little fish-and-chips shop – ideal for a simple but satisfying meal.
Pier Road; 074 915 8800

The Water's Edge *moderate*
Hotel and restaurant on the shores of Lough Swilly. Watch the lake lapping gently below while tucking into locally caught seafood, poultry, or game. Accommodation in comfortable lakeside guestrooms.
Rathmullan; 074 915 8182; www.thewatersedge.ie

Eat and Drink: inexpensive, under €25; moderate, €25–50; expensive, over €50

Above Winding country road on the hillside near Portsalon **Above center** A typical thatched cottage on the roadside near Portsalon **Above right** Portsalon's long, wave-washed Stocker Strand

HORSEBACK RIDING ON ROSGUILL PENINSULA

Carrigart Riding Stables
Pony trekking on the beach.
Carrigart; 074 915 3583; open Easter–Nov

WHERE TO STAY

FANAD HEAD (CIONN FHANADA)

Rockhill Holiday Park *inexpensive*
Log cabins and mobile homes to rent in Kerrykeel, between Milford and Fanad Head. Provides children's activities including arts, crafts, and cooking classes, as well as go-kart racing, water sports, climbing, tennis, and football, and organizes children's day trips and summer camps. On the R246 on the outskirts of Kerrykeel.
Kerrykeel; 074 915 0012; www.rockhill.ie

ROSGUILL PENINSULA

Tra na Rosann Hostel *inexpensive*
Hostel set in pretty countryside with views of the coast and Tory island. Near several quiet beaches and Tranarossan Bay.
Downings; 074 915 5374; www.anoige.ie; open Jun–Sep

Downings Bay Hotel *moderate*
This three-star hotel overlooks the bay and is a good base for exploring the area. It also has a leisure center with an indoor pool half a mile (1 km) down the road.
Downings; 074 915 5586; www.downingsbayhotel.com

Rosapenna Hotel and Golf Resort *moderate*
Four-star hotel on Sheephaven Bay with two superb links golf courses, a leisure center and a pool.
Downings; 074 915 5301; www.rosapenna.ie

④ Portsalon
Co Donegal

This tiny seaside resort on the east side of Fanad Head is a hive of activity in summer, with kayaks, sailing boats, and pedalos bobbing in the water, and children building sandcastles on the strand. The action centers on **Portsalon Pier** (take a right turn in the village), where a small water sports shop rents out wet suits, kayaks, and diving equipment, charters boats, and runs boat trips around the bay. Anglers can spin for mackerel from the pier; high tide or night-time are best. Just along the coast, **Portsalon Golf Club**, an 18-hole links course established in 1891, has an outstanding setting with panoramic views.

🚗 *Take the coast road out of Portsalon, passing through Doagh Beg and on to Fanad Head. At Fanad Head, turn right along the road to Fanad lighthouse (half a mile/1 km). Park on right at lighthouse gates.*

The Gaeltacht

Fanad Head is in the Donegal "Gaeltacht," the name given to the Irish-speaking areas of Ireland. Until the 16th century, Irish was the main language of Ireland, but under British rule English was enforced and Irish was outlawed. Today, some 75 percent of people in the Gaeltacht speak Irish. Children are taught Irish in schools, and road signs are in Irish; cultural traditions are also preserved. The Donegal Gaeltacht is one of the largest in the country, stretching almost unbroken along the coast from Fanad Head to Slieve League.

⑤ Fanad Head (Cionn Fhanada)
Co Donegal

Piled on a rocky outcrop at the tip of Fanad Head, **Fanad Lighthouse** *(closed to public)* is an attractive ensemble of whitewashed buildings clustered around a classic lighthouse tower. It was built in 1818, in response to the

Below The picturesque 19th-century lighthouse atop a rocky outcrop at Fanad Head

tragic sinking of the *Saldana* in Lough Swilly – it is said that all lives were lost save that of the ship's parrot, whose silver collar inscribed with the ship's name identified the vessel. The view from the grounds of the lighthouse takes in Tory island to the west and Dunaff Head to the east.

Leaving the lighthouse, take the main road back through Fanad Head. Instead of following the R247 to Kerrykeel follow the coast road around **Ballyhiernan Bay**, where there's a picnic area, south to **Milltown** and back. This detour is a lovely drive with views over **Mulroy Bay** and across to the **Rosguill Peninsula**.

🚗 *Take the R246 to Kerrykeel (An Cheathru Chaol). Continue to Milford and turn right onto R245 for Carrigart.*

Above Rolling farmland and heathland on the Fanad Peninsula

bend. The 7-mile (11-km) drive starts in **Carrigart** (Carraig Airt), a Victorian village that once formed part of the estate of the Earls of Leitrim. The gateway to the Rosguill Peninsula, it benefits from tourism in summer. Behind the main street, Strand Park looks over the dune-backed shoreline. Take the R246 out of Carrigart. After 4 miles (6 km), there is a stunning view over **Tranarossan Bay**, a perfect arc of fine white sand.

Follow the road round to **Rosapenna**, which has a long beach, two 18-hole links golf courses – the Old Tom Morris course dating from 1891 and Sandy Hills, a challenging modern links – and on to **Downings** (Na Dúnaibh) in Sheephaven Bay. In autumn, Downings is the launching point for game fishing charters in search of giant bluefin tuna.

From Downings, follow the road around the peninsula through a wild and stony landscape. The road is narrow and bumpy in places, but this is the most thrilling part of the drive, a succession of scenic inlets and dramatic seascapes. On the run back to Carrigart, there's a great viewpoint at **Clontallagh** (Cluain tSalach).

FISHING ON FANAD HEAD AND ROSGUILL PENINSULA

The Meadows Trout Fishery
This man-made lake, fed by a stream, is regularly stocked with rainbow trout. There's a cabin with a gas ring and microwave to make lunch or dinner. Advice and tuition can be provided by the manager. Reservations recommended. *Cloughfin, Rossnakill (on the R246 from Fanad Head to Kerrykeel); 086 804 7516*

Central Fisheries Board
For information on sea angling, including big game fishing off Downings, contact the Central Fisheries Board. Its website lists charter boats and skippers in the area. *01 884 2600; www.cfb.ie*

EAT AND DRINK AROUND FANAD HEAD (CIONN FHANADA)

Ripples Restaurant *moderate*
Overlooking Mulroy Bay, at the entrance to Kerrykeel village, this family-friendly restaurant offers steaks, duck, fish and chips, and much more. *Kerrykeel; 074 915 0110; www.ripplesrestaurant.com*

Above The treacherous rocks of Fanad Head, one of Ireland's most northerly headlands

6 Rosguill Peninsula
Co Donegal

Known as the Atlantic Drive, the road around Rosguill Peninsula, from Mulroy Bay to Sheephaven Bay, is an exhilarating route, with outstanding views of rocky headlands and white sandy bays around every hairpin

---

DAY TRIP OPTIONS

Seaside Rathmullan, is a lovely base for outdoor activities or following the Atlantic Drive around Rossguill Peninsula.

Historic Rathmullan
Make the most of the great beach and outdoor activities at Rathmullan ❷ for an ideal day trip. Visit the Flight of the

Earls Visitor Centre, play golf, or enjoy a walk in the surrounding area. In summer, take the Lough Swilly Ferry from the pier to Buncrana on the Inishowen Peninsula, a 10-minute hop.

Rathmullan is 12 miles (20 km) from Letterkenny, which links with the N56 and N14. See p226 for details of ferries to Buncrana.

The Atlantic Drive
For dramatic seascapes and unspoiled beaches, drive around the Rossguill Peninsula ❼. Don't miss Tranarossan Bay, one of Ireland's best beaches.

From the N56, take the R245 to Carrigart (9 miles/15 km), the start of the drive.

Eat and Drink: inexpensive, under €25; moderate, €25–50; expensive, over €50

Classic Northern Ireland

Carrickfergus to Lough Neagh

Highlights

- **Bushy glens**
  Drive through some of the nine forested Glens of Antrim

- **Geological marvel**
  Explore the dramatic and mythic splendor of the Giant's Causeway

- **Spectacular views**
  Enjoy panoramic seascapes from the heights of Bishop's Drive Road

- **Romantic castle**
  See the breathtaking clifftop ruins of Dunluce Castle

Vertigo-inducing rope bridge over turbulent waters at Carrick-A-Rede

Classic Northern Ireland

A drive along the Causeway Coast and through the Glens of Antrim takes in spectacular scenery, from dramatic coastal cliffs and unspoiled beaches and bays to romantic glens, hillside waterfalls, and forest parks. This tour begins just north of Belfast and follows a dramatic and breathtaking coastal route dotted with pretty villages, historic castles, and stunning natural wonders – including the Giant's Causeway – to discover a place steeped in myth and legend. At the southern end it turns inland through the lovely Sperrin Mountains to reach tranquil Lough Neagh, at the heart of Northern Ireland.

KEY

Drive route

ACTIVITIES

Take a walk high above the sea across the Carrick-A-Rede rope bridge

Sample Irish whiskey, and learn the secrets of how it is made, at the Old Bushmills Distillery

Stroll through centuries of history along the walls of Derry

Take a boat trip on the calm waters of lovely Lough Neagh

Above Far-reaching views and sheer cliffs add drama to the coastline around the Giant's Causeway, Co Antrim, *see p238*

see p235

PLAN YOUR DRIVE

Start/finish: Carrickfergus to Lough Neagh.

Number of days: 5, allowing half a day at the Giant's Causeway.

Distance: Approx. 210 miles (340 km).

Road conditions: Roads are generally in good condition, although some mountain and glen roads may be impassable in winter.

When to go: Spring, summer, and autumn offer the best weather, and most visitor attractions are open. The weather is always changeable, so be prepared for rain at any time of year.

Opening times: Most shops and attractions open 9 or 10am–5 or 6pm. Shops open Mon–Sat; in large towns also noon–6pm on Sun. Convenience stores in villages open 8am until late.

Main market days: Coleraine: second Sat of month; **Limavady:** Fri; **Derry:** first Sat of month; **Dungannon:** first Sat of month; **Strabane:** last Sat of month.

Shopping: Coleraine's Causeway Speciality Market *(see above)* is a vibrant gathering of artists and craftspeople, while Derry has shops selling traditional Irish linen, crystal, and tweeds.

Main festivals: Waterfoot (Glenariff): Féis of the Glens, Jul; **Ballycastle:** Aul Lammas Fair, Aug; **Derry:** Jazz and Big Band Festival, Apr/May; Foyle Film Festival, Nov; **Omagh:** Appalachian & Bluegrass Festival, Sep.

DAY TRIP OPTIONS

Birdwatchers should pack a picnic and take the ferry from Ballycastle to Rathlin Island to see the puffin colony. Lovers of **nature and history** could easily spend a day exploring Glenarm and Glenariff, the "Queen" of the Glens of Antrim. For full details, *see p241*.

Left Fishing vessels moored at the harbor at Carnlough, Glenarm, *see p235*

Above Sturdy walls of Carrickfergus Castle, overlooking the harbor and Belfast Lough

WHERE TO STAY

AROUND CARNFUNNOCK COUNTRY PARK

Ballygally Castle Hotel *moderate*
Facing the sandy beaches of Ballygally Bay, 2 miles (3 km) on the A2 coastal road from the country park, this castle dates back to 1625 and reputedly even has its own friendly ghost. Original beamed ceilings and period rooms add to the charm and character.
Causeway Coastal Route, Ballygally, BT40 2QZ; 028 2858 1066; www.hastingshotels.com

AROUND GLENARM

The Londonderry Arms Hotel *moderate*
This is a friendly, historic hotel in the village of Carnlough (3 miles/5 km on the A2 from Glenarm Glen) at the foot of Glencoy, restored to its original Georgian style by the current owner. Rooms are very comfortable, and are individually furnished. There is a choice of fine dining or relaxed bistro food (*see Eat and Drink, opposite*). Curiously, Sir Winston Churchill once owned the Londonderry Arms.
20 Harbour Road, Carnlough, BT44 0EU; 028 2888 5255; www.glensofantrim.com

① Carrickfergus
Co Antrim

The oldest city in County Antrim, predating even Belfast, of which it is now almost a district, Carrickfergus is a pretty seaside town set on Belfast Lough. Dominating the waterfront is **Carrickfergus Castle** (*open daily*), a striking Norman edifice built for defense in the 12th century and used for this purpose as recently as World War II. It is possible to take a guided tour of the castle, the best-preserved of its kind in Northern Ireland, and from its ramparts there are good views of the harbor and marina and across Belfast Lough. Nearby on Antrim Street is the **Carrickfergus Museum and Civic Centre** (*open daily*) with exhibitions on local history. Carrickfergus is known worldwide as the subject of a haunting Irish ballad that begins, "I wish I was in Carrickfergus."

🚗 *Follow the A2 north to reach the Causeway Coastal Route. There are great sea views en route to Whitehead; the road then follows the western shore of Larne Lough. After the port town of Larne itself, the best of the Causeway Coastal Route begins, with spectacular cliffs and sea views over to Scotland. Continue on the A2, passing through Black Cave tunnel and along Drains Bay. The entrance to Carnfunnock Country Park is just after the bay, on the left. Drive through the entrance (marked with a pyramid) and park in the parking lot.*

② Carnfunnock Country Park
Drains Bay, BT40 2QG; Co Antrim

A perfect place for families to enjoy, **Carnfunnock Country Park** (*open daily*) is a lovely country park of 470 acres (190 ha) filled with woods, gardens, and walking trails, parts of which are set on the coastal shore. Many of the estate's original features, such as the walled garden and the ice house, remain. There are plenty of activities including a mini-golf course, a laser clay pigeon shooting range, a miniature railway, a remote-control boating lake and remote-control truck course, an adventure playground, and a maze. There are also picnic areas and a café.

🚗 *Continue along the A2 coastal road through Ballygally and Milltown to Glenarm village, gateway to Glenarm. Follow its main street to the glen.*

Above The Gothic stone Barbican Gate, the main entrance to Glenarm Castle

③ Glenarm
Co Antrim

This lovely forested glen stretches along the Glenarm river, which is fed by streams gushing down from the glen. The Glenarm Scenic Route runs from the village of Glenarm, up the B97 through the glen itself, back

Below The Glenarm river skirting the walls of noble Glenarm Castle, seat of the Earls of Antrim

Above View over the beautiful forested slopes of Glenariff toward the sea

down to the coast through the next glen, Glencoy, and along the A42 to **Carnlough**. Along the way is Gothic **Glenarm Castle**, seat of the Earls of Antrim. Its extensive grounds include a delightful 18th-century **Walled Garden** (open May–Sep; closed Tue) and tea rooms in the old Mushroom House. The Walled Garden is especially lovely in spring when a sea of spring bulbs and clouds of apple and pear blossom are a breathtaking sight.

🚗 *Continue on the A2 via Carnlough to Waterfoot.*

④ Waterfoot
Co Antrim

Waterfoot (also known as Glenariff), the village at the mouth of the glen of Glenariff, is set on Red Bay, so-named for its sandstone cliffs and the resulting shade of the sand on its long stretch of beach. Glenariff is known as the "Queen of the Nine Glens of Antrim." It is a U-shaped valley bounded on either side by precipitous hills, and the landscape really is spectacular, with everything from seashores and cliffs to dense forest and waterfalls. **The Glenariff Forest Park Scenic Route**, along which the route runs, is typical of the wonderful glen scenery that is a highlight of driving in Antrim.

🚗 *At the end of Waterfoot village, turn left at the T-junction onto the A43, toward Glenariff Forest Park. Follow this road; the entrance to the forest park is on the left.*

⑤ Glenariff Forest Park
BT44 0QX; Co Antrim

This stunning **forest park** (open daily) in the upper part of the glen, has many scenic, circular, marked trails and walks that lead through mixed woodlands, along the Inver and Glenariff rivers, past waterfalls and to viewpoints with panoramic views down the mountainsides and all the way to the Mull of Kintyre in Scotland. Especially well worth seeing are two of the park's largest and most spectacular waterfalls, Ess na Larach, which has a viewing-point bridge, and Ess na Crub.

🚗 *Leaving the Forest Park, turn left onto the A43, then right onto the B14 along the glen of Glenballyeamon to Cushendall.*

EAT AND DRINK

AROUND CARNFUNNOCK COUNTRY PARK

Garden Restaurant in Antrim
moderate
The restaurant at the Ballygally Castle Hotel is the most attractive place for a meal in these parts. It is located inside the castle walls and looks out over the gardens. The chefs pride themselves on their use of local produce. A set menu is offered at lunch, while in the evening guests can choose between *table d'hôte* or bistro menus. An informal lunch menu is also available in the hotel bar.
Causeway Coastal Route, Ballygally, BT40 2QZ; 028 2858 1066; www.hastingshotels.com

AROUND GLENARM

Frances Anne and Tapestry Restaurant *expensive*
The award-winning cuisine at this elegant restaurant in the Londonderry Arms Hotel focuses on ingredients sourced from the Glens of Antrim, such as wild salmon. Fine wines and whiskeys are also served. For those looking for something more relaxed, the hotel's welcoming **Coach House Bistro** *(moderate)* serves up good-quality pub favorites including various steaks, seared salmon, and confit of duck.
20 Harbour Road, Carnlough, BT44 0EU; 028 2888 5255; www.glensofantrim.com

Below left St. Patrick's Church, Glenarm village
Below Pretty fishing village of Carnlough

Above Wild and rocky shoreline near the popular seaside resort of Ballycastle

WHERE TO STAY

BALLYCASTLE

Colliers Hall *inexpensive*
This guesthouse offers both B&B-style and self-catering accommodation in an old converted stone barn.
50 Cushendall Road; 028 2076 2531; www.colliershall.com

AROUND BALLYCASTLE

Manor House *inexpensive*
This 18th-century Georgian house – a ferry ride away from the mainland – overlooks the sheltered harbor at Rathlin Island, and every room has a sea view. Local seafood is a specialty of the restaurant.
Rathlin Island, BT54 6RT; 028 2076 3964; www.rathlinmanorhouse.co.uk; closed Mon and Tue

Whitepark House
inexpensive–moderate
This is a beautiful guesthouse set on picturesque Whitepark Bay, with a friendly welcome and personal service.
150 Whitepark Road, Ballintoy, BT54 6NH; 028 2073 1482; www.whiteparkhouse.com

Below Torr Head, with its dramatic landscape and stunning sea views

Glens of Antrim

The coastline of Antrim is marked by nine glens, each full of natural wonders such as rivers, waterfalls, and forests. The nine are Glenarm, Glencloy, Glencorp, Glendun, Glenballyeamon, Glenaan, Glenshek, Glentaisie, and Glenariff. The last is known as the "Queen of the Glens" because of its particular majesty and beautiful waterfalls. The glens are full of myths, legends, and stories of fairies, which were once a large part of local folklore.

⑥ Cushendall
Co Antrim
Cushendall is an attractive little conservation village and resort. Much of the activity centers on the waterfront, with its pier and sailing club. There is a golf course and beach, and the ruined Layde Church has some lovely Celtic crosses. Caves in nearby Tiveragh Hill are said to be occupied by the "little people."
🚗 *Follow the A2 north, then turn right onto the B92 (also marked Torr Head Scenic Route) through Knocknacarry and on to Cushendun.*

⑦ Cushendun
Co Antrim
This tiny, picturesque fishing village is known for its quaint, whitewashed houses built in Cornish style. It was designed for Lord Cushendun by the architect Clough Williams-Ellis, best known for his Italianate town of Portmeirion in Wales. The waterfront and sheltered harbor are perfect for a stroll. On a clear day there are superb views across to Scotland.
🚗 *Take the Torr Road, following signs for Torr Head. Turn right for Torr Head.*

Above Traditional storefront in the pretty village of Cushendall

⑧ Torr Head
Co Antrim
The road to **Torr Head** ascends steeply and there are some spectacular coastal views over the North Channel to the Mull of Kintyre in Scotland, north to Rathlin Island, and down over stunning **Murlough Bay**. The ruined buildings below Torr Head used to be customs houses and a lookout station that recorded the passage of transatlantic ships. The small lane down to Murlough Bay from Torr Head passes a megalithic

tomb and a group of old radio masts and outbuildings that were once a transmission and listening station for the Royal Air Force.

🚗 *Leaving Torr Head or Murlough Bay, turn right onto Torr Road and, on reaching the village of Ballyvoy, turn right onto the A2 for Ballycastle. Park on the seafront in Ballycastle.*

Above The lookout station at Torr Head

9 Ballycastle
Co Antrim

Ballycastle is a busy market town and a popular seaside resort. From the harbor here, ferries leave for the 40-minute crossing to **Rathlin Island**. It is in a cave on the island that, in 1306, the fugitive Robert the Bruce is said to have seen the struggling spider that prompted him to "try again" and return to win Scottish independence from the English. Scattered with ancient ruins, the island is now home to a puffin colony. Ballycastle – at the head

of glens Glenshesk and Glentaisie – has a small heritage trail taking in churches, monuments, and the ruins of a Franciscan friary.

🚗 *Take the B15 coastal road west to Carrick-A-Rede Rope Bridge.*

10 Carrick-A-Rede Rope Bridge
BT54 6LS; Co Antrim

The famous **Carrick-A-Rede Rope Bridge** (open Mar–Oct: daily, weather permitting) runs across a chasm 66 ft (20 m) wide and 75 ft (23 m) deep. It was originally used as a working bridge enabling salmon fishermen to cross to the small rock outcrop, but nowadays it is primarily a tourist attraction, as much for the beauty of the site as for the challenge of crossing the wobbly bridge itself. Arrive early in peak season to avoid lines, and wear sensible footwear and warm clothes to cross the bridge. The bay of **Larrybane**, below, was used as a limestone quarry for much of the 1950s, and visitors can walk to the old quarry area and view the fine stalactite cave in the cliffs.

🚗 *From Carrick-A-Rede, turn right onto the B15. As a short detour, turn right for Whitepark Bay, a pristine crescent-shaped beach, sheltered below cliffs and backed by sand dunes (strong currents make it unsuitable for swimming). Returning to the B15, go through Ballintoy and turn right onto the A2, signed to Bushmills. Then turn right onto the B146 for the Giant's Causeway. There is paid parking next to the Visitor Centre, although the site itself is free.*

Above The hair-raising rope-bridge crossing at Carrick-A-Rede

EAT AND DRINK

CUSHENDALL

McCollam's Bar *inexpensive*
This is a lively pub with traditional music and singing every weekend, and impromptu music sessions on other nights, especially in summer. A wide range of classic and inventive dishes are served in the friendly first-floor restaurant.
Upstairs at Joe's, 23 Mill Street, BT44 0RR; 028 2177 1992 (bar); 028 2177 2630 (restaurant); www.mccollamsbar.com

CUSHENDUN

Mary McBride's Bar *inexpensive*
This tiny bar is big on character and atmosphere. Try one of the traditional dishes and, on a Saturday, don't miss the live music.
2 Main St, BT44 0PH; 028 2176 1511

BALLYCASTLE

Central Wine Bar *inexpensive*
Come to this family-run restaurant for a great evening out. The menu changes according to the season.
12 Ann Street; 028 2076 3877; www.thecellarrestaurant.co.uk

Cellar Restaurant *moderate*
This is a cozy restaurant in the seaside town of Ballycastle. Fresh seafood such as Ballycastle lobster is a specialty.
11B The Diamond, BT54 6AW; 028 2076 3037; www.thecellarrestaurant.co.uk

Above The jagged, quarried limestone cliffs, concealing fine stalactite caves, of Larrybane

Eat and Drink: inexpensive, under £25; moderate, £25–£50; expensive, over £50

Above Giant's Causeway on a stormy day
Below right The remarkable basalt "stepping stones" of the Causeway

VISITING GIANT'S CAUSEWAY

Giant's Causeway Visitor Centre
A shuttle bus runs from the center to the rock formations, half a mile (1 km) away. Wear appropriate shoes and raincoats, as it can be wet and slippery on the stones.
44 Causeway Road, BT57 8SU; 028 2073 1855; www.nationaltrust.org.uk/giantscauseway

WHERE TO STAY

GIANT'S CAUSEWAY

The Smuggler's Inn *inexpensive*
This is a small, family-run hotel with great sea views, ideally situated down the road from the Giant's Causeway. There is also a restaurant.
306 Whitepark Road, BT57 8SL; 028 2073 1577; www.smugglers-inn.co.uk

BUSHMILLS

The Bushmills Inn *moderate*
This cozy hotel, with open peat fires and gas lighting, describes itself as "a living museum of Ulster hospitality." However, every modern luxury is also present in the charming rooms. The restaurant is excellent, too.
9 Dunluce Road, BT57 8QG; 028 2073 3000; www.bushmillsinn.com

AROUND BUSHMILLS

Bayview Hotel *moderate*
This quiet hotel in the small harbor village of Portballintrae, just north of Bushmills, overlooks the sea and is a great base for exploring the area.
2 Bayhead Road, Portballintrae, BT57 8RT; 028 2073 4100; www.bayviewhotelni.com

⓫ Giant's Causeway

BT57 8SU; Co Antrim

This natural geological phenomenon consists of around 40,000 polygonal basalt columns, forming a huge causeway that juts out into the sea. Scientists believe that the columns were created some 60 million years ago by volcanic activity. However, local legend tells it better, with the story that they were created by the Irish giant, Finn McCool, who was fighting a rival Scottish giant, Benandonner. McCool is said to have created a pathway of stepping stones from Ireland to Scotland, so he could walk across the sea to confront his rival. There are similar stones on the island of Staffa in the Hebrides.

A two-hour walking tour

From the parking lot and **Visitor Centre** ①, follow the cliff path to the right. There are great views as the path ascends. Descend the **Shepherd's Steps** ② carefully (there are 162 in total, and they are steep). At the bottom, follow the path toward the **Giant's Organ** ③, an impressive set of columns in the cliff face, that resemble 39-ft (12-m) organ pipes. Walk past the Organ towards the **Amphitheatre** ④. On turning the corner into the Amphitheatre, the **Giant's Eyes** ⑤ are on the right – eye-shaped sockets in the red iron ore layer, where basalt boulders have fallen out. Turn and follow the path back past the Organ, then take the path that descends toward the Causeway itself. Look out for the **Giant's Boot** ⑥ rock on the shore of Port Noffer to the right. Before passing through the **Giant's Gate** ⑦, turn and look back for a view of the Giant's Chimney Tops, chimney-stack-like columns protruding from a headland to the east. Through the Gate are the main "stepping stone" rock formations. Any wish made while sitting in the **Wishing Chair** ⑧ in the Middle Causeway is said to come true. Return up the path to the Visitor Centre. From here there is a good view of the hunched form of the **Giant's Granny** ⑨. Continue past Port Ganny to see the **Camel** ⑩, which "sits" in Portnaboe, before heading back to the Visitor Centre.

🚗 *From the parking lot, turn right on the B146, then turn right again onto the A2. Drive through Bushmills to the Distillery.*

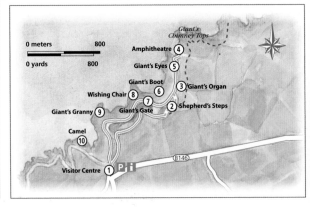

⑫ Old Bushmills Distillery

BT57 8XH; Co Antrim

Ireland's oldest whiskey distillery, the **Old Bushmills Distillery** *(open daily),* was founded in 1608 when a royal license was granted by King James I to Sir Thomas Phillips to distil *uisce beatha* (Irish for "water of life"), or whiskey as it is now known. Old Bushmills is still a fully operational distillery, where brands such as Bushmills, Black Bush, and Bushmills Malt are made, using unpeated malted barley. Guided tours for visitors explain the craft of Irish whiskey-making, including the Irish triple-distillation process, and looking at the warehouses full of barrels. There's a chance to taste the product at the end of the tour.

🚗 *Leave Bushmills on the A2, toward Portrush. Dunluce Castle is a short distance along this road on the right.*

Irish Whiskey

Irish whiskey is made from three ingredients: barley, yeast, and water. The barley is milled to a grist, which is then steeped in Mash Tuns with hot water, to produce fermentable sugars. The addition of yeast converts these sugars into alcohol. The raw spirit is then distilled in a pot still. Irish whiskey is distilled three times, giving it its unique flavor. It is then matured in oak casks. Bushmills is aged for five years in sherry and bourbon casks, which refines the spirit and adds complexity, color and more flavor, but some whiskeys are aged for much longer, such as Bushmills 21-Year-Old Malt.

---

⑬ Dunluce Castle

BT57 8UY; Co Antrim

The romantic ruins of **Dunluce Castle** *(open daily)* have a dramatic clifftop setting, jutting out into the sea. A short audiovisual presentation on the history of the castle can be viewed before exploring the ruins. Most of the present castle building dates from the 16th and 17th centuries and there are breathtaking (if scary) views down to the water crashing onto the rocks far below.

🚗 *Continue on the A2 toward Portrush. From a parking lot on the right-hand side there are sweeping coastal views. After the following bend, there is a space on the left just large enough for one*

car. If it is empty, park and cross the road. Look back toward Dunluce to see the Giant's Head, a huge face eroded into the cliffs. At Portrush, turn right onto Causeway Street and drive to Ramore Head for more sea views.

⑭ Portrush

Co Antrim

Portrush is a large seaside town and one of Northern Ireland's most popular family holiday destinations. It gets very busy in the summer, especially on bank holiday weekends. There are plenty of outdoor activities and the beach is very good for surfing. **Waterworld** *(open Jun–Sep: daily),* the water park on the seafront, and other amusements provide plenty of family entertainment.

🚗 *Continue on the A2 to Portstewart. Follow signs for the Promenade, turn right onto Atlantic Circle, and drive along Kinora Terrace to Portstewart Point and Harbour Hill, affording lovely views over to the Inishowen Peninsula.*

⑮ Portstewart

Co Derry

Portstewart is another very busy seaside holiday resort with a lengthy beach and promenade. The long golden strand is the main focal point, popular with walkers and surfers.

🚗 *From Portstewart take the B185 in the direction of Coleraine but, at the roundabout, take the A29 (second exit) for the Coleraine ring road. At Greenmount Roundabout, take the B201 (third exit) for Castlerock. Turn left onto the A2. Turn right onto the B119, Sea Road, marked for Castlerock. Hezlett House is on this road just before Castlerock village.*

Above Surfers enjoying the waves at Portrush Beach, a popular family holiday destination

---

EAT AND DRINK

BUSHMILLS

The Bushmills Inn *moderate*
The award-winning **Taste of Ulster** restaurant at this hotel *(see left)* is housed in its 17th-century stables, overlooking a garden courtyard. The mix of traditional and new Irish cuisine might feature pan-fried peppered fillet of beef flamed in Bushmills whiskey. Reservations advised.
9 Dunluce Road, BT57 8QG; 028 2073 3000; www.bushmillsinn.com

PORTRUSH

Ramore Wine Bar *inexpensive*
The Ramore is a popular, reasonably priced wine bar – part of a complex which includes a pasta restaurant below and Oriental restaurant above.
The Harbour, BT56 8BN; 028 7082 4313; www.ramorerestaurant.com

---

Below Ruined Dunluce Castle, breathtakingly perched on its rocky promontory

Above Mussenden Temple, perched on the clifftop **Above center** Glenelly Valley in the Sperrins **Above right** River Foyle in Derry

WHERE TO STAY

AROUND DOWNHILL DEMESNE

Downhill Hostel *inexpensive*
A friendly hostel in a lovely Victorian building with views over Downhill beach to Donegal, and good facilities.
Glenhassen Hall, 12 Mussenden Road, Downhill, Castlerock, BT51 4RP; 028 7084 9077; www.downhillhostel.com

DERRY (LONDONDERRY)

Beech Hill Country House Hotel *moderate*
A charming and elegant hotel, set in mature gardens southeast of Derry's city walls. Home cooking is a specialty.
32 Ardmore Road, BT47 3QP; 028 7134 9279; www.beech-hill.com

City Hotel *moderate*
This large, 4-star hotel with a heated pool overlooks the River Foyle.
Queen's Quay, BT48 7AS; 028 7136 5800; www.cityhotelderry.com

AROUND DERRY (LONDONDERRY)

Dungiven Castle *moderate*
This historic family home has elegant, 16th-century-style rooms and is set in lovely gardens with mountain views.
145 Main Street, Dungiven (on the A6 Belfast–Derry road), BT47 4LF; 028 7774 2428; www.dungivencastle.com

Radisson Roe Park Resort *moderate*
A spacious hotel and spa, this is the north coast's only 4-star luxury resort.
Roe Park, Limavady (signed off A2); BT49 9LB; 028 7772 2222; www.radissonroepark.com

AROUND LOUGH NEAGH

Ardtara Hotel *moderate*
A delightful 19th-century country house hotel, Ardtara is full of character with lots of old-style charm and decor.
8 Gorteade Road, Upperlands, Maghera, BT46 5SA (on A29 north of Desertmartin); 028 7964 4490; www.ardtara.com

Where to Stay: inexpensive, under £100; moderate, £100–£200; expensive, over £200

16 Hezlett House

BT51 4TW; Co Derry
Pretty **Hezlett House** *(open May–Jun & Sep: Sat–Sun; Apr & Jul–Aug: Fri–Tue)* is a picture-postcard traditional thatched Dower House and farmyard owned and run by the National Trust. It is thought to be one of the oldest buildings in Northern Ireland, with timber frames dating from 1690. Visitors can take a guided tour of the simply furnished, Victorian-style interior to learn more about life in 18th-century rural Ireland. There is also a small museum of historic farm equipment.

🚗 *Return to the A2 and turn right. The entrance to the Downhill Estate is on the right before the road begins to descend a hill.*

Above Symbolic statue "Hands Across the Divide," in the city of Derry

17 Downhill Demesne

BT51 4RP; Co Derry
The lovely **Downhill Demesne** *(open daily)* was built between 1774 and 1778 by the Earl of Bristol. Downhill House itself is now a ruin, but its gardens remain and there are spectacular clifftop walks. Clinging to the top of the cliffs, the picturesque **Mussenden Temple** *(028 7084 8567 for opening details)* was originally used as a library. Saved from collapsing over the edge when the site was taken over by the National Trust, it is now a popular wedding venue.

🚗 *Follow the road to Downhill and turn left here, just after the row of buildings, for the Bishops Road Drive. There are spectacular elevated views over Lough Foyle to the Inishowen Peninsula and, farther along, to the Sperrin Mountains. Continue on this road, turning right onto the B201 Windyhill Road and rejoining the A2 for Limavady. From here, the road skirts the edge of Lough Foyle for part of the way to Derry. Park on the street or in one of two multistory parking lots at Quayside and Foyle Road.*

18 Derry (Londonderry)

Co Derry
The city of Derry is a large, commercial city with a historic walled center lying along the banks of the River Foyle. The walls, forming an elevated walkway, date back to the early 17th century. "The Troubles" *(see p246)* had a huge impact on the city of Derry and, like Belfast, it has powerful murals representing the feelings of both sides of the community. However, since the 1998 Good Friday Agreement that launched the peace process, the city is more optimistic. The **Museum of Free Derry** *(open Jul–Sep: daily; Apr–Jun: Mon–Sat; Oct–Mar: Mon–Fri)* tells the story of the city's turbulent history.

🚗 *From Derry, take the A5 toward Omagh, following signs for the Ulster American Folk Park.*

⑲ Ulster American Folk Park

BT78 5QY; Co Tyrone

This fascinating **Folk Park** *(Apr–Sep: daily; Oct–Mar: Mon–Fri)* tells the story of emigration from Ireland to America in the 18th and 19th centuries. Visitors move around the site through a series of traditional buildings ranging from an Irish weaver's cottage to a period American street, and there is even a full-sized reconstruction of a 19th-century sailing ship, of the kind in which the emigrants crossed the Atlantic, that can be boarded in order to experience the hardships they endured. In these authentic settings, costumed characters perform traditional crafts and go about their daily routine, bringing the past to life, while tours and exhibitions provide fascinating background information.

🚗 *Leaving the Park, turn left onto the A5 south, then left onto Gortnagarn Road and left again onto the B48. The entrance to the Gortin Glen Forest Park is on the right hand side. To reach the Forest Drive, drive through the parking lot and follow the signs.*

Above Pennsylvania log farmhouse at the Ulster American Folk Park

⑳ Sperrin Mountains

Co Tyrone/Co Derry

The Sperrins are a designated Area of Outstanding Natural Beauty and the largest mountain range in Northern Ireland. There are numerous scenic drives, cycle trails, and walking routes in the area. The **Gortin Glen Forest Park** *(open daily)* covers part of the 3,700-acre (1,500-ha) forest. The park has a range of delightful walking trails, including one that follows the pretty Pollan Burn, as well as an 5-mile (8-km) Forest Drive that includes a number of "vista parks" en route, where motorists can stop to enjoy magnificent views. The coniferous woods are home to plenty of wildlife including red squirrels and Sika deer.

🚗 *Turn right out of the Park on the B48 to Gortin and then Plumbridge. Turn right at Plumbridge onto the B47, passing through the Glenelley Valley. At Draperstown, turn right onto the B40 for Magherafelt and, from there, head south on the B160 to Ballyronan village on the shores of Lough Neagh.*

㉑ Lough Neagh

Co Derry

Lough Neagh, in the very center of Northern Ireland, is the third-largest lake in Europe, and five of the six counties border it. It is a popular place for birdwatching (around 1,000 whooper swans settle around the lake in winter) and fishing, and there are many visitor attractions all around the lough. Boat trips run from **Ballyronan Marina** to sites of interest around the lake, such as the beautiful Celtic High Cross at Ardboe, while an evening cruise with live folk music offers the chance to see the sun set over the Sperrins.

Above Tranquil Lough Neagh, a popular spot for boat trips and birdwatching

EAT AND DRINK IN DERRY (LONDONDERRY)

Browns Restaurant
inexpensive–moderate
A smart, contemporary restaurant, popular for its consistently great cooking and stylish atmosphere.
1 Bond's Hill, Waterside, BT47 6DW; 028 7134 5180; www.brownsrestaurant.com

Halo Pantry and Grill *moderate*
This restaurant, within the old city walls, was once a shirt factory. Its high ceilings and tall windows give it a light and spacious feel, and the food is mouthwatering. Dine in the grill or the more informal pantry.
5 Market Street, BT48 6EF; 028 7127 1567

La Sosta Ristorante *moderate*
A buzzy, authentic, family-run Italian restaurant serving delicious food. Friendly service.
45/a Carlisle Road, BT48 6JJ; 028 7137 4817; www.lasostarestaurant.co.uk

---

DAY TRIP OPTIONS

Glenarm Glen and Ballycastle are ideal bases to see rich birdlife and visit lovely glens.

A trip to puffin island
Take the ferry (40 mins, reservations essential) from Ballycastle ❾ to Rathlin Island – bring a picnic and explore this tranquil haven for birds and other wildlife. Puffins are in residence from April to August. If it's

not picnic weather there is a pub and a restaurant (the Manor House, *see p236*) on the island.

Only island residents can bring cars to the island. Leave the car at the ferry terminal or seafront in Ballycastle.

A day in the glens
Combine several lovely glens in a day's tour, starting at Glenarm ❸, pausing to visit Glenarm Castle with

its delightful gardens and tearoom. Then drive down Glencoy before heading back up along the coast to Waterfoot (Glenariff village) for Glenariff ❹ and the lovely woodland walking trails of Glenariff Forest Park ❺.

Head south on the A2 to Glenariff, and then from here follow the drive's instructions along the route to Glenariff Forest Park.

Eat and Drink: inexpensive, under £25; moderate, £25–£50; expensive, over £50

The Land of St. Patrick

Belfast to the Mountains of Mourne

Highlights

- **Buzzing Belfast**
  Discover the historic *Titanic* Quarter, the colorful Cathedral Quarter, and the vibrant Queen's Quarter

- **Outstanding gardens**
  Stroll through beautiful Mount Stewart Gardens, laid out by Lady Londonderry in the 1920s

- **Coastal wildlife**
  Explore the myriad small bays and inlets at Strangford Lough, rich in wildfowl and marine life

- **Majestic mountains**
  Head through the high passes of the Mountains of Mourne, pausing near the Spelga Dam for superb views

Rural scene below the magnificent Mountains of Mourne in the south of County Down

The Land of St. Patrick

With Strangford Lough at its center and the open sea to the east, County Down has more than 200 miles (320 km) of coastline, with good beaches and nature reserves to enjoy. In the south of the county, the magnificent Mountains of Mourne dominate the horizon. The county is also rich in historic monuments and stately homes, while St. Patrick's Trail traces the footsteps of Ireland's patron saint. From the hustle and bustle of Belfast in Co Antrim, along the Ards Peninsula flanking the eastern shores of Strangford Lough, and through the pretty seaside villages on Dundrum Bay, this drive ends with a spectacular trip through the Mountains of Mourne.

Above The peaceful waters of Strangford Lough, the UK's largest sea inlet and designated an Area of Outstanding Natural Beauty, *see p248*

ACTIVITIES

Discover the epic story of the *Titanic* at the Titanic Visitors Centre in Belfast

Explore the fascinating open-air Ulster Folk and Transport Museum and step back to the 18th century

Wander around the classical house and gardens of lovely Castle Ward

Hike up Slieve Donard, the highest mountain in Northern Ireland

Stranraer,
Isle of Man,
Liverpool

KEY

— Drive route

PLAN YOUR DRIVE

Start/finish: Belfast to the Mountains of Mourne.

Number of days: 3 days.

Distance: 93 miles (150 km).

Road conditions: Generally good, but some mountain roads may be impassable in winter.

When to go: Spring, summer, or autumn when the weather is milder and most attractions are open.

Opening times: Most shops and attractions open 9 or 10am–5 or 6pm. Shops open Mon–Sat; in large towns also noon–6pm on Sun. Convenience stores in villages open 8am until late.

Main market days: Belfast: Fri (variety) and Sat (food and garden), St. George's; Newtownards: Sat; Portaferry: Sat.

Major festivals: Belfast: Film Festival, Mar–Apr; *Titanic* Made in Belfast, Apr; Cathedral Quarter Arts Festival, Apr–May; **Castle Ward:** Opera Festival, May–Jun; **Castlewellan:** Celtic Fusion, Jul; **Newcastle:** Mourne International Walking Festival, Jun.

DAY TRIP OPTIONS

Nature lovers can experience the area's natural splendor and diverse wildlife by hiring a canoe on Strangford Lough, or hiking through the Tollymore Forest Park in the foothills of the Mountains of Mourne. **Families** with children will enjoy visiting the Exploris Aquarium in Portaferry. For full details, *see p249.*

Below left Belfast's Crown Bar, *see p246*
Below Newcastle, a 19th-century resort beneath the Mourne Mountains, *see p249*

Above The Big Fish sculpture on Belfast's regenerated waterfront

VISITING BELFAST

Parking
There are several parking lots near City Hall, including Bedford Street, Dublin Road, and Great Victoria Street, and metered parking around Ulster Hall.

Tourist Information
Belfast Welcome Centre, 47 Donegall Place, BT1 5AD; 028 9024 6609; www.gotobelfast.com; open Sun 11am–4pm; Jun–Sep: Mon–Sat 9am–7pm; Oct–May 9am–5:30pm

WHERE TO STAY

BELFAST

Ten Square *moderate*
Boutique luxury hotel with 23 stylish bedrooms and a superb, central location on Donegall Square.
10 Donegall Square South, BT1 5JD; 028 9024 1001; www.tensquare.co.uk

Malmaison *moderate–expensive*
Funky and stylish hotel in an old seed warehouse. Period features mix with contemporary decor.
34–8 Victoria St, BT1 3GH; 028 9022 0200; www.malmaison.com

The Merchant Hotel *expensive*
Set in a historic listed building in the Cathedral Quarter, and elegantly decorated with antiques.
35–9 Waring St, BT1 2DY; 028 9023 4888; www.themerchanthotel.com

AROUND THE ULSTER FOLK AND TRANSPORT MUSEUM

The Old Inn *moderate*
Charming hotel that offers an old-fashioned welcome with open fires and beamed ceilings.
15 Main Street, Crawfordsburn, BT19 1JH (9 miles/15 km after the Ulster Folk Museum on the A2, turn left on the B20 at the sign for Crawfordsburn); 028 9185 3255; www.theoldinn.com

① Belfast
Co Antrim

A bustling trading port in the 18th and 19th centuries, Belfast has a rich heritage. The city built and launched the RMS *Titanic* in 1912, making it a global center for ship-building; it is also famous for its linen and tobacco industries. However, the Troubles, from the 1960s to the 1990s, led to decline. Regeneration projects in the wake of the peace process have helped the economy recover and there is a buzz about the city, especially in the arty Cathedral Quarter, Queen's Quarter (around Queen's University), and the Gaeltacht Quarter, which promotes Irish language and culture.

Two-hour walking tour
Start at City Hall on Donegall Square, a Neo-Classical masterpiece completed in 1906. Beside it, the **Belfast Wheel** ① *(daily until 9 or 10pm)* offers bird's-eye views of the city and beyond. From the north side of the square, walk along Donegall Place, the main shopping street. On the left is the Belfast Welcome Centre. Continue and turn right into Castle Lane, taking one of the narrow "Entries" to join High Street. Turn right here to see **Albert Clock** ②, a curious tower, built in 1867 as a memorial to Prince Albert. Turn left along Victoria Street, left into Waring Street, and right into

Above Political mural, West Belfast, the frontline of the sectarian conflict known as the Troubles

Donegall Street to reach the period Cathedral Quarter and **St. Anne's Cathedral** ③ *(open Mon–Fri; public entry limited during services on Sun)*. Work began in 1899 on St. Anne's, which contains some beautiful mosaics of St. Patrick. From the cathedral, turn left at Royal Avenue, then right into Castle Street and left into Fountain Street. At No. 52 is Belfast's oldest library – the **Linen Hall Library** ④ *(open Mon–Sat)*, with superb archives on Irish history and culture. Walk along Wellington Place, turn left at the end onto College Square and continue along Great Victoria Street. On the right is the **Grand Opera House** ⑤, a handsome building dating from 1895. No. 46 is Belfast's most famous pub – the **Crown Bar** ⑥ – with its fabulous high Victorian interior. Continue to University Road and the University Quarter around prestigious **Queen's University** ⑦, founded in

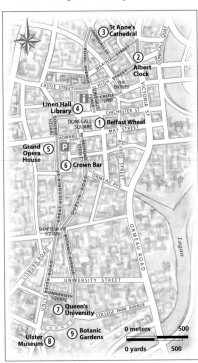

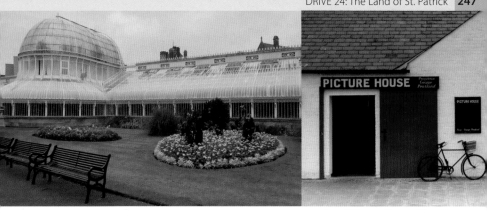

1845. The Visitor Centre *(www.qub.ac.uk; 028 9097 5252)* holds exhibitions and can arrange guided tours of the campus. From University Square, turn right onto College Park and continue to Botanic Avenue and the **Ulster Museum** ⑧ *(www.nmni.com; 0845 608 0000)*, which has a fine collection of art, craftwork, and archeological finds. Next door are the **Botanic Gardens** ⑨ *(open daily)*, opened in 1827. The early Victorian wrought-iron and glass palm house was added soon after. To return to City Hall, follow Botanic Avenue onto Dublin Road and Bedford Street.

🚗 *From Donegall Quay, take Victoria Street leading to A2 for Bangor, crossing Queen Elizabeth Bridge. Continue on A2 to Holywood, following the signs for the museum (7 miles/11 km from Belfast).*

Taxi and Boat Tours
To see West Belfast's political murals, symbols of the city's past and present sectarian divisions, take a Black Taxi tour from City Hall. Or tour the *Titanic* Quarter by boat, visiting landmarks connected with the building of the RMS *Titanic*. Tours leave from the Lagan Lookout on Donegall Quay.

❷ Ulster Folk and Transport Museum
Cultra, Holywood, BT18 OEU; Co Down
This outdoor museum-village *(open Tue–Sun)* has a collection of early 20th-century buildings from all over Ulster, reconstructed here. A transport section commemorates local ship- and aircraft-building, and a miniature train runs on Saturday afternoons, weather permitting.

🚗 *Rejoin the A2 in the direction of Bangor. Leave it at Crawfordsburn*

and take the B20 (Ballyrobert Road) for Bangor and then the A21 to Newtownards. Take the A20 for Portaferry, driving beside Strangford Lough, and turn left for Mount Stewart after 5 miles (8 km).

❸ Mount Stewart House and Gardens
Portaferry Rd, Newtownards, BT22 2AD; Co Down
Created by Lady Londonderry in the 1920s, these gardens contain a vast range of plants and trees, set off by architectural features such as the octagonal **Temple of the Winds** and outstanding views across Strangford Lough. Highlights include the **Italian and Spanish Gardens**, the **Shamrock Garden,** and the **Sunken Garden**. The house has an eclectic collection of furniture and artwork – including a painting of the celebrated racehorse Hambleton by George Stubbs – and information about the statesmen who have lived or stayed here.

🚗 *Leaving Mount Stewart, turn left onto the A20. Greyabbey is just over 2 miles (3 km) from Mount Stewart.*

Above The Neo-Classical facade of Mount Stewart House, with a grand stairway leading to its gardens

Above left The wrought-iron and glass palm house in Belfast's Botanic Gardens **Above** An old-fashioned picture house recreated at the Ulster Folk Museum

EAT AND DRINK IN BELFAST

The Crown Bar *inexpensive*
The interior of Belfast's most famous pub, built in 1895, is ornately tiled, with etched glass, polished brass and private rooms. The menu includes baguettes and burgers, plus traditional Irish stew and beef and Guinness pie. *46 Great Victoria St, BT2 7BA; 028 9024 3187; www.crownbar.com*

The Cellar Restaurant *moderate*
This is one of the city's best-kept secrets. Set on the slopes of Cave Hill, it has great views over the city. Expect dishes such as venison, guinea fowl, pan-fried salmon, lamb, and one or two vegetarian options. *Belfast Castle, Antrim Rd, BT15 5GR; 028 9077 6925; www.belfastcastle.co.uk*

Deane's *expensive*
Award-winning eatery, run by chef Michael Deane, known for its high-quality cuisine using locally sourced produce. Sleek, modern decor. *36–40 Howard St, BT1 6PF; 028 9033 1134; www.michaeldeane.co.uk; open Tue–Sat*

Eat and Drink: inexpensive, under £25; moderate, £25–50; expensive, over £50

VISITING STRANGFORD LOUGH

Tourist Information
Portaferry: The Stables, Castle Street, BT22 1NZ; www.ards-council.gov.uk; 028 4272 9882; open Easter–end Sep

Boat Trips
From Portaferry to Strangford, **ferries** run at quarter past and quarter to the hour. **Boat trips** on the lough from Portaferry can be arranged through Ards Boat Tours, 028 9182 6846

WALKING IN THE MOUNTAINS OF MOURNE

Route cards with ten Mourne Mountains walks can be bought from Mourne Heritage Trust, 87 Central Promenade, Newcastle; 028 4372 4059; www.mournelive.com. Guided walks are also available (028 4372 5143; www.walksinthemournes.co.uk).

WHERE TO STAY

STRANGFORD LOUGH

The Cuan Inn inexpensive
This small, friendly, family-run hotel in Strangford village has an intimate feel. The Square, Strangford, BT30 7ND; 028 4488 1222; www.thecuan.com

DOWNPATRICK

The Mill at Ballydugan inexpensive–moderate
Just outside Downpatrick, this 18th-century flour mill has been turned into a small hotel, bistro, and restaurant. Drumcullen Road, Ballydugan; BT30 8HZ; 028 4461 3654; www.ballyduganmill.com

NEWCASTLE

Slieve Donard Resort & Spa expensive
Built as a luxury Victorian hotel and still oozing class in its unrivaled setting. Downs Road, BT33 0AH; 028 4372 1066; www.hastingshotels.com

AROUND NEWCASTLE

Glassdrumman Lodge inexpensive–moderate
Friendly guesthouse in the foothills of the Mourne Mountains. Each room has either a coastal or mountain view. Mill Road, Annalong, BT34 4RH (take A2 south from Newcastle and turn right onto Mill Road just before Annalong); 028 4376 8451; www.glassdrummanlodge.com

Burrendale Hotel moderate
A relaxed hotel and country club on the A50 just outside Newcastle, with a cozy bar, two restaurants, and pool. 51 Castlewellan Road, BT33 0JY; 028 4372 2599; www.burrendale.com

Above Kilkeel Harbour, a major fishing port **Above right** Gothic arches of Cistercian Grey Abbey, founded

④ Greyabbey
Co Down

The attractive village of Greyabbey takes its name from **Grey Abbey**, a Cistercian abbey founded in 1193. The remains of its Gothic buttresses and arches nestle in parkland on the north of the village. A museum in the gatehouse documents its history.

🚗 **Return to the A20 and drive south to Portaferry, following the signs to the Strangford Ferry (see left).**

⑤ Strangford Lough
Strangford, Downpatrick, BT30 7LS; Co Down

This Area of Outstanding Natural Beauty forms the UK's largest sea inlet and is rich in wildlife. It is almost landlocked except for a gap between **Portaferry** and **Strangford** known as the "Narrows." The lough can be accessed from either side. Arrange a canoe trip or take a boat tour around its waters from Portaferry (see left).

🚗 **From Strangford, take the A25 towards Downpatrick for 1 mile (2 km). At the crossroads there is a sign for the entrance to Castle Ward pointing to the right.**

⑥ Castle Ward
Strangford, Downpatrick, BT30 7LS; Co Down

The **Strangford Lough Wildlife Information Centre** (028 4488 1411) is in the grounds of this stately home (grounds open daily; house Jul–Aug: daily pm only; other times: weekends only; closed Nov–mid-Feb). Built in the 1760s, the house famously combines two contrary architectural styles. The front of the house is Neo-Classical, while the rear, overlooking Strangford Lough, is Neo-Gothic. Inside, the decor is similarly mixed. An extensive walled area surrounds the house, with woodland trails and lovely views of the lough.

🚗 **Turn right, taking the A25 to Downpatrick, 8 miles (13 km) away. In the town, follow signs for the Saint Patrick Centre and park opposite it.**

⑦ Downpatrick
Co Down

St. Patrick (c.AD 390–461), Ireland's patron saint, landed in Strangford Lough in around AD 428. He is strongly linked with Downpatrick. **The Saint Patrick Centre** (open

Above The Neo-Classical front of Castle Ward, which gives no clue to its Neo-Gothic rear

Mon–Sat; Apr–Sep: also Sun) on Market Street, traces his footsteps in the area. He is said to be buried in the graveyard of **Down Cathedral**, on English St (turn left out of the St. Patrick Centre and walk up the steps by the building), where a memorial marks the spot. However, Armagh also claims to be his burial place.

From Downpatrick, take the A25 to Clough and join the A2 for Newcastle.

The Powers of St. Patrick
Inspired by a vision, St. Patrick came to Ireland to convert the pagan population to Christianity. Legend credits him with many supernatural deeds, including ridding the country of snakes.

Above Portaferry, departure point for the ferry across the "Narrows" to Strangford

❽ Newcastle
Co Down
This seaside resort has a magnificent setting, with the **Mourne Mountains**, dominated by Slieve Donard (2,796 ft/852 m), the highest mountain in Northern Ireland, rising behind the town and Dundrum Bay. It is known for its two golf courses, including the links course at the **Royal County Down Golf Club**, and the splendid

Slieve Donard Hotel, a spa hotel set between sea and mountains (see left).
Newcastle has a pleasant **beach**, but for more privacy drive 3 miles (5 km) south of town, where the **Mourne coastal footpath** gives access to secluded coastline. There is a parking lot, picnic table, and walks.

Continue south along the A2 to the pretty town of Kilkeel and then turn right onto the B27 to Hilltown. This leads up into the Mourne Mountains.

❾ Mountains of Mourne
Co Down
The Mourne Mountains lie in an Area of Outstanding Natural Beauty. There are many popular walking trails (see left) including those up **Slieve Donard** and its slightly smaller neighbor **Slieve Commedagh**, with views as far as the Isle of Man on a clear day. The highlight of this area is the **Silent Valley** (after 4 miles/6.5 km on the B27, turn right onto Head Road for the Visitor Centre), a reservoir flanked by the Mourne Wall, a 22-mile (35-km) drystone wall linking 15 mountain peaks. To experience its magical silence take the 3-mile (5-km) walk around the reservoir. Return along Head Road to the B27 and turn right to reach the **Spelga Dam**.

The **Silent Valley Visitor Centre** (open daily; 08457 440 088; www.niwater.com) has an exhibition about the area and a café with stunning views. As the valley is closed to traffic, a **shuttle bus service** runs between Ben Crom and the parking lot (runs pm only; Jul–Aug: daily; rest of year: weekends).

It is possible to continue to pretty **Rostrevor**, staying on the B27 to Hilltown and turning left onto the B25. Rostrevor is known for its mild micro-climate and has parks and picnic areas with views across to Carlingford on the Cooley Peninsula.

Above Gothic flying buttresses at the ruined abbey in the pretty village of Greyabbey

EAT AND DRINK

NEWCASTLE
Sea Salt Delicatessen & Bistro
inexpensive
Tasty lunches daily and a varied tapas-style menu Fri–Sat eve.
51 Central Promenade, BT33 0HH; 028 4372 5027

Hugh McCanns Café Bar Deli
moderate
Live entertainment, a varied menu; and a great setting near the promenade.
119 Central Promenade, BT33 0EU; 028 4372 2487; www.hughmccanns.com

AROUND NEWCASTLE
The Buck's Head Inn moderate
In an 18th-century building, this is a friendly spot with imaginatively cooked seafood and other local produce.
77 Main St, Dundrum, BT33 0LU (4 miles/6 km) north of Newcastle on the A24); 028 4375 1868

Mourne Seafood Bar moderate
Delicious, fresh, locally caught seafood with unusual as well as well-known species appearing on the menu.
10 Main Street, Dundrum, BT33 0LU (4 miles/6 km) north of Newcastle on the A24); 028 4375 1377; www.mourneseafood.com

---

DAY TRIP OPTIONS
Newcastle makes a good base to explore the various attractions in this area. Here are two day trips, with an option for rainy weather.

Sea and mountains
Take a canoe trip on Strangford Lough ❺ to spot the abundant

wildlife. Or head to Tollymore Forest Park for a scenic hike at the foothills of the Mountains of Mourne ❾. There are several hiking trails (the longest is 8 miles/13 km), through forests and along the River Shimna.

The park can be found 2 miles/3 km south of Newcastle.

Family fun
A great option on rainy days is the Exploris Aquarium (open daily) in Portaferry, near Strangford Lough ❺. There is a marine discovery lab and a seal rescue center.

Retrace the drive on the A2/A25 to Strangford and Portaferry.

Eat and Drink: inexpensive, under £25; moderate, £25–£50; expensive, over £50

Fermanagh Lakelands

Belleek to Boa Island

Highlights

- **Spectacular views**
  Contemplate one of the finest views in Northern Ireland from the Cliffs of Magho

- **Spellbinding caverns**
  Wonder at the stalactite-filled caverns and subterranean pools of the Marble Arch Caves

- **Neo-Classical stately homes**
  Experience the 18th-century grandeur of Florence Court and Castle Coole

- **Tranquil waterways**
  Savor the peaceful waters of Lough Erne, a paradise for nature-lovers, bird-watchers, and anglers

Boats moored at the marina of Castle Archdale Country Park, Lower Lough Erne

Fermanagh Lakelands

The inland county of Fermanagh in Northern Ireland is known as the Lakelands, for more than a third of its total area lies under water. The scenic waterways of Lough Erne, divided into Upper and Lower Lough Erne, are the county's main feature. Lower Lough Erne, set against a hilly backdrop, is dotted with islands and flanked by castles, stately homes, walks, and forest parks. This tour includes all the highlights of Lower Lough Erne – exploring the lake by land and water, and taking in its main sights, loveliest views, and most interesting activities. For outdoor enthusiasts there are underground rivers, caves, forests, and ruined castles, while others can visit stately homes, a lace museum, and a china workshop.

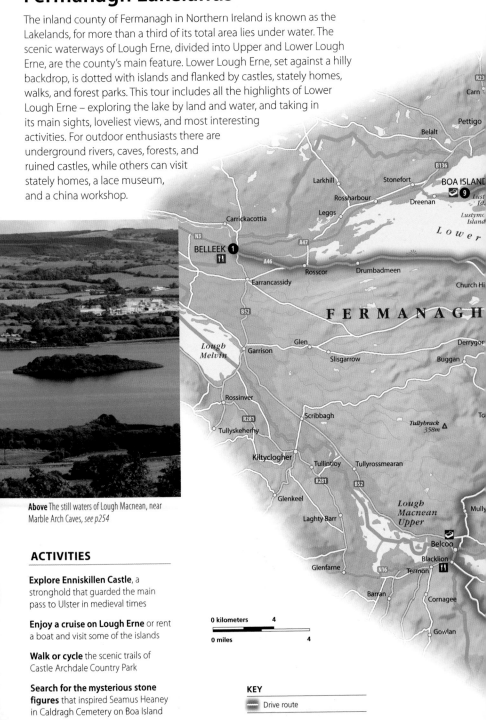

Above The still waters of Lough Macnean, near Marble Arch Caves, *see p254*

ACTIVITIES

Explore Enniskillen Castle, a stronghold that guarded the main pass to Ulster in medieval times

Enjoy a cruise on Lough Erne or rent a boat and visit some of the islands

Walk or cycle the scenic trails of Castle Archdale Country Park

Search for the mysterious stone figures that inspired Seamus Heaney in Caldragh Cemetery on Boa Island

KEY

Drive route

Above Forest Walk, Castle Archdale Country Park, *see pp256–7*

PLAN YOUR DRIVE

Start/finish: Belleek to Boa Island.

Number of days: 2 days.

Distance: 67 miles (108 km).

Road conditions: Mostly good although there are some uneven surfaces along the A46. Some of the smaller roads around Monea and Boho are liable to flooding. Lough Navar Forest Drive is one-way and uneven in parts.

When to go: Spring through to autumn, when most attractions are open and the weather is best.

Opening times: Most shops and attractions open 9 or 10am–5 or 6pm. Shops open Mon–Sat; in large towns also 12–6pm on Sun. Convenience stores in villages open 8am until late.

Main market days: Belleek: third Tue of month; **Enniskillen**: Tue and Thu; Farmers' Market, every second Sat.

Shopping: Belleek is renowned for fine parian china. Enniskillen is a center for many crafts, including jewelry, ceramics, and textiles. Handmade lace and linens can be found in Bellanaleck.

Major festivals: Enniskillen: Drama Festival, Mar; **Upper and Lower Lough Erne**: Waterways Ireland Classic Fishing Festival, Apr/May; **Lower Lough Erne**: Vintage Car Rally, Aug.

DAY TRIP OPTIONS

For a first-rate **family attraction** visit the Marble Arch Caves Geopark. **Nature-lovers** will enjoy walking, boating, or cycling around the shores of Lower Lough Erne. For full details, *see p257*.

Above Walkway down to the Marble Arch Caves, one of Europe's top show caves

WHERE TO STAY

AROUND MARBLE ARCH CAVES

Customs House Country Inn
inexpensive–moderate
This country hotel is at Belcoo, on the drive route from Belleek to Marble Arch Caves and 12 miles (20 km) from the caves off the N16. It is known for its warm welcome, good food and lovely views over Lough Macnean.
25–7 Main St, Belcoo; BT93 5FB; 028 6638 6285; www.customshouseinn.com

Knockninny Country House
inexpensive–moderate
Lovingly restored Victorian hotel, complete with marina, situated on Upper Lough Erne's shoreline, 14 miles/23 km from the caves on the A509.
Knockninny Quay, Derrylin; BT92 9JU; 028 6774 8590; www.knockninnyhouse.com

AROUND ENNISKILLEN

Killyhevlin Hotel and Health Club
moderate
A peaceful place set in extensive grounds on the shores of Lough Erne just half a mile (1 km) from Enniskillen along the A4 to Castle Coole. The pool and Jacuzzi are good places to unwind after a day's driving.
Killyhevlin, BT74 6RW; 028 6632 3481; www.killyhevlin.com

Right Setting a gentle pace on a back road in County Fermanagh

① Belleek
Co Fermanagh
This quiet village on the banks of Lough Erne has quaint, hand-painted storefronts. It is famous for its fine parian china, an industry introduced to the village by the local landowner in 1857, in the wake of the potato famine. At the **Belleek Pottery Visitor Centre** (*Jan–Feb: Mon–Fri; Mar–Oct: daily, Sun pm only; Nov–Dec: Mon–Sat*), guided tours take visitors to see the delicate Belleek china being crafted and decorated. A museum displays Belleek ware from the company's earliest days, including an urn-shaped vase made for the 1900 Paris Exhibition, and there is a showroom and tearoom.

🚗 *Cross the bridge by the Pottery, veer left, then turn left and follow signs for the A46, a lovely drive alongside Lower Lough Erne. After 13 miles (21 km), just after Tully Castle, turn right onto the B81 at Binmore Road for Derrygonnelly. Continue to Monea and 1 mile (2 km) after Monea turn right at the crossroads, then right again after another 1 mile (2 km) at a T-junction. Follow the signs to Belcoo, then turn left in Blacklion for Florence Court. Turn right for the Marlbank Scenic Loop. The entrance for Marble Arch Caves is 5 miles (8 km) along this drive, on the left.*

② Marble Arch Caves
Marlbank, Co Fermanagh; BT92 1EW
These unique show caves are among Europe's finest and are part of an Area of Outstanding Geological Interest recognized by UNESCO. They were sculpted out of limestone, which formed when Ireland was covered by ocean some 330 million years ago.

Guided tours (*Mar–Sep: daily, last tour 4.30pm; Jul–Aug: last tour 5pm; book during peak times, 028 6634 8855*) begin with an underground boat ride through a mesmerizing landscape of stalactite-filled caverns, stone pools, streams and cascades, each feature atmospherically lit. The 30-ft (9-m) Marble Arch itself stands in a glen at the confluence of three streams. Tours last 75 minutes and are suitable for anyone of reasonable fitness (wear walking shoes and a warm sweater). Facilities include a restaurant and exhibition area.

🚗 *Leaving Marble Arch Caves, drive down the entrance road and turn left. At the next T-junction, turn right. Drive through the small hamlet of Florence Court and turn right into Florence Court.*

Lough Navar Forest Drive
This is an extensive area of woodland with a diverse array of habitats. A 7-mile (11-km) scenic tour, known as the Forest Drive (*open daily, 10am–sunset*), begins off the Glennasheevar Road between Derrygonnelly and Garrison, and emerges at the spectacular 1,000-ft (300-m) high Magho Cliffs, with an outstanding viewpoint over Lower Lough Erne, Donegal and the surrounding mountains. From the main forest drive there are many short walks that reach various points of interest.

③ Florence Court
Enniskillen, Co Fermanagh; BT92 1DB
A beautiful stately home and demesne dating from the early 18th century, Florence Court (*grounds open daily; house open Mar–Aug: pm daily; Sep–Oct:*

Above left Monea Castle ruins, near Belcoo
Above Enchanting setting of Enniskillen Castle

pm weekends only, closed winter; call in advance on 028 6634 8249), was occupied by the Earls of Enniskillen until the early 1950s, when it was acquired by the National Trust. A guided tour reveals rich Rococo plasterwork – especially on the ceilings of the dining room, Venetian room, and staircase – all restored following a fire in 1955, and fine Irish furniture. The grounds have a water-powered sawmill, an ice house, a forge, a walled garden, and a forest park with walking trails.

🚗 *At the exit, turn right, toward Enniskillen/A4. Then turn left onto the A32 for Enniskillen and after 2 miles (3 km), turn right. Continue for 2 miles (4 km) to reach Bellanaleck. Park at the lace museum.*

④ Bellanaleck
Co Fermanagh

The quirky **Sheelin Antique Irish Lace Museum** *(closed lunchtime and Sun)* in Bellanaleck has around 700 examples of lace made in Ireland between 1850 and 1900. It also sells vintage lace and linen, including wedding dresses and veils, baby bonnets, lace coasters, and more. There is a sweet little tea shop next door.

🚗 *From Bellanaleck, take the A509 north and turn right onto the A4 for Enniskillen. For Enniskillen Castle, keep left through the town and park at the free parking lot beside the castle.*

⑤ Enniskillen
Co Fermanagh

This lively county town is situated on an island between Lower and Upper Lough Erne. Its main sight is **Enniskillen Castle** *(open Tue–Fri 10am–5pm, Mon and Sat pm only; Jul–Aug: also Sun; Oct–Apr: closed weekends)*,

built in the early 15th century by the Maguire family. Standing at the narrowest crossing point between the two loughs, it has had an interesting history and has been used as an English garrison fort and military barracks. The castle's most stunning feature is the Watergate, a fairy-tale twin-turreted tower, best admired from the far bank of the river. It now houses the **Fermanagh County Museum** and **Royal Inniskilling Fusiliers Regimental Museum**.

Also in Enniskillen is the **Buttermarket**, a delightful enclave of small art galleries, craft studios, and coffee shops set in the restored 19th-century dairy market.

🚗 *Leaving Enniskillen, follow signs for Belfast/A4. Castle Coole is just over 1 mile (2 km) from Enniskillen. An admission charge per car is taken on the driveway.*

⑥ Castle Coole
Enniskillen, Co Fermanagh; BT74 6JY

One of Ireland's finest Neo-Classical houses, Castle Coole *(open Mar–Sep; house pm only; call in advance on 028 6632 2690)*, was commissioned by the first Earl of Belmore in the 1790s. Its expense nearly bankrupted him. The splendid Regency furnishings can be appreciated on a guided tour, highlights of which include the State Bedroom, the Oval Saloon, and the servants' quarters. There is a lovely lakeside walk in the grounds.

🚗 *Take Castle Coole Road back toward Enniskillen. Keep left at the mini roundabout and then turn right at the lights. At the roundabout, take the 4th exit for the A32 for Irvinestown and Kesh. After 3 miles (5 km), turn left at the roundabout onto the B82 for Killadeas.*

Above left Monea Castle ruins, near Belcoo
Above Enchanting setting of Enniskillen Castle

EAT AND DRINK

BELLEEK

Thatch Coffee Shop *inexpensive*
Pretty thatched tea room in the center of Belleek, with daily specials and home baking.
20 Main St, BT93 3FX; 028 6865 8181

Moohans Fiddlestone
Traditional-style pub with an open fire and regular live music.
15–17 Main St, BT93 3FY; 028 6865 8008

AROUND MARBLE ARCH CAVES

MacNean House and Restaurant *expensive*
Run by award-winning chef Neven Maguire. Outstanding food prepared with local ingredients and great ambience in a village location 12 miles (19 km) west of Enniskillen on N16.
Main St, Blacklion; Co Cavan; 071 985 3022; www.macneanrestaurant.com

ENNISKILLEN

Blake's of The Hollow/Café Merlot *moderate*
Blake's, the pub, is full of character, with an original Victorian bar. Below the pub, Café Merlot serves tasty European dishes, slow-roast meats, and seafood.
6 Church St, BT74 7EJ; 028 6632 2143; **Café Merlot:** *028 6632 0918*

Franco's Restaurant *moderate*
Seafood is the specialty, but there is also rib-eye steak, rack of lamb, and duck, as well as pasta and pizza.
Queen Elizabeth Road, BT74 7DY; 028 6632 4424; www.francosrestaurant.co.uk

Scoffs Restaurant & Cocktail Bar *moderate*
This is one of Enniskillen's best restaurants. On the lower floor is the more relaxed Uno wine bar, which has the same menu.
17 Belmore St, BT74 6AA; 028 6634 2622; www.uno-restaurant.co.uk

Eat and Drink: inexpensive, under £25; moderate, £25–£50; expensive, over £50

VISITING LOUGH ERNE

Exploring by boat
Boats can be rented for the day or half-day *(Mar–Oct; 028 6862 8100; www. manormarine.com)*. No experience required as instructions are given. Trips around the lake, on the *Lady of the Lake* cruise boat, passing Devenish, depart from Rossclare Jetty at Killadeas *(11:30am Sat year-round and 3pm daily Jul–Aug weather permitting)*.

WHERE TO STAY

LOWER LOUGH ERNE

The Cedars Guesthouse *inexpensive*
Comfortable guesthouse with in-house bistro, near Castle Archdale on the shores of Lower Lough Erne. Follow the lough-side B82 along the drive route from Enniskillen.
301 Killadeas Rd, Irvinestown, BT94 1PG; 028 6862 1493; www.cedarsguesthouse.com

Manor House Country Hotel *moderate*
Situated 7 miles (11 km) from Enniskillen on the shores of Lough Erne along the B82 drive route, this 18th-century manor house combines period elegance and modern comforts including a pool and sauna. Boats for rent by the day or take a leisurely cruise around the lake *(see above)*.
Killadeas, BT94 1NY; 028 6862 2200; www.manorhouseresorthotel.com

BOA ISLAND

The Courtyard B&B *moderate*
A private ferry takes visitors and their cars to this idyllic 75-acre (30-acre) island. Tennis courts, indoor pool, and nature trail.
Lusty Beg Island, Boa Island, Kesh, BT93 8AD; 028 6863 3300; www.lustybegisland.com

❼ Lower Lough Erne
Co Fermanagh

Lough Erne is divided into two distinct water systems. Upper Lough Erne is a maze of small channels and joins the mighty Shannon River, while Lower Lough Erne is a vast lake set in unspoiled countryside, closer to the sea. It is the perfect location for activities such as water sports, birdwatching, boating, and fishing, while on land there are numerous trails for hiking and cycling, as well as pony-trekking. There are over 150 small islands and inlets to explore, and some of the larger islands boast their own resorts.

To explore Lower Lough Erne, join a cruise on board the comfortable *Lady of the Lake* from Killadeas or rent a boat independently from Manor House marina *(see left)*. One of the most interesting islands is **Devenish Island**, once called Ox Island. It has the remains of a monastic settlement founded by St. Molaise in the 6th century, including a superb 82-ft (25-m)

12th-century round tower. Notice the human faces carved above the four windows, the only instance of such embellishment on an Irish round tower.

White Island also has the remains of a 12th-century church, with eight enigmatic figures along the interior north wall. They are believed to date from the 6th–9th centuries.

🚗 *Leaving Killadeas, turn left onto the B82. After 2.5 miles (4 km), look for the entrance to Castle Archdale Country Park and park at the Visitor Centre.*

❽ Castle Archdale Country Park
Irvinestown, Co Fermanagh; BT94 1PP

This large country park on the shores of Lough Erne has mature woodlands, a marina, and a slipway, as well as many walking and cycling trails, and a red deer enclosure and butterfly garden. The castle, built in the early 1600s, is now a ruin, accessible through Castle Archdale Forest. The Visitor Centre, in the courtyard buildings of the old manor house, has information on walks and wildlife. A heritage trail links points of interest, including evidence of the park's use by the RAF in World War II. In summer, boats are available for hire to explore Lough Erne, and a ferry runs to White Island *(see right)*.

A two-hour walking tour

Start this 4-mile (6-km) walk at the **Visitor Centre** ① and continue toward the **Walled Garden** ②, where the road leads to the marina and RV park. Enter the forest here and at the first junction turn left toward the castle. Continue straight on to a cottage and a sign for **Tom's Island** ③. Turn left here (if the path is waterlogged, take the forest road and then rejoin the path after the jetty). Cross the causeway onto Inish Beg or Tom's Island, keeping left. The lakeside path has excellent views over to White Island (there is a ferry to the island from the marina, *see*

White Island
Castle Archdale ④
Tom's Island ③
Davy's Island
Archdale Forest
Marina
Ⓟ ① *Visitor Centre* ② *Walled Garden*
B82

| 0 meters | 800 |
| 0 yards | 800 |

Where to Stay: inexpensive, under £100; moderate, £100–£200; expensive, over £200

right) and of Lough Erne, stretching into the distance. Keep walking along the path past the jetty and then inland slightly, following the river. Continue along this and cross the access road. At the bridge and tarmac road into the Forest Service parking lot, turn right. The ruins of **Castle Archdale** ④ are here. In the summer this area is particularly enchanting with colorful wild flowers in bloom. Turn left uphill and take the path behind the castle. At the junction turn left, then left again at the next forest road, and then right. To return to the visitor center, trace the route back to the forest and follow the road past the walled garden.

🚗 *Leaving Castle Archdale, turn left onto the B72 for Kesh and after 1 mile (2 km) turn left for the Kesh scenic route. The road surface is uneven but there are lovely views of Lough Erne, with a viewpoint about half a mile along. At Kesh, turn left at the junction and then left again at the T-junction for Pettigo/Belleek, crossing the bridge. Take the next left onto the A47 for Boa Island. On Boa, there is a marked turn for Lusty Beg Island. About 1 mile (2 km) after this, turn left*

for Caldragh Cemetery. Park at the bottom of the road and access the graveyard through the turnstile on the left.

⑨ Boa Island
Co Fermanagh

The largest of Lough Erne's islands, Boa is joined to the mainland by bridges at both ends. It is notable for two mysterious stone figures, to be found in the center of **Caldragh Cemetery**, an early Christian graveyard at the western end of the island. The first, the **Boa Island Figure**, is a carved stone, 3 ft (1 m) high, with two faces, back to back; it is also known as the Janus Figure after the Roman god with two faces. It is believed to represent a Celtic deity and symbolize fertility, but its true significance is uncertain. It is said to have inspired Seamus Heaney's poem "January God."

The second, smaller figure beside it, the **Lusty Man**, was originally discovered in a cemetery on Lusty Mor Island, just south of Boa Island, and was moved to its present location in 1939. It is thought to be older than the Janus figure, but is similarly shrouded in mystery.

Above far left Turret-like lodges by Lough Erne's championship golf course **Above left** The tranquil waters of Lower Lough Erne, a haven for wildlife **Above** Courtyard buildings of the old manor house at Castle Archdale

VISITING CASTLE ARCHDALE

Visitor Centre
Castle Archdale Country Park, Irvinestown, is 11 miles (17 km) northwest of Enniskillen; 028 6862 1588; open Easter–Oct daily, Nov–Easter Sun 10am–4pm only

Boat and Bike Rental
Boats and bikes can be rented on weekends from Easter to the end of September, daily in July and August. Boats take up to six people and instructions are provided.
Bike Rental: 028 6862 1892

Ferry Trips
The *Gypsy Lady* makes the 20-minute crossing to White Island *(Easter–Sep weekends only, Jul–Aug daily)*. There is also a ferry from **Trory Point** to Devenish Island *(4 miles/6 km from Enniskillen on A32; Apr–Sep daily).*

EAT AND DRINK

The hotels in the area offer several options for drinking and dining *(see Where to Stay, left).*

DAY TRIP OPTIONS

Enniskillen is an ideal base, the area's best sites being within easy reach. The first trip takes in Marble Arch Caves, followed by a visit to pretty Bellanaleck. The second option is a day on Lower Lough Erne – choose to explore by boat, bike, or on foot.

Caverns and lace

Marble Arch Caves ② are a global geopark and a popular attraction

for families. Book ahead for the tour, which includes a boat ride and walk through immense caverns. On the way back to Enniskillen, stop at the Sheelin Antique Irish Lace Museum in Bellanaleck ④ (vintage items for sale), and have lunch or afternoon tea in the tearoom.

Follow the A32 southwest for 11 miles (17 km) to reach the caves. Return on the A32/A509 via Bellanaleck.

A day on Lough Erne

Take one of the access points for a lakeside walk along Lower Lough Erne ⑦ or rent a boat to do some independent island-hopping. Alternatively, rent a bike from Castle Archdale Country Park ⑧ and cycle around the shoreline.

Head north from Enniskillen on the A32/B82 for Castle Archdale Country Park and Killadeas.

Eat and Drink: inexpensive, under £25; moderate, £25–£50; expensive, over £50

General Index

Page numbers in **bold** refer to main entries

The information in this
DK Eyewitness Travel Guide is checked regularly.

Acknowledgments

Dorling Kindersley would like to thank the many people whose help and assistance contributed to the preparation of this book.

Main Contributors
Brian Daughton is a versatile travel writer and award-winning photographer. He has contributed to many publications, including Time Out's *Flight-Free Europe*, the *Guardian*, *Photo District News (PDN)*, *Foto Mundo* and the *Suddeutsche Zeitung*. He also lectures at the University of the Arts and London Met.

John S. Doyle is a freelance journalist and lives in Dublin.

Yvonne Gordon is a features and travel writer and a radio broadcaster. Born in Dublin, she has traveled the length and breadth of Ireland since childhood. As well as writing travel features for newspapers such as the *Irish Times*, magazines and international travel websites, she has contributed to four guidebooks to Ireland.

Editorial Consultant
Donna Dailey

Fact checker
Sylvia Earley

Proofreaders
Jane Ellis and Linda McQueen

Indexer
Hilary Bird

Special Assistance
Derek Earley, Ciara Kenny, and Lewis Reed for test-drives; Fiona Riordan at EGMC for supplying road signs

Photography
Brian Daughton, Stephen Power

Additional Photography
Joe Cornish, Tim Daly, Steve Gorton, Jamie Marshall, Ian O'Leary, Rough Guides/Roger Mapp, Antony Souter, Clive Streeter, Alan Williams

Additional Editorial and Design Assistance
Louise Cleghorn, Brian Daughton, Lydia Halliday, Sands Publishing Solutions, Susana Smith

Maps
John Plumer, JP Map Graphics Ltd, www.jpmapgraphics.co.uk

Picture Credits
Every effort has been made to trace the copyright holders of images, and we apologize in advance for any unintentional omissions. We would be pleased to insert the appropriate acknowledgments in any subsequent edition of this publication.

The Publishers would like to thank the following individuals, companies and picture libraries for their kind permission to reproduce their photographs:

t=top; tc = top center; tl=top left; tr=top right; c=center; cl=center left; cr=center right; bc = bottom center; bl=bottom left; br=bottom right.

Alamy Images: Design Pics Inc. - RM Content 138-9; Dennis Flaherty 92bc; JoeFox CountyMayo 208br; Fabrice Lambert 206br; Mira 226ca; Keith Nuttall 227tr; scenicireland.com/Christopher Hill Photographic 214ca; Stuwdamdorp 10tr; Peter Titmuss 10bl. **Barberstown Castle:** 142tl. **Borris House:** 85clb. **Corbis:** Richard Cummins 125tr; Destinations 73t, 75tl, 227bc; JAI/Doug Pearson 180-1; Ladislav Janicek 5bc; Arthur Morris 94-5. **Michael Diggin:** 15tl. **Dublin Mountains Partnership:** Karen Woods 143br. **Mark Fearon**/www.photographersdirect.com: 207bl. **Flickr.com:** www.flickr.com/photos/jule_berlin/560207760/ 218ca; www.flickr.com/photos/dnlbyl/2213073893 Donal Boyle 218br. **Galway City Museum:** 185br. **Getty Images:** Axiom Photographic Agency/Richard Cummins 9br; Axiom/IIC 2-3, 136br, 183br, 183tl, 192cl, 225bl; Lonely Planet Images/Gareth McCormack 217tl; Lonely Planet Images/Richard Cummins 70-1; Photographer's Choice/Andrew Holt 16br, 26tr; Photographer's Choice/Brian Lawrence 222-3; Riser/Joe Cornish 190-1; Robert Harding World Imagery/Gary Cook 193tl; Robert Harding World Imagery/Martin Child 26br; Robert Harding World Imagery/Richard Cummins 76tl; Robert Harding World Imagery/Roy Rainford 7cl. **The National Trust Photo Library ©NTPL:** 247bc, 248br. **Newmills Corn and Flax Mills:** David Armour 214tc. **Photolibrary:** Design Pics Inc/The Irish Image Collection 77tr. **Sathya Sai Sanctuary Trust for Nature:** 209tl. **Strokestown Park:** 169tl, 169tr. **Tipperaryphotos.com:** 13tl.

Sheet Map
Alamy Images: Tom Mackie front; Robert Harding Picture Library Ltd/FireCrest back.

Map Cover
Alamy Images: Hemis/Patrick Frilet.

Jacket
Front: Alamy Images: Hemis/Patrick Frilet; **Back: Alamy Images:** Kuttig – Travel tl; **Getty Images:** Axiom Photographic Agency/Richard Cummins tc, Travel Ink tr; **Spine: Alamy Images:** Hemis/Patrick Frilet.

All other images © Dorling Kindersley
For further information see: www.dkimages.com

Road Signs - Eire

SPEED LIMITS AND GENERAL DRIVING INDICATIONS

Yield

Stop

Junction ahead with major road

Junction ahead with smaller road

No left turn

No passing

No access for vehicles over 14.3 ft in height

Speed limit

Entrance to 30 km/h speed limit zone

End of 30km/h zone

WARNING SIGNS

Two-way traffic

Series of dangerous corners ahead

Slippery road

Crosswinds

Danger of falling rocks

Sharp rise ahead e.g. Hump-Back Bridge

Road narrows on both sides

Road narrows from left

Level crossing with barrier

Level crossing with no barrier

Steep descent ahead

Deer or wild animals

Children crossing

Pedestrian crossing ahead

Road divides

Dual-lane road ends

Overhead electric cables

Tunnel ahead

Single lane

Roadworks ahead